A SHORT
HISTORY
OF THE
WORLD

A SHORT
HISTORY
OF THE
WORLD

THE STORY OF MANKIND FROM
PREHISTORY TO THE MODERN DAY

ALEX WOOLF

ARCTURUS

PICTURE CREDITS

akg-images 14, /Bildarchiv Monheim 17 (top), /Erich Lessing 46, 78, 177, 187; The Art Archive/National Anthropological Museum Mexico 12 /National Palace Mexico City 34 (top)/ Egyptian Museum Cairo, 57 /Musée des Arts Décoratifs Paris 58 /The British Library 87; The Bridgeman Art Library 15, 44 (top), 45, 118 (bottom), 120 (top), 134, 176; clipart.com 11, 16, 17 (bottom), 22, 25 (top), 37, 64 (bottom), 67, 69 (bottom), 74 (top), 76, 77, 79, 80, 81 (bottom), 82, 88 (top right), 91, 92, 105 (top), 107, 109, 111 (top), 116, 117, 120 (bottom), 125, 126, 127, 128 (top), 129, 138 (top), 146, 147, 151, 154, 155 (top), 157, 158, 159, 164 (bottom), 167, 169 (bottom), 175 (bottom), 182, 190, 191 (top), 202, 203 (top), 208 (top), 215, 223, 227, 230, 238, 258 (bottom), 270; Corbis 8, 10 (bottom) 13, 18, 19 (middle) 21 (top), (left) 24 (right), 27, 28, 30 (bottom), 33 (top) 39, 40, 41, 49 (top), 52, 60, 64 (right) 65, 84, 141 (bottom), 144, 148, 164, 216, 217, 229, 244, 246, 248, 249, 250, 251, 252, 255, 261, 263, 264, 266 (top), 267, 268, 271, 272, 273, 276, 277, 278 (bottom), 282, 283, 288, 289, 291 (top), 293, 294, 295, 298; Dover Publications Ltd 31; Getty Images 62 (top), 71 (middle), 81 (top), 115 (top), 120 (top), 213 (bottom), 275 (top), 285 (bottom), 291 (bottom); istock 35, 42, 153; Library of Congress 221, 243; Mary Evans Picture Library 10 (top), 25 (bottom), 54, 70, 111 (bottom), 149 (bottom), 212, 239, 242; Amal Mongia 179; Umair Mohsin 86; Jamie Naish 169 (top); Photolibraries.com 168; Science Photo Library 9; Shutterstock.com front and back cover, 69 (top), 97, 101, 132, 203 (bottom), 254, 299; Jo St Mart 49 (bottom), 50, 133 (bottom), 142; Topfoto 23, 47, 55, 85, 99 (bottom), 155 (bottom), 183 (middle), 188, 190, 224 (top), 226 (top).

ARCTURUS

This edition published in 2014 by Arcturus Publishing Limited
26/27 Bickels Yard, 151–153 Bermondsey Street,
London SE1 3HA

Copyright © Arcturus Holdings Limited

ISBN: 978-1-4351-4290-9
AD004317UK

Printed in Malaysia

4 6 8 10 9 7 5 3

CONTENTS

INTRODUCTION   7

THE PREHISTORIC WORLD: 7,000,000–10,000BC

Human Origins 7,000,000–2,000,000BC   8
Peopling the Earth 2,000,000–40,000BC   10
Human Development 40,000–8000BC   12

THE ANCIENT WORLD: 10,000–500BC

From Hunting to Farming 8000–3000BC   14
Early Farming Communities 8000–2000BC   16
The Dawn of Civilization 4500–2000BC   18
Early Cultures of the Middle East 9000–4300BC   20
Sumer 4300–2334BC   22
The First Empires of Mesopotamia 2334–1595BC   24
Kingdoms and Empires of
   Mesopotamia 1595–1000BC   26
The Assyrian and Babylonian Empires 1000–539BC   28
The Hebrews 1200–539BC   30
The Achaemenid Empire 559–480BC   32
Early Egyptian Civilization 6000–2040BC   34
Middle Kingdom Egypt 2040–1532BC   36
New Kingdom and Late Period Egypt 1532–332BC   38
The Indus Valley Civilization 3300–1700BC   40
Vedic Period India 1700–500BC   42
The First Civilizations in East Asia 6000–221BC   44
Peoples of Central Asia 6000–400BC   46
Neolithic and Bronze Age Europe 6500–500BC   48
The Rise of Aegean Civilization 3000–1100BC   50
The Rise of Greece 1100–480BC   52
Phoenicians and Carthaginians 900–480BC   54
Peoples of the Americas 4000–200BC   56
Peoples of Africa 7000–500BC   58

THE CLASSICAL WORLD: 500BC– AD500

Classical Greece 500–435BC   60
Greece and Macedon 435–336BC   62
Alexander the Great
   and the Hellenistic World 336–30BC   64
Parthian and Sasanian Persia 238BC–AD636   66
The Etruscans and the Rise of Rome 800–290BC   68
The Later Roman Republic 290–27BC   70
The Roman Empire 27BC–AD300   72
The Fall of the Western Roman Empire AD300–476   74
The Celts 500BC–AD500   76

Germans and Steppe Peoples 400BC–AD500   78
The Early Byzantine Empire AD480–629   80
Mauryan India 500BC–AD50   82
Kushan and Gupta India AD50–550   84
The Han Empire 221BC–AD220   86
China and Japan AD220–589   88
South-east Asia and the Pacific 300BC–AD500   90
The Maya 200BC–AD900   92
Mexico and South America 200BC–AD700   94
Africa 500BC–AD500   96
Advances in Technology 500BC–AD600   98
Religions of the East 600BC–AD500   100
Religions of the West 500BC–AD500   102

THE MEDIEVAL WORLD: 500–1500

The Carolingian Empire 600–814   104
Europe in the Age of the Vikings 793–1100   106
The Holy Roman Empire 962–1806   108
Christendom 500–1300   110
Feudal Europe 1000–1300   112
War and Plague in Medieval Europe 1000–1400   114
The Rise of Europe's Towns and Cities 1000–1500   116
The Birth and Spread of Islam 622–750   118
The Abbasid Empire 750-1037   120
The Byzantine Empire 629–1453   122
Turkish Empires 1037–1453   124
The Crusades 1095–1291   126
Renaissance Europe 1400–1500   128
Africa 500–1500   130
India 550–1500   132
Sui and Tang China 589–907   134
Song China 907–1279   136
The Mongol Empire 1204–1405   138
Japan and Korea 600–1500   140
South-east Asia 500–1500   142
North America and the Pacific 500–1500   144
Toltecs and Aztecs 800–1520   146
South America and the Incas 1000–1533   148
World Religions 500–1500   150

THE EARLY MODERN WORLD: 1500–1783

Dawn of a New Era 1494–1559   152
The Age of European Exploration 1415–1600   154
The Reformation in Europe 1517–1618   156

CONTENTS

Europe in the Time of the Thirty Years' War
1618–1648 158

Swedish Expansion in the Baltic 1521–1721 160

The Expansion of Russia 1492–1783 162

Europe in the Age of Absolute
Monarchs 1648–1715 164

18th-Century Europe 1715–1783 166

The Rise of European Capitalism 1492–1775 168

The European Enlightenment 1650–1800 170

The Rise of the Ottoman Empire 1492–1640 172

The Decline of the Ottoman Empire 1640–1783 174

Safavid Persia and the Rise of
Mughal India 1500–1779 176

Mughal India 1605–1765 178

Ming China 1368–1644 180

The Rise of Manchu Qing China 1644–1783 182

Japan 1500–1800 184

South-east Asia 1500–1800 186

African Kingdoms 1500–1800 188

Spanish Colonization of the Americas 1550–1783 190

European Exploration of
North America 1500–1700 192

Colonial North America 1650–1775 194

The American Revolution 1763–1783 196

THE 19TH-CENTURY WORLD: 1783–1914

The French Revolution 1789–1799 198

Napoleonic Europe 1800–1815 200

The Industrial Revolution 1770–1914 202

Consequences of the Industrial
Revolution 1800–1914 204

The Growth of Nationalism in Europe 1815–1849 206

German and Italian Unification 1815–1871 208

The Russian Empire 1783–1917 210

The European Alliance System 1871–1914 212

The Demise of the Ottoman Empire 1783–1923 214

The Westward Expansion of
the United States 1783–1910 216

The American Civil War 1861–1865 218

The Industrial Expansion of
the United States 1800–1914 220

The Development of Canada 1763–1914 222

Independence in Latin America 1783–1830 224

Latin America Post-independence 1830–1910 226

The British in India 1765–1905 228

The Decline of Manchu Qing China 1783–1911 230

The Modernization of Japan 1800–1914 232

Colonialism in South-east Asia 1790–1914 234

Colonialism in Australia and
New Zealand 1788–1914 236

Africa 1800–1880 238

The Scramble for Africa 1880–1914 240

Science and Technology 1783–1900 242

THE MODERN WORLD

World War I 1914–1918 244

The Russian Revolution and
the Soviet Union 1917–1939 246

Europe Between the Wars 1918–1939 248

USA and Canada 1914–1945 250

World War II in Europe 1939–1945 252

The Holocaust 1942–1945 254

Japan 1914–1941 256

World War II in the Pacific 1941–1945 258

The Republic of China 1911–1949 260

Independence in India 1905–1949 262

The Cold War 1945–1989 264

The USA and Canada 1945 onwards 266

The Soviet Union and Post-Soviet
Russia 1945 onwards 268

Europe 1945 onwards 270

The People's Republic of China 1949 onwards 272

Japan and Korea 1945 onwards 274

South-east Asia 1914 onwards 276

The Indochina Wars 1954–1979 278

Central and South Asia 1948 onwards 280

Australia and New Zealand 1914 onwards 282

The Middle East 1923 onwards 284

The Arab-Israeli Conflict 1948 onwards 286

The Rise of Islamism 1979 onwards 288

Africa 1914 onwards 290

Latin America 1910 onwards 292

Environmental Challenges 1970 onwards 294

Advances in Science, Technology
and Medicine 1900 onwards 296

Into the Future 298

World History Timeline 300

Index 302

INTRODUCTION

When asked to comment on the significance of the French Revolution, the Chinese leader Chairman Mao replied that it was 'too early to tell'. He may have been right. Certainly, when it comes to thinking and writing about history, it is advisable to take the long view. The patterns and cycles that characterize the narrative of our past often take a while to play themselves out. This may not be immediately apparent from our 21st-century standpoint, with its 24-hour rolling news and seemingly endless stream of world-shaking, history-making events. History seems to unfold almost faster than we can absorb it. Yesterday's news already seems old; last month's headlines feel positively antiquated. And as for Paris in 1789 – what could we possibly learn about that long-ago episode that we don't know already? But this is surely just a trick of historical perspective. The recent past looms large in our collective consciousness and naturally feels more momentous than anything from the 18th century or earlier. Previous generations undoubtedly felt the same significance about their own time as we do about ours.

A history of the world is an opportunity to stand back and take a long view. It is a chance to discern the broad patterns and cycles that might be less visible in histories of more limited scope. And when we do stand back, surprising parallels start to become apparent. We see the same universal themes playing themselves out in very different periods and places. The fight for land and resources is as clearly observed in the struggle between Mitanni and Egypt in the 1400s BC as it is in the Sino-Japanese wars of the 19th and 20th centuries AD. The struggle for freedom and self-determination is as evident in the rebellions of the Jews against Roman rule in first and second-century Palestine as it is in the popular uprisings that toppled governments in Tunisia and Egypt in early 2011. The desire to make sense of existence stirred the philosophers of ancient Greece as much as their counterparts today. And the power of individuals to create mass movements can be seen in King Ashoka's promotion of Buddhism in the third century BC as much as in Mohandas Gandhi's mass campaign of civil disobedience 22 centuries later.

In 300 pages, this book tells the story of human history from its earliest beginnings in Africa some six or seven million years ago to the complex, globalized world of today. The book is intended to be an accessible, enjoyable read; no previous in-depth knowledge of history is necessary. It offers an overview of the human story, and a sense of its broad sweep, hopefully leaving readers with a much stronger sense of how we as a species progressed from hunting and gathering in the forests and savannahs of prehistoric Africa to networking on the Internet or listening to our ipods in today's crowded towns and cities.

How will future scholars judge our attempts to make sense of history? Have we achieved an understanding of our past in its broadest sense that will stand the test of time, or will our version undergo further revision? It is, of course, far too early to tell.

Alex Woolf

HUMAN ORIGINS

7,000,000–2,000,000BC

The first written records of human activity date from about 5,500 years ago; anything that happened before that time is known as prehistory. We know about this distant era only through archaeological excavations of ancient settlements and the painstaking work of anthropologists examining ancient bones and fossils.

Most scientists believe that humans and apes evolved from a common ancestor who lived between ten and five million years ago. The first hominids – the family of primates that includes human beings and their human-like ancestors – probably appeared around seven million years ago. What distinguished hominids from other primates was their ability to walk on two legs.

The first hominids

The earliest hominids probably lived in the tropical rainforests of East and North-Central Africa. At that time, the Earth's climate, though warmer than today, was cooling, and the rainforests that had covered much of Africa were shrinking. The hominids began to come down from their trees and cross large areas of open savannah in order to find food. As they ventured across longer distances, they developed the ability to walk on two legs.

The oldest-known hominid fossil is between six and seven million years old. Discovered in Chad in northern Africa in 2001, it has a skull partly resembling an early human and partly an ape. Similar early hominid fossils have been discovered in

Right Donald Johanson displays a plaster cast of the skull of the hominid fossil he discovered in Ethiopia, which he named Lucy

LUCY

One of the most complete examples of an Australopithecine that has ever been found was discovered by American anthropologist Donald Johanson in 1974, during an expedition searching for fossils in Ethiopia. While excavating in the Afar Depression, Johanson came across a 40 per cent complete skeleton of an *Australopithecus afarensis*. The anatomy indicated that the fossil was female and that she had lived 3.2 million years ago. Johanson named her Lucy after the Beatles song 'Lucy in the Sky with Diamonds'. At the time, she was the oldest hominid yet found. Lucy measured 1.1 m (3.6 ft) in height, weighed 29 kg (64 lbs) and looked similar to a chimpanzee, yet her pelvis and leg bones were identical in function to those of modern humans, proving that she had walked erect.

Kenya and Ethiopia but it is unclear how any of these species relate to later hominids or to human beings.

The Australopithecines

About four million years ago, a hominid genus called *Australopithecus* appeared in East Africa. In contrast to the flatter faces of early humans, Australopithecines had faces that jutted out beneath their foreheads. They were about a metre or so in height and had long arms and large, flat molars, useful for grinding their diet of fruit, nuts, seeds, vegetables and insects. They also scavenged meat from the carcasses of the herd animals of the savannah. They remained good tree-climbers, but had the great advantage over their ancestors of being bipedal.

Scientists have identified six separate *Australopithecus* species, based on differences in their size and the shape and size of their jaws, teeth and brains. The original species, *Australopithecus afarensis*, lived in Ethiopia and Tanzania, while later species appeared in southern, eastern and north-eastern Africa. Two of the six species are known as the robust Australopithecines, while the other four are called gracile (or slender) Australopithecines. Robust Australopithecines had larger molars and more powerful jaws and may have had larger bodies than their gracile cousins.

Scientists disagree on the relationship between the different *Australopithecus* species. Some believe they were all originally one species that moved to different parts of Africa and then evolved to adapt to local conditions, while others say they evolved one from the other. Still others argue that the differences between robust and gracile Australopithecines are so great that they form two distinct groups.

Our ancestors

Robust Australopithecines, since they became extinct between one and a half and one million years ago, can be ruled out as the ancestors of *Homo sapiens*. Of the graciles, the most likely candidate for an ancestor of modern humans is *Australopithecus garhi*, which lived in north-eastern Africa some two or three million years ago. However, some anthropologists argue that we may actually be descended from another hominid species that lived at the same time as the Australopithecines. A fossil skull found in north-west Kenya in 1999 revealed a species with a relatively flat face, much more like early human beings. Known as *Kenyathropus platyops*, it may have itself evolved from an Australopithecine more than two million years ago.

Above This artist's impression shows the skull of Kenyathropus platyops and a reconstruction of its broad, flat face

PEOPLING THE EARTH

2,000,000–40,000BC

The first hominids to be considered human beings appeared in Africa about two million years ago. These are commonly divided into three species: Homo habilis, Homo rudolfensis *and* Homo erectus. *All three had larger brains and flatter faces than* Australopithecus *but of the three,* Homo erectus *had the largest brain and the most upright posture. Most scientists believe that* Homo erectus *evolved into modern humans.*

Above right
*Homo erectus
had discovered
how to create fire*

Below *This
reconstruction
shows the physiog-
nomy of* Homo
erectus, *thought to
be the ancestor of
modern humans*

The first tools

All three of these early human species made and used stone tools. At first, these were nothing more than sharp-edged stones used for cutting, scraping or chopping the flesh and bones of the animals they killed – made by striking one stone against another, chipping away pieces to form a cutting edge. Later toolmakers used wood or bone mallets to produce straight, sharp cutting edges.

Homo erectus learned to make double-edged hand axes, which they used to shape wood or bone and cut up meat, showing that they may have been the first hominids to hunt large animals.

Out of Africa

Homo erectus were the first hominids to live outside Africa. Some time after 1.8 million years ago, they began a migration that led them through the Middle East to South and South-east Asia and northern China, although they did not reach the Americas or Australia. The earliest non-African examples of *Homo erectus* have been found on the island of Java, Indonesia, and are around 1.8 million years old – although some scientists think this is a separate species.

The ice ages of the Pleistocene era, which lasted from about two million to 11,500 years ago, prevented much human migration to Europe, because of the massive glaciers that covered large parts of the continent during this period. The earliest human remains in Europe, found in northern Spain, date to around 800,000 years ago.

To survive in colder, northern areas, *Homo erectus* mastered fire and began to wear clothing – the first hominid species to do so. The earliest evidence of the use of fire was found in a cave in northern China occupied by *Homo erectus* around half a million years ago.

Homo sapiens

Modern human beings are classified as *Homo sapiens*. This group evolved higher, more rounded skulls, while the ridged brows and protruding faces of earlier hominids gradually disappeared and a noticeable chin developed. Certain differences, such as skin colour and eye shape, continued to distinguish the various groups of *Homo sapiens,* depending on where they lived in the world, and these differences can still be seen among humans today.

There are two main theories about how *Homo sapiens* developed: the single origin theory and the multiple origin theory. According to the more widely accepted single origin theory, the humans that spread out of Africa to different parts of Asia and Europe did not maintain contact with each other. Those that remained in Africa evolved into another species, *Homo heidelbergensis,* which spread throughout Africa and then into Europe (but not Asia) around one million years ago. Those that spread into Europe adapted to the cold and severe conditions to form *Homo neanderthalensis,* or Neanderthals.

The first *Homo sapiens* appeared in Africa between 200,000 and 100,000 years ago, having evolved from the African *Homo heidelbergensis.* The new species then spread throughout Africa, as well as into Asia and Europe, displacing those

THE NEANDERTHALS
The Neanderthals lived in ice age Europe between 150,000 and 35,000 years ago. With large noses and short, sturdy bodies averaging around 1.6 m (5.2 ft) in height, they were well adapted to the cold climate. They were the most advanced toolmakers of their time, using hammers made from bones, antlers and wood to produce a range of tools for butchering animals, scraping hides and carving wood. Advanced hunters, they also made spears for hunting animals such as horses, reindeer and mammoths. Most lived in caves, but some built circular tents from hides, leaves or bark supported by wooden posts. Interestingly, the Neanderthals were the first people known to bury their dead.

who lived there. These earlier peoples, including the Neanderthals in Europe and *Homo erectus* in Asia, eventually became extinct.

According to the multiple origins theory, sufficient contact was maintained between early human subgroups, including *Homo erectus,* Neanderthals and *Homo heidelbergensis,* to ensure they remained part of the same species. The differences in appearance between each subgroup were due to their adaptation to local conditions. At some point between 700,000 and 400,000 years ago, these scattered groups evolved into *Homo sapiens.*

Below *The fossilized skulls of Neanderthals showed ridged brows and projecting jaws*

TIMELINE (ALL DATES BC)	
c. 2,000,000 ya	*Emergence of first human beings, including our direct ancestor,* Homo erectus
c. 1,800,000 ya	Homo erectus *begin to migrate to Asia from Africa*
800,000 ya	*First evidence of* Homo erectus *in Europe*
500,000 ya	*First evidence of* Homo erectus' *use of fire*
700–400,000 ya	Homo sapiens *evolve (according to multiple origins theory)*
200–100,000 ya	Homo sapiens *start to appear in Africa (according to single origins theory)*
150–35,000 ya	*Neanderthals exist in Europe.*

HUMAN DEVELOPMENT

40,000–8000BC

The period known as the Upper Paleolithic or Late Stone Age, which dates from about 40,000 to 10,000 years ago, was a time of notable advances in human mental development and technology. More sophisticated tools and artefacts were produced, the first settlements were established, the first languages were spoken and the first works of art created. Humans also began to travel, building boats or rafts that took them to Australia and crossing the freezing land-bridge into the Americas.

humans moved into Europe, where they hunted the vast herds of reindeer, horse, bison and mammoth that moved across the Eurasian steppes and tundras.

North-eastern Siberia was settled around 20,000 years ago, perhaps by people moving up from northern China. At that time, Asia was connected to North America by a frozen land-bridge, which was first crossed by people some 15,000 to 20,000 years ago. These original Americans gradually spread through the new continent, reaching the southernmost tip of South America 11,000 years ago.

The earliest organized settlements date to around 27,000 years ago. These took the form of campsites, some with storage pits, and they were often located in the bottoms of narrow valleys, perhaps to make it easier to hunt passing herds. Most were probably not settled all year round, but were inhabited at certain times of the year to take advantage of seasonal food sources.

Above *This fresco in the National Anthropological Museum in Mexico shows hunters crossing the Bering Strait some 20,000 years ago during the first ice age*

Settlement

Modern humans had arrived in China and South-east Asia by around 75,000 years ago. Here they learned how to build rafts or boats, and by 40,000 years ago they had reached New Guinea and Australia (then joined into one giant continent), probably by a series of great island-hopping voyages. At about the same time, modern

Tools

Before the Upper Paleolithic period, all tools were made of stone. Most were crude in appearance and could be used for a number of functions. Around 40,000 years ago, the archaeological record shows a dramatic improvement in the range and sophistication of tools. Bone, ivory and antler were used to obtain more refined and complex designs than was possible with stone or wood, and tools came to serve more specialized functions, such as cutting, slicing, carving, piercing, engraving or drilling. Eyed needles of bone, oil lamps and rope all appeared for the first time during this period, and bone needles in particular were important in the development of close-fitting clothing. As people became more skillful and ambitious at hunting and fishing, they created better equipment, including sturdy spears, darts, harpoons and fish hooks.

Art

One of the most fascinating developments of this period was the first art. As people progressed beyond mere subsistence they began to decorate themselves with jewellery, such as beads made from polished shells. Then, from about 30,000 years ago, the first carvings appeared – sculptures and engravings of animals and people, made from bone, ivory or stone. At about this time, the first cave art appeared in Europe – paintings of hunted animals, such as mammoths, horses and bison, many of them of very high artistic quality. Some show animals that have been speared. The colours they used – black, red and yellow – were obtained from charcoal, clay, iron and other minerals. Late-stone-age Europeans also made clay, ivory or stone figurines of women, which may have represented fertility.

Language

Exactly when spoken language developed is a mystery. It is possible that Neanderthals had a crude language. Studies of the anatomy of their vocal tracts show they were certainly capable of it. However, many anthropologists believe that speech first developed during the late Stone Age. They argue that the development of complex tools, the increasing specialization of human activity and the invention of art, all required greater cooperation between individuals, necessitating speech.

Life

We can only speculate about what life was like in the late Stone Age. It is estimated that there were around ten million humans in the whole world at that time. There is evidence of limited trade, with finds of exotic materials in some settlements, far from their origins. However, most people lived isolated existences, rarely if ever meeting anyone outside of their own group or tribe. These groups were certainly larger and more settled than those of earlier epochs. The earliest remains of built settlements, from around 10,000 years ago, suggest that these groups might have included between 400 and 600 people. The social organization of these groups can only be guessed at.

Above *An ivory amulet and idol, found at Dolni Vestonice in south Moravia. They are about 25,000 years old*

WHAT HAPPENED?

Scientists have puzzled over the causes of the 'Upper Paleolithic Revolution' — the sudden acceleration in human development 40,000 years ago. Some say climate change played a part in this. The Earth, already in the midst of an ice age, grew colder during this period. Necessity of survival in these harsh conditions may well have been the mother of human invention. Lower global temperatures may have, for example, reduced the availability of timber and made flint brittle and unusable as a tool, forcing people to consider other materials. According to another theory, the development of language may have actually changed people's behaviour, giving humans the capacity to plan for the future and communicate complex and abstract ideas.

FROM HUNTING TO FARMING

8000–3000BC

Until the last ice age ended around 11,500 years ago man had been a hunter-gatherer, hunting animals and gathering wild plants for food. There was no need to look beyond the savannahs, steppes and tundras, where big game was abundant and easily caught. However as the glaciers melted, sea levels rose, flooding vast areas of lowland hunting grounds, while at the same time the forests advanced. In these new conditions, humans had to find new ways to survive. During the next 5,000 years, known as the Neolithic period, all of these factors kick-started a transition to organized farming.

Above *This artist's impression shows a Neolithic farming settlement*

The first farmers

Farming began around 10,000 years ago, or 8000BC, in an area known as the Fertile Crescent, comprising modern-day Iraq, Syria, Israel, Jordan and Egypt. This region, as well as being fertile, enjoyed a great diversity of annual plants, which were well adapted to the new climate of long dry seasons. Among the first plants to be farmed were probably barley, wheat and oats, which were all easy and quick to grow and readily storable.

So how did the jump from gathering wild plants to deliberately planting them take place? The first farmers were probably hunter-gatherers who began growing crops to supplement the food they obtained from dwindling herds of game. They started by planting the seeds of their favourite wild plants to guarantee a steady supply. Gradually, they domesticated these plants by breeding strains with desirable characteristics, such as high yield and rapid growth. As their methods improved, farming became their most important source of food.

The move from driving game for hunting to domesticating and herding these animals was similarly momentous. The first pastoral farmers were probably shepherds in northern Iraq in about 8000BC. The wild ancestors of sheep, goats, cows and pigs were gradually domesticated, exploited not just for their meat, but also for their skins, wool and eventually their milk. The domestication of oxen and horses for traction would come later, starting in about 3000BC.

The spread of agriculture

Over the next 5,000 years, farming spread to different parts of the world. By 6000BC, people were herding cattle and growing rice and sorghum in northern Africa. Between 5000 and 4000, agriculture developed independently in Asia, where rice rather than wheat was the staple crop. Rice and millet were grown in the Yangtse Valley in China and modern-day Thailand, followed by mung, soy and azuki beans. In the Indus Valley in northern India, people grew wheat, legumes, oranges, dates and mangoes. By 3500, the Indus Valley farmers were growing cotton for textiles.

Between 4500 and 4000, cattle and wheat farmers spread from the Fertile Crescent through modern-day Turkey into the densely forested areas of central, western and northern Europe. The hunter-gatherers of these parts learned farming techniques from the newcomers. Agriculture reached southern Africa by around 3000. In 2700, maize was domesticated in Central America, followed by corn and beans in about 1500. By 1000, people in eastern North America were cultivating gourds and sunflowers. Potatoes, tomatoes and maize were being grown in South America by this time.

Technological advances

Compared to hunting and gathering, farming was hard work and in many parts of the world it was adopted only gradually and probably unwillingly. However, farming did make life easier in many ways. It provided a steady supply of food and allowed people to live in one place for a long time, paving the way for some important technological advances.

Heavy tools and equipment, for example, would have been impractical for hunter-gatherers with their nomadic existence, but Neolithic farmers, with their settled lifestyles, were able to develop many new and useful devices. Heavy axes for forest clearing, hoes for digging soil, sickles to cut grain and millstones to grind flour were all invented by the first farming communities. The kilns that farmers built to bake clay pots to store their grain provided them with the means to smelt and cast metals: first copper in about 6000, then bronze in about 3500 and, eventually, iron. The wheel – arguably the most important prehistoric innovation – was invented by the Sumerians in about 5000. It was first used to make pottery and only later applied to transport. Wool and cotton producers mastered the art of spinning and weaving plant and animal fibres to produce the world's first textiles.

TIMELINE (ALL DATES BC)	
c. 9500	The last ice age ends
c. 8000	Farming begins in the Fertile Crescent
c. 6000	Farming spreads to northern Africa. Copper ore is first smelted
c. 5000	Farming develops in parts of Asia, including the Yangtse and Indus Valleys. Intensive farming first practised in Sumer
c. 4500–4000	Farming spreads to Europe
c. 3500	First bronze implements appear
c. 3000	Animals first used for traction. Farming spreads to southern Africa
c. 2700	Farming develops in Central America
c. 1000	Farming has developed in eastern North America and in South America by this time.

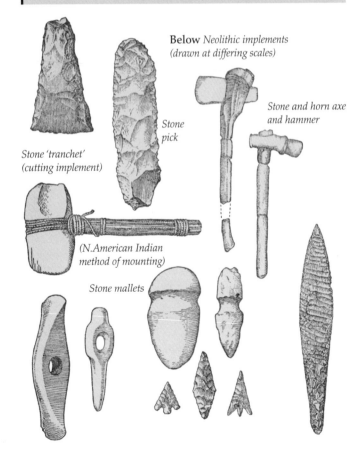

Below Neolithic implements (drawn at differing scales)

Stone and horn axe and hammer

Stone pick

Stone 'tranchet' (cutting implement)

(N.American Indian method of mounting)

Stone mallets

EARLY FARMING COMMUNITIES

8000–2000BC

The impact of the rise of agriculture on Neolithic society cannot be overstated. It revolutionized the way people lived, worked and related at the most profound level and launched humanity into an era of progress that continues to this day. This is most vividly illustrated by considering the experience of those communities that did not adopt agriculture during this period. When Europeans arrived in North America in the 16th century AD, they encountered hunter-gatherers living much as their ancestors had done ten thousand years before.

Colonizing new areas

The first important effect of farming was that it led to the settlement of many new areas of land. Early farmers would settle in an area for as long as the crops grew well there. When the land surrounding their village grew less productive because the crops had used up the nutrients in the soil, the farmers (who had yet to develop fertilizers to replace the nutrients) would move to a new area and build another village, and so the process of gradual colonization continued.

Below *The development of farming led to settled communities*

Population growth

As farming methods improved and food became more plentiful, farming communities could support far greater numbers of people. In this way, agriculture enabled an enormous increase in the human population. A single hunter-gatherer required an area of 25 km² (9.6 square miles) to live, and a typical band of hunter-gatherers numbered between 30 and 50. By contrast, the most basic forms of agriculture could support up to 20 people per km², and typical farming villages contained hundreds of people. In areas such as Sumer where food production was intensified through the use of ploughing and irrigation, the population of a town could number in the thousands.

It was not only the increased supply of food that allowed a greater population. Because of their nomadic lifestyle, hunter-gatherer families could only carry one child at a time, limiting the number of children each family could have, whereas the settled existence of sedentary farmers meant that larger families were now possible. This increase in family size was, however, somewhat offset by a higher death rate due to disease. Farming communities inevitably lived close to the animals they domesticated and a number of diseases, including influenza, smallpox and measles, spread from animals to humans.

Social changes

Despite disease, the human population rose steadily, especially in areas that adopted intensive farming techniques. As a result, increasing numbers of people could be supported by farming that were not actually needed to work as farmers or food producers. Instead they were able to become skilled at crafts and made baskets, cloth, leather goods, tools or pottery. Farming communities became more specialized. They also became wealthier as people acquired material possessions on a scale beyond anything conceivable in a

HOUSES AND HOMES

From the earliest times, humans have sought shelter and protection from the elements. Early nomadic peoples took advantage of the natural shelter that was afforded by caves, rocky outcrops and woodland, or they built tents from branches covered in animal hide.

With the coming of agriculture, people were able to settle in one place and build longer-lasting homes. The Celts, an early European people, built round houses with low walls of stone or branches and twigs woven together and covered in mud. The roof was a frame of branches covered with bundles of tied straw.

Neolithic communities of the Middle East learned how to make bricks by pressing mud into wooden moulds and leaving the mud to dry out in the sun. Mud bricks became the most important building material in the region, being strong, durable, yet easy to produce. When a house fell into disrepair, it was quickly knocked down and replaced with a new one.

Above *This ancient European settlement shows a typical Celtic house with round stone walls and a reconstructed straw roof*

hunter-gatherer society. Differences in wealth became more marked and gave rise to notions of social status. The simple egalitarianism of hunter-gatherers gave way to a more complex, hierarchical society.

The Neolithic revolution spread unevenly around the globe. In those places with good soil and a favourable climate, farming developed more quickly and the social changes were consequently more dramatic. It is no coincidence that the first cities arose in Mesopotamia in the Fertile Crescent, the birthplace of agriculture. In places with poor soil and climate, such as parts of North America, hunter-gatherer society would continue for many more hundreds of years. Most parts of the world fell between these two extremes.

By around 2000BC, in South and Southeast Asia, New Guinea, North Africa, northern Europe and parts of Middle and South America, the majority of farming communities consisted of a few hundred – in some cases, a few thousand – individuals, living in villages. Although they may have traded with and spoken the same language as neighbouring tribes, they were essentially independent and self-sufficient. Remains of these early communities show evidence of communal building projects, such as the large stone tombs found in western Europe. This suggests the existence of leaders within the community who could, from time to time, coerce others in their tribe to undertake such works.

Left *A Neolithic painted pottery jar dating from c. 2000BC*

THE DAWN OF CIVILIZATION

4500–2000BC

Exactly when civilization began is a matter of debate. It depends firstly on what we mean by the term. Some have sought to define civilization by listing certain attributes such as writing, cities and monuments. This may be true, although these could be called products of civilization rather than essential characteristics. The single factor that differentiates civilizations from earlier societies is complexity. Through advances in agriculture and technology, civilizations are societies that have attained a surplus of resources that frees up a significant proportion of the population to interact in complex, organized and creative ways. They are able to establish, for example, cities, a social hierarchy, a governing class, laws, bureaucracy, industry, money, markets, organized religion and education.

Chiefdoms

But how did the simple farming communities described on the previous pages turn into civilizations? These communities may have been sufficiently organized to produce the occasional large-scale building project, such as a communal tomb, but most of their energy and resources went into food production. Gradually, however (and only where conditions were favourable), these simple communities began to grow larger and more complex. As before, agriculture provided the key. In the areas where intensive farming techniques could be used, hierarchical communities of up to 20,000 people began to develop. These were known as chiefdoms.

In these communities, status was hereditary, and the senior person of the highest-ranking family was the chieftain of the whole community. Chieftains often exercised their power through a warrior class and could order major constructions such as tombs and temples. Stonehenge in Wiltshire, England, (c. 2200BC) is an example of such a project. Chiefdoms usually had a central stronghold or ceremonial centre surrounded by smaller satellite settlements. There is evidence, found in ancient shrines and temples, that these communities partook in collective worship.

The first chiefdoms arose in Mesopotamia in about 4500, followed by Egypt in about 3300. A little later, chiefdoms developed among the Minoans on Crete, in the Indus Valley in India and in China. By 2500, farming communities in western Europe and in Central America were turning into chiefdoms.

Below *Stonehenge was constructed as some form of ceremonial centre in about 2200BC*

TIMELINE (ALL DATES BC)	
c. 4500	*First chiefdoms arise in Mesopotamia*
c. 3300	*Chiefdoms emerge in Egypt*
c. 3400	*Earliest known examples of writing*
c. 3100	*Chiefdoms are established in Indus Valley*
c. 3000	*Chiefdoms emerge on Minoan Crete*
c. 2500	*Chiefdoms develop in western Europe and Central America.*

The first civilizations

On the fertile floodplains of the Tigris and Euphrates in Mesopotamia, the Nile in Egypt, and the Indus in India, agriculture could support communities of tens of thousands. Here chiefdoms turned into city-states, and the first civilizations arose.

Ties of kinship and respect for lineage were no longer enough to hold such large communities together, and rulers required new methods to maintain their authority and the loyalty of their people. Religion was central to most ancient societies, and the community's chief priest was often also its leader, with the backing of a priestly class. Law codes were devised to maintain order, and bureaucracies were established to uphold and administer the new laws. To bolster their prestige, rulers commissioned large-scale public building projects such as roads, canals, temples and palaces.

Above *The periodic flooding of the Nile left fertile plains that would support large agrarian communities*

Left *A Sumerian tablet covered with cuneiform script, the earliest known form of writing*

Writing

As civilizations grew larger and more complex, government administrators, merchants and traders could no longer store all the information they needed in their heads, and systems of writing became necessary. The earliest known writing has been found on clay tablets in the Sumerian city of Uruk in Mesopotamia and dates from about 3400. This was already a complex system with over 700 signs, so it is likely that it began developing much earlier. The earliest Sumerian writings are accounts and records of transactions. It was only from about 2400 that writing began to be used to record law codes, chronicles, letters, religious scriptures or literature.

All early civilizations developed writing systems. Many of these, such as the Sumerian, began as pictographic systems, with each sign forming a simplified picture of the object or action it represented. Others, such as the Egyptian system, were hieroglyphic, with each sign representing a word or part of a word. The first alphabetic system, in which each sign (or letter) represents a sound, was devised in the 1600s in the eastern Mediterranean.

WAR

With the arrival of agriculture, people began to acquire material possessions and demarcate territory. It is likely that from time to time, other tribes would have wished to lay claim to these possessions and territory and this may have led to raids and skirmishes. However, few Neolithic settlements show signs of fortification, so this was probably a fairly unusual occurrence. *War* in the modern sense of the term, involving states attacking each other with armies, really began with the emergence of the first city-states. These states produced enough of an agricultural surplus to support and maintain organized armies – at least for the duration of a military campaign, after which the soldiers could go back to being farmers. These armies could be used defensively to protect wealth, or offensively to attack other states and expand the power and wealth of a particular state.

EARLY CULTURES OF THE MIDDLE EAST

9000–4300BC

That civilization first arose in the Fertile Crescent of the Middle East was due, at least in part, to climate and geography. Toward the end of the last ice age, this region of good soils and light but reliable rainfall was colonized by an abundance of wild cereal plants, pulses and nut trees. These highly favorable conditions encouraged bands of local hunter-gatherers to establish the world's first permanent farming communities. In time, these communities grew to become chiefdoms and, ultimately, the earliest city-states.

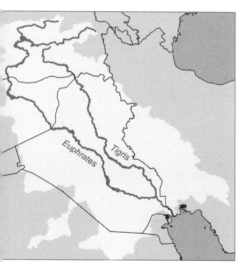

Above *The fertile flood plain between the Tigris and Euphrates rivers gave rise to the Ubaid culture, which lasted for about 1600 years*

The Natufians and other early cultures

Among the first of the hunter-gatherers to turn to farming were the Natufians of the Levant. From around 9000BC, the Natufians began to settle in villages of wooden huts with stone foundations. They hunted gazelle and harvested wild barley and emmer and einkorn wheat close to their settlements. In about 8000, the Natufians learned to selectively breed their crops. By 7500, they had abandoned their hunter-gatherer lifestyle altogether and begun to live entirely on farmed produce.

Other cultures were also developing around this time. Jericho, in modern-day Palestine, was the site of a very early Neolithic settlement. By 8000, a community of some 1,500 people lived there in huts of sun-dried mud bricks, cultivating barley, emmer wheat, pulses and figs. And from 9000, hunter-gatherers in southern Anatolia and the Zagros Mountains began to herd flocks of wild sheep and goats. These animals were fully domesticated by the seventh millennium.

Hassuna culture

Between 6500 and 5500, a series of cultures arose in Mesopotamia, gradually spreading agriculture across the region. The first of these was the Hassuna culture (6500–6000), based in northern Mesopotamia, which grew emmer and einkorn wheat and barley and bred sheep, goats, pigs and cattle. The Hassuna people smelted copper and lead and were the first to produce painted pottery and fire it in purpose-built kilns.

Halafian and Samarran culture

In about 6000, the Hassuna culture was replaced by the Halafian culture, also centred on Mesopotamia's north. Archaeological evidence suggests that Halafian chieftains grew very wealthy through control of their community's trade. At around the same time, further to the south, the Samarran culture developed. The Samarrans developed large-scale irrigation systems, boosting crop yields on the dry lands of central Mesopotamia.

Ubaid culture

By contrast, southern Mesopotamia – the floodplain between the Tigris and Euphrates that would one day nurture the first civilizations – remained unfarmed during the seventh millennium. Centuries of annual flooding had made the soil there extremely fertile, yet with very little rainfall

Left *A jar of the Hassuna culture in Mesopotamia, showing incised decoration*

there was no natural means of watering crops in the dry season. The key to unlocking the riches of the floodplain was irrigation, and the earliest culture to master this technique was the Ubaid, which appeared in about 5900.

The Ubaid culture lasted for some 1,600 years and provided the link between the early Neolithic cultures of northern and central Mesopotamia and the first true civilization, the Sumerians. The Ubaid were, at first, simple hunters and herders, who learned irrigation techniques from the Samarrans. With the invention of the plough in the fifth millennium, productivity was boosted still further and settlements soon grew into towns.

One of these was Eridu, near the western shore of the Persian Gulf, which became an important religious centre. The Ubaid built a multi-roomed temple complex there on a one-metre tall base. Over the centuries, layers would gradually be added to this until – long after the Ubaid had disappeared – it evolved into the first ziggurat, a kind of stepped pyramid.

Because southern Mesopotamia lacked many raw materials, including timber, metals and stone, trade with other settlements was vital, and through these trade links Ubaid culture spread through the region. By 5400, Ubaid culture had replaced Halafian culture in northern Mesopotamia.

Some elements of civilization were starting to appear in Ubaid culture towards its end.

ÇATAL HÜYÜK

Overlooking wheatfields in the Konya Plain in south-central Turkey lies Çatal Hüyük. This extraordinary site stands out from history as a surprising, early oasis of high culture, foreshadowing the great civilizations of the future. The 8.5-hectare (21-acre) site is the largest and most advanced Neolithic settlement yet found. Dating from between 6500 and 5500, it shows evidence of trade, irrigation, wall-painting, sculpture, weaving, basketry, pottery, and the earliest-known evidence of copper smelting. Yet, unlike the city-states that would follow, Çatal Hüyük lacked the local conditions for long-term growth and, after 1,000 years, it was abandoned.

Major building works such as canals and temples required a strong central authority, and high levels of trade encouraged them to develop an accounting system based on clay tokens. However, the society lacked the complexity and hierarchical nature of a fully developed civilization.

Above *Part of the site of Çatal Hüyük, which was first discovered in the late 1950s and is still under excavation today*

TIMELINE (ALL DATES BC)

c. 9000	*Natufians begin to settle in villages. Hunter-gatherers in southern Anatolia and Zagros mountains start to herd sheep and goats*
c. 8000	*Jericho is an established settlement of 1,500*
c. 7500	*Natufians become a full farming economy*
c. 6500–6000	*Hassuna culture*
c. 6000–5500	*Samarran culture*
c. 6000–5400	*Halafian culture*
c. 5900–4300	*Ubaid culture.*

SUMER

4300–2334BC

The world's first civilization arose in Sumer, which is the ancient name for southern Mesopotamia, during the Uruk period (4300–3000BC). In these fertile, low-lying marshes, the land had to be drained and irrigated before it could be farmed, and flood barriers had to be built. All this required cooperation between different villages. As the population rose and pressure for reclaimed land grew, it must have made sense for these villages to unite to form towns, usually on the site of the shrine of the local god. These towns then grew to form cities.

Below right
The story of Gilgamesh, written in cuneiform script on 12 stone tablets, attributes superhuman courage and strength to him

City-states

The first cities were built in about 3500. They were, in fact, city-states – independent states consisting of a city and its surrounding territory. There were around twelve of these city-states, the largest being Uruk, with a population of around 10,000. Uruk was the dominant city until around 3000. Other cities, such as Kish, Ur, Eridu, Lagash and Nippur had populations of between 2,000 and 8,000. Each city worshipped its own deity and had at its centre a large temple complex administered by priests. Gradually the gods of each city became organized into a hierarchy, which changed as the power of the cities waxed and waned.

Religion

Religion was more dominant in Sumerian society than elsewhere in the ancient world, perhaps because few others felt more at the mercy of the gods. The Tigris and Euphrates rivers were subject to devastating floods and unpredictable changes of course. It was a land of high winds, dust storms, plagues and merciless

THE EPIC OF GILGAMESH

Gilgamesh is a legendary hero of Mesopotamian literature. His adventures were recorded by an Assyrian king in the seventh century BC, but his origins go back much earlier than that. It is possible that the character of Gilgamesh was based on a king who ruled the Uruk between 3000 and 2500. The epic tells of a king of Uruk, part-god part-human, who is consumed with a desire for adventure and goes in search of eternal life. The epic may preserve something of early Mesopotamian history in the character of the wild man Enkidu, who is tamed by the gods and then helps a group of herdsmen. He is later brought to a farming city where he first fights, then became friends with, Gilgamesh. Enkidu's progress could be seen to represent the gradual evolution of the Mesopotamians from wild hunter-gatherers to civilized city-dwellers.

droughts. It is understandable therefore that they turned to higher powers to impose some order and certainty on their lives. The first kings of these cities were, not surprisingly, priests.

Trade
The city temples doubled as distribution centres where surplus food and craft products were collected and then distributed to the townspeople or used for trade. Trade links were established with other parts of the Middle East, helping to spread Sumerian culture. The Sumerians also traded with places as far afield as Afghanistan and India. The problem of keeping track of the many transactions prompted the invention of writing (see page 19).

Early Dynastic Period
Between 3000 and 2334, known as the Early Dynastic Period, Sumerian history entered a new and turbulent phase. As the population of the city-states grew, they came into conflict with each other over territory, and wars broke out. The cities defended themselves with large walls and armed themselves with bronze weapons. The art of this period depicts rulers trampling their enemies. The scribes, whose original purpose was to record commercial transactions, turned their skill to poetry, glorifying the epic deeds of conquering kings. The first slaves were recorded at this time, most likely prisoners of war.

Kings became more secular in character as their authority came to depend on their armies as much as their priests. They established the first law codes and built opulent palaces next to the temple complexes. On their deaths they were given elaborate burials, accompanied by luxurious objects and even their sacrificed servants.

TIMELINE (ALL DATES BC)	
c. 4300	*Start of Uruk period*
c. 3500	*First cities are built*
c. 2900	*Start of the Early Dynastic Period*
c. 2450	*Elamites conquer Sumer*
c. 2400	*City of Kish controls Sumer*
2350	*City of Umma controls Sumer*
2334	*Sumer is conquered by Akkad.*

The fall of Sumer
The first city to dominate in this period was Kish, possibly under a king named Etana. Next came Uruk, one of whose kings may have been Gilgamesh, who later became the subject of the world's first literary epic (see panel). Another dominant city of the time was Ur. The civil war so weakened Sumer that, in about 2450, it fell under the control of the Elamites, a people from the Zagros Mountains to the east. By around 2400, Kish had reasserted its dominance, but was soon overthrown by the city of Lagash under King Eannatum. Umma, which conquered Lagash in 2350, became the last city-state to rule over Sumer. Its rule lasted just 16 years, ending with the conquest of Sumer by Akkad, the new power in Mesopotamia.

Below *A detail from the 'Standard of Ur', dated c. 2500BC. It is made of shell with a background of lapis lazuli*

THE FIRST EMPIRES OF MESOPOTAMIA

2334–1595BC

From the 2300s BC, the rule of city-states in Mesopotamia was replaced by the rule of empires. These early empires were generally unstable and short-lived, their success depending greatly on the strength of their rulers. Conquered states were forced to pay tribute, but were not actually occupied, so, in times of weak rule, they could assert their independence by stopping payments. Mesopotamian empires also faced threats from beyond their borders. Peoples such as the Kassites and Amorites from neighbouring regions were attracted by the wealth of Mesopotamia and the land, with its undefendable frontiers, was frequently attacked.

Sargon of Akkad

The first great empire in history was founded by Sargon I of Akkad in 2334. Around this time, Sumer had become divided into two lands: Akkad (from Abu Salabikh to the edge of the northern Mesopotamian plains) and Sumer (from Nippur south to Eridu). Sargon began his career as an official in the court of King Ur-Zababa of the Akkadian city of Kish. He may have overthrown the king to become ruler of Kish. Then, in three hard-fought battles, he defeated Umma, the dominant city-state of Sumer. Sargon went on to conquer the rest of Sumer, Akkad and Elam before leading his army to a series of victories that extended his empire to cover parts of modern-day Iran and Turkey.

Above *The script on this clay cone refers to the long-running hostilities between the city-states of Lagash and Umma*

Right *The ruins of the ziggurat temple of Agar Guf, in the Kassite city of Dur Kurigalzu, now a suburb of Baghdad*

To celebrate his victories, Sargon built a magnificent capital city called Akkad (or Agade). An outstanding military leader, Sargon also proved himself an able administrator, governing the empire for 56 years until his death in 2279. Sargon was a Semite, a person who spoke a Semitic language such as Arabic or Hebrew, and during his rule, Semites replaced the Sumerians as the dominant people of Mesopotamia. Their language came to be called Akkadian.

Sargon's empire lasted a further 60 years under his successors, reaching its zenith during the reign of Sargon's grandson Naram-Sin (reigned 2254–2218). After this, it declined, collapsing in 2193, probably due to invasions by Gutians from the Zagros Mountains and the nomadic Amorites from the Syrian desert. For the next 80 years, individual city-states once again competed for dominance.

Ur-Nammu

In 2112, the Sumerian city of Ur came to hold sway over the region. Its ruler, Ur-Nammu, built an empire that extended from Assyria in the north to Elam in the

south-east. Ur-Nammu created a system of regional governors and tax collectors to help administer his empire. Under his reign, the first ziggurats were built. From 2034, the empire came under attack from the Amorites and was finally destroyed in 2004 when Ur was sacked by the Elamites.

Assyria

For the next 200 years, city-states fought each other without any achieving lasting dominance. Then, in 1813, an Amorite leader called Shamshi-Adad took control of the northern state of Assyria, and a new power emerged in the region. Assyria had established itself as a significant trading power since around 2000, with colonies in Anatolia trading tin and cloth for silver and gold. With Shamshi-Adad's accession, the Assyrians expanded their territory to encompass western Syria, northern Mesopotamia and the borders of Akkad. Shamshi-Adad's empire was short-lived, however, as he came under increasing attack from the Elamites and the Akkadian city-state of Eshnunna, and was already in decline by the time of his death in 1781.

Babylonia

By 1757, most of Assyria was under the control of Babylonia, the new regional power, centred on the city of Babylon in Akkad. Babylon had been ruled by an Amorite dynasty since 1894 and, with the accession of the powerful king Hammurabi in 1792, it asserted control over the whole of Akkad, which would soon become known as Babylonia. In 1787, the belligerent Hammurabi conquered Sumeria to the south. After taking over Assyria, he completed his conquest of Mesopotamia with his capture of Eshnunna in 1755.

THE CODE OF HAMMURABI

To keep control of his many subjects, Hammurabi created one of the earliest written collections of laws, known as the Code of Hammurabi. The code, which he based on older collections of Sumerian and Akkadian laws, consisted of 282 laws. These dealt with many aspects of Babylonian life, including work disputes, divorce, treatment of children and punishment of criminals. One law stated that if a house fell down, its architect would be sentenced to death. Another decreed that a man who stole from a burning house would be burned alive. The code was carved on stone tablets and placed in temples around the empire.

Above *The Code of Hammurabi tablets are among the best-preserved of their type*

Hurrians and Hittites

In the 17th century BC, new external powers emerged to threaten the Babylonian Empire under King Hammurabi. In about 1680, the Hurrians, a people from Armenia, took over Assyria and began to spread through northern Mesopotamia. Then, in 1650, the Hittites, an Indo-European people originally from Thrace in south-eastern Europe, established themselves as a powerful kingdom in Anatolia. The Hittites, under their king Mursilis, invaded and sacked the city of Babylon in 1595.

Below *A bust of King Hammurabi of Babylonia, dating from the 18th century BC*

TIMELINE (ALL DATES BC)	
2334–2112	*Empire of Sargon of Akkad*
2112–2004	*Empire of Ur-Nammu of Ur*
1813–1781	*Empire of Shamshi-Adad of Assyria*
1792–1595	*Empire of Hammurabi of Babylonia.*

KINGDOMS AND EMPIRES OF MESOPOTAMIA

1595–1000BC

In the six centuries that followed the fall of Babylon in 1595, empires and kingdoms rose and fell in Mesopotamia. The main competing powers of this period were the Hurrians, the Hittites, the Assyrians and the Babylonians. Both the Hurrians and the Hittites had to contend with a rising superpower to the south-west: Egypt. Then, from around 1200, the major powers were thrown into further turmoil by the large-scale invasion of the region by nomadic peoples. Unlike city-states, these peoples possessed no infrastructure to attack nor central authority to negotiate with, and when faced with mighty armies, they could simply melt away into the hills. As such, the nomads proved the undoing of more than one empire.

Mitanni

The Hurrians, who had been establishing themselves in northern Mesopotamia since the early 17th century, founded the kingdom of Mitanni in about 1550. The Hurrians used horses and were among the first people to use chariots in warfare. During the late 16th century, they extended their power westwards into the Levant (the part of the Fertile Crescent bordering the Mediterranean). Here, in the early 1500s, they confronted the rising power of Egypt. For the next century,

Below *This engraving shows Rameses II, ruler of Egypt from 1279 to 1213BC, going into battle against the Hittites at Kadesh*

Mitanni and Egypt fought for control of the land between the Orontes and Euphrates Rivers (modern-day Syria). However, by the early 1400s, both kingdoms began to fear the rise of the Hittites to the north, and Egypt and Mitanni decided to form an alliance.

Hittites

Following their conquest of Babylon in 1595, the Hittites gained control of northern Syria, and by 1500 they had become a leading power in the Middle East. Their dominance was based on a mixture of diplomacy (they often developed peaceful and profitable relationships with the peoples they conquered) and military innovation (they created a new design of chariot that could carry three fighters rather than two).

Between 1353 and 1335, Egypt suffered a period of political instability, leaving its ally Mitanni vulnerable to Hittite aggression. In 1340, the Hittite king Suppiluliumas (reigned 1344–1322) destroyed the Mitanni capital of Washukanni, then attacked Mitanni territory in the Levant. By 1328, the Hittites controlled western Mitanni and Suppiluliumas had installed a puppet ruler in Washukanni.

A new rivalry now grew between the Hittites and Egypt, culminating in an epic battle at Kadesh on the Orontes River in about 1274. The Hittites, led by King Mutwatallis, triumphed and Hittite power was extended as far south as Damascus. Tensions between the two powers remained strong until 1258 when – alarmed at the resurgence of Assyria in the east – they formed an alliance.

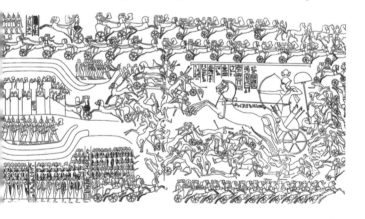

Assyria

The second rise of Assyria began under the reign of Ashuruballit I (reigned 1363–1328), who seized the city of Nineveh from Mitanni in 1330. By 1300, the Assyrians had conquered the Washukanni and were encroaching on Hittite territory in the east. King Tukulti-Ninurta I (reigned 1243–1207) scored victories against the Hittites and the Kassites of Babylonia to build a brief empire that stretched from the Upper Euphrates to the Persian Gulf, but it did not outlast his death.

Babylonia

Following the Hittite sacking of Babylon in 1595, control of the city-state passed to the Kassites, a people from the east, in about 1570. From the 14th to the 12th centuries BC, Babylonia came under repeated attack by the Kingdom of Elam, eventually leading to the downfall of the Kassite dynasty in 1158. A new, native dynasty emerged some 30 years later, beginning with Nebuchadnezzar I (reigned 1124–1103). In revenge for earlier defeats, Nebuchadnezzar led a devastating campaign against the Elamites, capturing their capital, Susa, and destroying their kingdom.

Nomad invasions

From the late 13th century, the Hittites, Assyrians and Babylonians faced fresh challenges as successive waves of nomads migrated into the region. In about 1205, the Hittite heartland in Anatolia was attacked by Phrygian tribes from south-eastern Europe, leading to the abandonment of their capital Hattusas. The empire disintegrated and their language and cuneiform disappeared.

At the end of the 12th century, Assyria came under combined assault from Mysians (relatives of the Phrygians),

TECHNOLOGICAL INNOVATIONS

This period witnessed significant advances in technology. Glass, glazed pottery and iron-smelting all appeared for the first time. Indeed, 1200 is generally regarded as the start of the iron age because from this time onwards, iron gradually began to replace bronze as the main metal for weapons and tools.

Kaskas and Hurrians (both from Anatolia). The Assyrian king Tiglath-pileser I (reigned 1115–1076) drove them back to Anatolia, but he and his successors were unable to withstand repeated attacks from a Semitic people, the Aramaeans. By 1000, Assyria had been reduced to its heartland around Ashur and Nineveh. During the 11th century, the Aramaeans were also challenging Babylonia from the north, while the Babylonians simultaneously had to fight off the Chaldeans to the south. Like Assyria, Babylonia was considerably weakened by its confrontation with the nomads.

Above *Flanked by his followers, Nebuchadnezzar, King of Babylon, addresses his court*

TIMELINE (ALL DATES BC)	
1550–1328	*Kingdom of Mitanni*
1595–1205	*Hittites flourish*
1363–1000	*Second empire of Assyria.*

THE ASSYRIAN AND BABYLONIAN EMPIRES

1000–539BC

kingdoms of Mesopotamia had the opportunity to revive. Of the three major powers to suffer nomad aggression, the Hittites had been worst afflicted, with the loss of their heartland to the Phrygians, and consequently were least able to recover. Reduced to a number of minor city-states in southern Anatolia, the Hittite people struggled on until their conquest by the Assyrians in the eighth century BC, after which they lost their separate identity and disappeared from history.

Over the next 400 years, the Assyrians rose again to create the largest and most powerful empire the world had yet seen. This was succeeded by a more short-lived Babylonian revival under Nebuchadnezzar in the sixth century. The fall of Babylonia in 539 brought the curtain down on nearly two millennia of Mesopotamian imperial history. From this point on, foreign powers would come to dominate the region, beginning with the Persians.

Above *Assyrian King Shalmaneser III meeting King Marduk-zakir-sumi of Babylon, shown in relief on Shalmaneser III's throne*

By the 900s, the Aramaeans and Chaldeans were starting to abandon their nomadic ways and settle down in city-states throughout Mesopotamia and the Levant. Although these peoples adopted many aspects of Mesopotamian culture, the Aramaeans retained their language and alphabet, and by around 500BC, Aramaic had supplanted Akkadian as the common tongue of the region.

As the nomads became more civilized, their threat diminished, and the native

Assyria

Assyria, by contrast, had maintained its heartland during the Aramaean incursions and so was able to launch a renewed bid for regional power. This began under Adad-nirari II (reigned 911–891) and continued under Ashurnasirpal II (reigned 883–859). By the 860s, the Neo-Assyrian Empire stretched across northern Mesopotamia and the Levant as far south as the Phoenician city of Tyre. Shalmaneser III (reigned 858–824) won control of the Mediterranean trade routes, but he faced a challenge when an alliance of Levantine states fought him at the Battle of Qarqar (853) on the Orontes. Although the Assyrians claimed victory, the battle dented their control of the Levant.

During the 80 years that followed

TIMELINE (ALL DATES BC)	
911–627	*Neo-Assyrian Empire*
627–539	*Neo-Babylonian Empire.*

Shalmaneser's reign, Assyria experienced a relative decline, owing to weak rulers, civil war and outbreaks of disease. Recovery began under Tiglath-pileser III (reigned 744–727), who took control of Babylon, reconquered the Levant and the Phoenician port cities, and imposed a heavy tribute on the kingdoms of Israel and Judah. Tiglath-pileser greatly strengthened central authority over the new empire by installing governors in each province under his direct control. Inspectors were regularly sent out to check on local administrators. The more rebellious vassal states were reorganized as provinces of the empire and, in some cases, large numbers of the native population were resettled to prevent local uprisings.

The Neo-Assyrian Empire expanded further under Sargon II (reigned 722–705), with successful campaigns against southern Anatolia to the north-west, the Armenian kingdom of Urartu to the north, Babylonia (now under the Chaldeans) and Elam to the south-east, and the Hebrews to the south-west. With all the money he exacted in tribute from his conquests, Sargon built a new capital at Dur Sharrukin, near Nineveh.

The empire falls

There were setbacks under Sennacherib (reigned 704–681), with rebellions in Judah, Babylon and Elam, but the empire reached its peak under Esarhaddon (reigned 680–669) and Ashurbanipal (reigned 668–627), under whom the Assyrians conquered the super-rich state of Egypt. Hoards of Egyptian treasure were brought back to the new capital of Nineveh. Assyrian triumph was short-lived, however. The empire was now over-stretched and long battles with the rebellious Babylonians and Elamites had left its armies exhausted. Egypt regained its independence by 651

Left The Tower of Babel is believed to have been built in Babylon. This portrayal by Pieter Bruegel the Elder, painted in 1563, is said to have been modelled on the Colosseum in Rome

BABYLONIA

The Babylonians struggled on against the Chaldeans, with Assyrian military support, until 745, when Babylonia was annexed by Assyria. For over a century, Babylonia submitted to Assyrian rule, enjoying a prominent status as the religious and cultural centre of the empire. Then, in 627, with the death of Ashurbanipal, Babylonia rebelled under Nabopolassar (reigned 626–605), who later sacked Nineveh with the help of the Medes. Under Nabopolassar and his son, Nebuchadnezzar II (reigned 604–562), Babylonia took up the mantle of the fallen Assyrian Empire, reoccupying virtually every territory previously held by Assyria.

Nebuchadnezzar rebuilt the city of Babylon, restoring its temples, walls and bridges to their former splendour. But the Neo-Babylonian Empire did not long outlive its founders. Its final king, Nabonidus (reigned 556–539) showed little interest in the politics and religion of his kingdom and was absent in Arabia when Babylon was invaded by King Cyrus the Great of Persia in 539. The city surrendered without a fight, thus ending the final empire of Mesopotamia and ushering in a new era of Persian domination.

and, on Ashurbanipal's death, the empire began to fall apart. Medes, Cimmerians and Scythians – peoples from the north and north-east – began to penetrate its borders, and Babylonia asserted its independence in 616. Four years later, the Babylonian king Nabopolassar, together with Cyaxares the Mede, destroyed Nineveh, and Assyria fell.

THE HEBREWS

1200–539BC

The Hebrews, later known as the Israelites and then the Jews, were an ancient people originally from Mesopotamia, who settled in Canaan (modern-day Syria, Lebanon and Israel). Their kingdoms were never powerful or long-lasting and were dominated by one powerful empire after another. Yet the Hebrews arguably had a greater impact on history than all those who conquered them. Their belief in a single god, which they preserved through centuries of dispersal, foreign rule and persecution, inspired three world religions – Judaism, Christianity and Islam.

Above *The Judgement of Solomon, painted in 880AD by Ingobertus as part of an illuminated manuscript*

Below *The remains of King David's Castle, with Jerusalem in the background*

Beginnings

The Hebrews migrated from Ur in Mesopotamia to Canaan probably some time around 1500BC. According to Jewish tradition, they were led there by a man called Abraham. His grandson Jacob took the name Israel, and Israel's 12 sons each founded a tribe.

At some point in their early history, possibly during the 1200s, some of the Hebrew tribes may have settled in Egypt, where they were forced into slavery by the pharaoh (possibly Ramses II – see page 38). According to the Bible, they were freed by a great teacher and leader called Moses, who led them back to Canaan. Moses was also a law giver, who established a set of laws, which the Jews believe were handed down to him by God.

The kingdoms of Israel and Judah

The Hebrew tribes fought many other peoples for dominion over Canaan, especially the Philistines to the south-west. To defend themselves more effectively against the Philistines, the Hebrews agreed to unite under a single monarch. Their first king, Saul (reigned c. 1020–c. 1006), was succeeded by David (reigned c. 1006–c. 965), who established the first Hebrew kingdom. David conquered the Philistines, Ammonites, Moabites and Edomites and obtained the loyalty of most of the local Aramaean tribes, cementing Hebrew control over Canaan. He captured the city of Jerusalem from the Jebusites and made it his capital.

David was succeeded by his son Solomon (reigned c. 965–928), who presided over large-scale building projects, including a temple in Jerusalem. Under Solomon's successor Rehoboam (reigned 928–911), the court in Jerusalem suffered a financial collapse and, when it tried to raise taxes, the people in the north refused to pay. As a result, the kingdom split in two: Israel (in the north) and Judah.

Foreign domination

The Hebrews could ill afford disunity at a time when both Egypt and Assyria were flexing their imperial muscles. In 924, Egyptian pharaoh Sohshenq I briefly exacted tribute from Israel and Judah, and during the reign of Israelite king Jehu (*c.* 842–*c.* 815), Israel was forced to pay tribute to Assyria. Under Tiglath-pilesa III, Assyria conquered the Levant and the kings of Israel and Judah became vassals of the emperor. After a rebellion by Israel in 724, Assyrian ruler Sargon II destroyed the kingdom by transporting the entire population to Assyria. The northern Israelite tribes thereafter disappeared from history, and the remaining Israelites of Judah came to be known as Jews.

As Assyrian power began to wane in the 630s, Judah regained its independence under Joshua (reigned 640–609) and expanded its territory to include the former kingdom of Israel. But after Joshua's death in battle against the Egyptians at Megiddo, Egypt briefly occupied Judah. In the Battle of Carchemish four years later, the Babylonians defeated Egypt and ousted them from the Levant. Judah became a vassal state of Babylonia.

In 597, a rebellion by Judah against Babylonian rule was brutally crushed by King Nebuchadnezzar II. Jerusalem was captured, its temple plundered, and 10,000 Jews were deported to Babylon. Ten years later, Judah rose again, and this time Nebuchadnezzar destroyed Jerusalem and its temple. He blinded Judah's king Zedekiah and took him, his nobles and many other Jews into captivity.

Exile in Babylon

This could have been the end for the Jewish people, but unlike the earlier Israelite tribes deported to Assyria, the Babylonian exiles held on to their Jewish identity. Religious teachers called prophets explained that the Jews' suffering was due to their failure to observe God's laws. If they would only follow the holy laws given to them by Moses, God would give them back their homeland. The Babylonian exile was an important period in the history of Judaism, when most of the scriptures that would one day form the Old Testament were written down.

Many Jews may even have found their new life in Babylon to their liking. When Cyrus the Great of Persia captured Babylon in 539BC and allowed the Jews to return to their homeland, thousands chose to stay where they were. They were the first of many communities of Jews who chose to live outside Israel, forming the beginnings of what would become known as the Diaspora.

Above Moses Breaking the Tables of the Law, *by the French artist Gustave Doré (1832–1883)*

TIMELINE (ALL DATES BC)	
c. 1500	*The Hebrews travel from Mesopotamia to Canaan*
c. 1200	*Possible date of the Exodus from Egypt, led by Moses*
c. 1020	*The Hebrew tribes unite under a single monarch*
c. 1005–*c.* 965	*Reign of David, who establishes the first Hebrew kingdom with Jerusalem as its capital*
c. 928	*The kingdom splits in two, with Israel in the north and Judah in the south*
722	*The Assyrians destroy the northern kingdom of Israel*
587	*The Babylonians destroy Jerusalem and deport many Jews to Babylon*
539	*Cyrus the Great captures Babylon and allows the Jews to return home.*

THE ACHAEMENID EMPIRE

559–480BC

The Achaemenid Empire was by far the largest the world had ever seen. Created in just over a decade by its first and most able ruler, Cyrus the Great, at its peak it stretched from Libya in the west to the Indus in the east. For the first time, the world's major civilizations – apart from the Chinese – were able to speak, trade, influence and share ideas with one another, helping to create the most diverse and cosmopolitan society yet.

Land of the Aryans

The Persians who invaded the Babylonian Empire in 539 were descended from the Aryans, a people originating from Central Asia. In the 1500s BC, the Aryans began migrating to a region east of Mesopotamia bordered by the Caspian Sea to the north and the Persian Gulf to the south. By the eighth century BC, two groups of Aryans had settled here – the Medes in the north-west and the Persians in the south. Both groups called their new homeland Iran, meaning land of the Aryans.

The Achaemenid dynasty

By the 600s, Persia was ruled by a dynasty founded by a king called Hakhamanish, known in Greek as Achaemenes. Although the dates of his reign are not known, he gave his name to the Achaemenid dynasty. In 648, when Ashurbanipal destroyed the Elamites and occupied the western part of their kingdom, the Persians took the opportunity to seize eastern Elam. For most of this period, however, the Persians were dominated by the more powerful Medes.

Cyrus the Great

This changed in 550 when the Persian king Cyrus the Great (reigned 550–529) defeated the Median king Astyages at the Battle of Pasargadae. Cyrus moved on to capture the Median capital at Hamadan. The tables were turned and little Persia now ruled the Medes. More accurately, the two peoples had united under the leadership of Cyrus the Great, who – it was claimed – had a Median mother.

Three years later, Cyrus conquered the kingdom of Lydia in western Anatolia, capturing its capital, Sardis, after a siege of just 14 days. His generals followed this up with the conquest of the Greek cities of Ionia. Cyrus spent the next few years expanding his empire's territories in Central Asia. His greatest triumph, however, was the conquest of Babylonia in 539. In just eleven years, Cyrus had built the world's largest empire. Moreover, he proved magnanimous in victory and diplomatic in his administration, exacting only modest tribute from conquered territories and allowing them to retain their own local customs and institutions.

Below A map showing the extent of the Achaemenid Empire under Darius I

TIMELINE (ALL DATES BC)	
550–539	*Cyrus the Great builds his empire*
529–513	*Cambyses and Darius I expand the empire*
490	*The Persians are defeated by the Greeks at Marathon*
480	*The Persians are defeated by the Greeks at Salamis and Plataea.*

Above *An engraving of Cyrus the Great, King of Persia and empire builder who combined military success with benevolent rule*

Further expansion

Cyrus was killed on campaign in Central Asia in 529 and succeeded by his son Cambyses (reigned 529–522). Cambyses added Egypt and Libya to the empire's dominions before dying, possibly at the hand of his brother Smerdis, in Syria. Darius I (reigned 521–486), a relatively junior member of the Achaemenid dynasty, killed Smerdis to take the throne. After putting down several rebellions, Darius began to campaign against the Scythians, a warlike nomadic people from the Eurasian steppe. In 518, he extended the empire east as far as the Indus and in 513, he conquered Thrace in south-eastern Europe.

Trouble in Greece

After putting down a rebellion by the Ionian Greeks in 494, Darius sent a force to invade mainland Greece to punish them for supporting the rebels. The Persian force was defeated at Marathon in 490, provoking Darius to make plans for a full-scale conquest of Greece. The plan was put into effect by his

son and successor Xerxes in 480, but failed decisively when the Greeks destroyed Xerxes' fleet at Salamis, then his army at Plataea.

So neither Darius nor Xerxes were able to force the Greeks to offer them earth and water, the sign of submission to the Persian emperor. After Xerxes' defeat, Achaemenid expansion effectively came to an end.

Below Scythian Emissaries Before Darius, *by an 18th-century artist*

ADMINISTERING THE EMPIRE

At its peak, under Darius I, the Achaemenid Empire spanned three continents and threatened to become over-extended. Darius, however, proved equal to the task of governing his vast dominions. He organized the empire into 20 satrapies, each ruled by a governor, or satrap, who was often a close friend or relation. Royal inspectors toured the empire and reported on local conditions. Darius introduced a system of regular taxation and fixed tributes, based on the wealth of each province. He implemented a unified system of coinage and expanded the Assyrian imperial postal system. He improved the 2,500-km (1550-mile) road network that linked the 20 satrapies, so that relays of mounted couriers could reach the remotest areas in just 15 days. At the centre of the empire, Darius built a new capital for himself at Persepolis where he installed a personal bodyguard of 10,000 men, called the Immortals.

EARLY EGYPTIAN CIVILIZATION

6000–2040BC

The civilization that arose in ancient Egypt was shaped, above all, by two geographical features: the River Nile and the desert all around it. The annual flooding of the Nile made the land fertile and highly favourable for agriculture, while the desert isolated Egyptian civilization from other cultures and acted as a shield against invasion – allowing it to flourish in relative independence for nearly three millennia. Unlike the Tigris and Euphrates, the Nile autumn floods ebbed at just the right time for planting crops, so there was no need for flood defences.

Above *Its vast expanse of desert kept Egypt safe from invasion*

Red land, black land

Egyptians saw their land as divided into two parts, the red and the black: the red being the desert and the black being the fertile silt-covered land along the banks of the Nile. Settlements grew up on the black land, strung out along the length of the river, which also acted as Egypt's main highway.

Farming began around or before 6000BC. By 4000, the Nile valley was heavily populated by farming settlements. The first chiefdoms appeared by 3300. Eventually, these chiefdoms came together to form two kingdoms. One of these controlled the area that lay on the Nile Delta, known as Lower Egypt, while the other kingdom controlled the area south of the Delta, known as

Right *The pharaohs wore a double crown, a striped headcloth and, during rituals and ceremonies, a false beard made of goat hair*

Upper Egypt. The two kingdoms competed for supremacy.

Early Dynastic Period

The kings of Egypt were known as pharaohs. The first pharaoh known to have ruled all of Egypt was Narmer. He was a pharaoh of Upper Egypt, who conquered Lower Egypt in about 3100 or 3000. Narmer's rule marked the beginning of the early dynastic period of ancient Egyptian history, which lasted until 2650BC and encompassed the reigns of the first two dynasties of pharaohs.

The pharaohs were regarded as descendents of the gods and sometimes

TIMELINE (ALL DATES BC)	
c. 6000	*Farming begins*
c. 3300	*First chiefdoms appear*
c. 3000–2650	*Early Dynastic Period*
c. 2650–2150	*Old Kingdom*
c. 2150–2040	*First Intermediate Period.*

even as gods themselves. Pharaohs claimed to be able to control the flooding of the Nile. This gave them great power during years of plenty, but could cause their authority to be questioned if the flood failed.

Narmer established Memphis (near present-day Cairo) as his capital. He and his successors built a temple to the city's main god, Ptah, and several palaces. A central government bureaucracy was established to administer the kingdom. The pharaoh's most senior official was the vizier, who was responsible for raising taxes and administering justice.

At the same time, a hieroglyphic writing system was developed. This was similar in principle to the pictographic system created by the Sumerians, except that the hieroglyphs were developed from symbolic patterns used to decorate pottery. Writing allowed the government to send messages throughout the kingdom, record instructions and keep count of food, animals and people.

Food productivity was increased during the early dynastic period, with the building of a canal network to increase the area under cultivation, and the invention of the ox-drawn plough.

Old Kingdom

In the history of ancient Egypt, there were four periods of rule by strong leaders: the Old Kingdom (2650–2150), the Middle Kingdom (2040–1640), the New Kingdom (1532–1070) and the Late Period (712–332). Between these were Intermediate Periods – times of disruption when power passed from the pharaohs to provincial governors or foreign occupiers.

The Old Kingdom spanned the third to the eighth dynasties. During the third dynasty, the pharaoh cemented his authority over Egypt by dividing it into

PYRAMIDS

Nothing proclaims the awesome power of the Old Kingdom pharaohs so clearly as the pyramids. The first known Egyptian pyramid was built for Pharaoh Djoser (reigned 2630–2611) at Saqqarah. The pyramid rises 60 m (200 ft) in six giant steps and is called the Step Pyramid. The golden age of pyramid building occurred during the sixth dynasty with the construction of the 146-m (480-ft) -high Great Pyramid, built for Pharaoh Khufu in about 2550, at Giza. Huge pyramids were also built there for Pharaohs Khafre and Menkaure. It is probable that the enormous cost of building these pyramids contributed to the eventual decline and fall of the Old Kingdom.

provinces, or *nomes*, run by nomarchs selected from the royal or noble families. The pharaohs were all-powerful at this time, as symbolized by the enormous pyramids that were built to entomb their bodies (see panel).

The kingdom was treated as the personal property of the pharaoh. However, this began to change during the fifth dynasty (2465–2323), when pharaohs began handing out lands to the nomarchs as a means of rewarding them for their loyalty. The nomarchs grew more independent and powerful, and the pharaoh became correspondingly weaker.

During the seventh and eighth dynasties, a series of ineffective pharaohs caused a power vacuum and government officials fought for control. The final blow for the Old Kingdom was a severe drought, beginning in about 2150, which caused the annual flooding of the Nile to fail. Royal authority collapsed and the kingdom became divided between rival dynasties in Upper and Lower Egypt, a time known as the First Intermediate Period.

Above *The Giza Necropolis, comprising the Pyramid of Khafre, the Pyramid of Menkaure and the Pyramid of Khufu, or Great Pyramid of Giza*

MIDDLE KINGDOM EGYPT

2040–1532BC

The Middle Kingdom lasted 400 years, encompassing the 11th to the 14th dynasties. Royal power was restored, and the period was marked by an increase in foreign trade, great prosperity, a flourishing of the arts, and enormous construction projects. The outside world began to impinge more urgently on Egypt during the Middle Kingdom, and governments were obliged to engage more regularly in diplomatic and military activity.

Egypt was reunified in 2040 by Mentuhotep II (reigned 2061–2010) of the 11th dynasty, who ruled from Thebes. This was a golden age for Egyptian art. Impressive sculptures of the pharaoh played their part in reasserting royal authority over the nomarchs.

Amenemhet I (reigned 1991–1962), a vizier in Upper Egypt, began the 12th dynasty when he siezed power and moved the capital to Itjtawy, near Memphis. The rulers of the 12th dynasty, including Senusret I (reigned 1971–1926), Senusret III (reigned 1878–1841) and Amenemhet III (reigned 1860–1814), proved strong and able leaders, helping to restore Egypt's wealth and power.

New chiefdoms and city-states began to appear in Egypt's neighbouring regions during this time. The pharaohs opened up trading links with the Levant, but at times also adopted a more belligerent stance towards these emerging kingdoms. Under Amenemhet I, Egypt conquered Lower Nubia. Senusret III was a warrior king, who often led his troops into battle. He

THE AFTERLIFE AND MUMMIFICATION

The Egyptians believed that life continued after death. The dead were taken to the underworld where gods judged them by weighing their heart against the 'feather of truth'. Those who passed the test went to the Field of Reeds to live forever, while the heart of a person who failed the test was eaten by a creature called Ammut and the person was thus destroyed.

To allow people to enter the afterlife, Egyptians believed it necessary to preserve their bodies after death. At first, they buried the dead in the desert sands, which soaked up the fluids and preserved the bodies naturally. Later they developed a method of preserving bodies by embalming them, known as mummification. First the embalmers removed all the internal organs, leaving only the heart in place so that it could be judged. Then they dried the body, coated it in resin and wrapped it in layers of linen strips. Embalming was expensive and only the pharaoh and senior officials could afford the best treatment.

Above *A mummy in the Egyptian collection at the British Museum, London, exhibiting the characteristic eye make-up. Tombs often contained clothing, wigs and slate palettes for grinding make-up*

campaigned in the Levant, forcing many of its rulers to become vassals of Egypt, as well as building a series of massive forts to protect Egypt's frontiers.

Second Intermediate Period

In about 1640, during the reign of the weak 14th-dynasty pharaohs, Egypt was invaded by the Hyksos, a Semitic people from the Levant. The Hyksos used weapons and tools of war unknown to the Egyptians, including horse-drawn chariots, improved bows and scale armour. They occupied Lower Egypt, ruling it from their capital at Avaris in the Delta, while Upper Egypt became a vassal state. Egypt lost control over Lower Nubia to the emerging kingdom of Kush.

Hyksos rule was known as the Second Intermediate Period. The Hyksos followed Egyptian culture and religion and their rule did not mark a significant break with tradition. However, they did open Egypt up to foreign influences. Bronze became more widely used, new crops and domestic animals were introduced, and fashions in dress changed.

Life in ancient Egypt

Archaeology and the study of hieroglyphs have revealed much about ancient Egyptian culture. Most Egyptians lived simple lives in villages and towns along the banks of the Nile. Their homes, made of sun-dried mud bricks, had flat roofs and small windows placed high in the walls to keep out the sun. Most of their time was spent outside, cooking, eating and even sleeping on the roof. Their main food was bread, but they also ate a variety of vegetables and fruits, fish, poultry, milk and cheese. Their favourite drink was beer, brewed from barley. Most clothes were made from linen cloth, woven from

the flax plant. Men wore skirts or robes while women wore long tunics. Both men and women wore make-up and jewellery. Many shaved their heads or cut their hair short to keep cool, while wealthy Egyptians wore wigs.

Religion

The Egyptians worshipped many gods and goddesses, each controlling a different aspect of daily life. Most powerful was the sun god Re. Other deities included Isis, goddess of mothers and wives; Osiris, who ruled over vegetation and the dead; Horus, god of the sky; and Hapi, god of the Nile. It was important to keep the gods happy to ensure, for example, the annual flooding of the Nile. People prayed and made offerings to them at outdoor shrines. Temples were built as homes for the gods. Ordinary people had access to the outer rooms of the temples, but only the pharaoh and the priesthood could enter the inner areas.

Above This falcon pectoral was among the riches found in the tomb of the pharaoh Tutankhamen. The falcon represented the sun god Horus

NEW KINGDOM AND LATE PERIOD EGYPT

1532–332BC

During the 500 years of the New Kingdom, encompassing the 18th to the 20th dynasties, Egypt grew to become the world's strongest power. Having absorbed military skills and technology from the Hyksos, Egypt developed a standing army and a great empire. History then took an unexpected turn when Pharaoh Akhenaten tried to change the state's religion, angering many in the process. Once again, a series of weak pharaohs and ambitious nomarchs led to Egypt's decline. Long periods of foreign control ensued, before a final flowering of native Egyptian rule, known as the Late Period.

Above *A mosaic of Alexander the Great fighting Darius III at Battle of Issus, dating from first century BC and found in the House of the Faun at Pompeii*

In the 1550s, the Theban king Seqenenre II struck the first blow against Hyksos rule by declaring Thebes independent from the vassal 16th dynasty that ruled Upper Egypt. Seqenenre set himself up as the first king of the 17th dynasty, sparking a war of liberation that would drive the Hyksos out of Egypt. The process was completed in 1532 by the 18th-dynasty pharaoh Ahmose I. This victory marked the beginning of the New Kingdom.

New Kingdom empire

After the experience of the Hyksos occupation, the 18th-dynasty pharaohs were determined to make Egypt stronger. They developed a permanent army that included horse-drawn chariots and other Hyksos-inspired innovations. Wishing to create a buffer zone between Egypt and the aggressive states of Mesopotamia to the north-east, the pharaohs embarked on wars of conquest.

Egypt reached its greatest extent in about 1500 under the warrior pharaoh Thutmose I (reigned 1506–1493), who conquered the entire Levant as far as the Euphrates, placing local rulers under the supervision of Egyptian officials. To the south, Thutmose I reconquered Lower and Upper Nubia and pushed deep into Kush. The motive for this southern expansion was primarily to take control of Nubia's rich gold deposits and following the campaign, Nubia was ruled directly through a court-appointed viceroy. However, Egypt struggled to retain control of the Levant, faced with local rebellions and the competing ambitions of Mesopotamian peoples such as the Hittites.

Decline

During the political turmoil that followed the reign of Akhenaten (see panel), Egypt lost control of the Levant to the Hittites. The 19th-dynasty pharaohs Seti I (reigned 1305–1290) and Ramses II (reigned 1290–1224) tried to restore Egyptian power with vigorous campaigns against the Libyans and Hittites, but ultimately these wars proved too costly and Ramses was forced to sign a peace treaty with the

Hittites in 1258, sharing control of the Levant.

In about 1200, Egypt suffered a succession of invasions by the Sea Peoples, a mix of Aegean, Anatolian and Levantine peoples. Ramses III (reigned 1186–1155) managed to drive them out in two great battles on land and sea, but could not prevent them from settling in Canaan. The heavy cost of these battles contributed to the gradual decline of Egypt's power in the Levant.

Third Intermediate and Late Periods

At home, the pharaohs inadvertently weakened their own power by granting large areas of land to the temples. By the 11th century, a third of Egyptian land was owned by the temples, and the priests had become a formidable force in their own right. In 1070, a series of power struggles erupted between priests and nomarchs, causing the country to fracture into small states. This marked the start of the Third Intermediate Period.

By 1000, Egypt had lost its empire and its weakness began to attract a number of foreign invaders. In 728, Egypt was conquered by the Nubian kingdom of Kush. Next came the Assyrians who, from 664, ruled Egypt through a client king, Psamtik I (reigned 664–610), the first king of the 26th dynasty. However, by 651, Psamtik had managed to shake off Assyrian control and Egypt was able to enjoy a century of independence known as the Late Period. This ended in 525 when Egypt was conquered by the Persians under Cambyses. A successful uprising in 402 led to a further period of independence, which ended with a Persian reconquest in 343. In 332, control of Egypt passed to Alexander the Great of Macedonia.

AKHENATEN

The start of the New Kingdom's decline can be traced to the reign of Amenhotep IV (1353–1335). Amenhotep was a devotee of an obscure sun god named Aten. In the fourth year of his reign, he raised Aten to the position of supreme deity. The following year, Amenhotep built a new capital, Akhetaten, and changed his name to Akhenaten. The pharaoh initially introduced Aten as a composite of two gods, Amun and Ra, but by 1344, he was insisting that Aten was in fact the only god and that he, Akhenaten, was the sole intermediary between Aten and his people. He ordered the defacing of other gods' temples throughout Egypt. Akhenaten's religious reformation was highly controversial and caused deep political divisions throughout the country. Soon after the pharaoh's death the old polytheistic religion was restored, the temples to Aten were pulled down and Akhetaten was abandoned. Subsequent pharaohs even went so far as to write Akhenaten out of history.

Above *A detail from a limestone relief found in the Royal Tomb at Amarna, depicting Akhenaten, his queen, Nefertiti, and two of their daughters making an offering to the sun-god Aten*

TIMELINE (ALL DATES BC)	
1640–1532	*Second Intermediate Period*
1532–1070	*New Kingdom*
1070–651	*Third Intermediate Period*
651–525	*Late Period*
525–402	*Egypt under Persian control*
402–343	*Period of Egyptian independence*
343–332	*Persia reasserts control over Egypt*
332	*Egypt is conquered by Alexander the Great.*

THE INDUS VALLEY CIVILIZATION

3300–1700BC

As with Mesopotamia and Egypt, the Indus Valley civilization of north-western India and Pakistan arose alongside a river that flooded regularly, providing rich, fertile soil for farming. In fact, the floodplain of the River Indus bore close similarities to those of the Tigris and Euphrates, with its aridity and the unpredictability of its floods. And as with Mesopotamia, these conditions necessitated cooperation between settlements in order to build large-scale irrigation and flood defence projects, spurring the development of city-states.

Below *The remains of the Granaries of Harappa in Pakistan*

The first farmers settled in the Indus Valley in about 3500BC. They lived in small villages of mud-brick houses, growing wheat, barley, legumes, fruit and cotton and raising cattle, sheep and goats. By 3100 the first towns had appeared, marking the beginning of the so-called Early Harappan Period (named after the Pakistani town of Harappa where archaeologists first discovered evidence of the culture). These towns interracted with highland peoples, with whom they traded grain and other foodstuffs for timber, metal and semi-precious stones.

In about 2600, the towns began to lose their regional differences and the Indus Valley became more culturally unified. The first cities were built at this time. The largest, at Harappa and Mohenjo Daro, had populations of between 40,000 and 50,000, making them among the biggest Bronze Age cities anywhere. Smaller cities were built at Ganweriwala, Rakhigari and Dholavira. There were also hundreds of Indus towns.

The Indus Valley civilization gradually expanded until it encompassed a territory much larger than its name implies, with towns and villages spreading southwards along the coast of India as well as north into Central Asia. In total, the region covered more than a million km², (386,000 square miles) giving it the greatest geographical extent of all the Bronze Age civilizations.

Planned cities

Unlike other cultures, where villages grew into towns, which then grew into cities, the Indus valley cities were planned as cities from the start. The ground was levelled, then planners laid out a grid of streets running north-south and east-west. Each city had a smaller citadel or 'upper town' on its

WRITING

Very little is actually known about the Indus Valley Civilization, despite the wealth of archaeological evidence. The reason for this is that the writings of these people have yet to be deciphered. This task has been made harder by the fact that historians do not know what language the people spoke, due to the obscurity of their origins. Also, Indus writings only appear in short inscriptions on pottery or stone seals. The most that can be said is that the pictographic script has over 300 signs, each probably representing a syllable.

west side. Built on a raised mud-brick platform and surrounded by a wall, the upper town contained large government buildings and granaries. The lower town, where most people lived, contained houses of varying sizes, suggesting a hierarchical society where status depended on wealth. The lower town also contained workshops where ornate jewellery and glazed pottery was produced. They traded these goods with southern India, Afghanistan, Mesopotamia and Iran.

Perhaps the most remarkable aspect of Indus Valley cities was their sophisticated water supply and sanitation systems. Each city had its own large reservoir, supplied by river and rain water, and each house obtained its water from a private or communal well. Almost all houses had a toilet and bathing platform. Sewers and street gutters carried away toilet waste. Such advanced sanitary infrastructure would not be matched again until Roman times, over 2,000 years later.

The uniform structure and layout of each Indus Valley city implies a strong degree of central control, leading some historians to argue that the Indus Valley civilization was, in fact, a unified empire with its capital at Mohenjo Daro or Harappa. This theory is undermined by the lack of evidence of kings or even of a state religion. There are no statues or paintings of rulers or gods, no royal tombs, nor any clear evidence of palaces or temples. Furthermore, there is little evidence of warfare or conflict: few weapons have been found and no imagery of fighting or soldiers.

Above A stone seal from the Indus Valley Civilization, now on display in the National Museum of New Delhi

Decline

The Indus Valley civilization came to an end between 2000 and 1700. There are many theories as to why this happened, but no one knows for sure. Some suppose a natural disaster may have been responsible, such as climate change, plague, or a radical change in the course of the Indus. Other theories include foreign invasion or a collapse of the farming system due to overpopulation. The fact that life in the countryside continued unchanged for several centuries suggests that foreign invasion was not to blame. Whatever the cause, by 1700 the magnificent Indus Valley cities had all been abandoned.

TIMELINE (ALL DATES BC)	
c. 3500	*Farming begins in the Indus Valley*
c. 3100	*First towns appear*
c. 2600	*First cities are built*
2000–1700	*Indus Valley civilization ends.*

VEDIC PERIOD INDIA

1700–500BC

Some two hundred years after the Indus Valley civilization had disappeared, a warlike Central Asian people known as Aryans arrived in India. The Aryans were close relatives of the people who settled in Iran and became the Persians (see page 32). Gradually the Aryans displaced the native peoples of northern India, extending their rule over the whole subcontinent except the south. They established a complex social hierarchy known as the caste system, developed a language called Sanskrit and composed a set of sacred poems called the Vedas, which became the earliest scriptures of Hinduism.

Right *An example of Sanskrit writing from the Vedas*

Some time around 1500BC, a semi-nomadic Indo-European people, who called themselves Arya, or 'noble ones', migrated into the Indian subcontinent from their homeland to the north-west. The Aryans settled first in the Punjab where they lived in small villages. They continued to follow their pastoral traditions, tending sheep, goats, cows and horses, but now they also began to grow crops such as barley, using an ox-drawn plough. Gradually they spread east, conquering the native Dravidians and driving many of them southward. The Aryans were a warlike people who used horse-drawn chariots and archers in battle. They reached the great plain of the River Ganges between 1000 and 800BC, where they settled in villages and grew rice.

The Vedas

Unlike the Indus Valley civilization, the Aryans did not build with stones or fired bricks, but from timber and sun-dried mud. As a result they left little trace of their presence in India. However, a mythic chronicle of their history has been preserved in the Vedas, a collection of religious poems believed to date from between 1700 and 900. The Vedas were memorized and passed on by word of mouth for centuries and were only written down in the 500s when a written form of their language, Sanskrit, was developed. The Vedas are the source of almost all knowledge about the Aryans. So important are they that Indian history between 1700 and 500 is known as the Vedic period.

अमुष्यमाणा सा सीता विवेश ज्वलनं
तो ऽग्निवचनात्सीतां ज्ञात्वा विगतक
र्मणा तेन महता त्रैलोक्यं सचराचर
देवर्षिगणं तुष्टं राघवस्य महात्मनः ।
भो रामः संप्रहृष्टः पूजितः सर्वदैवतैः

Kingdoms

According to the Vedas, the Aryans originally lived on the plain of the Ganges in *janas,* or clans, each of which was descended from a single ancestor. The *janas* were ruled by a *raja,* a word that later came to mean 'king'. By around 900, the *janas* had formed into small tribal kingdoms known as *janapadas,* and by 700 the *janapadas* had merged to form sixteen *mahajanapadas* or great realms that stretched across northern India from

TIMELINE (ALL DATES BC)	
c. 1500	*Aryans migrate to India*
1700–900	*The Vedas are created*
1000–800	*Aryans settle by River Ganges*
c. 900	*First tribal kingdoms are formed*
c. 700	*16 large Hindu kingdoms dominate northern India.*

HORSE SACRIFICE

The *rajas* of the Aryan kingdoms held many elaborate ceremonies, the most famous of which was the horse sacrifice. A horse was released and allowed to wander freely for a year. It was followed by a group of soldiers who kept a careful record of its route. The Aryans believed that the horse's journey was a sign sent by the gods, and any lands that the horse roamed across could be claimed by the *raja*. At the end of the year, the horse was recaptured and sacrificed by the grateful *raja*.

modern-day Afghanistan to beyond the Ganges delta. By 500, the dominant *mahajanapada* was Magadha, under its powerful *raja* Bimbisara. Meanwhile, the Aryan villages and towns grew into cities, including Ujjain and Kausambi.

Caste system

Over many centuries the Aryans developed a hierarchical society composed of four classes, or castes. The Brahmans, or priests, were the highest caste. Next were the Kshatriya – the nobles and warriors. Below them were the Vaisya – the craftspeople and merchants. At the bottom were the Sudra, or servants and labourers, who may have been native Dravidians. These social divisions were hereditary and there was no possibility of moving out of the caste one was born into. People could only marry members of their own caste.

Religion

The Aryans believed in many gods and goddesses, of whom the most powerful was Indra, the god of rain. The other important deities were Agni, god of fire; Varuna, god of the waters; Vayu, the wind god; Rudra, god of storms; Usha, goddess of dawn; Sarasvati, a river goddess; Kuvera, god of wealth; Soma, the moon god; and Surya, the sun god. The Brahmans were in charge of worship. They presided over the *havan* (sacred fire ceremony), during which they threw grains into a fire as offerings to various deities. As they did so, the Brahmans would chant *mantras* or strings of sacred sounds.

From 500BC, the focus of worship moved from the Vedic gods to three main deities: Vishnu, Shiva and Shakti, and the religion of Hinduism emerged in the form in which it is practised to this day. At around the same time, two other world religions were founded in India. The religious teacher, Siddhartha Gautama, who became known as Buddha (Enlightened One) founded Buddhism. Another teacher, Mahavira, founded Jainism. Both faiths rejected the authority of the Vedas and the Brahmans.

Left An 18th-century Rajasthani painting showing Krishna, the eighth incarnation of Vishnu, with his consort Radha

Below The goddesses Sarasvati, Lakshmi and Parvati, known as the tridevi. Sarasvati's children were the Vedas

THE FIRST CIVILIZATIONS IN EAST ASIA

6000–221BC

The early history of China is a complex narrative. A mosaic of neolithic cultures gradually coalesced in the fifth millennium BC to produce the Yangshao culture and, by the late fourth millennium, the Longshan people had emerged in northern China. There is some archaeological evidence to support the Chinese legend that the Xia produced China's first dynasty in the third millennium. However, the first historically attested dynasty was the Shang, followed by the Zhou. Between them, the Shang and the Zhou would lay the foundations for over 2000 years of imperial rule in China.

Yangshao and Longshan cultures

Humans and their primitive ancestors have lived in the area now called China for about two million years. By about 10,000 years ago, a number of Neolithic cultures had developed across China. From two of them – the Yangshao and the Longshan – Chinese culture eventually emerged. By 5000BC, the Yangshao were living in villages and farming millet in north-western China. Yangshao culture reached the peak of its development in about 3000BC.

The Longshan emerged in about 3200 from rice-farming cultures in the Yellow River valley in eastern China. They farmed rice and raised cattle and sheep. Where local conditions allowed, the Longshan practised intensive rice cultivation using irrigation. They made copper implements and traded with other cultures. They heated cattle bones, perhaps as a method of divination. The defensive walls of compressed earth around their settlements show evidence of warfare.

Right *A kneeling terracotta archer in the tomb of Emperor Shi Huangdi (ruled 247–221BC)*

Xia dynasty

According to Chinese legend, civilization was established by Emperor Huang Di, the 'Yellow Emperor', in 2698 and China's first dynasty was the Xia, founded by Yu the Great in 2205. Huang Di is almost certainly a mythological figure, and most experts thought the same about the Xia until excavations in Henan Province in the 1960s and 1970s revealed some surprising finds. Archaeologists uncovered urban settlements, bronze implements and tombs suggesting the existence of an early Bronze Age civilization in the same locations mentioned in ancient Chinese texts. Whether or not this was the Xia remains an open question.

Shang dynasty

There are no doubts, however, about the existence of the Shang dynasty. Founded in about 1766, the Shang developed China's first complex, hierarchical society. Elaborate burials suggest they were governed by a powerful hereditary elite. They built cities such as Eritou, Luoyang and Zhenzhou,

Below *A jade bi from the Warring States period. Bi are thought to have symbolized both heaven and high social status*

CONFUCIANISM

The turmoil that characterized the later Zhou period inspired the great philosopher Confucius (c. 551–c. 479BC) to found his ethical system, which stressed the need for individuals to develop moral character and responsibility. From around 100BC, Confucianism became a powerful influence on Chinese society and would remain so until the 20th century AD. (See also page 101)

went to war in horse-drawn chariots, produced magnificent bronze vessels and developed a system of pictographic writing that formed the basis of modern Chinese. Shang rule extended over much of northern China and as far south as the Yangtze River. They ruled their homeland in the eastern Huang He valley directly while controlling other areas through a system of semi-independent vassal states.

Zhou dynasty

In about 1122, the cruel and autocratic Shang ruler Di-xin was overthrown by one of his vassal kings, Wu of Zhou from western China. Wu established his own dynasty, the Zhou. To give their rule legitimacy following their seizure of power, the Zhou developed the idea of the 'Mandate from Heaven'. This gave kings a divine right to rule so long as they were just. If a king became unjust, Heaven would send him a warning, and if he failed to reform, the Mandate would pass to another. The Mandate from Heaven remained an essential justification both for imperial rule and, when necessary, usurpation by another king, for many centuries to come.

The Zhou ruled western China directly from their capital at Hao, while the eastern states were governed by noblemen who were either relatives or trusted supporters of the king. As time passed, the Zhou kings became weaker, and the rulers of the eastern states grew increasingly independent.

Decline of the Zhou

In 771, the Zhou king was killed and his capital sacked by the ruler of Shen, one of the eastern states, with help from a nomadic tribe, the Quanrong. The Zhou were forced to move eastward from Hao to a new capital, Luoyang. With the royal line broken, the power of the Zhou diminished still further and and their kingdom began to fragment. The Zhou king controlled less land than most of his nobles, who became, effectively, rulers of independent states. A power struggle began between the seven eastern states for control of the whole of China. From 480, the emperor's sovereignty was no longer recognized and the separate states engaged in open warfare, a time known as the Warring States Period. This only ended in 221 when Qin, under the leadership of Shi Huangdi (see page 86), defeated the last of its rival states to establish China's first empire with direct control over the entire country.

Above *Sun Tzu (c. 544–496BC) was the author of* The Art of War, *a book on military strategy that has survived to this day*

TIMELINE (ALL DATES BC)

c. 5000–3000	*Yangshao culture flourishes in north-western China*
c. 3200–2000	*Longshan culture flourishes in eastern China*
1766–1122	*Shang dynasty*
1122–480	*Zhou dynasty*
480–221	*Warring States Period.*

PEOPLES OF CENTRAL ASIA

6000–400BC

Central Asia is a vast region of steppe grasslands, forests, mountains and deserts, and its geography has shaped the cultures that have developed there. Its aridity made agriculture difficult and its distance from the sea cut it off from much trade. As a consequence, few cities arose in Central Asia. For thousands of years, nomadic horse peoples of the steppe dominated the region.

Above *Detail of a carpet dating from the fourth century BC, discovered at a Scythian burial site*

Early communities
The first agricultural communities of Central Asia arose in the mountainous area in the south-west of the region (north of Iran) in the sixth millennium BC. Some of these, such as Tepe Hissar and Altyn Depe, had grown into towns by the fourth millennium. By the third millennium, Altyn

Depe covered an area of nearly 30 hectares (74 acres) and was engaged in craft production, elaborate burials and the building of monumental platforms similar to the early ziggurats of Sumer (see page 24). To support such towns, farmers created a precarious irrigation system, which collapsed in about 2000. When the Persians conquered the region in the late first millennium, they developed more sophisticated irrigation with the construction of a network of underground canals called *qanats*.

The rise of the horse
Where local conditions allowed, especially on the margins of Europe, farming communities began to appear by 4500, herding livestock and growing some crops. Some of these communities were the first to domesticate the horse. Initially horses were raised for their meat, but by 4000, they were being used for transportation. The first wheeled vehicles appeared (as evidenced by burial sites) in southern Russia in the fourth millennium. Horses were bred for strength in order to pull larger and larger vehicles, and by the third millennium they were strong enough to pull war chariots. Spoked wheels, first developed by the Andronovo culture of western Siberia, soon replaced solid wheels, making chariots much more manoeuvrable and allowing them to dominate battlefields.

Nomadic pastoralism
In the second half of the second millennium, the Srubnaya people living north of the Caspian Sea developed bits and bridles, enabling them to start riding horses. This innovation allowed steppe

TIMELINE (ALL DATES BC)	
c. 950–700	*Cimmerians flourish on western Steppe*
700–c. 350	*Scythians build empire on western Steppe.*

mentioned in historical sources.

Meanwhile, the Scythians went on to found a powerful empire stretching from southern Russia to the borders of Persia. The military success of the Scythians lay in their mastery of horse-riding, which gave them a speed and mobility that astounded their rivals. Their power was such that they managed to repel an invasion by the mighty Persian army in 513BC. But the Scythians were not just warriors. They developed a sophisticated society ruled by a hereditary monarch and a class of wealthy nobles. They buried their leaders in underground chambers together with weapons, richly worked jewellery, horses, wagons, wives and servants. The Scythian Empire flourished until the fourth century BC, when it was eclipsed by the Sarmatians.

Left *An illustration of a typical nomadic yurt, made of animal skins*

peoples to manage herds over vast distances. Horse-riding spread through Central Asia and led, by the early first millennium, to the rise of nomadic pastoralism, a way of life that would dominate the region for the next several thousand years. Nomadic groups moved their herds of sheep, goats, horses and camels between summer and winter pastures, greatly increasing grazing land available to them. The nomads lived in animal hide tents called yurts that were easily disassembled and transported.

Cimmerians and Scythians

The first known nomad power was that of the Cimmerian people from the Russian steppe north of the Black Sea, who rose to prominence in the 900s. Some 200 years later, they were confronted by another nomadic people, the Scythians, Iranian speakers from western Central Asia, who migrated to Cimmerian territory in the 700s. The Scythians fought the Cimmerians for some thirty years before driving them south into Anatolia. Here, the Cimmerians conquered Phrygia (696) and then Sardis, capital of Lydia (652), before being routed by the Lydians in about 626. The Cimmerians, who probably then settled in Cappadocia, thereafter cease to be

SEDENTARY CIVILIZATIONS

While the steppes continued to be dominated by nomads, the second millennium witnessed the appearance of settled agricultural communities, and even city-states, in less arid parts of Central Asia. The so-called Oxus civilization, which arose in present-day Turkmenistan, northern Afghanistan, southern Uzbekistan and western Tajikistan, was the first sedentary civilization of the region. They used irrigation to farm wheat and barley, produced monumental architecture, bronze tools, ceramics and jewellery. They may even have developed a system of writing, as evidenced by some pictographs found on a stone seal in Turkmenistan in 2001. The Oxus civilization interacted with the pastoral nomadic Andronovo culture to their north. Both these peoples, and the Srubnaya people, have been cited as possible originators of the Indo-European language and ancestors of the Aryan people who later settled in Iran and India (see pages 32 and 42).

NEOLITHIC AND BRONZE AGE EUROPE

6500–500BC

Left *One of the Neolithic houses at Skara Brae on the island of Orkney, Scotland. Each has a shelved dresser on the wall facing the doorway*

Agriculture did not spread smoothly or quickly through Europe. It took time to develop crop strains suited to the colder, wetter climates of the continent. The switch from hunting and gathering to farming took place over a long period, with many cultures adopting a semi-sedentary, semi-nomadic existence before eventually forming permanent settlements. Often agriculture spread due to migrants colonizing an area. In other cases, indigenous hunter-gatherers were forced to adopt farming due to a decline in availability of local food sources.

AGRICULTURAL INNOVATIONS

The successful transition from a hunter-gatherer to a farming culture in Europe was greatly helped by a number of advances made between 3900 and 2500. The first of these occurred in the late fourth millennium, when people began to use animals for more than just their meat. This was the start of dairy production, of oxen being used for traction, and of sheep as a source of manure and wool. By the early third millennium, wool was replacing flax as the raw material of most textiles. Ploughing had begun by the late fourth millennium and wheeled vehicles were being used in northern Europe by 2500. In arid south-eastern Spain, irrigation systems were probably in use by this time, allowing intensive agriculture to develop.

The spread of farming

European agriculture first arose in Greece and the Balkans in about 6500, possibly influenced by migrants from the Fertile Crescent. They grew cereals and legumes and raised cattle, sheep and goats. It spread around the Mediterranean coast, reaching Spain by 5000. A separate farming culture began in the northern Balkans in about 5400 and spread north and west into central Europe by around 5000. The encroachment of farmers into these territories put pressure on local hunter-gatherers' resources, forcing them to turn to farming as well. By 4500, farming had spread into western Europe, Britain and Scandinavia.

Neolithic society

Neolithic settlements typically contained about 40–60 individuals. They dwelt, with their livestock, in longhouses made of wood or – in treeless areas – of stone. Judging from the lack of variation in the quality and quantity of grave goods found at Neolithic sites, society was fairly egalitarian. Many buried their dead in communal tombs, which may also have acted as territorial markers. Some of these tombs, such as those in Britanny and Ireland, contained elaborately decorated stones.

In the third millennium, large stone circles called henges began to appear in north-west Europe. It is hard to determine whether their function was religious, astronomical, or both. However, the fact that such ambitious structures could be undertaken at all suggests the emergence of chiefdoms led by a powerful ruling elite. Increasing differences in wealth and status are also demonstrated by a greater variety in grave goods found at sites dating from this period.

Bronze Age Europe

The first Europeans to use bronze were the Unetice culture of central Europe in about 2500. From here, bronze usage spread to south-eastern Europe, the Aegean and Italy by 2300, followed by the western Mediterranean and western Europe by 1800 and, finally, Scandinavia by 1500. The advent of bronze hastened the transition from stone to metal in the production of tools and other artefacts.

By around 2300, chiefdoms were established across most of Europe. Fortifications, defended enclosures and weapons, found at sites in central and southern Europe, suggest that warfare

between communities was fairly common, probably owing to competition for good agricultural land as populations rose. Militarism spread to western Europe in about 1100, demonstrated by the appearance of hillforts, bronze swords and bronze display armour.

There is evidence of regular trade from the late third millennium, particularly in tin and amber, which led to a growing uniformity of culture across Europe. Societies also became increasingly hierarchical. The rich elites were buried under large earth mounds called barrows.

Urnfield culture and the end of the Bronze Age

A different type of burial technique appeared in Hungary in about 1350. The people of the so-called Urnfield culture cremated their dead and buried the ashes in urns in cemeteries of hundreds, sometimes thousands, of graves. Some of these were buried with valuable grave goods and covered with barrows, continuing at least some earlier traditions. Urnfield culture spread, mainly through trade or migration, through most of continental Europe.

The European Bronze Age came to an end in the first millennium BC. Although the first iron artefacts started to appear in Europe in about 1200, bronze tools continued to predominate until 1000 in Greece and 750 in northern Europe, after which iron tools became common.

Above These bronze Etruscan weapons, dating from the sixth century BC, were discovered at the town of Bolsena in Latium, Italy

Below This bronze burial urn from about 500BC was found in eastern Germany

TIMELINE (ALL DATES BC)	
6500	*Farming begins in Greece and Balkans*
4500	*Farming reaches western Europe*
2500	*Bronze is first used in central Europe. First wheeled vehicles appear*
2300	*Chiefdoms established across most of Europe*
1350	*Urnfield culture appears in Hungary*
1200	*Iron is first used Europe.*

THE RISE OF AEGEAN CIVILIZATION

3000–1100BC

The Aegean Sea provided the setting for the first true civilizations in Europe. Between about 3000 and 1100BC, three cultures flourished: the Cycladic culture in the Cyclades, a group of islands in the southern Aegean; the Minoans, centred on the island of Crete; and the Mycenaeans on mainland Greece. After discovering how to make bronze, the Aegean people became highly skilled in architecture, painting, sculpture, pottery and other crafts. They built magnificent palaces, developed systems of writing, and laid the foundations for the later civilization of Classical Greece.

Above right

A fresco from the Minoan palace at Knossos, Crete, built between 1700 and 1400BC. Its 1300 rooms, which include a theatre, cover 2.4 hectares (6 acres)

Cycladic culture

Cycladic culture developed during the early Bronze Age on a number of islands in the southern Aegean, including Milos, Naxos, Siros and Thera. The people there were skilled in pottery and metalwork, making decorated clay vases and a wide variety of practical bronze objects, including tweezers, chisels, fishhooks and daggers. Their greatest artistic achievement, however, were beautiful marble figurines dating from around 2600. Many depict female shapes and may represent a mother goddess. From 1700, the islands became influenced by Minoan culture and, from around 1450, they were colonized by the Mycenaeans.

Minoan civilization

The Minoans are named after one of their legendary kings, Minos. Their civilization arose on the island of Crete in about 3000. The island's fertile soil produced abundant crops of wheat, olives and grapes. Through trade with other islands, the Minoans became rich and by 2000, they had built several fine palaces on the island. The biggest and most elaborate of these was the palace at Knossos, and smaller edifices were built at Khania, Mallia and Phaistos. It is likely that these were centres of government for individual city-states. They also functioned as storehouses for food, probably supplied by local farmers and used to feed the many servants, craftspeople and administrators who worked at the palaces.

The Minoans were highly skilled artists. Palace rooms at Knossos are decorated with wall paintings showing young men and women dancing, talking and somersaulting over bulls. They were also resourceful engineers, incorporating advanced sanitation systems within their palaces. Interestingly, their palaces lacked defensive walls, which suggests that for much of their history they felt themselves immune from outside attack. By 2000, the Minoans had developed a hieroglyphic

TIMELINE (ALL DATES BC)

c. 3000–1450	*Minoan civilization and Cycladic culture flourish*
c. 2000	*Mycenaeans move to Greece from Balkans*
c. 1600–1200	*Mycenaean civilization dominates Greece.*

script, superseded by a syllabic script in about 1700. Neither has been deciphered.

In about 1700, the palaces and towns fell into ruin, due perhaps to an earthquake or war between the city-states. They were rebuilt soon after, and during this 'second palace period', Knossos became dominant, reducing the other states to tributary status. The Minoan palaces and towns were destroyed for a second time in 1450, following their conquest by the Mycenaeans.

Mycenaean civilization

The Mycenaeans were a Greek-speaking people who moved to Greece from the Balkans some time before 2000. By around 1600, small city-states began to develop. Dominant among these was Mycenae in the north-eastern Peloponnese, and others included Tiryns, Pylos, Athens and Thebes. Unlike the peaceful Minoans, the Mycenaeans appear to have been a warlike people, who rode to battle on horse-drawn chariots but fought on foot with swords, daggers and spears. Their towns were well fortified with thick walls and gateways.

Elaborate tombs found at Mycenae suggest a society ruled by wealthy and powerful kings, supported by a warrior aristocracy. The kings were buried in vaulted tombs along with ornately crafted weapons, jewellery and other artefacts of gold, silver and bronze. They ruled from palaces and employed hundreds of craftspeople and hundreds more slaves. The Mycenaeans traded olive oil, wine, pottery and precious artefacts with Minoan Crete and other Aegean islands and with Malta, Sicily, Italy and Egypt. Through their contact with the Minoans, they adopted a system of writing based on the Cretan syllabic script.

In about 1450, the Mycenaeans became an expansionist power, conquering Crete and possibly launching attacks on Egypt, the Hittites and Troy – the last may have inspired the later myth of the Trojan War. Mycenaean civilization ended violently in about 1200 when they were attacked, probably by the same Sea Peoples who overran Egypt and the Levant (see page 29). Most of their cities were destroyed, the art of writing was lost and the whole of Aegean entered a dark age, which lasted for around 400 years.

Below The bull-leaping fresco from the Court of the Stone Spout at the palace at Knossos, painted in about 1550–1450BC

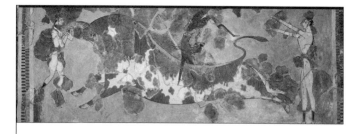

BULL WORSHIP AT KNOSSOS

The Minoans at Knossos worshipped bulls for their strength and virility. Throughout the palace, bulls feature in wall paintings, carvings and sculptures. In the palace's central courtyard, young men and women leapt and somersaulted over charging bulls. The palace is also the origin of the Greek myth of the monstrous Minotaur – half-man, half-bull – who was supposed to have lived there. According to the legend, the Minotaur lived beneath the palace within a maze of corridors called the labyrinth. In fact, Labyrinth, meaning 'house of the double axe', is the ancient name of the palace, and the word probably became associated with the palace's complex network of corridors.

Below This marble statue of Theseus fighting the Minotaur by Jean-Etienne Ramey is in the Tuileries Gardens in Paris

THE RISE OF GREECE

1100–480BC

For 400 years after the fall of the Mycenaeans, Greece remained poor and isolated, its city-states having regressed to tribal monarchies. Recovery began when power passed from the kings to a class of hereditary nobles, or aristocrats. Under their rule, city life revived and trade links were reestablished. Within a century, Greek cities were once again bustling centres of wealth and productivity, ready to start expanding their influence across the region.

Above *A 19th-century engraving of the Trojan Horse of mythology, described in Homer's* Odyssey

Monarchs

After the collapse of their civilization in 1200, many Mycenaeans fled to western Anatolia where they became known as Ionians. Shortly afterwards, the Dorian people from northern Greece moved into the Peloponnese. The people who came to be known as Greeks (they called themselves Hellenes) were descended from the Dorians and Ionians. During the 'dark age' that followed the Mycenaean era, contact between Greece and the outside world all but ceased. Mycenaean palaces fell into ruin. Knowledge of writing was lost, though memories of past glories were kept alive through oral poetry. People lived in isolated tribal communities under the rule of monarchs, who took advice from a council of hereditary soldier-aristocrats.

Aristocrats

During the ninth century BC, the monarchs gradually lost power to the aristocrats, and by around 800 most had been overthrown. Under aristocratic rule, trade recommenced, the population rose, urban life revived and the city-states were reborn. Among the most important of these were Athens, Sparta, Thebes and Corinth.

Writing – necessary for trade – was reinvented in the late 700s, this time employing an alphabet based on the one used by the Phoenicians (see page 54). The Greeks added vowels, turning it into a simpler and more flexible writing system. Their oral history could now be written down, and two epic poems, the *Iliad* and the *Odyssey*, attributed to the poet Homer, were composed. The simple writing system encouraged a rise in literacy levels in Greece, helping to bring about a remarkable blossoming of Greek culture in the fifth century.

Prosperity brought its own problems. Soon there were too many people and too little farmland. City-states frequently fought for control of the best land and some, such as Sparta, grew powerful at the expense of others.

By the seventh century, aristocratic rule had grown increasingly unpopular. A merchant class, who had grown rich through trade, was frustrated at being excluded from political power because they lacked aristocratic birth. Another discontented group were ex-farmers who, after failing to repay loans due to poor harvests, had lost their land and been forced into slavery.

The aristocrats were further undermined by the decline in importance of their status as a warrior elite – the original basis of their legitimacy – due to the emergence of new methods of warfare. Greek armies became dominated by heavily armed, spear-carrying foot soldiers called hoplites, who fought in a close-packed phalanx. The hoplite system was pioneered by Sparta and enabled her to become the dominant power in Greece during the sixth century.

Tyrants and oligarchs

Between 660 and 485, there were revolutions in many city-states as the aristocrats were replaced by *tyrants* – a term that means rulers who had gained power through their own efforts rather than by virtue of birth. The tyrants enacted some popular measures, such as distributing farmland to the landless and creating employment through public works. But ultimately they were more concerned about holding onto power than serving the people. Most were overthrown within a few decades, and by the sixth century the majority of city-states were run by small groups of wealthy citizens called oligarchies.

Democrats

A few city-states took their political reforms an unprecedented step further. The first and most notable of these was Athens. In 594, the Athenians appointed a statesman called Solon to reform the city's constitution. Solon ended the practice of enslaving debtors and freed many slaves. He divided citizens into four classes according to their wealth. Each class had the right to serve at a certain level of government or to elect officials. Solon's laws were too radical for many and led to a period of civil war and a further spell of tyrannical rule. However,

GREEK COLONIES

The shortage of good farmland in eighth-century Greece encouraged many Greeks to found new colonies overseas, and between the eighth and sixth centuries Greek city-states were established along the Mediterranean coast. The colonies were founded as independent city-states, yet often retained close ties with their parent states. The first major Greek colonies were in southern Italy and Sicily. Later colonies were founded in Spain, southern France, Corsica, Cyprus, North Africa, Egypt and on the Black Sea coast. Despite their dispersal around the Mediterranean, the Greeks retained a strong sense of a common cultural identity, reinforced by their language, their worship of the same gods and their participation in pan-Hellenic festivals, such as the Olympic Games.

Left *A Roman bronze reduction of a lost Greek statue, Myron's* Discobolus. *Cast in the second century AD, it is now in the Glyptothek in Munich and is one of several Roman copies of the original*

they laid the foundations of the world's first democratic government, which emerged in 508. In that year, another Athenian statesman, Cleistenes, gave all male citizens the right to serve in government and vote on major decisions.

PHOENICIANS AND CARTHAGINIANS

900–480BC

The Greeks were not the only people to colonize the Mediterranean during the first millennium BC. The Phoenicians, a seafaring power from the Levant, were simultaneously founding colonies in Cyprus, North Africa, southern Spain, the Balearics, Sardinia and Sicily. By the seventh century, the most powerful of these colonies was Carthage in present-day Tunisia. When Phoenicia was itself conquered in the sixth century, the colonies became independent and Carthage emerged as the centre of a new empire in the western Mediterranean.

Above An illustration of a single-masted Phoenician trading ship entering port

Phoenicia, where civilization arose in about 3000BC, was situated in present-day Lebanon as well as parts of modern Syria and Israel. The Phoenicians spoke a Semitic language similar to Hebrew. In the second millennium, they developed a 22-letter alphabet that consisted only of consonants and would form the basis of the later Greek and Latin alphabets.

Sailors and traders

The Phoenicians were great sailors and, by the first millennium BC, they were capable of travelling thousands of kilometres in their single-masted wooden ships. They set up colonies and trading posts as far as the Atlantic coast of Africa and may even have travelled as far as the Azores and Britain. They were the first to discover the use of the North Star as an aid to navigation and built some of the earliest lighthouses on the shores of their colonies to mark the coastline for their ships.

During the third millennium BC, the Phoenicians developed ports at Byblos, Berot, Sidon and Tyre, trading cedar wood, grain, fruit, cattle and purple dye with Egypt. They were especially famous for this dye, which they extracted from the murex shellfish, and the name *Phoenicians* actually comes from the Greek for 'purple people'. Phoenician merchants brought exotic goods to their cities, including silk, perfumes and spices from the Orient, and ebony, ivory, amber and precious stones and metals from North Africa.

Phoenician expansion

By 1500, the port cities of Phoenicia had become independent states, but they had little military strength and for most of the second millennium they were dominated either by Egypt or the Hittites. By around 1200, the city-states won their independence and began to establish colonies in the western Mediterranean, particularly in Tunisia, Sicily and Sardinia. From the late ninth century, the Phoenician cities were regularly dominated by Assyria and forced to pay tribute to them. The need to find gold and other precious metals to fulfill Assyrian demands forced the Phoenicians to sail ever further west in search of new

RELIGION

The Phoenicians worshipped several gods and goddesses, most notably Astarte, goddess of fertility. Astarte was married to Melqart, god of the sun and of death. There was a temple to Melqart at Tyre, where spring and autumn festivals were dedicated to him. The Carthaginians followed the same religion, but worshipped Melqart as Baal Hammon (their most important god) and Astarte as Tanit. As part of their worship of Baal Hammon, the Carthaginians regularly sacrificed animals. According to Roman accounts, they also sometimes sacrificed children.

territory. By the eighth century, they had colonies in southern Spain and Morocco and their trade routes extended hundreds of kilometres along the Atlantic coasts of Europe and Africa.

Carthage

The colonies remained nominally subject to the parent cities, but in the sixth century, when Phoenicia was conquered in rapid succession by the Babylonians and then the Persians, the Phoenician colonies were forced into independence. By this time, the most powerful colony was Carthage, and it quickly took on a leadership role among the western Phoenician territories. Founded in the late eighth century by settlers from the city of Tyre, led by their queen Elissa (known in Greek and Roman sources as Dido), Carthage was built on the shores of what is now the Gulf of Tunis. Its strategic position on a peninsula and its two excellent harbours enabled Carthage to grow quickly. By around 500, the city-state had become the capital of a maritime empire consisting of former Phoenician colonies in southern Spain, Morocco, Sardinia and western Sicily.

Through its trade in gold, silver, tin and iron, Carthage became the richest city in the world and a major military power. Frequently at war with the Greeks for control of Sicily, Carthage allied itself with the Etruscans, a people in central Italy. Etruscan power declined in the late fifth century, however, and in 480 the Greeks inflicted a crushing defeat on the Carthaginians at Himera, Sicily. Carthage went through a period of decline, but rose again at the end of the fifth century. From 410, the Carthaginians waged another series of wars with the Greeks, again for control of Sicily, but they were never able to conquer the whole island. Carthaginian power was finally broken by the Romans in the third century. In the course of three wars (see page 70), the Romans drove Carthage from Sicily, took control of its colonies and finally destroyed the city.

Above A silver coin showing the Carthaginian god Baal Hammon, dating from c. 230BC

TIMELINE (ALL DATES BC)	
c. 3000	*Civilization emerges in Phoenicia*
c. 1200	*Phoenician cities become independent states and begin establishing colonies*
c. 800	*Phoenician cities dominated by Assyria*
500s	*Phoenician colonies, including Carthage, become independent*
500–202	*Carthaginian empire flourishes.*

PEOPLES OF THE AMERICAS

4000–200BC

The prehistoric migrants who crossed the Bering Strait into America some 15,000 to 20,000 years ago pursued a largely unchanging nomadic existence across the vast North American plains for many thousands of years. It was only in the narrower spaces of south-eastern Mexico and Central America, with their fertile floodplains and tropical forests, that competition among settlers stimulated cultural activity and the first civilizations were formed. Maize was domesticated in Central America by around 2700, leading to the first sedentary farming communities by around 2300. The soil was sufficiently fertile to produce four crops of maize a year, enough to support the first complex society in Mesoamerica: the Olmecs.

Olmecs

The Olmec people lived in the warm, humid lowlands along the Gulf Coast of Mexico. They established simple farming communities here in about 1500, growing crops on the raised riverbanks and using rafts and canoes to catch fish and water birds. By 1250 the Olmecs were living in chiefdoms – settlements of two or three thousand people ruled by a hereditary elite. They traded foodstuffs and carved figurines of jade and ceramic for obsidian (a hard volcanic glass used to make tool blades). They also built ceremonial centres – earthen pyramid mounds on stone platforms – and created huge carved heads that were probably depictions of their gods

Right *This greenstone figure of a priest holding a 'jaguar child' is known as* Las Limas Monument 1. *It bears incised drawings of Olmec supernaturals*

or chiefs. The ceremonial centres and carvings were regularly destroyed or buried, perhaps due to war or, more likely, as part of a ritual marking the death of a chief or dynasty.

The Olmecs greatly influenced the Mesoamerican cultures that followed them. They may have been the first civilization in the Western hemisphere to develop a writing system – symbols found at an Olmec site are similar to a later Mayan hieroglyphic script. They also developed a long count (non-repeating) calendar, later used by other Mesoamerican cultures, and may have invented the concept of zero. The Olmec civilization appeared to reach a peak in about 1000 before going into decline. By 300, the Olmecs had entirely disappeared as a distinct culture.

TIMELINE (ALL DATES BC)	
3750–1800	*Complex societies emerge in Peru*
c. 1500	*Olmec farming communities established*
c. 1250	*Olmec chiefdoms emerge*
c. 1200	*Mayan civilization arises*
800–200	*Chavín flourish in Peru*
600–400	*Maya build cities*
c. 500	*Zapotec states emerge.*

Maya and Zapotecs

The Maya emerged in about 1200 in the highlands of Guatemala and began to spread into the lowlands of Yucatán in about 1000. By draining the swamps and channelling the water into canals, they were able to create sufficiently fertile farmland to support a complex society. Between 600 and 400, the Maya began to build cities with monumental temple pyramids at Tikal, Palenque, Nakbe, Komchen and other places. Influenced by the Olmecs to their west, they became experts at craftwork, astronomy and mathematics. They developed a hieroglyphic writing system and several types of calendar.

Another complex society developed to the west in the Oaxaca Valley of southern Mexico. The Zapotecs used simple irrigation systems and terracing to increase food production and by 500, at least seven small states had emerged in the valley, the most developed of which was Monte Albán. Like the Maya, the Zapotecs developed a system of hieroglyphic writing, built stone pyramids and developed a calendar. Their stone carvings show evidence of violent rituals.

South America

In South America, the earliest complex societies were based on fishing rather than farming. They developed on the coast of Peru between 3750 and 1800. The marine life in this area was unusually rich, allowing many to engage in other pursuits besides fishing. Village leaders organized labour forces to build temples and ceremonial centres, for example at Aspero, built in 2600. In the early second millennium cotton, squash, gourds and some root crops began to be cultivated, while mountain dwellers began to herd alpacas and llamas.

During the first millennium, agricultural

land was expanded by diverting rivers from the Andes on to the arid coastal lowlands. Trade increased between the coastal communities, the farming settlements and the highland peoples. In some places, such as Garagay, monumental ceremonial centres were built. The largest of these would have needed many hundreds of thousands of workdays to construct, and would have required a considerable marshalling of any society's resources, yet burial sites do not indicate a strongly stratified society.

Above *People of the Zapotec civilization making gold jewellery and mosaics, from a fresco painted in 1942 in the National Palace in Mexico City*

CHAVÍN

From around 800, a complex and sophisticated culture emerged in Peru, known as the Chavín after its main religious centre at Chavín de Huantár. The Chavín people were talented artists, carving stone, weaving and painting cloth, and producing pottery decorated with warriors and animals. They were also fine metalworkers, producing elaborate gold and silver plaques, drinking vessels and jewellery. At Chavín de Huantár, they created the largest religious and ceremonial centre in first millennium Peru, including temple buildings and dwellings that extend over an area of 457m² (546 square yards). Chavín culture reached its height around 400, before experiencing a rapid decline. Less than 200 years later, new building work ceased and the culture disappeared.

PEOPLES OF AFRICA

7000–500BC

Around 9,000 years ago, bands of hunter-gatherers lived in the area now occupied by the Sahara Desert. At that time the Sahara was mainly grassland, broken up by large lakes and teeming with wildlife. Many people settled on the shores of the lakes, hunting, fishing and living off wild plants. They used tools of stone and bone and produced pottery decorated with a distinctive pattern of wavy lines. Out of these communities, the continent's first farmers emerged.

Right *An 18th-century illustration of a tent and costumes from the Nubian desert in north-east Sudan*

Early farming in the Sahara

During the seventh millennium BC, some of the eastern Saharan groups became Africa's first farmers. The region was subject to lengthy droughts and, to survive these periods, people began planting the seeds of their favourite wild plants, including wheat and barley. By 6000BC, people in western Sahara were planting bulrush millet, sorghum and African rice. Over many hundreds of years, they developed a permanent dependence on these crops.

Cattle, sheep and goats were domesticated in the central Sahara by about 5000, creating a new way of life in which semi-nomadic herders drove their animals between summer and winter pastures. By around 3000, the Saharan

climate had grown much drier, lakes and rivers shrank and desertification spread, pushing the herders southwards into the semi-arid Sahel region. From here, cattle herding spread eastwards towards the Ethiopian highlands and from there into southern Africa.

Farming in Ethiopia and West Africa

Farming arose independently in the isolated highlands of Ethiopia. By 5000BC the people here were growing cereals unique to the area, such as teff and finger millet, as well as noog (an oil plant), ensete (a relative of the banana) and indigenous strains of barley, flax, emmer wheat, peas and lentils. By 3000, agriculture had developed in the tropical areas of West Africa, where people cleared and burned areas of forest to grow yams, oil plants, cow peas and African rice.

TIMELINE	
6000s BC	*Farming develops in eastern Sahara*
5000s BC	*Farming develops in Ethiopian highlands*
c. 5000BC	*Domestication of livestock in central Sahara*
c. 3500BC	*Complex society arises in Nubia*
c. 3000BC	*Desertification intensifies in Sahara; farming develops in tropical West Africa*
1700–1500BC	*Kerma flourishes*
900BC–AD350	*Kush/Meroë flourishes.*

Nubia

Among the early farmers who kept animals and grew crops on the banks of the Nile in north-east Africa, a complex culture arose in about 3500 in an area known as Nubia (present-day Sudan). The early Nubians were heavily influenced and regularly conquered by Egypt, directly to their north. However, two powerful, independent Nubian states did emerge in the second and first millennia: Kerma and Kush. Although the Nubians did develop their own writing system in the 300s BC, this has never been deciphered so almost all of what we know about the Nubians comes from Egyptian texts and archaeology.

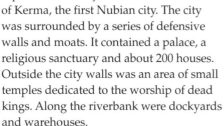

Kerma

The Kingdom of Kerma, in Upper (southern) Nubia, lasted from 1700 to around 1500. Its capital was the city of Kerma, the first Nubian city. The city was surrounded by a series of defensive walls and moats. It contained a palace, a religious sanctuary and about 200 houses. Outside the city walls was an area of small temples dedicated to the worship of dead kings. Along the riverbank were dockyards and warehouses.

Three kilometres (just under 2 miles) to the east of Kerma was an enormous cemetery containing over 30,000 graves. Each grave was a round or oval pit in which the bodies were laid on their right sides, their hands in front of their faces, always looking north. This posture did not vary, suggesting a religious significance. Many

ROYAL GRAVES AT KERMA

Several of the graves found at the cemetery east of Kerma were royal tombs. The three largest, built in the 16th century BC, were mounds of about 90 m (300 ft) in diameter and 4 m (13 ft) high. In the centre of each mound was a small vaulted chamber housing the king's body on a carved stone bed, and his most valuable possessions. Connected to the chamber was a corridor running east to west along the entire diameter of the mound, containing the bodies of dozens of sacrificed servants, guards, wives and children. One tomb contained over 300 such bodies. The tombs were surmounted by enormous white marble monuments.

were laid on wooden beds, as if sleeping, and were buried with food and their belongings – in many cases their pet dogs.

Kush

The Kingdom of Kerma was conquered by the Egyptian pharaoh Thutmose I in about 1500. After a long period of Egyptian control, the Kingdom of Kush emerged in Nubia in about 900, with its capital at Napata. In 728, the Kushite king Piankhy conquered Egypt and he and his successors became the 25th Dynasty of Egyptian pharaohs. After 64 years in control, the Kushites retreated from Egypt in the face of Assyrian invaders. Kush (which became known as Meroë after 590) continued to flourish as an independent state in Nubia until it was conquered by the Ethiopian kingdom of Axum in AD350 (see page 96).

The Kushites were heavily influenced by Egyptian culture. They built pyramids and developed an alphabet based on Egyptian hieroglyphics (although they spoke a different language). They worshipped their own gods, but also worshipped the gods of Egypt. Their gods included Sekhmet, god of the fierce summer heat, and Tefnut, god of water and floods. Their wealth was based on exploitation of local resources, such as iron, copper and gold, as well as trade.

Left *The Meroitic funerary stela of Waleye, son or daughter of Kadeye, from Sai in Upper Nubia, now at the British Museum*

CLASSICAL GREECE

500–435BC

The fifth century BC witnessed a remarkable flowering of culture among the city-states of Greece, particularly Athens. For perhaps the first time in history, a social elite began to think deeply about the world around them, to experiment with new architectural, artistic and literary forms, and to consider rational explanations of nature without recourse to gods and goddesses. So much of what we take for granted in contemporary Western civilization – democracy, science, medicine, drama, philosophy – has its roots in this brief, yet extraordinary era. So revolutionary were its achievements that historians have come to view it as the start of a new chapter in human history. Thus, in 500BC, ancient history made way for the classical world.

Below *An 18th-century engraving showing Socrates, under sentence of death at Athens, composing a hymn to Apollo*

Culture

Many possible reasons have been cited for the magnificent achievements of Greek – and especially Athenian – culture in the fifth century BC. Some have argued that the fiercely independent nature of the Greek city-states placed a strong emphasis on individual freedom and encouraged creative thought. Others have speculated that the emergence of democracy (see page 53), and the political debate it generated, led to an insistence on rational argument and the need for proof in other areas of human activity. Certainly, the widespread use of slaves for manual work allowed a wealthy elite sufficient time to devote themselves to matters of an intellectual and artistic nature.

Whatever the cause, the ancient Greeks were among the world's first philosophers, scientists and physicians. They were the first to speculate deeply about the underlying nature of the universe, the nature of knowledge and reality, and the meaning of good and evil. Among the most important Greek philosophers were Socrates (c. 470–399) and Plato (428–348).

Greek scientists believed the universe operated according to laws that they could discover using logic and reasoning. Some of their conclusions anticipated the discoveries of modern science. For example, Aristarchus of Samos (310–230) claimed that the Earth revolved around the Sun, and Democritus (460–370) believed all substances consisted of tiny, indivisible atoms.

Wars with Persia

It is perhaps astonishing that the achievements of Classical Greece took place against a backdrop of almost constant warfare. Provoked by Athenian assistance to the rebellious Greek cities in Persian-dominated Ionia, Persia attacked Greece in 490. When Athens defeated the Persians at Marathon, their emperor decided to mount a full-scale invasion, which took place ten years later. The Persian force was said to have been the largest ever assembled in ancient times – 200,000 soldiers, supported by around 1000 ships.

The northern Greek states thought it wisest to remain neutral, leaving the southern states, led by Athens and Sparta,

THE ARTS

The Greeks invented many new artistic and literary forms, which remain influential to this day. Whatever medium their artists worked in, they strove for an ideal of beauty based on harmonious proportions. Their architects built magnificent temples, such as the Parthenon in Athens, with tall columns arranged around a rectangular inner chamber. Their sculptors, such as Phidias, produced astonishingly lifelike figures of gods, goddesses and heroes. Their vase paintings depicted vivid portrayals of their myths and legends. Writers such as Aeschylus, Euripides, Sophocles and Aristophanes introduced new literary forms: the tragic and comedy drama. So universal were their themes that their plays are still enjoyed today.

to confront the invaders. The Spartans tried to block the Persian advance, but were defeated after a heroic stand at Thermopylae. This gave the Athenians time to evacuate their population, leaving the Persians to occupy their empty city. The Persian fleet was ambushed and destroyed by the Athenians at Salamis. Half the Persian army then retreated, while the other half was crushed by the Spartans at Plataea in 479.

With the threat to their homeland now lifted, the Athenians took the fight to the Persians, reopening the Bosphorus to Greek shipping in 475 and liberating the Ionian Greeks in 468. There were further outbreaks of fighting in the following years until a formal peace was negotiated with the Persians in 448.

Delian League

To pay for the war against Persia, Athens formed the Delian League in 479, consisting of Greek cities bordering the Aegean. Each member state contributed to a common fund on the island of Delos. As its wealthiest and most powerful member, Athens dominated the league and often used its navy to forcibly collect contributions from other members. It also insisted that other member states follow the Athenian system of coinage, weights and measures. As the threat from Persia receded, members began to resent making payments to the league, particularly when, in 454, the treasury was moved from Delos to Athens and funds were diverted into building schemes for the city, including the Parthenon. However, few dared openly to confront Athens and the league became, in effect, an Athenian Empire.

Athens may have had the strongest navy in Greece, but the strongest army belonged to Sparta, a city in the Peloponnese. After Athens tried to extend its power to the Peloponnese in 457, war broke out between the two cities. Sparta provoked anti-Athenian rebellions in the Delian League, which Athens forcefully quelled. However, Athens could not sustain its position on the Peloponnese and eventually accepted Spartan dominance there in 445.

Above *The western side of the Parthenon, which was rebuilt from 437BC after the Persians razed it to the ground in 480BC*

TIMELINE (ALL DATES BC)	
490	*Athens defeats Persian forces at Marathon*
480	*Athens defeats Persian fleet at Salamis*
479	*Sparta defeats Persian army at Plataea; Delian League is formed*
457–445	*War between Athens and Sparta*
454	*Delian League treasury moved from Delos to Athens*
448	*Peace treaty between Greek cities and Persia.*

GREECE AND MACEDON

435–336BC

During the course of the following century, the city-states of Greece fought each other almost continuously, forging alliances of convenience with each other, and sometimes with Persia, to gain a temporary advantage over their rivals. For brief periods, Athens, Sparta and Thebes were able to exert a tentative hegemony, but it was not until the rise of Macedon in the 340s that a power capable of unifying Greece emerged.

Above *King Philip II of Macedon (reigned 359–336BC)*

Above *The siege of Syracuse, shown in a 17th-century engraving*

The Peloponnesian War

The peace that followed the first war between Athens and Sparta (457–445) was but an uneasy truce. Tensions continued to simmer between the two rival states and war broke out again in 431. The strength of Sparta lay in its army, while Athens was essentially a naval power. Each pursued strategies that played to their particular strengths. Sparta occupied Attica (the land surrounding Athens) and ravaged its farms, depriving the city of its food supply. Athens, expecting this, took the Attic farmers within its city walls and used its fleet to import food from overseas and raid the Peloponnesian coast. However, plague broke out in the overcrowded city, killing over 30,000 Athenians between 430 and 426.

By 421, the war had reached a stalemate, with neither side able to inflict a decisive blow on the other. A peace was negotiated, but on terms that alienated a number of Sparta's Peloponnesian allies, including Argos, Mantinea, Elis and Corinth. The cities formed an anti-Spartan alliance with Athens. In 418, Sparta defeated them at Mantinea. The rebel coalition broke up, many of them returning to the Spartan fold.

Sicilian expedition

In 416, Athens launched an attack on Syracuse, a powerful Greek city in Sicily, allied to Sparta. The invasion was a disaster for the Athenians, who were soundly defeated on land and sea, losing most of their 45,000-strong force. The Spartans raised the pressure on their enemy by fortifying the city of Decelea in Attica, cutting off Athens' overland supply routes, including silver from Athenian mines.

The Athenian cause looked lost in 412 when the Spartans fomented a revolt by Athens' allies in Ionia and obtained money and ships from the Persians to create a Spartan fleet. Athens survived for a time because the Ionians were slow in attacking them and the Persians were similarly tardy in supplying Sparta. However, in 405, the Athenian navy was destroyed by a Spartan fleet at Aegospotami. Without its navy, Athens had no means of communicating with its empire or supplying its city with food. The following year, Athens surrendered. The Peloponnesian War was over.

Sparta and Thebes

Sparta was now the strongest city in Greece, but its hegemony was soon under threat. Its rivals were unhappy that Sparta's agreement with Persia allowed the Persians to control Ionia. War broke out between

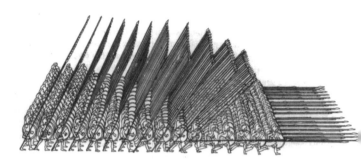

Sparta and four states – Athens, Thebes, Corinth and Argos – in 395. The peace in 387 that ended this conflict confirmed the status quo, with Sparta remaining dominant in Greece, and Persia holding sway in Ionia.

Spartan hegemony ended when its army was crushed by Thebes at Leuctra in 371. For a time Thebes dominated Greece, but by 362 Greece was in a state of confusion and almost perpetual civil war, with no city strong enough to exert its will over the others. The stage was set for the emergence of a new power – not a city-state, but a kingdom – that would eclipse the achievements of Athens, Sparta and Thebes by bringing together all the quarrelsome city-states of Greece into a single, unified power.

The rise of Macedon

The kingdom of Macedon lay in the northernmost part of Greece and had a mixed population of Greeks, Illyrians and Thracians. Most Greeks regarded it as a barbarian kingdom, not really Greek at all – yet by the 350s, Macedon had developed a strongly Hellenic culture. Under the leadership of King Philip II (reigned 359–336), Macedon began to expand its influence within Greece. Philip was an innovative and ruthless soldier-king. He introduced the phalanx infantry corps armed with a long spear called the *sarissa* and used siege engines to take cities quickly by storm rather than by prolonged blockade. Against long-established convention, he was prepared to fight through the winter.

By seizing the Greek cities of Amphipolis, Methone and Potidaea, Philip gained control of sufficient wealth to fund his military ambitions. By 348, he controlled all of Greece as far south as Thermopylae. In 340, Athens and Thebes formed a Hellenic League in a desperate attempt to halt Macedonian expansion, but Philip crushed the alliance at Chaeronea in 338. Following this, Philip organized the Greek cities into the League of Corinth. He announced that he would lead an invasion of Persia to liberate the Greek cities of Ionia and avenge earlier Persian attacks. Philip believed that Persia, despite its great size, was militarily weak. However, in 336, the Macedonian king was assassinated before he had a chance to prove this. It was left to his 18-year-old son Alexander to carry through Philip's plan.

Above *Philip II introduced the Macedonian phalanx formation of sarissas – pikes measuring 4–7m (13–21ft) long. The phalanxes were well-nigh impregnable from the front*

TIMELINE (ALL DATES BC)	
431	*Peloponnesian War breaks out*
430–426	*Plague in Athens kills a quarter of the population*
418	*Sparta defeats Athens and a rebel coalition at Mantinea*
414	*Athenian fleet is destroyed at Syracuse*
405	*Sparta wins the Peloponnesian War*
395–387	*Alliance of Athens, Thebes, Corinth and Argos fail to defeat Sparta in the Corinthian War*
371	*Thebes defeats Sparta at Leuctra*
359	*Macedon conquers Paionia*
352	*Macedon conquers Thessaly*
342	*Macedon conquers Thrace*
338	*Macedon defeats Greek city-states at Chaeronea*
336	*Philip II of Macedon is assassinated.*

ALEXANDER THE GREAT AND THE HELLENISTIC WORLD

336–30BC

Alexander III, king of Macedon, commonly known as Alexander the Great, was arguably the most successful military commander of the ancient world, possibly of all time. He ruled for just thirteen years, from 336BC until his death in 323, but in his short reign, he reunified Greece under Macedonian rule and then conquered the vast Persian Empire, including Anatolia, Syria, Phoenicia, Judea, Egypt, Bactria and Mesopotamia. By the time of his death, probably from malaria, Alexander's empire stretched some 4,830 km (3000 miles) from Greece to India. Alexander brought Greek ideas and culture to the territories he conquered and ushered in a new era, known as the Hellenistic Age.

Right *The illustration shows the legend of Alexander the Great cutting the Gordian knot – the sign that he would become ruler of all Asia*

Below *This 19th-century woodcut shows Alexander the Great riding his favourite horse, Bucephelus*

Wars of the Diadochi

When Alexander died, most probably from malaria, he left no clear successor, and a power struggle immediately began between the diadochi (Greek for 'successors') for control of his empire. Alexander's son and heir was still an infant, so several regents – former officers in Alexander's army – were appointed to rule in his stead. One of these, Perdiccas, eliminated his rivals and took sole control. After Perdiccas himself was killed in 321, Antipater was named as the new regent, and he appointed various officers as satraps of different parts of the empire. Over the next 20 years, these officers and their successors fought each other to obtain larger shares of territory. Out of this conflict there finally emerged, by 301BC, three Hellenistic states: the Seleucid Empire in Mesopotamia and Persia; the Ptolemaic kingdom in Egypt, Palestine and Libya; and the Antigonid dynasty in Macedonia and Greece.

Seleucid Empire

Seleucus had been one of Alexander's most distinguished generals. In 320, he was appointed satrap of Babylonia and by 312 he had expanded his control over the entire eastern part of Alexander's empire. By 281, Seleucus' empire reached its greatest extent when military victories won him control of Anatolia and northern Syria. His heirs struggled to retain control of such a large domain. They lost the eastern provinces of Bactria and Parthia and were unable to prevent semi-independent kingdoms forming in many parts of Asia Minor.

A Seleucid revival began in 223 with the arrival of a young, energetic ruler, Antiochus III. First he restored Bactria and Parthia to the empire. Then, in 198, he conquered Egypt. But his glory was short-lived. The following year, Antiochus invaded Greece and was defeated by the Romans, who forced him to cede territories in Europe and Asia Minor and pay them a large indemnity.

None of Antiochus' successors could prevent the empire's further decline. The Romans pushed them out of Egypt; the eastern territories once again asserted their independence; and insensitive Seleucid rule in Judea led to a Jewish uprising there. By the 160s, the empire had become wracked by civil war as rival claimants to the throne fought for control. Meanwhile, their dominions continued to shrink in the face of Parthian expansion. The Seleucids limped on until 60BC, when their remaining territories were absorbed by the Romans.

Ptolemaic Dynasty

Alexander conquered Egypt in 332BC. He founded a new capital city, Alexandria, and appointed Greeks to positions of authority. On Alexander's death, Perdiccas appointed Ptolemy, a close friend of Alexander's, to be satrap of Egypt. Ptolemy consolidated his rule during the Wars of the Diadochi. In 305, he adopted the title of king and founded a dynasty that would rule Egypt for the next 275 years. During the time of the Ptolemies (all the kings took this name), thousands of Greek army veterans were rewarded with farmland in Egypt. Many married Egyptian women, producing a Greco-Egyptian governing class. Hellenistic culture spread through the country, although those of Greek origin remained a privileged elite, living under Greek law and receiving Greek education. The Ptolemies did, however, follow one Egyptian custom: they married their sisters

TIMELINE (ALL DATES BC)	
336–323	*Alexander the Great conquers his empire*
323–321	*Perdiccas, as regent to the infant Alexander IV, takes control of the empire*
321–301	*Wars of the Diadochi*
312	*Seleucus founds his dynasty*
306	*Antigonus founds his dynasty*
305	*Ptolemy founds his dynasty*
168	*Antigonid dynasty ends*
60	*Seleucid dynasty ends*
30	*Ptolemaic dynasty ends.*

(who were usually called Cleopatra or Berenice), and often ruled jointly with them. This produced very divisive politics, and increasingly feeble monarchs. The later Ptolemies were such weak, corrupt rulers that by 80BC, Egypt effectively became a protectorate of Rome. It finally became part of the Roman Empire in 30BC, when the last Ptolemaic queen, Cleopatra VII, killed herself.

Left *An engraving of the emperor Seleucus, former general of Alexander and governor of Babylonia*

ANTIGONID DYNASTY

Alexander the Great's general Antigonus 'the One-Eyed' gained control of Greece, the eastern Mediterranean and most of the Middle East, on Alexander's death. Antigonus pronounced himself king in 306, but was killed in the Battle of Ipsus in 301 and most of his lands were siezed. His son Demetrius managed to regain control of Macedonia a few years later, and by 276 Demetrius's son Antigonus II Gonatas had consolidated the family's hold over Macedonia as well as most of Greece. The Antigonid kings were mainly successful, establishing Macedonia as the dominant kingdom of Greece. Their fortunes began to wane in 215, when they suffered the first of a series of defeats to the Romans. The dynasty finally ended in 168.

PARTHIAN AND SASANIAN PERSIA

238BC–AD636

For 800 years, two successive empires dominated Persia, occupying the period between the last Hellenic successors of Alexander the Great and the rise of Islam in the seventh century AD. Under the Parthian and Sasanian empires, a uniquely Persian culture developed, with its own style of art and architecture and its own religion: Zoroastrianism. For long periods, the Persian armies dominated the lands around them. At their height, their empires extended from Syria in the west to the Indus in the east. Under the Sasanians, the influence of Persian culture would stretch even further, reaching as far as Western Europe, Africa and China.

Above *This fourth-century gilded silver horse's head is from the Sasanian dynasty. Found in Kerman, Iran, it is now in the Louvre in Paris*

The ancient land of Parthia lies in present-day Iran. It was a satrapy of the Achaemenid Empire from the sixth century BC until its conquest by Alexander in about 330. Following Alexander's death, Parthia became a province of the Seleucid Empire. In the late fourth and early third centuries, the Parni, a nomadic people from Central Asia, moved into Parthia and adopted its language and culture. Their king, Arsaces I (reigned c. 247–c. 211), toppled the Seleucid satrap Andragoras and, in 238, declared Parthia independent. In 209, the Seleucid emperor Antiochus III reconquered Parthia. But in the early second century, as Seleucid power crumbled, Parthia was quick to take advantage, winning back its former territories and going on the offensive.

Parthian expansion

The Seleucids managed for a time to hold back Parthian expansion, but under Mithradates I (170–138) and his successors, the Parthians conquered Persia and Mesopotamia. By 124, Parthia controlled lands from Herat in the east to the Euphrates in the west. In the years that followed, the eastern provinces were invaded by nomadic Scythians (also known as Sakas), but Parthia, under Mithradates II (reigned 110–87), won these lands back. To the west, Mithradates II's forces expanded into part of Armenia and pushed back the declining Seleucids as far as northern Syria. Here, for the first time, Parthia was confronted by the might of Rome, and the two empires agreed a common border on the Euphrates.

Roman-Parthian wars

When the Romans crossed that border in AD53, the Parthians destroyed their army at Carrhae – the Roman heavy infantry were no match for the highly mobile Parthian horse archers. The Parthians might have gone on to challenge Roman dominance in the Middle East, except that, after the time of Mithradates II, they showed little appetite for conquest. This may have been due to the decentralized nature of their empire, which was made up of vassal sub-kingdoms ruled by semi-independent dynasties.

The Romans, keen to avenge Carrhae, launched frequent attacks against Parthia, but were unable to make decisive headway until AD115–117 when the emperor Trajan took Armenia and Mesopotamia. These conquests were abandoned by his successor Hadrian, but northern Mesopotamia was again acquired by the Romans under Emperor Septimus Severus in 198.

Sasanians

The wars against the Romans took a heavy toll on the Parthian dynasty, and in AD224 Ardashir I (reigned c. 220–240), the vassal king of Persia, defeated the Parthian army at Hormizdagan, slaying the emperor. Soon afterwards, Ardashir founded the Sasanian (or Sasanid) dynasty, named after his grandfather, Sasan. The Sasanians called their empire Eranshahr (Dominion of the Iranians). Unlike the Parthians, they pursued an expansionist policy.

Under Shapur I (reigned 241–272), the Sasanians defeated the Kushans to take Sogdiana, Bactria and north-west India. By the 270s, their empire stretched from the Upper Euphrates in the west to the Indus in the east, and from Sogdiana in the north to the Mazun region of Arabia in the south.

Decline and downfall

For the next two centuries, the Sasanian empire flourished. Towards the end of the fifth century, the Ephthalites, or 'White Huns', conquered Sogdiana and Bactria and killed the emperor, bringing instability. The empire revived under Khosru I (reigned 531–579), who destroyed the

SASANIAN SOCIETY AND CULTURE

Unlike the Parthians, the Sasanians ran a highly centralized empire, with provincial governors directly responsible to the emperor. Zoroastrianism became the only permitted religion, and a hereditary caste system rigidly classed people as either priests, soldiers, scribes or commoners.

The Sasanians promoted a great renaissance of Persian art and architecture. Artists created sophisticated ceramic art, beautiful engraved metalwork, and spectacular rock sculptures in places such as Shahpur, Taq-e Boastan and Naqsh-e Rajab. Splendid palaces were built at Ctesiphon, Firuzabad and Sarvestan.

Above *An image of Zoroaster, or Zarathustra, founder of Zoroastrianism, taken from an ancient carving*

Ephthalite empire and reconquered the eastern provinces.

The Sasanians finally fell by overreaching themselves in their long-running conflict with the Byzantine Empire (the Eastern Roman Empire). In 607, Khosru II (reigned 591–628) launched an all-out invasion of the Byzantine Empire, overrunning Syria and Palestine in 608 and Egypt in 618. The Byzantines turned the tide, however, and destroyed the Sasanian army at Nineveh in 627. Khosru fled and the empire sank into anarchy. In 637, the glorious Sasanian era was swiftly terminated as Muslim Arab armies swept in from the south and took control of Persia.

TIMELINE	
238BC–AD224	*Parthian Empire flourishes*
AD53	*Parthian army under Surena wipes out Roman army under Crassus at Carrhae*
AD224–637	*Sasanian Empire flourishes.*

THE ETRUSCANS AND THE RISE OF ROME

800–290BC

The Etruscans emerged from the Villanovans, an early Iron Age culture based in Tuscany, in about the eighth century BC, to form the first great civilization in the Italian peninsula. With land rich in iron and copper ores and a coastline blessed with fine natural harbours, the Etruscans grew wealthy from trade. They built cities, such as Vulci, Tarquinii and Veii, which were ruled by kings as independent states. They expanded to the south, taking control of the city-state of Rome in about 600. In the sixth century, competition with the Greeks over trade routes led to numerous clashes. Assisted by the Carthaginians, the Etruscans won some victories, but from the late sixth century, they suffered a series of crises, including the loss of Rome (509) and the destruction of their fleet (474). In about 400, they suffered an invasion of the Po valley by Celts, while to the south they were pressed by the growing might of Rome. By the mid-fourth century, Etruscan civilization had been virtually destroyed.

Above The Intervention of the Sabine Women, *by Jacques-Louis David, shows Hersilia, daughter of the Sabine leader Titus Tatius and wife of the Roman ruler Romulus, trying to effect a reconciliation between them*

Early Rome

The other major group of peoples occupying the peninsula during this period were the Italic speakers, who had probably migrated to Italy from central Europe early in the second millennium. These included Apulians, Latins, Veneti, Ligurians, Umbrians, Sabines and Samnites. Most were still organized as tribes by the eighth century BC, but the Latins, influenced by the Etruscans, had developed a number of city-states, including Rome.

Founded in about 753BC, Rome was built on a strategic position at the lowest crossing point on the River Tiber. For most of the sixth century, it was a minor city, ruled by a succession of Etruscan kings. The seventh king, Lucius Tarquinius Superbus, was a cruel tyrant and, in 509, the Romans overthrew him in a popular uprising. Rather than installing a new king, the Romans decided to abandon monarchic government and establish a new system of annually elected magistrates called consuls. The consuls would be advised by an assembly of prominent citizens called the Senate. The Roman Republic was born.

Rome expands

In the latter half of the fifth century BC, the Romans began to expand. They had no plans to build an empire at this stage, but may have been motivated by the growth of

TIMELINE (ALL DATES BC)	
c. 753	*Rome is founded*
c. 600–509	*Rome is ruled by Etruscan kings*
509	*Roman Republic is founded*
494	*Plebeian Council established in Rome*
400–390	*Celts invade northern Italy and sack Rome*
343–290	*Samnite Wars*
290–275	*Rome conquers southern Italy.*

their population and the need to make their city more secure from attack. Rome's first two major wars were against Fidenae (437–426), a nearby Latin city, and against Veii, a rich Etruscan city, which they defeated in 396. In 390, Rome was sacked by an invading tribe of Celts, who were only persuaded to leave after being offered a large sum of gold. It took some time for Rome to recover from this setback, but by the 340s, helped by the virtual collapse of the Etruscans, they had reasserted their dominance over much of central Italy. In a bid to maintain their independence, a coalition of Latin cities declared war on Rome in 340, but were defeated within two years.

Samnite wars

A more formidable challenge for Rome were the Samnites, a people based in the southern Apennines, to the east of the Latins, who were also ambitious for supremacy in Italy. The Romans and the Samnites fought three great wars over the course of half a century (343–341; 327–304; and 298–290), involving almost all the states of Italy. The first war was inconclusive, but won Rome the important territory of Campania. The Second Samnite War was marked by a string of victories by the Samnites lasting until 311, when the Romans turned the tide against the Samnites and their Etruscan allies. In the final war, the Samnites, Etruscans, Umbrians and Gauls formed an alliance in a last desperate attempt to prevent Roman hegemony. The crucial battle took place in 295 at Sentinum, Umbria. Superior Roman tactics, training and leadership won the day. Samnite power was broken and Roman domination of central Italy was complete.

Southern conquests

The Romans consolidated their position in central Italy by colonizing defeated territories with their own citizens and promising full citizenship to conquered peoples if they proved their loyalty. Rome then began a campaign against the Greek states of southern Italy. The Greek city of Tarantum appealed for help to King Pyrrhus of Epirus in Greece. Pyrrhus defeated the Romans at Heraclea in southern Italy in 280, but his army suffered such crippling losses that his name was forever afterwards associated with costly victories. Another 'Pyrrhic victory' followed at Asculum (279). The Romans held out, and in 275 Pyrrhus retreated from Italy. Three years later, Tarantum fell, and the Romans became masters of mainland Italy.

Below Sculpture of a wolf nursing Romulus and Remus, mythical founders of Rome

PATRICIANS AND PLEBEIANS

The first 200 years of the Roman republic was dominated by a struggle between the two major social classes, the patricians (ruling families) and the plebeians (lower classes), in which the latter group fought for greater political representation. In 494, a Plebeian Council was established, with power to pass laws that affected the plebeians only. The council was able to safeguard plebeian rights against abuses by the patricians. In the fourth century, the plebeians also won the right to run for the major offices of state. The political accommodation of the plebeian class established a social cohesion that helped the Republic to weather numerous crises in the centuries that followed.

Left The Roman Senate was composed of noblemen and elected magistrates

THE LATER ROMAN REPUBLIC

290–27BC

In 264, the Carthaginians – then the dominant power in the Mediterranean – established a presence on Sicily, an island that Rome regarded as part of its sphere of influence. War broke out between the two powers, the start of an epic series of conflicts known as the Punic Wars, from which Rome would ultimately emerge victorious.

Below *The Carthaginian leader Hannibal led his army and war elephants across Europe to attack the Romans*

Punic Wars

The Romans had no seafaring tradition, but quickly mastered the art of naval warfare, defeating the Carthaginian fleet at Mylae in 260. An audacious Roman attack on Carthage itself was repelled in 255 and the First Punic War dragged on until 241 when a Roman victory at Lilybaeum caused the collapse of Carthaginian control of Sicily. In 238, the Romans also annexed Corsica and Sardinia.

In 219, the Carthaginian leader Hannibal took Saguntum, a Spanish city within the Roman sphere of influence, sparking the Second Punic War. Rome controlled the sea, so Hannibal led his army, including 36 war elephants, on an epic overland journey through Spain and Gaul and across the Alps. He arrived in the Po valley in 218 with 20,000 infantry and 6,000 cavalry. Gallic tribal peoples and the southern Greek cities rallied to his cause and Roman troops could not prevent Hannibal's occupation of northern Italy. Marching south, he won several battles and even wiped out a Roman army at Cannae in 216, yet refrained from attacking Rome. After Cannae, the Romans avoided open battle with Hannibal, preferring to wage a campaign of attrition against his forces.

The Roman fightback began in 210, when Scipio attacked Carthage's Spanish territories. By 206, the Carthaginians had been driven from Spain. Two years later, Scipio invaded North Africa, threatening Carthage. Hannibal was recalled from Italy to confront Scipio and the two generals met at Zama in 202. Hannibal was defeated and Carthage surrendered, ceding Spain and the Mediterranean islands to Rome and giving up its navy. Rome now dominated the western Mediterranean. In 147, a Roman army razed Carthage to the ground, selling the survivors into slavery. The territory became the Roman province of Africa.

Growing empire

The empire of the Roman Republic continued to expand throughout the second century. Northern Italy was retaken by 191 and, over the next 70 years, the Spanish peninsula was gradually conquered.

TIMELINE (ALL DATES BC)	
260–241	*First Punic War*
219–202	*Second Punic War*
149–147	*Third Punic War*
62	*First Triumvirate is formed*
58–51	*Julius Caesar conquers Gaul*
44	*Caesar appointed 'dictator for life'; assassinated soon afterwards*
43	*Second Triumvirate is formed*
31	*Octavian defeats Antony at Actium*
27	*Octavian is declared* princeps.

Southern Gaul fell to Rome in 121. To the east, the Romans captured the territories of the declining Hellenic empire, including Macedonia and Greece (146) and large parts of the Middle East (130s). The Romans organized their new territories into provinces under the control of governors. The governors wielded absolute power – the rights of Roman citizens did not extend to conquered peoples – backed by garrisons, ready to use force if necessary.

The expanding empire caused tensions back in Rome. The aristocracy grew extremely wealthy from the treasure and slaves won on campaign. Meanwhile poor Roman farmers found themselves unable to compete with the cheaper foods imported from the provinces or produced by slave-run estates. Many migrated to the city where they joined a growing underclass of urban poor. For a while the city authorities attempted to mask the increasing gap between rich and poor by offering the masses free bread and laying on entertainments, but ultimately they could not prevent rising demands for social reform.

End of the Republic

The army reforms of Marius (see panel) gave enormous political power to successful generals of the Roman army. Three of these generals, Pompey, Crassus and Caesar, formed an alliance in 62 known as the First Triumvirate, which ruled Rome until the death of Crassus (during the Battle of Carrhae against Parthia) in 53. Pompey had been the senior member of the triumvirate, but power then began to shift towards Caesar, whose conquest of Gaul, completed in 51, vastly increased his wealth and prestige. A power struggle between the two men ensued. Caesar defeated Pompey in 48 and was appointed 'dictator for life' in 44. However, a month later he was assassinated by republicans fearful of his growing power.

Caesar's lieutenant Mark Antony, together with Antony's ally Lepidus and Caesar's great-nephew Octavian, took power as the Second Triumvirate. Lepidus was forced into exile in 36, and a power struggle commenced between Octavian and Antony. When Octavian's forces routed Antony's at Actium in 31, Antony committed suicide and Octavian achieved supreme power. After a lengthy and exhausting civil war, the Senate and the popular assemblies of Rome were happy to relinquish power to a strong ruler. In 27 BC, Octavian was declared *princeps* (first citizen). His successors would call themselves *imperator* (emperor). The era of the Roman Republic was over.

ARMY REFORMS

In 107, a Roman general called Gaius Marius reformed the Roman army, allowing for the first time recruitment of landless citizens. These soldiers would be rewarded for their years of service with grants of land, making them dependent on – and consequently fiercely loyal to – their generals. This dramatically increased the power of the generals in Roman politics, who could now rely on their armies to support their political ambitions. It also helped to drive territorial expansion as generals had to find new lands with which to reward their veterans.

Left The general Gaius Julius Caesar (100–44 BC) formed the First Triumvirate with Pompey and Crassus

Below La Morte di Cesare (The Death of Caesar) by the Italian painter Vincenzo Camuccini (1771–1844)

THE ROMAN EMPIRE

27BC–AD300

Under Octavian, who reigned as Augustus (27BC–AD14), Rome enjoyed an era of peace and stability. He introduced a system of government known as the principate, retaining many of the institutions of the Republic, including the Senate, but vesting ultimate political power in the emperor. Over time, emperors became increasingly autocratic and the Senate was reduced to an advisory body. After his death, Augustus came to be worshipped as a god, and this became an established tradition for all successful emperors thereafter. With such power concentrated in the hands of one man, the state of the empire inevitably depended on the quality of its emperor. Under its best rulers, including Trajan (reigned 98–117), Hadrian (reigned 117–138) and Marcus Aurelius (reigned 161–180), the empire prospered. The reigns of cruel and decadent emperors such as Nero (54–68) and Commodus (180–192) were marked by social and political crises.

Further expansion

The empire continued to expand during the imperial era. Under Augustus, Rome annexed Egypt (30BC), Galatia in modern Turkey (25BC) and north-west Spain (19BC) and the empire's northern frontier was extended to the Danube. Attempts to conquer Germany ended after a crushing defeat at the Battle of the Teutoburg Forest in AD9, which convinced Augustus that the empire had reached its natural limits and that no further expansion was desirable. His successors did not agree. Under

Claudius, Roman control of the entire Mediterranean coastline was completed with the annexation of Lycia (43) and Mauretania (44). In 43, Claudius also began the conquest of Britain. By 84, the southern two-thirds of Britain had been occupied, but Scotland was never brought under Roman control. The final expansionist phase of the Roman Empire occurred in the second century – known as the period of the 'Five Good Emperors'. Trajan conquered Dacia, Armenia and Mesopotamia, but his successor, Hadrian abandoned all these territories except for Edessa. Then, Antoninus Pius (reigned 138–161) briefly extended the empire's northern frontier into Scotland (142–155). Finally, Septimus Severus (reigned 193–211) seized northern Mesopotamia from the Parthians in 198.

Ruling the empire

With Severus' conquest, the Roman Empire achieved its maximum extent. Its power and prosperity by this time – together with its cultural influence over its subject peoples – was unrivalled in history. Treasure from the provinces poured into the imperial coffers and Rome grew into the largest and richest city on earth. In return, Rome offered its provinces peace, stable government and protection from invaders, allowing trade and commerce to flourish. A vast network of roads, bridges and tunnels connected up the empire. Originally built to carry troops and military supplies, the road system greatly benefited long-distance trade and communication. The Romans founded new towns across the empire, equipped with baths, theatres, amphitheatres, sewers, plumbing and heating systems. With the extension of

Below *The Colosseum was built between AD72 and 80 by the Flavian emperors as a gift to the citizens of Rome*

citizenship to the vast majority of conquered peoples and the gradual adoption of Latin as the lingua franca, people throughout the empire began to think of themselves as Romans.

Crisis of the third century

During the third century, a serious political crisis erupted that brought the empire to the brink of collapse. Augustus had never laid down clear rules for the imperial succession. During the relatively stable first and second centuries, the succession tended to be hereditary. When a dynasty died out or a bad emperor was overthrown, frontier armies would put up their own candidates for the succession, there would be a short civil war and the victor would become emperor. In the third century, these civil wars became far longer and more frequent. At the height of the crisis, between 235 and 284, twenty-six emperors ruled, all but one of them dying by violence. One emperor, Valerian, was captured by invading Persians at Edessa in 260 and died in captivity. To buy the loyalty of their troops, emperors minted more money, causing runaway inflation and a major economic crisis.

As rival generals vied for power, the empire's borders were often left undefended and subjected to frequent raids by Carpians, Goths, Vandals and Alamanni, as well as attacks from Sasanians in the east. From 260, the empire began to fragment. The usurper Postumus formed a Gallic Empire containing Gaul, Britain and Spain. Odenathus, meanwhile, ruled Egypt, Syria and much of Anatolia.

Diocletian's reforms

The empire was reunified in the 270s under Aurelian, although Dacia was permanently abandoned. However, the first wholesale attempt at tackling the empire's political

TIMELINE	
AD9	*Germanic tribes wipe out Roman army at Battle of Teutoburg Forest*
44	*Roman control of entire Mediterranean coastline is completed*
198	*The Roman Empire achieves its maximum extent*
260–274	*Empire splits in three with Palmyrene Empire breaking away in the east and Gallic Empire breaking away in the west*
286	*Diocletian splits authority over empire between two emperors.*

problems was carried out by Diocletian (reigned 284–305), who reformed the entire imperial structure. Diocletian decided the empire was simply too large to be governed by one man and in 286 he split it in two, appointing his friend Maximian to rule the west while he ruled the east. In 293, he appointed junior emperors for both himself and Maximian to provide a line of succession. This became known as the tetrarchy. He also tried to bolster imperial authority by introducing court rituals, expanded the army and reorganized the provinces to make them more directly responsible to the emperor. The tetrarchy collapsed on Diocletian's death, but his reforms were sufficient to restore stability and ensure the survival of the empire – for the time being at least.

Below *The Roman Baths at the city of Bath. Fed with hot water from the Sacred Spring, the Baths were visited by pilgrims from across the empire*

THE FALL OF THE WESTERN ROMAN EMPIRE

AD300–476

During the fourth century, the traditional polytheistic religion of the Romans was replaced by a new faith, Christianity, helping to restore a level of cultural cohesion to the empire. But despite this and Diocletian's reforms, by the late 300s the empire was weakening, no longer able to withstand repeated assaults from barbarian tribes from the north and east.

Above right *The Ostrogoths were among the barbarian tribes that challenged the Roman Empire*

Right *Attila invaded Gaul but was defeated by coalition forces fighting under the Romans*

On Diocletian's resignation in 305, the empire fell victim once again to a power struggle between rival emperors. Constantine I (reigned 306–337) seized power in the west and reunified the empire in 324. (This did not last, however, and by 395, the split between east and west had become permanent.) In 330, recognizing that the empire's strength now lay in its eastern provinces, Constantine shifted his capital to Byzantium (modern-day Istanbul), which was renamed Constantinople. Meanwhile,

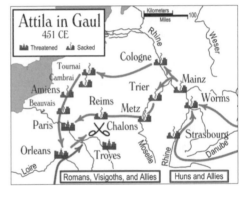

the western empire grew steadily weaker. The population declined and army recruitment suffered. The western armies were forced to fill their ranks with barbarian mercenaries. In the 370s and 380s, the manpower shortfall and frontier incursions were proving so serious that the Romans were forced to contract out the defence of their frontiers, offering loyal border tribes the status of federates, or allies.

Ostrogoths

Despite the weakness of the west, the first serious barbarian incursion occurred in the east. In 372, the Huns, a nomadic people from the Central Asian steppe, arrived in southern Russia and defeated the Ostrogoths, a tribe from eastern Germany.

TIMELINE

312	*Christianity is legalized in the empire*
330	*Constantine I founds a new imperial capital at Constantinople*
378	*Ostrogoths defeat the Romans at the Battle of Adrianople*
391	*Christianity becomes the official religion of the empire*
395	*Empire permanently splits between east and west*
406–415	*Invading Germans settle in Gaul and Spain*
410	*Visigoths sack Rome*
438	*Vandals conquer Roman North Africa*
441–451	*Huns overrun large parts of the empire*
476	*Romulus Augustulus, the last emperor of the west, is deposed.*

In 375, the vanquished Ostrogoths appealed to the eastern emperor Valens to allow them refuge within the empire's borders and Valens authorized their entry into Thrace. Once there, the Ostrogoths were mistreated by corrupt officials and soon turned to rioting and pillaging. Valens confronted them and was killed at the Battle of Adrianople in 378. The Ostrogoths overran Thrace and Pannonia so that, in 382, Emperor Theodosius (reigned 379–395) had no choice but to federate them.

Invasions of Italy, Gaul and Spain

In 395, the Visigoths, another Germanic tribe, invaded Greece and Dalmatia under their chieftain Alaric. By 401 they had reached northern Italy, but were checked at Pollentia by a Roman force. After this, the invasions came thick and fast. In 406, the Ostrogoths invaded Italy under Radagausus, attacking Florence before the Romans were able to drive them away. The same year, the advance of the Huns prompted a multitude of Germanic tribes – Vandals, Suevi and Alans, followed soon after by Franks, Burgundians and Alemanni – to cross the Rhine and sweep into Gaul. Between 409 and 415, many of these barbarians crossed the Pyrenees to settle in Spain. In Britain, the Romans came under attack from Picts, Scots and Saxons. Honorius decided to abandon the province and withdraw troops for use elsewhere in the empire.

In August 410, Alaric returned with his Visigoths and descended on Rome itself, which they pillaged for three days – the first successful attack on the capital for 800 years. Honorius, by now based in Ravenna, saw little choice but to make peace with the Visigoths. He asked them, as allies, to attack the Suevi, Alans and Vandals in Spain. In return he offered them lands in Aquitaine, southern Gaul, as federates – in effect this meant autonomy, as the Romans were by

ROME AND CHRISTIANITY

The Romans were generally tolerant of the religions of conquered peoples, so long as those peoples also honoured the Roman pantheon. The one exception to this was Christianity – a religion inspired by the life and teachings of Jesus of Nazareth, who lived in Palestine in the early first century AD. The Christians were not prepared to accept any theology but their own and the Romans frequently persecuted them as a result. Despite this, Christianity spread steadily throughout the empire. In 312, the emperor Constantine legalized the religion and eventually converted to Christianity himself. In 391, Christianity became the empire's official religion when Theodosius (reigned 379–395) outlawed Roman and other non-Christian religious practices.

now too weak to enforce their sovereignty over these lands.

Final collapse

In 428, the Vandals crossed from Spain to Africa and, in 438, took Carthage and the fertile provinces of Vyzacena and Numidia, threatening Rome's grain supply. Three years later, the Huns, under Attila, overran the Balkans, seizing all the lands east of the Rhine. In 451, Attila invaded Gaul, but was defeated by the Roman general Aetius, commanding a coalition of Romans, Visigoths, Burgundians and Franks. Shortly after Attila's death in 453, the Huns collapsed, and with their threat gone, the Germanic tribes had less reason to show loyalty to Rome. By the 470s, the western empire had shrunk to little more than Italy, and the emperors had become puppets of Germanic generals such as Ricimer, Orestes and Odoacer. The last emperor of the west was Romulus Augustulus. He was deposed in 476 by Odoacer, who proclaimed himself king of Italy.

Above *This sixth-century mosaic in Ravenna portrays Jesus dressed in a cloak of Tyrian purple, a colour associated with royalty*

THE CELTS

500BC–AD500

The Celts were a diverse group of peoples from ancient Europe, connected by a common language, religion and culture. Fierce warriors and talented artists, they were the first and greatest Iron Age civilization. Celtic history occurred in three stages. The earliest Celts emerged from the Urnfield culture (see page 49) of the northern Alps in the middle of the second millennium BC. Between 1000 and 600BC, groups of these Celts began to migrate, carrying Urnfield culture across western Europe to northern Spain.

Above *The Celts were notable warriors who spread east and west across Europe by force from their origins in the northern Alps*

Hallstatt culture

The second stage of Celtic culture, named for the village of Hallstatt, Austria, where many graves and artefacts were found, emerged in about 1200. Hallstatt was one of Europe's first iron-using cultures and was characterized by its hillforts and elaborate burials for its elite. Between the 700s and 500, it spread across France, Spain, Portugal, Germany, the Low Countries and southern Britain.

La Tène culture

The third and final stage of Celtic history, known as La Tène culture, developed from Hallstatt culture in France and Germany in about 450BC. La Tène culture is known for a distinctive art style called curvilinear, which was used to decorate weapons, jewellery and other artefacts, by engraving their surfaces with abstract and symmetrical curves, spirals and circles. La Tène culture spread through trade and migration across central and western Europe (apart from Spain), reaching Britain and Ireland by around 400. In Spain, a separate and distinct 'Celtiberian' culture formed.

Above *La Tène culture metalwork was characterized by abstract compositions of tendrils, spirals and S-scrolls*

Invasions

In about 400BC, Celts invaded northern Italy and the lower Danube region. In northern Italy, Celtic raids severely weakened the Etruscan civilization. The Celts established themselves in the fertile Po valley, a region that thereafter became known as Cisalpine Gaul (*Gaul* being the Roman term for Celt). They then marched south to Rome and besieged the city until the Romans bribed them to go away.

The Celts of the lower Danube began moving south into the Balkans and Greece in the early third century BC. They attacked Delphi and conquered the Hellenistic kingdom of Thrace. Three Celtic tribes migrated east from there to settle in central Anatolia from where they launched invasions of neighbouring kingdoms.

Decline

The high point of Celtic culture came in the early to mid-third century BC. Thereafter, the Celts began to come under pressure from the Romans, Greeks and Carthaginians and were pushed firmly on to the defensive. The Carthaginians began the process of ejecting the Celtiberians from Spain in the 230s, a

SOCIETY

The Celts were a tribal people, with some tribes organized into federations. Tribes were ruled by a chief, supported by a warrior elite and a priestly class known as Druids. The Druids performed religious rites, judged criminals and advised the chief. Most people lived in small settlements surrounded by farmland. By the second century BC, the Celts began building larger, fortified settlements called *oppida,* which functioned as centres of trade and sometimes administration. The Celts appeared to be on the verge of creating a complex civilization of their own, with the development of large towns, coinage and writing, when they were conquered by the Romans.

process continued by the Romans after their defeat of the Carthaginians in 206. Celtiberians continued to hold out in north-west Spain until they were brought under Roman rule in 19BC. The Greeks expelled the Celts from central Anatolia in 230 and from Thrace in about 220.

From 225, Rome began its assault on Cisalpine Gaul. The Celts resisted until 192, when their last base at Bononia (modern Bologna) was crushed. Between 58 and 51BC, the Roman general Julius Caesar conquered the Celts of Gaul. The Celts of Pannonia (modern Hungary) were defeated by 9BC. Just a small enclave of independent Celts now remained in mainland Europe, situated in Germany, north of the Danube.

Britain and Ireland

The Celts of continental Europe gradually became Romanized and their identity began to disappear. However, Celtic culture continued to flourish in Britain until the Roman invasion of AD43. Although the Romans dominated much of Britain, they were never able to subdue its northern and western extremities – Cornwall, Wales and Scotland – where Celtic traditions survived and their languages continued to be spoken. After Roman rule ended in 410, La Tène art revived in Britain, by now heavily influenced by late Roman and Anglo-Saxon art styles.

The Romans never reached Ireland, and the Irish Celts were left relatively undisturbed throughout the Roman period. In the fifth century, an early Christian called Patrick led a group of Celts to Ireland and established a church there. By 600, Ireland had become the cultural centre of Celtic Christianity, sending missionaries to mainland Britain and Europe.

Above *This woodcut of 1832 shows druids making human sacrifice to their gods by means of the Wicker Man*

TIMELINE (ALL DATES BC)

c. 1000–700	*Celts spread Urnfield culture through western Europe*
c. 700s–500	*Celts spread Hallstatt culture through western Europe*
c. 600	*Celts occupy Spain, forming Celtiberian culture*
c. 450	*La Tène culture develops in France and Germany*
400	*Celts invade northern Italy*
273	*Celts conquer Thrace*
133	*Rome defeats Celtiberians*
51	*Rome defeats Celts of Gaul*
9	*Rome defeats Celts of Pannonia.*

GERMANS AND STEPPE PEOPLES

400BC–AD500

Almost alone among the peoples of Europe, the Germanic tribes proved resistant to the conquering armies of Rome, and when the great empire to their south began to crumble, they were well placed to hasten its defeat and colonize its former territories. Out on the Eurasian steppe, the Sarmatians dominated in the west, but real threats to the empires of India, China and Europe were emerging among the Turko-Mongol peoples to the east.

Above *Fighting together, the Cimbri and Teutones were able to score successes against the Roman armies*

Germans

The Germanic people originated in Scandinavia and northern Germany. In the latter half of the first millennium BC, they migrated to the south and west, displacing Celtic settlers in southern Germany. By the second century BC, the Germans had reached the edge of the Roman world. Two tribes, the Cimbri and Teutones from Jutland, crushed a Roman army at Noreia in the eastern Alps in 113. The tribes then moved west and achieved further victories against the Romans in southern Gaul between 109 and 105. Thereafter they split,

with the Cimbri moving into Spain and the Teutones to northern Gaul. This weakened them and by 101, the Romans were able to defeat both tribes.

In 56BC, Julius Caesar conquered the Germanic tribes to the west of the Rhine – the only Germans to be brought under permanent Roman rule. For the next fifty years, the Romans struggled to pacify the tribes to their north, but after an alliance of German tribes led by Arminius wiped out three Roman legions in the Teutoburg Forest in AD9, the Romans ceased trying to conquer the Germans. Roman policy thereafter was to federate (ally themselves with) friendly border tribes, trading with them and giving them military aid to fight their enemies. Many of these friendly Germans were themselves recruited into the Roman army.

From the early third century AD, Germanic tribes began to form themselves into federations – for example, several Rhineland tribes merged to form the Franks. As such they became more effective fighting forces and conducted numerous devastating raids on the Roman Empire during the late third and fourth centuries. In the late fourth and fifth centuries, German tribes such as the Visigoths, Ostrogoths, Vandals and Franks began to overrun the Western Roman Empire, creating kingdoms within its borders and ultimately bringing about its downfall.

Steppe nomads

To the east of Germany lay the vast Eurasian steppe. Here, horse-mounted nomadic peoples had managed herds over huge distances since the second millennium

BC. Some of these peoples exploited their mastery of the horse to become formidable military powers. Although they were able, at various times, to terrorize the sedentary civilizations of Europe, India and China, they failed to make lasting conquests of these regions because of the lack of grazing land required by their vast mounted armies. Where they did occupy non-steppe lands for lengthy periods, such as the Toba who dominated China from AD386 to 534, they were obliged to abandon their nomadic lifestyle.

In the first millennium, the western steppe was dominated first by the Cimmerians, who were displaced by the Scythians in the early 700s (see page 47). By the fourth century BC, Scythian power was waning and their people were gradually absorbed by another Steppe people of Iranian descent, the Sarmatians.

Xiongnu

The eastern steppe was inhabited by Turkic and Mongol peoples. In the third century BC, the Xiongnu, a coalition of Turkic tribes, rose to dominance. Formidable warriors, they used the short composite bow, a weapon ideal for horse-mounted troops, to devastating effect against their enemies. In the late second century BC, they conducted frequent raids against Han China (see page 87), exacting substantial amounts of tribute. Between 133 and 53BC, the Han retaliated, conducting a long series of campaigns against the Xiongnu and eventually reducing them to tributary status.

Huns

In the late fourth century, another warlike Turkic people, the Huns, migrated west to eastern Europe, terrifying the Germanic peoples there and prompting the Germans to invade the Roman Empire in search of

JUAN-JUAN AND TUJUE

From AD400, a coalition of Mongol tribes known as the Juan-Juan dominated the eastern steppe. In 553 they were defeated by a Turkic tribe called the Tujue. One of the tribes in the Juan-Juan coalition, known as the Avars, fled west after their defeat. From the 580s to the early 600s, the Avars combined with the Sasanians to almost bring down the Byzantine Empire. Meanwhile, the Tujue went on to build their own empire that, by 600, extended from Crimea in the west to Manchuria in the east.

sanctuary. The Huns invaded the empire themselves under the leadership of their warrior king Attila (reigned 434–453), but Hun power collapsed soon after his death. Another Hunnish people, the Ephthalites (or White Huns) invaded the eastern Sasanian empire towards the end of the fifth century and, early in the sixth century, destroyed the Gupta Empire of India.

Left *Attila the Hun, leader of the Hunnic Empire from 434 to 453, was one of the most troublesome of the Roman Empire's enemies*

THE EARLY BYZANTINE EMPIRE

AD480–629

The Byzantine Empire was the eastern part of the Roman Empire. It was based in Asia Minor and, at its greatest extent in the sixth century AD, it included parts of southern Europe, North Africa and the Middle East. The people of the empire called themselves Romans – later historians named it the Byzantine Empire after Byzantium, its capital. There is no agreed beginning to the Byzantine Empire. Some historians argue it began in AD330 when the Roman emperor Constantine established his new capital at Byzantium, renaming it Constantinople. Others say it began in 395 when the Roman Empire was formally split between east and west. Still others place its foundation at the time of the Heraclian reforms of the early seventh century. The Byzantine Empire outlasted the Western Roman Empire by 1,000 years, ending with the fall of Constantinople to the Turks in 1453.

Above In 325, the First Council of Nicaea had been convened to define Christian doctrine and had rejected Arian beliefs

Efforts at expansion

From the late fifth century onward, the Byzantine emperors made periodic efforts to reconquer the west in the name of Rome and Orthodox Christianity. The Goths, Vandals and other Germanic tribes of the west were followers of Arianism, a form of Christianity that denied the divinity of Christ, and were thus regarded as heretics by the eastern Romans. In 488, Emperor Zeno (reigned 474–491) persuaded Theodoric, the Romanized, Orthodox Christian king of the Ostrogoths, to overthrow Odoacer, the Germanic, Arian king of Italy. Theodoric achieved this in 493, but he ruled Italy for the next 33 years as an independent monarch, paying only lip service to the eastern emperor's overlordship.

During the early sixth century, Byzantine efforts to reassert Roman authority in the west were diverted by an increasing threat in the east from Sasanian Persia. Despite fighting wars on two fronts, the Byzantine Empire enjoyed a period of economic prosperity, thanks to the policies of Zeno's successor Anastasius (reigned 491–518).

TIMELINE

493–526	Theodoric the Great of the Ostrogoths rules Italy
532	Justinian I makes peace with the Sasanians
533	Belisarius conquers the Vandal kingdom in North Africa
535–562	Byzantine Romans reconquer Italy
554	Byzantines retake southern Spain
572	Lombards conquer most of Italy
580s	Avars invade Balkans
602–610	Byzantine Empire brought to its knees as Avars, Slavs and Sasanians overrun its territories
610–620	Heraclian reforms strengthen process of Hellenization
627	Byzantines destroy Sasanian threat.

He ended currency inflation, reduced taxes to stimulate trade and established a more efficient tax collection system, enriching the treasury by 320,000 pounds of gold during the course of his reign.

Justinian I

It was the Byzantines' good fortune that this era of prosperity coincided with the arrival of a young, ambitious and intelligent ruler. The overriding ambition of Justinian I (reigned 527–565) was to reestablish the Roman Empire in Europe. In 532, he negotiated a peace treaty with the Sasanians, freeing up his armies for an assault on the Barbarian kingdoms of the west. In 533, Justinian's general, Belisarius, conquered the Vandal kingdom in North Africa. Two years later, the Byzantines invaded Italy. After a long and bitter struggle with the Ostrogoths, Italy was back in Roman hands by 562. In 554, Justinian retook southern Spain, when he was asked to intervene during a civil war between rival claimants to the throne of the Visigothic kingdom.

Invasions

Justinian's conquests restored Roman power in the Mediterranean, but the high cost of these wars had drained the imperial treasury. Soon after his death, the empire was attacked on all fronts. Slavs raided the Balkans and the Sasanians made significant inroads in the east. In 572, Lombards from Germany seized most of Italy. During the 580s, a nomadic people from Central Asia called the Avars (see page 79) invaded the Balkans. A counter-attack by the emperor Maurice (reigned 582–602) during the 590s nearly succeeded in destroying the Avar threat, but Maurice was overthrown in 602 following an army mutiny and his usurper, Phocas, proved an incompetent tyrant. The administration of the empire became paralysed as Avars and Slavs overran the Balkans and Sasanians retook northern Mesopotamia.

Heraclius

Phocas was deposed in 610 by Heraclius, son of the governor of the province of Africa. Heraclius (reigned 610–641) struggled to defend the empire's territory, but by 618, the Sasanians had taken Syria, Palestine and Egypt and launched raids deep into Anatolia, almost reaching Constantinople. Heraclius worked on reforming the army, offering grants of land to individuals in return for hereditary military service. By 622, the army was strong enough to go on the offensive, and Heraclius launched an audacious assault on Persia itself. Five years later he inflicted a decisive defeat on the Sasanians at Nineveh, bringing the war to an end.

During the early years of Heraclius' rule, he introduced a number of reforms to rebuild the empire's administration. The Heraclian reforms effectively marked the end of the empire as an eastern remnant of the Roman Empire and the start of its new incarnation as the medieval Greek Byzantine Empire. Greek, which had always been the dominant language in the eastern empire, replaced Latin as the official language. Heraclius dropped the traditional imperial title of 'Augustus', preferring the Hellenic *Basileus*, and persuaded the head of the Orthodox Church, the patriarch of Constantinople, to use church wealth and authority to support the state.

Above A carving of Justinian I, the Byzantine emperor whose expansionist policies led to the reconquest of Italy and southern Spain

Below The Slavs overran the Balkans, thereby disrupting the administration of the empire

MAURYAN INDIA

500BC–AD50

Under the Mauryan Empire (321–185BC), almost the whole of India was ruled by one government for the first time in its history. At its height, in the third century BC, all but the southern tip of India and modern-day Pakistan was ruled by the Mauryan Empire. Its third king, Ashoka, was one of the most remarkable rulers in history – a man who renounced violence and attempted to rule by moral authority alone.

Above *An illustration showing the ambitious leader Chandragupta Maurya being carried in a litter*

In 500BC, northern India was dominated by 16 *mahajapadas*, or kingdoms, the most powerful of which was Magadha (in modern-day Bengal and Bihar), with its capital in Pataliputra (modern-day Patna). Southern India was inhabited by tribal peoples, many of whom practised Hinduism but otherwise lived a simple, isolated existence.

Nanda dynasty

In 364, the Magadha kingdom came under the control of the expansionist Nanda dynasty. By 340, the Nanda had extended their influence over a large area of central and north-eastern India. Alexander the Great conquered north-western India in 326, but before he could invade Magadha, his exhausted army mutinied and he was forced to retreat. Nevertheless, Alexander's near-conquest of India left a deep impression on a young soldier from Magadha called Chandragupta Maurya.

He was inspired by the vision of uniting the whole of India under one empire.

Chandragupta

In 321, Chandragupta raised an army and seized the throne from Dhana, the unpopular Nanda king. By 311, Chandragupta had conquered the whole of northern India as far as the Indus. This brought him into conflict with Seleucus, the Macedonian general who, after Alexander's death, had seized control of the eastern part of Alexander's empire (see page 64). Chandragupta fought a great battle against Seleucus in 305. The outcome is unknown, but afterwards the two kings made a treaty and a marriage alliance. In return for 500 war elephants, Seleucus ceded Chandragupta control of the whole Indus Valley.

Chandragupta created a strong central bureaucracy, which enforced a strict law code and supervised the work of state-owned farms, forests, mines and workshops. His government carried out an extensive program of road building and irrigation works, greatly improving communications and agricultural productivity throughout the empire. In 293, Chandragupta abdicated in favour of his son Bindusara (reigned 293–268). According to tradition, Chandragupta had converted to the Jain faith and decided to live out his remaining days as a monk. The Mauryan Empire continued to grow under Bindusara, who extended its borders deep into southern India.

Ashoka

Bindusara's son Ashoka (reigned 268–232) at first continued in the expansionist

TIMELINE	
364–321BC	*Nanda dynasty controls much of central and north-eastern India*
321–311BC	*Chandragupta Maurya conquers northern India*
c. 261BC	*Ashoka converts to Buddhism*
185BC	*Mauryan dynasty ends.*

footsteps of his father and grandfather, conquering Kalinga on the east coast of India in 261. But after he witnessed the bloodshed his victory had caused, Ashoka was overcome with sorrow and regret and converted to Buddhism. Ashoka rejected war as a means of gaining power, revised his grandfather's harsh law code and attempted to rule, as far as possible, according to the Buddhist principles of right conduct and non-violence.

Post-Mauryan India

The Mauryan Empire did not long survive Ashoka's death. The last Mauryan king, Brihadrata, was overthrown by Pushyamitra Shunga, one of his generals, in 185. Shunga established his own dynasty, which ruled Magadha in eastern and north-central India until 73.

After the collapse of the Mauryan Empire, most of northern India splintered into small states – a mix of tribal republics and monarchies – stretching between the Indus and Ganges Valleys. In the north-west, a Bactrian Greek king called Demetrius (reigned 190–167) established a dynasty that lasted from 180 until around 94. The Indo-Greeks were succeeded by nomadic Scythians (known in Indian sources as Sakas), who founded a powerful kingdom in the Indus Valley: this endured until the first century AD when it was destroyed by the Kushans.

The legacy of the Mauryan Empire was particularly strong in southern India, where improved trade and communication links ended the region's isolation and spurred its development. The first major state here was Kalinga, which dominated eastern India in the first century BC. Satavahanihara in south-central India rose to prominence in the late first century BC, and remained dominant in the south until the third century AD. The island of Sri Lanka was especially responsive to Ashoka's Buddhist missionaries, who arrived in about 250BC, and Buddhism quickly became the major religion there.

Left *One of the statues of Buddha at the sacred mountain of Mihintale, where Buddhism is believed to have been first introduced to Sri Lanka*

ASHOKA AND BUDDHISM
Based on the teachings of the sixth-century guru Siddhartha Gautama, Buddhism was one of several minor Hindu-influenced sects at the time of Ashoka, but the Mauryan king's patronage set it on its way to becoming a major world religion. Ashoka had edicts explaining Buddhist principles carved on pillars, rock faces and cave walls throughout his empire. He founded monasteries, built stupas (mound-shaped monuments) and promoted Buddhism abroad, sending missionaries to Indonesia, southern India, Sri Lanka and Central and western Asia. His involvement in the Third Buddhist Council of 240 helped to establish Buddhist doctrine and laid the groundwork for the expansion of the religion.

KUSHAN AND GUPTA INDIA

AD50–550

Between the first and sixth centuries AD, two great empires arose in north India. For 200 years, the Kushans, originally from Central Asia, controlled a looseknit empire of tributary kingdoms, promoting the Buddhist faith and growing wealthy from trade. The Guptas, whose territory encompassed northern and eastern India, flourished from 335 to 550. They presided over a peaceful, prosperous and highly creative era of Indian history.

Kushan Empire

The Kushans were descendants of a nomadic people called the Yueh-Chi. In the second century BC, the Yueh-Chi migrated south-west from their homeland in the Central Asian steppes. In about 135BC, they conquered the Greek kingdom of Bactria and formed themselves into five chiefdoms. The most powerful of these, called Kuei-shuang, eventually absorbed the others and gave its name to the whole people.

The first leader of the united Kuei-shuang, or Kushans, was Kujala Kadphises. In around AD50, he defeated the Northern Sakas and extended Kushan territory into north-west India. His successor, Vima Kadphises (reigned *c.* 75–100)

Below A Gandharan statue of a standing bodhisattva, or 'enlightened being'

conquered the Indus Valley and much of the Ganges plain, creating an empire that stretched from the Aral Sea in the north to the Ganges in the south. The empire reached its peak under Kanishka (reigned *c.* 100–130). As well as a superb military leader, Kanishka was a great patron of the arts (see panel).

The Kushan Empire had a decentralized structure, with each region ruled by a vassal king called a *yaghbu*. The system worked well enough until the third century, when the empire began to fragment, splitting into western and eastern halves in about 225. Soon afterwards, the Sasanians invaded, conquering the western half. The remaining eastern half split into numerous small kingdoms.

Kushan culture and religion

The Kushan Empire was well-placed to benefit from the trade between China and the west. Merchants and traders travelling the Silk Road (see page 86) had to pass through Kushan lands, and by taxing them, the Kushan emperors grew enormously wealthy. The Silk Road also brought the Kushans into contact with different civilizations and cultures, including the Persians and the Romans. These diverse influences were reflected in the multifaceted nature of Kushan art and culture, which mixed Roman, Greek, Indian and Central Asian styles.

KUSHAN ART

During the reign of Kanishka, artists began to create the first statues of Buddha in human form. Two distinct art styles developed. In the city of Gandhara, artists were influenced by Greek and Roman sculpture. Their depiction of Buddha was similar to a Greek god: handsome, youthful, with a long face and flowing robes. In the city of Mathura, the artists developed a style more closely related to Indian traditions. The Mathura Buddha has a round, smiling face, long earlobes and a shaved head or topknot.

The most important influence on the Kushans was Indian Buddhism. Kanishka was the first Kushan emperor to convert to Buddhism and he convened the Fourth Buddhist Council to clarify Buddhist doctrine. Most of Kanishkas successors also followed the Buddhist faith. Despite this, the Kushan rulers were tolerant of religion, showing respect for Indian, Persian, Roman and Greek deities.

Gupta Empire

The decline of the Kushans made possible the rise of a new Indian empire – the Guptas – in the fourth century. The Gupta dynasty began with Chandra Gupta I (reigned 320–335) who, by means of a marriage alliance, won control of Magadha, the heartland of the former Mauryan Empire. His son Samudra Gupta (reigned 335–380) spent most of his long reign on military campaigns, conquering one kingdom after another to create an empire that stretched right across northern and eastern India. His son, Chandra Gupta II, extended Gupta territory still further with his conquest of the Western Sakas.

The Guptas ruled their empire as overlords, with little territory under their direct control. Conquered rulers could continue ruling their sub-kingdoms but were expected to pay tribute to the Gupta kings. In the 450s, the Gupta Empire was attacked by the Ephthalites (or White Huns), a nomadic people from Central Asia. Skanda Gupta (reigned c. 455–467) managed to drive out the Huns, but they returned in 505–511, overrunning northern India and sacking the Gupta capital at Pataliputra. The empire fell apart soon afterwards and the Gupta territory was reduced to little more than Magadha. India was once again divided into small kingdoms.

TIMELINE	
135BC	Kushans conquer Bactria
AD50	Kushans conquer north-west India
100–130	Kushan Empire reaches its height
225–240	Sasanians conquer western Kushan Empire
320	Gupta dynasty is founded by Chandra Gupta I
380–415	Under Chandra Gupta II, the Gupta Empire reaches its zenith
511	Gupta Empire collapses
540–550	Reign of Vishnu Gupta, the last of the Gupta dynasty.

Gupta art and science

The period of Gupta rule is remembered by many as a golden age. It was a time of enormous creativity in both the arts and the sciences. The Guptas were devout Hindus and under their rule the Hindu epics, the *Ramayana* and *Mahabharata*, reached their final form. *Puja*, or image-worship, became popular, inspiring beautiful sculptures of the Hindu gods and the construction of many temples. Sanskrit literature flourished at the Gupta court, notably with the plays and poems of ancient India's most famous poet, Kalidasa (c. 400).

Gupta astronomers calculated that the apparent movement of the stars was caused by the Earth spinning on its axis and that the moon and planets shone by the reflected light of the sun. Their mathematicians simplified arithmetic by introducing the concept of zero. Their invention of the decimal system was later adopted by the Arabs and, later still, by the Europeans.

Below *A terracotta carving of a musician from a Hindu temple of the Gupta period*

THE HAN EMPIRE

221BC–AD220

Emperor Shi Huangdi, who unified China under the Qin, was followed by the Han dynasty, which ruled China for almost 400 years. The Hans oversaw an expansion of Chinese territory and the establishment of a powerful imperial government supported by a large and well-educated civil service. The arts and sciences thrived under the Hans, and an important trade route, the Silk Road, linked China with the West.

Above *The dramatic scenery of the East-West trading route that became known as the Silk Road*

As the power of the Zhou dynasty declined in the first millennium BC (see page 45), China collapsed into a civil war known as the Warring States period (480–221). The stronger states gradually eliminated the weaker ones until, in 221, just one state – the Qin – reigned supreme. Based in western China, the Qin was a centralized state with a powerful army. The process of unifying China under Qin rule was carried out in a series of swift military campaigns by Zheng (reigned 246–210), after which he adopted the title Shi Huangdi, the 'First Emperor'.

Shi Huangdi

Shi Huangdi applied the Qin method of rule to the whole of China, establishing a style of centralized, autocratic government that has endured to the present day. The aristocratic rulers of conquered states were overthrown and replaced by officials directly responsible to the emperor. A vast central and local civil service was recruited to micromanage the 36 districts of the empire. Currency, weights and measures, laws and the Chinese script were standardized throughout the realm. To demonstrate that he was – literally – the *first* emperor, Shi Huangdi ordered the burning of all works of history, as well as any works that might have turned people against him. Scholars who protested were executed. To keep out nomadic invaders from the north, the emperor linked up the numerous short walls built by earlier rulers, marking the beginning of the Great Wall of China. Perhaps most significantly, Shi Huangdi gave the Chinese a sense of themselves as a single, unified nation – the name *China* is derived from *Qin*, the name of his dynasty.

Han Gaozu

Shi Huangdi died in 210 and his son proved a weak ruler. By 209 there were widespread revolts by prisoners, peasants and the descendants of aristocrats. In 206 the Qin dynasty collapsed and power passed to one of the rebel leaders, Lui Bang. The son of a farmer, Lui Bang was the first commoner to become emperor. Known posthumously as Han Gaozu, he was founder of the Han dynasty and ruled until 195. Gaozu was a skillful ruler who revoked many of Shi Huangdi's harsh

SCHOLARSHIP

Gaozu, the first Han ruler, was an uneducated man and shared Shi Huangdi's distrust of scholarship. However, under subsequent Han rulers, education gained in status and a large university was built in Chang'an. Under Emperor Wudi (reigned 140–87), Confucianism (see page 101) became the official state philosophy and Confucian scholars were promoted to senior government posts. An examination was introduced as a means of selecting civil servants, and applicants were judged on their knowledge of Confucius' teachings.

TIMELINE	
221BC	*China unified under the Qin*
206BC	*Liu Bang (Han Gaozu) founds the Han dynasty*
133–53BC	*The Han pacifiy the Xiongnu*
AD9–23	*Wang Mang rules China*
24	*Restoration of Han dynasty*
189	*Han empire fragments*
220	*Xian, final Han emperor, is forced to abdicate; China splits into three kingdoms.*

statutes and reduced taxes to restore stability to the empire. He rewarded some of the military and civilian officials who governed China's districts with land in return for loyalty – reviving to some extent the feudal system of pre-Qin China, but without ever threatening the centralized state.

Former Han period

Han rule is divided into two periods. During the Former Han period, which lasted from 206BC to AD9, the capital was at Chang'an (modern Xi'an) in western China. During the Former Han period, China expanded southwards into modern-day Tibet, northern Vietnam and North Korea, but suffered frequent raids to its northern border by Xiongnu nomads from Mongolia. Over a long series of military campaigns beginning in 133, the Han gradually pacified the Xiongnu, reducing them to tributary status by 53BC.

The military campaigns of the Han weakened the economy, and encouraged a reformer, Wang Mang (45BC–AD23), to declare that the Han had lost the Mandate of Heaven (see page 45). Wang Mang overthrew the dynasty in AD9 and introduced a series of radical land reforms that damaged the economy even further. In AD24, the Han regained power under Liu Xiu (reigned 24–57), marking the start of the Later Han period, which lasted until 220.

Later Han period

The later Hans ruled from Luoyang in central China. Liu Xiu, his son Ming (reigned 57–75) and grandson Zhang (reigned 75–88) were competent rulers who oversaw a modest recovery in the empire's wealth and power. However, the rulers that followed were weak and power passed to rival court factions – eunuchs, empress' families and Confucian scholar-officials, as well as to provincial warlords. Economic problems worsened, leading to peasant rebellions. In 189, warlords seized Luoyang and the empire fell apart. While warlords from different parts of the country fought each other for control of the empire, Han emperors continued to rule as figureheads. The last one, Emperor Xian, was forced to abdicate in 220. None of the power-hungry warlords could wield sufficient authority to take over the empire in its entirety, and China split into three kingdoms.

Below *Emperor Shi Huangdi, from an 18th-century album of portraits of 86 Chinese emperors*

CHINA AND JAPAN

AD220–589

From the fall of the Han dynasty in 220 to the rise of the Sui in 589, China remained divided and almost constantly at war. After a brief period of unity following the Three Kingdoms period, the north fell once more into division, falling victim to external conquest, while the south flourished. The northern kingdom was revived by the Toba (397–534) and again by the Northern Zhou (577–589) before the whole country was reunited under the Sui.

Three Kingdoms

Following the abdication of the last Han emperor in 220, China split into three kingdoms. The most powerful of these was the northern kingdom of Wei. Larger by area but much less populated was the kingdom of Wu, to the south. Wu transformed southern China, hitherto dominated by non-Chinese tribal peoples, into an important centre of Chinese culture. The weakest and least populous kingdom was the western state of Shu (present-day Szechwan Province). Each kingdom was ruled by an 'emperor' who proclaimed himself the legitimate successor to the Han dynasty. Wars between the kingdoms were frequent and bloody. Whole towns were wiped out, and the population fell sharply. In 263, the Wei conquered the Shu. Two years later, Sima Yen, the Wei general who defeated the Shu, usurped the Wei throne and declared himself Wudi (reigned 265–289), the first of the Jin dynasty. In 280, Wudi conquered Wu and reunited the country.

Right A woman from the Wu kingdom, where customs included tattooing

Above *Cao Cao (154–220), who was posthumously titled Emperor Wu of Wei*

Below *An image from the ancient Chinese book* The Romance of the Three Kingdoms

Despite the turbulence of the 60-year Three Kingdoms period it was later romanticized in Chinese literature as an age of chivalry and heroism.

Sixteen Kingdoms

Unification did not last. After Wudi's death, a violent power struggle erupted between his sons, known as the 'rebellion of the eight princes' (291–306). The princes tried to bolster their campaigns by recruiting from nomad peoples of Central Asia, but this only encouraged the nomads to invade. In 306 a Xiongnu chieftain, Liu Yuan, began his conquest of northern China, capturing the two capitals, Luoyang (311) and Chang'an (316). Northern China collapsed into a patchwork of part-Chinese, part-nomad states known as the Sixteen Kingdoms. Widespread famine and banditry forced large numbers of people to flee to southern China, which remained under Jin rule. Here, many of them settled on the fertile but under-populated Yangtse plain. Their arrival accelerated the Sinicization of southern China begun by Wu. For the next 300 years, the south would enjoy a period of relatively stable rule under five successive dynasties. By the sixth century, it had overtaken the north as the wealthiest and most populous region of China.

The Toba

In the north, one of the nomad-Chinese states, known as the Toba, defeated the others during an 11-year campaign between 386 and 397, unifying northern China and reestablishing the Wei state. The Toba people were conscious of their position as outsiders, and with their nomadic background, they also lacked experience in administering a large region. However, they did have the support of many northern landowners, who welcomed the prospect of a strong government to safeguard their economic interests. Gradually, the Toba assimilated themselves into Chinese culture and began to rule like any other Chinese dynasty, even launching defensive wars against nomadic invaders from the north. The capital was symbolically transferred from the northern frontier to the ancient imperial city of Luoyang, and by the late fifth century, the court had actually banned the original Toba language, dress and surnames.

The Northern Zhou

In 534, pro-Toba and pro-Chinese factions in the Toba court fell out, causing civil war, and the Toba Wei state split into eastern and western halves. A powerful landowning family in the north-west known as the Northern Zhou took control of Western Wei in 557, then extended their territory into western China (formerly the Shu kingdom). In 577, the Northern Zhou conquered Eastern Wei, reunifying the north. Four years later, a general of mixed nomad-Chinese descent called Yang Jian (known posthumously as Wendi), usurped

JAPAN

Japan was first settled around 30,000 years ago by people from Siberia and Korea. Some 10,000 years ago, the Jomon culture developed on the largest island of Honshu. By around 3000BC, they began supplementing their hunting and gathering lifestyle with farming. They used stone tools and made pottery. By 2000BC, they had learned to build boats and to fish. After 300BC, settlers reached Japan from China and Korea, bringing new skills such as weaving, rice growing, mining and metalworking. Between 300BC and AD250, known as the Yayoi period, the first villages and towns were built and Japan's first states emerged. During the Kofun period (c. 250–538), Japan became a patchwork of small kingdoms, each ruled by a powerful clan. This was followed by the Asuka period (538–710), when the Yamato political system developed: the clan-kingdoms merged into a united Japan under a single emperor.

the Wei throne and founded the Sui dynasty. After spending some years consolidating his power in the north, Wendi crossed the Yangtse River in 589 and overthrew the Nan Chen dynasty in the south. After almost 400 years of division, China was once again united under one ruler.

Above A jar in the Kamegaoka style from the final Jomon period (1000–400BC)

TIMELINE	
300BC–AD300	*Yayoi period in Japan*
AD220–280	*Three Kingdoms period in China*
291–306	*Rebellion of the eight princes causes civil war in northern China*
316–386	*Sixteen Kingdoms period in northern China*
386–397	*Toba conquer northern China*
397–534	*Toba-Wei rule in northern China*
c. 500	*Yamato become rulers of Japan*
534	*Toba Wei splits into eastern and western halves*
577	*Northern Zhou reunifies northern China*
581	*Wendi founds the Sui dynasty*
589	*China is reunified under the Sui.*

SOUTH-EAST ASIA AND THE PACIFIC

300BC–AD500

The story of human settlement and culture in South-east Asia and the Pacific is really the story of one people, the Austronesians (speakers of the Austronesian language), and their gradual spread through the region between 3000BC and AD1000. The Austronesian-speaking peoples originated in Taiwan in about 3000BC. The introduction of rice cultivation during the fourth millennium had led to substantial population growth, prompting their expansion into the Philippines, Malaysia and Indonesia. By 2000BC they were the dominant peoples in these places. In the early second millennium BC, the Austronesians settled the coast of modern-day Vietnam. Some time around AD200, Austronesians from Indonesia sailed west across the Indian Ocean in outrigger canoes and became the first people to settle Madagascar, off the coast of Africa.

Lapita

In about 2000BC, Austronesians began colonizing the coastal areas and islands of New Guinea, mixing with the Australoid peoples who had settled there tens of thousands of years before (see page 12). As a result of this interaction, Lapita culture, characterized by distinctive pottery and shell tools, emerged by about 1600. The Lapita were extraordinary sea travellers, who managed to cross enormous distances on sail- or paddle-powered dugout canoes and settle the region of the Pacific known today as Melanesia. Along with their navigational skills, the Lapita made important technological advances. In the late second millennium, they invented the outrigger canoe – the outrigger was a wooden float attached to the canoe, increasing its stability and allowing more substantial cargo to be carried. This enabled much longer-distance voyages and Lapita culture was able to spread eastwards, reaching the Bismarck Islands, New Caledonia, Fiji, Samoa and Tonga by 1000. Evidence of Lapita settlement can be found in the remains of their distinctive pottery, found in all the places they colonized. Made from reddish-coloured clay, Lapita pots and bowls were decorated with elaborate and repeated patterns, often using a pointed tool.

Polynesians

By around 500BC, the Lapita had disappeared as a distinctive culture. In the west, it became part of the traditional Australoid culture, while in the eastern

Left *The famous moai of Easter Island are carved from ash taken from the extinct volcano Rano Raraku*

triangle of Fiji, Samoa and Tonga it developed into Polynesian culture. Inheritors of the seafaring skills and technology of the Lapita, the Polynesians put this to use with the some of the first planned long-distance voyages in the Pacific. Their understanding of the stars, ocean currents, winds, waves and bird behaviour, developed over hundreds of years, enabled them to navigate accurately across vast distances of open ocean. By 200BC, they had spread eastwards to Tahiti, the Tuamotu archipelago and the Marquesas Islands. By AD300, they had reached Easter Island and by 400, they had settled the Hawaiian islands. Later in the millennium, the Polynesians were to reach New Zealand, the Solomon Islands and, possibly, the coast of America.

Micronesians

Micronesia in the North Pacific contains over 2000 scattered islands occupying an area larger than that of the USA. Starting in about 4500, peoples from the Philippines, Indonesia and Melanesia (the area settled by the Lapita – see above) began to settle many of the Micronesian islands. Many of the islands were volcanic with fertile soil, and the people here were able to live by growing taro, yams, breadfruit and other crops. On the less fertile islands, fishing was a vital source of food. Micronesian society was based around clans, with the head clan claiming descent from the island's original settlers. Their settlements were made up of wooden houses built on rock platforms. They made pottery, shell tools, wood and stone carvings and jewellery. Like other Pacific peoples, they were skilled seafarers.

The first states

Most of South-east Asian and Pacific society remained tribal during the classical

ABORIGINALS

The people who settled Australia 40,000 years ago remained isolated from the rest of the world until the arrival of Europeans in the 18th century AD. They pursued a virtually unchanging hunter-gatherer lifestyle, adapting to the different climates and environmental conditions of each part of Australia. Each aboriginal tribe was granted its own territory by the 'ancestors', the mythical creators of the aborigines, and the land could not be sold, bartered or given away. Aboriginal tribes were made up of clans led by elders. Their mythology, the dreamtime, which told of the ancestors, was handed down by word of mouth. Each tribe had its own dreamtime stories.

Above *The traditional art of the aborigines is characterized by intricate geometric patterns and organic colours*

TIMELINE

c. 4500BC	*Islands of Micronesia are settled*
c. 2000BC	*Austronesians colonize New Guinea*
c. 1600BC	*Lapita culture emerges in New Guinea*
c. 1000BC	*Lapita culture spreads through Melanesia*
c. 500BC	*Polynesian culture emerges in Fiji, Samoa and Tonga*
c. AD400	*Polynesians settle Hawaii*
AD800–1000	*Polynesians reach New Zealand*
c. AD400	*Funan empire dominates mainland South-east Asia.*

period. The region's first states emerged in South-east Asia in the first century AD as a result of trade contacts with India and China. One of the earliest states was Funan, based in the lower Mekong (in modern-day Vietnam), which grew wealthy through trade. By AD400, Funan had become a formidable regional power, with an empire covering much of mainland South-east Asia.

THE MAYA

200BC–AD900

The Maya civilization of Central America reached its peak between AD250 and 800, a time known as the Classic period. They inhabited an area that encompasses present-day Guatemala, Yucatàn in Mexico, Belize, Honduras and El Salvador. The Maya did not rule over this area as a single empire, but lived in autonomous city-states, each with its own king. The Maya built impressive temples, developed a writing system and practised advanced mathematics and astronomy.

Above right *The Mayans believed that the gods gave their own blood to create human life, and that blood and life had to be given back in return*

Late Preclassic Maya

The city-states of the Maya emerged between 300BC and AD250, known as the Late Preclassic period. Many of these had fortifications, and wars between them were probably frequent. The preeminent city of this period was El Mirador in modern Guatemala, which flourished between about 150BC and AD150. It had a population of around 80,000, large temple pyramids, a fortified palace complex and causeways linking it to satellite settlements.

The Maya were greatly influenced by the Olmecs (see page 56). They worshipped similar gods, played the same sacred ball game, measured the years using a long-count calendar similar to the one invented by the Olmecs and inherited Olmec expertise in mathematics and astronomy.

Like their predecessors, the Maya also developed a system of writing. However, unlike the Olmec script, Mayan writing used both logograms (symbols representing words) and syllabic glyphs (symbols representing syllables) and so could fully represent their spoken language.

The main centre of Mayan writing in the Late Preclassic period was not El Mirador but the southern highlands of modern Guatemala, where numerous engraved monuments were erected to honour former kings. The earliest of these, in El Baúl, dates to around AD36. Possibly due to a volcanic eruption, this southern Mayan culture declined in the third century AD and no new monuments were erected after this.

Tikal

In AD300, the practice of erecting stone monuments revived in the central lowland rainforest area of present-day Guatemala, marking the beginning of the era known as the Classic period. The largest and most powerful city-state for most of the Classic

TIMELINE	
300BC–AD250	*Mayan city-states emerge*
300–562	*Tikal is the dominant city-state*
900–950	*Mayan city-states of central lowlands are abandoned and fall into ruin.*

period was Tikal, which covered an area of 15 km² (6 square miles), contained some 3,000 buildings and may have had up to 90,000 inhabitants. Tikal reached the height of its power under King Stormy Sky (reigned 411–457) when it dominated the region economically and politically and had trade links throughout much of Mesoamerica, including Teotihuacán. Tikal declined after its defeat by the city-state of Caracol in 562. It recovered under Ah Cacau (reigned 682–723), but never regained its former status. Other important Maya cities included Palenque, Copán and Kalakmul.

Government, trade and warfare

The Mayan kings ruled from palaces in the centre of the city with the help of a council of noblemen. Kings may have claimed descent from the gods. In Palenque and other cities, the king adopted the title of *kinich,* a reference to the sun god, Kinich Ahaw. The kings and nobles also had a priestly function, presiding over religious ceremonies.

The city-states traded with each other and with other large urban centres in Mesoamerica. They traded cacao beans (also used as a form of currency), salt, wood, feathers, jade and cotton. Despite links of trade and culture, warfare between states was common. Conflicts arose due to pressures of rising populations and competition for good agricultural land. Cities also needed a regular supply of prisoners of war to make human sacrifices to their gods.

Decline

The Classic period ended in the ninth century when the city-states of the central lowlands began to fail. Population levels declined, new building work ceased and the Maya abandoned their cities and returned to live in remote villages. By 950, all the major Mayan cities of the central lowlands were in ruins. Why this happened is a mystery. One theory is that competition for preeminence among the city-states placed too much pressure on the peasantry to supply food and labour, causing economic depression, famine and, ultimately, political collapse. In the north, cities such as Chichén Itzá, Uxmal and Mayapan continued to flourish until about 1000, when the area was invaded by Toltecs from central Mexico. Mayan civilization finally ended with the Spanish conquest in the 16th century.

Below *A page from the* Dresden Codex, *a record of Mayan civilization thought to have been made shortly before the Spanish Conquest*

RELIGION AND ASTRONOMY

The Maya worshipped around 150 deities, the most important of which were Itzamma, god of science and writing, and Kinich Ahaw, the sun god (they may have been different aspects of the same god). The Maya practised human as well as animal sacrifice to appease their gods. They saw great religious significance in the movements of heavenly bodies and sought to understand them through observation. From their study of the night sky, they created the long-count calendar. Their skill in mathematics allowed them to produce highly accurate charts of the movements of the moon and planets.

MEXICO AND SOUTH AMERICA

200BC—AD700

The Olmecs who inhabited the Gulf Coast of Mexico laid the foundations of Mesoamerican civilization in the Middle Preclassic period (900–300BC). Their culture was inherited by the Zapotecs of the Oaxaca valley, who flourished in the Late Preclassic (300–1BC). However, by the first century AD, the city of Teotihuacán in central Mexico had become the most significant centre of Mesoamerican culture.

TIMELINE	
c. 300BC	Teotihuacán is founded
c. 100BC–AD600s	Moche flourishes
c. AD1–750	Teotihuacán flourishes
c. AD200–800	Nazca people flourish
c. AD400–1000	Huari and Tiahuanaco flourish.

Above *A view of Teotihuacán's Avenue of the Dead and Pyramid of the Sun, seen from the Pyramid of the Moon*

Teotihuacán

Teotihuacán first arose in about 300BC as a small farming village, one of many in the fertile central valley of Mexico. In the first century BC, the settlement underwent rapid growth when refugees arrived there following a volcanic eruption in Cuicuilco. Teotihuacán was transformed into a grand city, built on a carefully planned grid pattern. It contained palaces, apartment buildings, a market place and a monumental ceremonial centre that included two enormous temple pyramids.

At its height, in about AD500, Teotihuacán covered 20 km² (8 square miles) and supported a population of between 125,000 and 200,000. Perhaps two-thirds of the population were farmers, but large areas of the city were also given over to workshops where craftspeople worked on ceramics, obsidian (a volcanic glass used for tools and weapons), pottery and stonemasonry. The city also contained residential quarters for merchants who travelled there from many parts of Mesoamerica.

Teotihuacán was governed by priest-kings who presided over elaborate religious ceremonies that often involved human sacrifices. For much of the Classic period, Teotihuacán was the largest and most significant cultural, religious and commercial centre in Mesoamerica. The city began to decline in the early seventh century, perhaps due to overcultivation of the surrounding land. It was sacked and burned in about 750, possibly during an invasion or rebellion by the nearby city of Cholula. The population fell sharply, but Teotihuacán continued to be honoured as a religious centre by the Aztecs in the 15th and 16th centuries.

Moche

The decline of the Chavín in about 200BC (see page 57) marked the beginning of the Early Intermediate period of South American history (200BC–AD500), during which the first states and empires arose. The first was Moche, which emerged in about 100BC in the coastal desert of northern Peru. The people of Moche fished and used irrigation to grow crops such as maize, potatoes, cotton, peppers and peanuts. They built a vast ceremonial centre containing two enormous mudbrick pyramids. Priest-kings were buried in large tombs near the pyramids. They were buried with gold, silver and precious objects.

The Moche civilization is best known for the high quality of its crafts and artwork. Specialist artists and craftworkers produced pottery, murals, textiles of cotton and wool and jewellery and other objects of precious metal. They used moulds to mass-produce pottery, which they then decorated with painted scenes of daily life and religious ceremonies or depictions of myths.

Moche began to expand in about AD200, spreading its culture by conquest along the coast and establishing fortified settlements at sites such as Loma Negra, Huaca del Brujo and Pañamarca. Moche itself was abandoned in about 500 after a devastating flood and the capital was moved to Pampa Grande. In the seventh century, the Moche state was absorbed by the Huari empire.

NAZCA

The Nazca people flourished between AD200 and 800 on the desert coast of modern Peru, to the south of Moche. They created enormous etchings on the surface of the desert depicting animals and geometric shapes, some measuring more than 120 m (390 ft) in length. Known as the Nazca lines, these etchings are so big that they can only be appreciated from the air, and they are thought to have been intended for the gods to view. The Nazca people also made decorated pottery bowls and musical instruments and wove textiles. In about 800, the culture disappeared, following its absorption into the Huari empire.

Huari and Tiahuanaco

The city of Huari emerged in about AD400 in the Peruvian Andes near modern Ayacucho. Its people developed South America's first terraced fields and built a major road network, both of which influenced the later Inca civilization (see page 148). The Huari were an expansionist people and by AD800 they had conquered a large area of northern Peru.

Above A stone mask found at Teotihuacán, dating from third–seventh century

Further south near Lake Titicaca, the city of Tiahuanaco arose around the same time as Huari. The city contained a ceremonial and administrative centre containing temples, tombs and palaces. This was surrounded by a residential area with housing for around 40,000 people. Between 400 and 700, Tiahuanaco built an empire that dominated the southern Andes and the southern coastal desert. Like the Huari, their motive for expansion was to achieve control of the resources of the lowland and coastal regions. Both Huari and Tiahuanaco were abandoned by around 1000, possibly because of prolonged drought.

AFRICA

500BC–AD500

During the classical era, powerful states continued to flourish in East Africa and the first states began to emerge in North Africa. In the latter region, the Berber kingdoms of Numantia and Mauretania emerged in the Maghrib in about 200BC, but these were barely given time to develop before being conquered by Rome. In West Africa, the Nok culture developed ironworking skills and in the early centuries AD, Bantu speakers from southern Nigeria began to spread their language and culture through most of southern Africa.

Above *King Ezana's stele in Northern Stelae Park at Axum, standing 21 m (70 ft) tall*

Right *A Nok culture terracotta sculpture dating from the sixth century BC*

Nubia

In Nubia (modern-day Sudan), the states of Kerma and Kush flourished in the second and first millennia BC (see page 59). In the seventh century BC, the Egyptians to the north attacked Nubia, forcing the Nubians to move their capital south to Meroë in about 590. The kingdom of Meroë, as it came to be known, remained a powerful, independent state, despite successive empires – Persians, Macedonians and Romans – ruling over Egypt to the north. Meroë only declined in the fourth century AD following attacks from desert nomads and was conquered by the kingdom of Axum in AD350.

Axum

Axum emerged in northern Ethiopia in the first century AD. Its major cultural influence was the Sabeans of Arabia from whom it inherited its alphabet, religious beliefs and architectural style. The main source of the kingdom's power and wealth was its control of the Red Sea port of Adulis, an important centre of trade. The Axumites exported spices, ivory, ebony, animal skins and tortoise shells in exchange for goods from Egypt, the Roman Empire, Arabia, India and even China. Axum conquered other smaller states along the Blue Nile River and the Red Sea coast. The rulers of Axum used their wealth to build impressive fortresses, palaces and stone monuments in the capital (also called Axum). Axum reached the height of its power under King Ezana (reigned c. 330– c. 356) under whom the Axumites conquered Meroë. Ezana was the first African king

TIMELINE	
590BC–AD350	*Kingdom of Meroë flourishes in Nubia*
500BC–AD400	*Nok culture flourishes in West Africa*
200sBC	*Kingdoms of Numantia and Mauretania briefly flourish in North Africa*
c. 100BC	*Camels are introduced to the Sahara*
c. AD1–500	*Bantu speaking peoples spread their culture through much of central and southern Africa*
c. AD1–650	*Kingdom of Axum flourishes in Ethiopia.*

to convert to Christianity and he made it the official religion of Axum. With the rise of Islam in the seventh century, Axum came under repeated attack by Arab Muslim armies and the kingdom gradually lost power and territory. Its most significant legacy, Christianity, survives to this day in Eritrea and Ethiopia.

Nok

The Nok culture (named after the Nigerian village of Nok where evidence of the culture was first discovered) flourished in West Africa from about 500BC to AD400. It spread through the region between the Niger and Benue rivers, south-west of the Jos Plateau. The Nok people were among the earliest ironworkers in Africa, smelting iron tools and weapons in circular clay furnaces. The earliest of these dates from 450BC. The Nok people are best known for producing terracotta sculptures of human and animal figures – the oldest sculptures found in Africa south of the Sahara. Most are around 30 cm in height, though some are nearly life-size. These hollow figurines have long, often cone-shaped faces with angular eyes and decorative hairstyles. It is likely the figurines were used for ritual or religious purposes.

Bantu

Between AD1 and 500, southern Africa witnessed a remarkable expansion of Bantu-speaking peoples. The first Bantu speakers probably lived in southern Nigeria and Cameroon in the second millennium BC, and by the first century AD, their growing population caused them to migrate southwards through the central African rainforest, reaching southern Africa by AD500.

They brought their knowledge of farming and ironworking, as well as their

CAMELS

The most significant development in North Africa during the Classical era was the introduction of the camel to the Sahara in about 100BC. The effect was analogous to the development of horse-riding to the Central Asian steppe (see page 46). Camels could endure long desert journeys far better than horses, mules and other beasts of burden. They proved well-suited to warfare, and enabled nomadic tribes to mount devastating raids on sedentary communities at the edges of the desert. More importantly, they allowed a major expansion in North African trade – until then, most goods had been transported by sea. By AD500 camel caravans were travelling along established trade routes between the Mediterranean and West Africa.

Left *Camels still fulfil their traditional role of providing transport for people and goods across desert areas of North Africa*

language (there are over 180 million Bantu speakers in Africa today), to many parts of the continent. The migration did not occur steadily or uniformly. Migrants would frequently split off into smaller groups and settle in different regions, which is why there are around 300 groups of Bantu speakers today, each with their own dialect.

ADVANCES IN TECHNOLOGY

500BC–AD600

The Classical era witnessed major changes in human society. Around the world, populations grew, food production intensified and states became ever more complex, with increasingly sophisticated political and social structures. People developed specialist skills in arts and crafts, architecture and poetry; others pushed back the boundaries of knowledge in astronomy, mathematics and engineering. In the most developed civilizations, there were key advances in technology. Cast iron and steel were discovered; wind and water power were harnessed; horse-riding and the art of warfare were revolutionized by the invention of the stirrup in about AD300. The arrival of the rudder and the compass transformed sea travel.

Above *A 17th-century illustration of a Chinese iron plough with a curved mouldboard*

metal when it was still in molten form. With its low melting point, good castability and wear resistance, cast iron was excellent for making weapons and figurines. By the third century BC, the Indians were mixing iron, charcoal and glass to create a much harder, stronger metal: steel.

Metallurgy

Iron, as a material for making sharp, tough tools and weapons, became increasingly widespread during the Classical era. In about 500BC, the Chinese learned how to produce cast iron by adding carbon to the

Power technologies

In the ancient world, most energy was provided by humans or animals. During the classical era, the Greeks found ways of amplifying the energy exerted by developing levers and rope-and-pulley systems. However, little actually changed in the methods of animal traction, beyond the development of more effective harnesses for oxen and donkeys and wheels that travelled more smoothly.

TIMELINE

c. 500BC	Chinese discover how to produce cast iron; Phoenicians and Greeks begin building two-masted ships
300–100BC	Rudder invented in China
c. 287–c. 212BC	Archimedes invents block-and-tackle pulley system, the screw (useful for irrigation), the catapult and the odometer
200s BC	Steel production begins in India
c. AD1–100	Waterwheels invented; magnetic compass invented in China; Hero of Alexandria invents the first steam engine
c. AD300	Stirrup invented
c. AD650	First windmills built in Sistan, Afghanistan.

HERO OF ALEXANDRIA

One of the most remarkable inventors of the ancient world was the Greek mathematician and scientist Hero (or Heron), who lived in Alexandria in the first century AD. Hero was the first man in history to use steam as a form of energy, an application not repeated until the Industrial Revolution 1,800 years later. His aeolipile, or 'windball', was an early type of steam engine. Steam from a cauldron of boiling water was passed through two pipes into a metal ball. As the steam was ejected through two curved exhaust pipes, the ball was sent spinning at high speed. The aeolipile was just one of 80 machines Hero is said to have invented. Other inventions included temple doors that opened automatically; the world's first coin-operated vending machine, which dispensed holy water; a wind-powered organ; and a mechanical puppet theatre that showed a complete, 15-minute performance of a play about the Trojan War.

Gradually, civilizations discovered ways of harnessing wind and water power to drive their machines. Although sails had been used to power boats and ships since the fourth millennium BC, important advances were made in the early classical era. By around 500BC, the Greeks and Phoenicians began building ships with two masts: a middle mast with a square sail and a smaller mast with a triangular sail. This allowed the building of much larger ships that could take far heavier loads.

In the first century AD, the first waterwheels were invented in China, India and the Roman Empire, harnessing the power generated by water as it falls from a height or moves downstream. In late-first-century Syria, waterwheels were being fitted with tubes or buckets to create a means of irrigation. The turning axle of a waterwheel could also be used to drive other machines, most commonly a millstone for grinding cereals and grains to make flour. The first windmills, however, would not be built until around AD650.

Transportation

Two very important innovations in sea travel emerged in the classical era. Between 300 and 100BC, the Chinese invented the rudder, making steering much easier. Then, in the first century AD, the compass was invented – also in China. It was discovered that a magnetic iron needle floated in water on a sliver of wood would point in a north-south line. The compass became invaluable to navigators.

In terms of land travel, the finest road builders of the classical era were the Romans. They invented a special surveying tool called a *groma* to build their roads as straight as possible. They built up their roads in three layers, reaching to a depth of about a metre: above a base of sand or mortar they laid rows of flat stones and, at the surface, a mix of gravel and lime. Because of their excellent roads, the Romans were able to develop a variety of wheeled vehicles to travel long distances quickly and comfortably. One of the largest of these was the *clabularium*. Pulled by eight oxen, it could carry loads of up to 500 kg (half a ton).

Above *Hero's aeolipile, which he described in his manuscript* Spiritalia seu Pneumatica, *written in about AD62*

Below *The invention of the waterwheel provided a new source of power*

RELIGIONS OF THE EAST

600BC–AD500

During the sixth century BC – just as democracy, science and philosophy were being invented in Greece – equally remarkable developments were occurring in India and China in the areas of religion and philosophy. In that century, Siddhartha Gautama founded Buddhism and Vardhamana Mahavira established the central tenets of Jainism, while Confucius and Lao Zi taught the belief systems that would come to dominate Chinese philosophical thought in the centuries that followed.

by three powerful gods: Vishnu, Shiva and Shakti. Under the Guptas (see page 85) the two great Hindu epics were written down: the *Ramayana* and the *Mahabharata*. The caste system became established, and belief in *karma* and reincarnation, central to modern Hinduism, developed around this time. Challenged by the rise of Buddhism, Hinduism became more flexible and tolerant, and by AD400 it began to recover in India. In the fifth century, Hinduism spread to South-east Asia.

Hinduism

By 500BC, Hinduism was the dominant religion in India. At the same time, it began to shed many of its Aryan roots and emerge in the form it is practised today. The numerous Vedic deities were superseded

Buddhism

Buddhism was founded in northern India by a man called Siddhartha Gautama (*c.* 563–*c.* 483), who taught that a state of enlightenment can be attained by

TAOISM

Taoism is a philosophy inspired by the teachings of the Chinese philosopher Lao Zi, who lived in the sixth century BC. However, the core work of Taoism, the *Tao Te Ching (The Classic of the Way and Virtue)* was compiled and revised between the fourth and second centuries BC by two thinkers, Zhuangzi and Zhang Daoling. The *Tao* teaches that the unity of nature determines what each individual thing is and what it does. The wise man desires nothing and does not interfere with nature. It also argues that simplicity and moving with the flow of events are the keys to wise government. In this sense, Taoism contrasted starkly with Confucianism, which encouraged a more proactive attitude to political leadership.

Right *A Taoist ritual for the dead painted in about 1700, illustrating a scene from the Ming dynasty novel* The Plum in the Golden Vase

suppressing worldly desires. He became known as the Buddha, or the 'Enlightened One' and his teachings were known as the Dharma. Buddhism remained a minor sect until the Mauryan emperor Ashoka converted to the religion in 260BC. He promoted Buddhism throughout India and sent missionaries to South-east, Central and western Asia. In northern India, Buddhism replaced Hinduism as the major religion. Buddhist monks carried their faith along the Silk Road to China in the first century AD. In the third century, Buddhism divided into two schools: Theravada, which applied a strict interpretation of Buddhist scriptures, and Mahayana, which took a more liberal approach. By the fourth century Buddhism had reached Korea from China, and in the fifth and sixth centuries Mahayana Buddhism reached Japan and became established in Myanmar and Vietnam. In India, Buddhism continued to thrive under the Hindu Guptas, but began to decline in about the sixth century when many of its centres in the north-west were attacked by White Huns from Central Asia.

Jainism

Jainism did not have a single founder. It claims the truth was revealed at different times by 24 tirthankaras (teachers who show the way), the last of whom, Vardhamana Mahavira, was born in Bharat, India, around 540BC. Jainism rejects the notion of a supreme being and advocates a deep respect for all living things. One of the main characteristics of Jain belief is the emphasis on the immediate consequences of one's behaviour. According to tradition, Mahavira established a community of 50,000 monks and nuns. Over the next millennium, the Jain community grew and spread to central and western India, but

began to lose momentum to the larger religions of Buddhism and Hinduism.

Confucianism

Confucianism is a system of thought more than a religion. It was founded by the Chinese philosopher Confucius (c. 551– c. 479) during the later Zhou period – a chaotic time in China's history (see page 45). Confucius believed that society could be saved if people acted with sincerity and showed good moral character in their personal and public conduct. This meant, among other things, filial piety and showing respect for authority. Confucius's ideas were spread by his disciples after his death and achieved government support under the Han dynasty. In 124BC, the government established the Imperial University to educate future government officials in Confucian ideals. However, between AD200 and 600, interest in Confucianism waned in China as many turned to Buddhism and Taoism.

Above *Nearly 2500 years after his death, the statue of Confucius appears in Chinese societies worldwide*

RELIGIONS OF THE WEST

500BC—AD500

During the period of the Republic and early Empire, the Romans were heavily influenced in their religious beliefs by the peoples they interacted with and conquered. As contact with the Greeks increased, the old Roman gods became associated with them. For example, Jupiter came to be seen as Zeus and Neptune as Poseidon. Foreign cults became popular among many Romans, such as the worship of the Egyptian Isis and the Persian Mithras. Cults also developed around several emperors. Christians and Jews were less tolerated than followers of pagan religions because of their faith in a single deity, which could not be so easily accommodated within a polytheistic belief system.

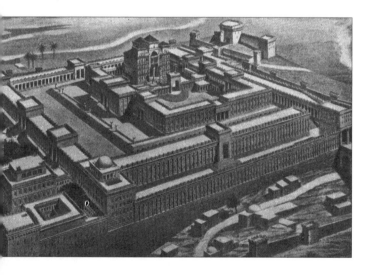

Above *This depiction of Solomon's Temple draws upon written records; archaeological remains are few*

Judaism

In 539BC Cyrus the Great, conqueror of Babylon, allowed the Jews who were exiled there to return to Israel (see page 31). Some 50,000 returned to Jerusalem. They rebuilt the city, including Solomon's Temple. In 332, Alexander the Great of Macedon conquered the Persian Empire, including Judah, and the Jews came under the rule of Hellenistic kings – the Ptolemies of Egypt and the Seleucids of Syria – who promoted Greek culture within their empires. Between 175 and 163, the Seleucid king Antiochus IV tried to ban the practice of Judaism. The Jews, led by Judah Maccabee, rebelled and overthrew the Seleucids. Judah Maccabee's family, the Hasmoneans, established an independent Jewish state that lasted for about 100 years.

In 63BC, the Romans conquered Judah, which they called Judea. At first the Romans ruled through puppet kings, the most significant of which was Herod the Great (reigned 37–4BC), who was hated for his ruthlessness, despite rebuilding the Temple on a grand scale. In AD6, Judea came under direct Roman rule. The Jews rebelled in 66 and when the Romans regained Jerusalem in 70, they burned the second Temple to the ground. In 132, in an uprising led by Simon Bar Kochba, the Jews managed to take control of Jerusalem, but the rebellion was crushed by the Romans three years later. By this time, many Jews had left Judea and dispersed to other lands, forming what became known as the Diaspora. Wherever they went, they maintained their traditions. Those who remained in Judea, now called Palestine, were banned from Jerusalem, which became a Roman city. New centres of Jewish learning arose in Galilee and Babylonia. Between 200 and 500, Jewish teachers and scholars compiled Jewish laws, customs and ethics into a book called the Talmud.

Christianity

Christianity originated with the teachings of a Jew, Jesus of Nazareth, who lived in Palestine in the early first century AD.

Christianity became the official religion of the Roman Empire. When the empire split between east and west in 395, the Church also separated to form the Orthodox Church in the east and the Roman Catholic Church in the west.

Left *Under Emperor Nero, the killing of Christians was considered to be entertainment for the masses*

According to tradition, Jesus performed miracles and preached about the coming of the Kingdom of God. His disciples believed he was the messiah, or 'anointed one', come to save people from their sins. They called him Christ, meaning 'saviour'. After Jesus' death, the disciples spread his teachings. Gradually the message of Christianity spread among the Jewish communities throughout the Mediterranean region. One convert, St Paul, was the first to actively encourage non-Jews to become Christians. Alexandria in Egypt, Antioch in Turkey, Jerusalem and Rome became major centres of early Christianity. By the start of the second century, Christian communities began to organize themselves, appointing bishops in each city, helped by deacons and priests.

Some Roman emperors saw the Christian Church as a threat and took harsh measures against them. Nero turned the killing of Christians into public entertainment and, in 303, Diocletian executed thousands of Christians for refusing to renounce their faith. These persecutions only seemed to make Christianity stronger, however, and by the fourth century, it had spread through-out the Roman Empire. Constantine I legalized Christianity in 312 and convened a council in Nicaea (Turkey) to establish basic Christian doctrine. In 391,

TIMELINE

539BC	Jews return to Israel
332–163BC	Hellenistic dynasties rule Judah
163–63BC	Judah is an independent Jewish state under the Hasmoneans
63BC	Romans conquer Judah (renamed Judea)
c. 4BC–AD29	Life of Jesus of Nazareth
AD66	Jews overthrow Romans in Jerusalem
70	Romans retake Jerusalem and destroy Second Temple
132–135	Jews under Simon Bar Kochba retake Jerusalem
135	Romans reconquer Jerusalem and turn it into a Roman city; Judea becomes Palestine
200–500	The Talmud, the book of Jewish law, is compiled
312	Constantine I legalizes Christianity
325	First Council of Nicaea agrees first uniform Christian doctrine, the Nicene Creed
391	Christianity becomes the official religion of the Roman Empire
395	Christianity splits into eastern and western Churches.

ZOROASTRIANISM

The religion of Zoroastrianism was founded some time between 1400 and 1000BC by a Persian prophet called Zoroaster, who taught a belief in a single god, Ahura Mazda, who created all things. At the heart of the religion is the belief that earth is a battleground between good and evil. Zoroastrianism flourished in Persia under the Achaemenids between 550 and 330, but did not prosper so well under the Seleucides and Parthians who ruled Persia after Alexander's conquest. It revived under the Sasanians, who ruled from the third century AD. An offshoot of Zoroastrianism called Mithraism was an early rival to Christianity in the Roman Empire, especially popular among Roman soldiers serving in the east. Aside from this, Zoroastrianism failed to win many followers outside Persia, although its ideas about good and evil influenced Jewish, Christian and Islamic thought.

THE CAROLINGIAN EMPIRE

600–814

The collapse of the Roman Empire in the west traditionally marks the end of classical civilization and the start of the medieval era in world history. For the most part, the Germanic tribes that settled in the territories of the former empire pursued their traditional ways of life, and Roman government, laws, commerce, culture and learning virtually disappeared. Urban life, trade and industry declined, while the Roman road network fell into neglect. The Church, however, survived as a powerful unifying force in continental Europe, and the pope, its leader in Rome, wielded significant political as well as religious authority. Christian communities, known as monasteries, emerged as important centres of learning from the fifth century.

Above Saint Remigius baptizes Clovis I *by the Master of Saint Gilles, painted in about 1500*

Frankish kingdom

The Franks were a Germanic people formed from several tribes, who began to raid Roman Gaul in the late third century. By 450 there were Frankish clans living throughout northern Gaul, each ruled by their own king. Following the collapse of the Western Roman Empire, a king of the Merovingian clan, called Childeric, and his son Clovis (reigned 482–511) managed to unite large numbers of Franks under their rule. Thus the Merovingians became a royal dynasty of the Frankish people and, under them, the Frankish kingdom expanded across much of modern France and Belgium.

The Merovingians did not create a strong central state. They followed the Germanic custom of dividing their lands between each male heir. This caused complex subdivisions, disputed successions and a weakening of royal power. Their conquests enabled Merovingian kings to reward their nobles with estates in return for military support. But when the conquests dried up, the kings had to pay for continued support with donations from their own lands. By the mid-seventh century, the balance of power had shifted away from the kings and

BRITAIN

After the withdrawal of the Roman legions in 410, Britain was invaded from the north by Picts and from Ireland by Scots. In the mid-400s, Angles, Jutes and Saxons arrived from Germany, driving native Britons to the western fringes – Wales and Cornwall. The Anglo-Saxons, as the invaders were known, occupied what would become England. They established several independent kingdoms. The most powerful – until its defeat by the Picts in 685 – was Northumbria. In the eighth century, Mercia became dominant under its kings, Aethelbald and Offa. The pagan Anglo-Saxons were converted to Christianity in the seventh century by missionaries sent out by the Celtic Church of Ireland as well as from the Church of Rome. The Celtic Church agreed to unite with the Roman Church in 664.

towards the families that ruled each of the kingdom's regions: Austrasia, Neustria, Burgundy, Aquitaine and Provence.

Carolingian dynasty

From the mid-seventh century, as Merovingian power declined, the kings became little more than figureheads and real authority passed to court officials known as mayors. One mayor, Pepin II of Herstal (ruled 679–714), was effective ruler of the kingdom from 687 and founded his own dynasty, the Arnulfings (later known as the Carolingians). Under his rule, Frankish power revived and most of the regions were returned to royal control. Pepin's son, Charles Martel (ruled 714–741) defeated an invading Arab army at Poitiers in 732, halting Islamic expansion in Europe.

Charles was succeeded by his son, Pepin the Short (reigned 741–768), who offered military aid to the pope in order to prevent the Lombards (rulers of most of Italy since 568) from conquering Rome. In return, the pope gave his blessing to Pepin when, in 751, he deposed the Merovingian monarch and took the Frankish throne for himself. When Pepin the Short died, the kingdom was divided between his sons Carloman and Charles (Charlemagne). When Carloman died in 771, Charlemagne became sole ruler.

Charlemagne

Charlemagne was an outstanding military leader and diplomat. He continued the work of his father, expanding Frankish territory and maintaining a policy of friendship and cooperation with the Church. Over 30 years of campaigning, he doubled the size of the Frankish kingdom. He conquered the Lombards in Italy; Avar territory in eastern Europe; the Breton kingdom in north-western France; and the Saxons in Germany. By 800, his domain extended through much of western Europe and Charlemagne was the most powerful European ruler since the emperors of ancient Rome.

Above *A 19th-century painting of the Battle of Poitiers, 25 October 732, won by Charles Martel (688–741)*

Charlemagne was driven by a zealous Christian faith. He conducted military campaigns and ordered mass executions to convert the pagan Saxons; made large donations of land to the papacy; and encouraged a renaissance of classical learning to improve the quality of the clergy. On Christmas day 800, Pope Leo III crowned Charlemagne emperor of a revived Roman Empire.

Like the Merovingian kings, Charlemagne granted estates to loyal nobles in return for military and political support, laying the foundations of feudalism in Europe. He tried to revive European trade by minting silver money and encouraging the establishment of markets. By the early ninth century, several important trading ports had developed on the northern coast of Europe.

Below *A portrait of Charlemagne, as seen in a late 16th-century engraving. His appearance was described in a biography by his courtier Einhard*

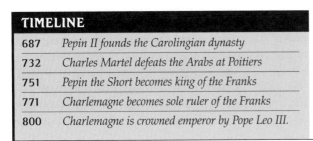

TIMELINE

687	*Pepin II founds the Carolingian dynasty*
732	*Charles Martel defeats the Arabs at Poitiers*
751	*Pepin the Short becomes king of the Franks*
771	*Charlemagne becomes sole ruler of the Franks*
800	*Charlemagne is crowned emperor by Pope Leo III.*

EUROPE IN THE AGE OF THE VIKINGS

793–1100

On 8 June 793, a party of ferocious seafaring warriors made landfall on Lindisfarne, an island off the north-east coast of Britain, and attacked the monastery there. They slaughtered or enslaved the monks, looted the monastery, then burned it to the ground, destroying one of Europe's foremost centres of learning. The raid sent shockwaves around Europe. Its perpetrators were Norsemen from Scandinavia, soon to be known as Vikings. The attack on Lindisfarne was only the beginning. Over the next 250 years, the Vikings would raid and colonize large areas of the continent.

Below *King Alfred fought repeated battles against the Vikings and eventually triumphed*

Rapid population growth in Scandinavia, leading to a reduction in the amount of available farmland, may have prompted the Viking raids. They continued into the ninth century, with incursions on British, Irish, Frankish and Mediterranean coastal settlements. Vikings even sailed their longships up rivers to sack inland ports like Dorestad, Hamburg and Cologne. Initially they came in search of plunder and slaves, but in 865 a large Danish Viking force invaded Britain with a different aim in mind: permanent settlement. Within five years, they had conquered Northumbria, Mercia and East Anglia. Only the kingdom of Wessex, ruled by King Alfred (reigned 871–899), held out. By 954, Wessex had won back control of the Viking territories and, in doing so, created the first united English kingdom.

Viking expansion

The ninth and early 10th centuries, were times of significant Viking expansion. Danish and Norwegian Vikings established colonies in Ireland, the Shetland and Orkney Islands, the Faroe Islands, Iceland and Greenland. In 911, a Danish Viking chieftain called Rollo won control of part of northern France now called Normandy (Land of the Northmen). In the east, Swedish Vikings set up trading centres in western Russia, eastern Belarus and eastern Ukraine, forging profitable trade routes between the Baltic and Black Seas. The local Slavs called them Rus and they gave their name to the first Russian state, which developed around the Viking stronghold of Novgorod in the 860s.

Viking assimilation

Between the 10th and 12th centuries, Norway, Denmark and Sweden developed into unified and stable states. During the same period, Scandinavian colonies in Europe gradually lost their Viking identity and converted to Christianity. By 1000, the Normans had adopted the language and culture of France, and Kievan Rus (a Viking colony centred on modern Kiev) had emerged as a Slavic Orthodox Christian state. A Danish-Norwegian force reconquered England in the early 11th century, and from 1016 to 1035 a Danish king – Cnut – ruled England, Norway and Denmark. Cnut's empire fell apart after his death and, following the Norman conquest

VIKING EXPLORATION

The Vikings were a great seafaring people and the best shipbuilders of their day. Their navigational skills, based on observations of the motion of the sun and stars, enabled them to determine the latitude in which they were sailing. As well as raiding and trading with the coastal settlements of Europe, the Vikings also embarked on long voyages of exploration, in order to discover and settle new territories. The Norwegian Vikings reached the Faroes in the early ninth century. They discovered Iceland, a further 1,600 km (1,000 miles) north-west, in the 860s; and in 982, the Viking Erik the Red discovered Greenland. Around the year 1000, on the coast of Newfoundland, Erik's son Leif Eriksson established the first European colony in North America, which the Vikings called Vinland.

Above *The ornately carved prow ornaments of Viking ships were removed at sea to avoid losing them, which might prove to be a bad omen*

of 1066, the Viking influence in England gradually dwindled. By the 12th century, Viking culture had virtually disappeared outside Scandinavia and Iceland.

Rise of the Holy Roman Empire

Just as the Viking onslaught reached its height, during the mid-ninth century, the Carolingian Empire was fracturing. Charlemagne was succeeded by his son Louis the Pious (reigned 814–840). After Louis died, a civil war between his sons over the division of the empire was only resolved by the Treaty of Verdun (843). The empire was divided into three parts, weakening royal authority and leaving no effective defence against the Vikings. Charles the Fat reunited the empire between 885 and 887, but he was deposed after failing to combat Viking raids, and in 889 the empire broke up into five kingdoms: West Francia (France), East Francia (Germany), Italy, Burgundy and Provence.

In the 10th century, East Francia emerged as the most powerful of these kingdoms, the leading defender of western Christendom and the core of a new Christian empire. In 936, Otto I (reigned

936–973) became king of East Francia. He defeated rivals to the throne, then turned his attention to the Magyars, a nomadic people from Russia who had settled in Pannonia (modern-day Hungary) and were launching raids against the European kingdoms. Otto routed the Magyars at the Battle of Lechfeld in 955, thereby securing his eastern border. In 961, after a ten-year campaign, he annexed most of northern and central Italy. In 962, the pope declared Otto emperor, an act that marked the foundation of the Holy Roman Empire (see pages 108–109).

TIMELINE	
793	*First Viking raid on Britain*
860s	*Swedish Vikings create first Russian state; Norwegian Vikings discover Iceland*
865	*Danish 'Great Army' lands in East Anglia*
870	*Vikings conquer most of England*
911	*Vikings win control of Normandy*
954	*Wessex regains England from the Vikings*
982	*Norwegian Vikings discover Greenland*
c. 1000	*Norwegian Vikings discover North America*
1016–1035	*Danish king Cnut rules England, Norway and Denmark.*

THE HOLY ROMAN EMPIRE

962–1806

The empire founded by Otto I in 962 (see page 107) covered modern-day Germany, Austria, Switzerland and northern Italy. In 1032, Burgundy in south-eastern France was added to its territories. By then it had become known as the Roman Empire – it acquired the 'Holy' prefix in 1254. Although the Holy Roman Empire was the dominant power in Europe for most of the Middle Ages, it was rarely a stable political entity, and its emperors faced serious challenges to their authority from German princes, the papacy and the northern Italian city-states.

Right *This woodcut from* Mediaeval and Modern History *by Philip Van Ness Myers (1905) shows a medieval king investing a bishop with the symbols of office*

By taking the title of emperor, Otto I had deliberately presented himself as the successor to Charlemagne, restorer of the Christian Roman empire in the west (see page 105). His son Otto II (reigned 973–983) even went so far as to style himself 'Emperor Augustus of the Romans'. Yet despite such evocative titles, the rulers of the Holy Roman Empire never exercised the grip on their territories enjoyed by Charlemagne or, indeed, the emperors of ancient Rome.

From the start, the empire suffered from a marked north-south divide. The north was the emperor's power base. Beyond the Alps, in northern Italy, he held less sway. However, his position was not always secure even in Germany, because of the tribal politics that continued to dominate the area. The emperor was elected by German princes from each of the main tribes: Franks, Saxons, Swabians, Bavarians and Lotharingians. Elections were not a straightforward process and the emergence of emperors owed much to personal influence, backroom deals and informal alliances. There was, consequently, plenty of scope for bitterness and resentment over the

election results, which sometimes led to civil war.

Investiture controversy

Periodically, emperors tried by diplomatic or military means to bolster their status in the southern part of their empire. The early emperors spent extended periods in the south and cultivated a strong relationship with the papacy in Rome. However, in 1075, that relationship broke down over the issue of investiture – the right to appoint people to senior positions in the Church.

The emperors had traditionally exercised this right and Emperor Henry IV (reigned 1056–1105) saw it as crucial: by appointing loyal church officials, the emperor could bring the lands of those officials within his control. The land would add to imperial tax revenues and also provide soldiers for wars. However, Pope Gregory VII (reigned 1073–1085) wished to claim the right of investiture for himself. He was trying to reform the Church and wished to appoint people who supported his reforms.

Henry IV, in a show of power, expelled the pope from office. In response, Gregory excommunicated him from the Church. Rivals of Henry among the German nobility used this as an excuse to rebel in support of the pope. The controversy severely weakened the position of the emperor, and by 1122 Henry's son Henry V (reigned 1106–1125) was forced to back down on the issue of investiture.

Decline

Emperor Frederick I Barbarossa (reigned 1152–1177) tried to increase his hold over the prosperous city-states of northern Italy, known as the Lombard League. He waged several campaigns against them, but was ultimately thwarted by their alliance with the papacy, together with outbreaks of disease within the imperial armies' ranks. Frederick Barbarossa's son Henry VI managed to conquer southern Italy and Sicily in 1194, but when Barbarossa's grandson Frederick II (reigned 1215–1250) once again tried to master Lombardy, he too was defeated by a coalition of the Lombard League and the pope. Frederick was deposed by the German princes shortly afterwards.

Thereafter, the Holy Roman Empire fell into decline. From 1254 to 1273, no individual prince was powerful enough to take control, and the imperial throne remained empty. Finally, Rudolf I of the House of Habsburg became emperor. However, he was forced to renounce any

GOLDEN BULL

In the late 13th century, the process of electing the emperor was formalized when the German princes formed a college of electors. Then, in 1356, Emperor Charles IV (reigned 1346–1378) issued a proclamation called the Golden Bull, which named seven permanent electors: the archbishops of Mainz, Trier and Cologne; the Count Palatine of the Rhine; the duke of Saxony; the margrave of Brandenburg; and the king of Bohemia. The Bull enshrined the rights of the seven never to have their lands divided. It therefore strengthened the constitution of the empire, ending controversies over the succession, and played an important role in the development of independent states within Germany.

further claim to rule in Italy, while in Germany he was no more than chief of a coalition of prominent princes. By the 15th century, with the rise of France and England, the empire was no longer the leading power in Europe. By the 16th century, the emperor had become little more than a figurehead. The empire itself finally came to an end in 1806.

Above *A woodcut from* The Swabian Chronicle, *first printed in 1486*

TIMELINE	
962	*Otto I founds the Holy Roman Empire*
1032	*The empire acquires Burgundy*
1075–1122	*The Holy Roman Empire fights with the pope over the issue of investiture*
1194	*Emperor Henry VI conquers southern Italy and Sicily*
1254–1273	*The emperor's throne is vacant*
1356	*The empire's constitution is strengthened by the proclamation of the Golden Bull.*

CHRISTENDOM

500–1300

During the Middle Ages, Christianity spread outwards from the lands of the former Roman Empire to encompass all of Europe and part of Russia. These Christian lands collectively became known as Christendom. The notion of Christendom reminded medieval Christians that they were subjects both of their king and of the Church – an institution that came to wield not only religious authority, but also considerable political power.

Above *St Peter's Basilica in Rome stands on the site of a basilica built by the Emperor Constantine*

In the fourth century, there were five major centres of the Christian Church, known as Great Sees, at Rome, Constantinople, Alexandria, Antioch and Jerusalem. Each had their own patriarch. The patriarchs of Rome, known as popes, as heirs of St Peter, claimed but failed to establish primacy over the others. In the seventh century, the cities of Alexandria, Antioch and Jerusalem fell to Arab Muslims, leaving Rome and Constantinople alone.

East and West

By this time, deep differences had developed between the two patriarchates, stemming from the division of the Roman Empire between east and west in 395. Consequently, the eastern Church, centred on Constantinople, and the western Church, centred on Rome, evolved separately and soon acquired their own characteristics. The eastern Church practised Orthodox Christianity and used Greek as its official language. The western Church practised Roman Catholicism and its language was Latin. Both Churches claimed primacy over the other. They also competed for converts. Catholic missionaries won Hungary and Poland to their Church, while Orthodox missionaries converted Serbia, Bulgaria and Russia.

Animosity between the Churches came to a head in 1054 when the pope excommunicated the patriarch for refusing to submit to his authority, and the patriarch, in turn, excommunicated the pope. This led to a permanent breach between east and west. The rift widened in 1204 when Catholic crusaders sacked Constantinople. For 50 years, Rome controlled the Orthodox Church. Constantinople never recovered and, in 1453, the city fell to Muslim Turks.

Christian expansion

Roman Catholic missionaries brought Christianity to England in the sixth and

TIMELINE	
927–941	*Monastery founded at Cluny*
988	*Russians are converted to Christianity*
1054	*Permanent split between eastern and western Churches*
1098	*Reformist Cistercian order is founded*
1204	*Catholic crusaders sack Constantinople, the centre of Orthodox Christianity*
1209–1229	*Albigensian Crusade.*

MONASTICISM

Since the fourth century, many medieval Christians had chosen to withdraw from the world and live in remote communities in order to devote themselves to God. A formal basis for monastic life was defined by certain leaders, such as the influential St Basil (*c.* 329–379) in the Orthodox Church, and St Benedict of Nursia (*c.* 480–c. 547) in the western Church. By the 11th century, monasteries like Cluny in Burgundy had become rich, worldly institutions far removed from their original ideals of a simple, isolated existence. This sparked calls for monastic reform. The Cistercian order, founded in 1098, marked a return to the austere rules of St Benedict, characterized by manual work, prayer and study.

seventh centuries, and to the Netherlands in the eighth, while Orthodox missionaries won over Kiev and much of Russia in the 10th century. Between the 11th and 14th centuries, Christian influence spread across Europe. More forceful means were used by Carolingian rulers to convert the Germanic tribes during the eighth and ninth centuries.

As well as winning converts, the Church was equally energetic in attacking heresy within Christian lands. The central doctrines of Christianity were set out in the Nicene Creed in 325. Those who followed different practices were branded heretics and ruthlessly persecuted. One heretical sect, the Cathars, were the victims of a campaign launched by the pope called the Albigensian Crusade (1209–1229), in which some 200,000 were killed.

Power, corruption and reform

As Christianity expanded, the Church acquired great wealth. Thousands of churches, including grand cathedrals, were constructed throughout Europe. By the ninth century, moral standards in the western Church had declined. The papacy itself was corrupt. A movement arose in the 10th century, centred on monasteries such as Gorze in Germany and Cluny in Burgundy, demanding Church reform.

The reformist pope Gregory VII (reigned 1073–1085) forbade marriage of the clergy, and the sale of church offices; and he banned lay people from investing bishops.

Gregory also claimed papal primacy in secular affairs, and over the next 200 years the papacy steadily grew in political stature, often challenging the authority of monarchs and leading to frequent clashes. Papal power reached its peak under Innocent III (1198–1216), whose personal charisma and status made him the dominant political figure of his age. At the same time, the Church came to control many aspects of ordinary people's lives. Its clergy presided over rites of passage; they ran hospitals, schools and universities and blessed troops before battle. The Church authorized military campaigns such as the Crusades (see pages 126–127), and was the ultimate authority on all matters of learning. It also encouraged people to make pilgrimages.

Above *Medieval manuscripts were largely produced in monasteries, sometimes highly illustrated for those who could not read*

Below *A 19th-century engraving of the Battle of Jaffa (1192) during the Third Crusade*

FEUDAL EUROPE

1000–1300

Feudalism was a political and social system that operated in western Europe during the Middle Ages. It governed the relationships between the aristocratic classes of medieval society, from the king to the lesser nobles. During the period before powerful nation states, feudalism fulfilled society's basic need for justice and security. At its core was the oath of fealty (loyalty), made between a lord and his vassal (servant). Thus the king would swear an oath of fealty with his barons, and the barons would swear a similar oath with nobles of lower rank.

PEASANTS AND SERFS

A separate system known as manorialism governed the relationship between the lord of the manor and his peasants. Manors were large estates owned by a lord and farmed by his peasant tenants; they included land for the lord's use and plots held by the tenants. The lord offered the peasants justice and protection from external enemies. In return, the peasants farmed both the lord's land and the plots he allocated to them. They paid the lord rent and taxes in the form of goods, services or money. Many of the peasants were serfs, meaning they were part of the lord's property, and would remain on the land even if a new lord acquired it.

Right *Illustration for the month of June in the* Breviarium Grimani, *an early 16th-century Flemish breviary*

Under the terms of the oath, a vassal promised to serve his lord in exchange for a fief. The form that service took depended on the vassal's status but might include providing soldiers for war; offering oneself as a soldier; providing manual labour for the lord's estate; or helping to pay ransom money if the lord was captured. The fief might take the form of land, money or employment. The oath of fealty was a lifelong bond that only ended when either the lord or vassal died. Because it was sworn between individuals, each vassal owed allegiance to his lord rather than to his country. This led to a decline in royal power under the feudal system and a corresponding increase in that of the nobles and barons.

Rise of feudalism

Feudalism grew out of the traditions of the Germanic tribes that dominated Europe in the early Middle Ages. The chieftain and the warriors of these tribes pledged loyalty to each other. The warriors fought for their chieftain and in return he rewarded them with estates and treasure. The oath of fealty developed further under Charlemagne and his successors in the ninth century. Under this system, land granted in the form of a fief remained the property of the lord: only the rights of use were passed on. The fiefs comprised the land, the buildings on it and the serfs who inhabited it; the vassal could receive what the land and peasants produced, including food and taxes. As the Franks expanded into parts of Italy, Germany and Spain, the feudal system took root in those areas, too. It extended to

England following the Norman Conquest of 1066, and from there it spread to Scotland and Ireland. Feudalism also occurred to a lesser extent in Scandinavia and eastern Europe.

Knights and chivalry

Feudalism emphasized the virtues of loyalty and service to a leader, and from this the idea of knighthood arose. The bands of mounted warriors that roamed the countryside during the early Middle Ages began to develop a new code of military behaviour. Instead of attacking and pillaging at random, they put their fighting skills at the service of their lord, who would then reward them with land. To be a knight meant embodying not only the military virtues of physical strength and courage, but also Christian virtues of humility and piety. By the 12th century, the idea of chivalry – a code that governed a knight's behaviour – had emerged. According to this code, knights had to carry out brave deeds, protect women and behave honourably on the battlefield.

Decline of feudalism

During the 13th century, several developments led to the decline of feudalism. The fief, which had originally reverted to the lord on the death of a vassal, increasingly came to be seen as a hereditary entitlement, passed on from the vassal to his son. As such, the idea of a lord's ownership of the fief gradually fell away. At the same time, states grew more powerful and centralized. Monarchs could raise money to hire professional soldiers, and so were less dependent on their barons. Kings demanded that allegiance be sworn to the state rather than to individual lords. With the increasing use of professionals in warfare, knighthood also declined. It did not help that many knights were falling short of the chivalric ideal, accused of drunkenness, bad behaviour and making fortunes from the spoils of war.

Above The Knights of Christ, *a panel from the Ghent Altarpiece, completed by Jan van Eyck in 1432*

WAR AND PLAGUE IN MEDIEVAL EUROPE

1000–1400

Warfare was a frequent occurrence during the later Middle Ages. As in every other age, disputes over land ownership or control of natural resources frequently led to hostilities between rival rulers. For the first part of this period, the feudal system dominated, allowing armies to be recruited as part of the vassals' service to their lords. Warfare was limited by rules and codes of honour. This was the golden age of the knight. During the 14th century, armies became more professional; new weapons were developed and the nature of warfare began to change. However, the most seismic event of that century was not a war but an epidemic – the Black Death.

Above *The Black Death killed about a third of Europe's population in three years*

The High Middle Ages (1000–1300)

The key development of the so-called High Middle Ages was a rapid rise in the population of Europe, due to increased agricultural yields and greater peasant prosperity. This was partly a result of agricultural and technological advances (the three-field crop rotation system; the introduction of the wheeled plough; the use of wind and water power for milling grain and working pumps, bellows and sawmills)

and partly thanks to the Medieval Warm Period, an era of unusually warm weather, lasting from the 900s to the 1300s.

It was also a period during which Europe suffered few barbarian invasions, with the brief exception of the Mongol invasion of 1241–1242 (see page 138). By 1000, the Vikings had assimilated and the Magyars had formed the settled state of Hungary. The Normans colonized southern Italy from 1017 and conquered England in 1066. Also in the 11th century, German princes expanded eastward beyond the Elbe River and European Crusaders founded Christian colonies in the Middle East. Christian Spaniards began the process of the *Reconquista*, regaining Spain from the Moors (completed in 1492).

The battles of this period were dominated by knights on horseback, supported by footsoldiers, who included archers and some crossbowmen. The footsoldiers either went ahead of the knights with the archers, to initiate the action, or formed a screen to protect the knights. The knights then charged, with lances lowered, in large, tightly packed groups that were almost impossible to stop. However, once opposing warriors were fighting one-on-one, their concern was to capture rather than kill their enemy, since a prisoner could be exchanged for ransom. This conduct became part of the chivalric code of warfare.

The Age of Crisis (1300–1400)

The 14th century was a period of calamity and upheaval in Europe. Growth and prosperity came to a halt and famines and plagues reduced the population by around

TIMELINE	
1017	*Normans colonize southern Italy*
1066	*Normans conquer England*
1241–1242	*Mongols invade Hungary*
1337–1453	*The Hundred Years' War*
1348–1351	*The Black Death sweeps through Europe*
1378	*Great Schism of the Roman Catholic Church*
1388	*Switzerland wins independence from Habsburg control*
1492	*Spanish complete the Reconquista of Spain from the Moors.*

half. The Church suffered a crisis when the papacy fell under the control of the French monarchy in 1303 and was moved to Avignon. A disputed papal election led to the Great Schism of 1378, when rival popes sat at Rome and Avignon. Such internal conflicts hurt the Church's prestige and influence.

The 14th century was also a time of almost continuous warfare. The Hundred Years' War (1337–1453) between England and France began with French attempts to recover English lands in France. The English scored victories at Crécy (1346) and Poitiers (1356), winning Aquitaine and Gascony. The French fought back, however, and by the century's end, the English held less land than they had in 1337. Within the Holy Roman Empire, German dynasties – the Wittelsbachs, Habsburgs and Luxembourgs – fought each other for primacy and control of imperial elections. In 1388, after nearly a century of rebellion, the Swiss won their independence from the Habsburgs. And in the later 14th century, Ottoman Turks overran most of the Balkans.

Styles of warfare changed during the century. Soldiers were recruited by agreed contracts, which created more professional armies. English armies fought increasingly on foot, with large groups of longbowmen, producing victories against French cavalry at Crécy and Agincourt (1415). Crécy was also one of the first European battles where cannons were used.

Above A depiction of the English victory over the French at the Battle of Agincourt (1415)

THE BLACK DEATH

The deadly epidemic known as the Black Death, which devastated Europe in 1348–51, was bubonic plague, transmitted to humans by the bites of fleas borne through European towns and cities by hordes of black rats. The plague originated in Central Asia in the mid-14th century. It spread along the overland and seafaring trade routes, reaching western Asia, North Africa and southern Europe by 1347. The first European outbreak occurred in Messina, Sicily. By 1348, the plague had spread to Italy, Spain, France and southern England. The impact was catastrophic. In the worst-affected areas, such as central Italy, eastern England and Norway, mortality rates reached 50 per cent or more. Overall, around a third of Europe's population perished. Outbreaks of the disease recurred every five to twelve years for the next 350 years and many cities did not regain their pre-plague populations until the 16th century. Depopulation caused severe labour shortages. Rents and prices fell and wages rose, weakening the traditional bonds of manorialism. The aristocracy tried to shore up their losses by raising taxes, but this provoked peasant uprisings such as the Jacquerie in France (1358) and the English Peasants' Revolt (1381).

Above Monks disfigured by the Black Death being blessed by a priest, from Omne Bonum, a 14th-century encyclopedia compiled by James le Palmer

THE RISE OF EUROPE'S TOWNS AND CITIES

1000–1500

Following the collapse of the Roman Empire, urban life declined dramatically throughout Europe and only began to recover in the 10th century. Local communities sought protection in times of warfare within castle walls. As the communities grew, urban centres developed near the castles and the castles themselves became incorporated within larger walled towns.

Right *The Guildhall of Corpus Christi in Lavenham, Suffolk, now belongs to the townspeople and houses a museum*

A town submitted to the authority of the local lord in return for his protection. Town-dwellers gradually developed the idea of citizenship, conferring on themselves special rights and privileges, from which outsiders were excluded, such as the right to own property or moor one's boat in the harbour. In actual fact, medieval towns relied on a certain level of inward immigration. They were such unhygienic places and mortality rates were so high that towns depended on newcomers in order to maintain their population levels.

Markets and fairs

Towns were important centres of commercial activity. Most trade took place at markets and fairs. Markets were held once or twice a week in the town square or in a covered market hall. Here local farmers and craftspeople sold their produce. Fairs were held on holy days at fair-grounds on the outskirts of towns. These attracted merchants from much further afield. Some, such as the Champagne fairs, became major centres of international trade.

Guilds

During the economic prosperity of the 11th and 12th centuries, towns grew steadily, attracting increasing numbers of merchants, skilled workers and professionals. These groups formed trade associations called 'guilds' in order to protect and advance their interests. Guilds laid down standards of quality and training and provided members with welfare benefits, but their most important function was to protect their members from external competition. The guilds became powerful in their own right and challenged the traditional authority of the local lord.

Communes

During the 12th century, the most powerful towns and cities sought to become independent from aristocratic control, forming self-governing, self-protecting communities called communes. Some negotiated deals with the local lord, by which he could share in the profits of the commune's commercial activities. In other cases, disagreement with the local nobility led to conflict. The first communes were in northern Italy, the most urbanized area in medieval western Europe. The most successful was Venice, which controlled the Adriatic Sea and grew wealthy from its trade with the east.

Other communes were established in Italian cities such as Genoa, Milan and Florence. Their prosperity provoked the rulers of the Holy Roman Empire into frequent attempts to take them over. Although the communes successfully thwarted these attacks, the social disruption of war led to a large-scale inward migration of refugees from the surrounding countryside. This in turn caused factional conflicts within the communes. The idea of communes spread to other parts of Europe. Communes were set up, for example, in the towns of Ghent, Bruges and Ypres in Flanders, where there was a flourishing woollen textile industry.

Banking and credit

As towns and cities grew more prosperous, ever larger sums of money had to be physically passed between buyers and sellers. The danger and inconvenience of this exchange instigated the first systems of credit (money promised but not presented). The use of credit required a better system of record keeping, and

Above Walled hill-top towns provided the communes with security against incursions by unwanted outsiders

Italian mathematician Luca Pacioli (*c.* 1445–*c.* 1514) devised the principles of book-keeping, giving rise to the accountancy profession.

By the end of the 12th century, banks began to appear in the northern Italian communes. Banks could store money safely, arrange loans or transfer funds between accounts over long distances, greatly facilitating commerce and trade. The leading bank of the medieval era belonged to the Medici in Florence (1391–1494). It handled the finances of the papacy and several of Europe's royal families, helping to fund military campaigns and collect taxes on behalf of its royal customers.

Above Medieval banking entailed hand-to-hand transfer until the use of credit was developed

THE HANSEATIC LEAGUE

In the late 12th century, the towns and cities of north Germany and the Baltic decided to join together for the common protection of their interests. They formed a powerful trade association known as the Hanseatic League. At its peak in the mid-14th century, the league included 37 of the largest towns and cities of the region and it had offices called *kontors* in the major cities of England, Flanders, Norway and Russia. The league gained control of the Russian fur trade; the fish trade with Norway and Sweden; and the wool trade with Flanders. It negotiated trading privileges for its members, prepared navigational charts, suppressed piracy and even waged war. When the Danish king seized the Hansa-dominated island of Gotland in 1361, a Hanseatic fleet blockaded Copenhagen, forcing Denmark to accept severe peace terms. The league's power declined in the 15th century, due to strong competition from England and the Netherlands.

THE BIRTH AND SPREAD OF ISLAM

622–750

Islam was founded by Muhammad (c. 570–632), a member of the Quraysh tribe of the city of Mecca in Arabia. From around 610, Muhammad received the divine revelations that would form the basis of the Koran, the holy book of Islam. Two years later he began to preach the message of Allah (God) and to attract followers; people called him the Prophet. At this time, most Arabs, including the Quraysh, believed in numerous deities. Muhammad's monotheistic message incurred the anger of the Quraysh.

Above *The name 'Muhammad' written in traditional Thuluth calligraphy*

Above *A 19th-century depiction of the first four caliphs of the Ummah*

To escape persecution, Muhammad and his followers fled in 622 from Mecca to Yathrib (later renamed Medina). This event, known as the *Hijrah* (flight), marks the beginning of the Muslim era and the first year in the Islamic calendar. Muhammad's message proved powerful enough to unite the Arab peoples and during the course of the next century, under the banner of their new faith, the Arabs would go on to conquer a vast empire, covering the Middle East, parts of western and Central Asia, North Africa and Spain.

In Medina, Muhammad created a new kind of community, called the Ummah. Unlike traditional tribes, into which one had to be born, to join the Ummah one only had to declare one's belief in Allah. Muhammad established the principles of Islam. For example, he declared that all lives were equal, he outlawed usury (charging interest on loans) and gave rights to women. In 630, Muhammad's forces conquered Mecca and its people accepted Islam. Two years later, the Prophet died.

First caliphs

Over the next 30 years, the Ummah was ruled in turn by four caliphs (successors) – Abu Bakr, Umar, Uthman and Ali – each chosen by the Muslim community. Abu Bakr (632–634) completed the unification of the Arabs under Islam. Umar (634–644) and Uthman (644–656) then led the Arabs on a period of rapid conquest to create an Islamic Empire. The Arabs destroyed the Persian Sasanian Empire and seized Syria, Palestine, Egypt and Libya from the Byzantine Empire.

While Uthman was caliph, he attracted criticism for appointing members of his own clan, known as the Umayyads, to senior positions. Some Muslims wished to replace Uthman with Ali, Muhammad's son-in-law. Supporters of Ali assassinated Uthman, and Ali became caliph. The new Umayyad leader Muawiyah opposed Ali, but the caliph refused to fight him. Ali's stance angered a group of rebels, the Kharijites, and they murdered him in 661.

Umayyads

Muawiyah became caliph (661–680) and founded the Umayyad dynasty – by claiming a divine right to rule. The Umayyads turned the caliph into a hereditary position and Muawiyah was succeeded by his son Yazid. But supporters of Ali believed Ali's son Hussain should be the next caliph instead. In 681, Yazid's vast army met Hussain's small force at Karbala and killed virtually all of them.

Between 683 and 685, the Umayyads faced further rebellions by Shia (see panel) and Kharijites, but Abd al-Malik (reigned 685–705) reasserted control. Under his son al-Walid I (reigned 705–715) the Umayyad Empire reached its greatest extent, securing conquests in Central Asia, North Africa and Spain. However, Umayyad attempts to extend their empire further into the Christian west failed with their unsuccessful sieges of Constantinople in 677 and 717, and their defeat by the Franks at Poitiers in 732.

Running the empire

The Arabs were influenced by the various civilizations they encountered; they absorbed Persian literary styles, Greek art, and the science of the Byzantines into their own evolving Islamic traditions. They adapted the Byzantine model of bureaucracy to create an administrative system capable of running a large empire. Medina, while remaining a holy city, became impractical as the hub of the empire, and so the Umayyads moved their capital to Damascus, in Syria.

The caliphs were both religious and political leaders, and they were determined to impose their faith on conquered peoples. At first, non-Arab converts to Islam were treated as inferiors but in due course, the strict rules that separated Arabs from the empire's subject peoples were relaxed and intermarriage was allowed. Under Abd al-Malik, Arabic became the official language of the empire and Islamic coinage was introduced. The first major Islamic monument, the Dome of the Rock mosque in Jerusalem, was completed in 691.

THE SUNNI-SHIA SPLIT

After the Battle of Karbala in 681, Islam split in two. Those who believed the leaders of Islam should be descendants of Muhammad became known as the Shiat Ali – the Party of Ali – or the Shia. Two of Ali's grandsons survived the massacre at Karbala and the Shia imamate (spiritual leadership) passed down through them. However, the majority of Muslims believed their leader should be chosen by the Ummah. They became known as Sunnis, derived from the Sunnah, meaning 'customs of the Prophet Muhammad'.

Below The Dome of the Rock, an Islamic shrine built between 685 and 691 on the Temple Mount in Jerusalem

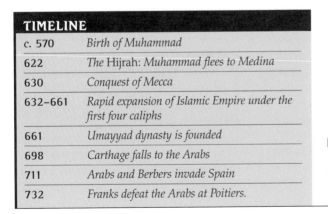

TIMELINE

c. 570	*Birth of Muhammad*
622	*The* Hijrah: *Muhammad flees to Medina*
630	*Conquest of Mecca*
632–661	*Rapid expansion of Islamic Empire under the first four caliphs*
661	*Umayyad dynasty is founded*
698	*Carthage falls to the Arabs*
711	*Arabs and Berbers invade Spain*
732	*Franks defeat the Arabs at Poitiers.*

THE ABBASID EMPIRE

750–1037

During the eighth century, the Umayyad caliphate was weakened by the contined hostility of the Shias and Kharijites, feuding between Arab tribes and the resentment of conquered peoples at the tax privileges enjoyed by the Arabs. The crisis came to a head in 747 when Abu Muslim of the Abbasid clan led a religious and political rebellion at Khorasan. This culminated in the defeat of the Umayyad caliph Marwan II at the Battle of Zab in 750 and the proclamation of the first Abbasid caliph, Abu al-Abbas (reigned 750–754).

The founder of the Abbasid clan, Abbas (566–c. 653) had been Muhammad's uncle, and when the Abbasids took power, they emphasized this family connection to the Prophet to give themselves legitimacy. As a further precaution, they ordered the massacre of the Umayyad family. One of the few Umayyads to survive was Abd al-Rahman. He fled to Spain and established an independent Umayyad emirate centred on Córdoba. The Abbasids also suffered territorial losses in North Africa. In 789, an independent Shia caliphate was founded in the Maghrib, and in 800 the Aghlabid emirs of Ifriqiya (modern Tunisia) declared their independence.

Above *An illustration for a tale from* A Thousand and One Nights

Below *The Oghuz Turks conquered the Ghaznavid emirate in 1037*

Golden age

Despite their territorial losses, the Abbasid caliphs presided over a golden era of Islamic civilization. Art, music, literature and science all flourished. While European scholarship stagnated, Islamic scholars rediscovered and extended the knowledge of the ancient Greeks in the fields of astronomy, geography, medicine, mathematics and philosophy. Their writers assimilated ancient stories and traditions from India, Persia, Mesopotamia, Egypt and Arabia to create masterpieces such as *One Thousand and One Nights*. In 763, the Abbasids founded a new capital, Baghdad. Within 40 years it had become the world's largest city and an important cultural and commercial centre.

The early Abbasid rulers paid strict observance to the religious aspects of the role of caliph. They gave support to Sunni Muslim scholars, who developed a sophisticated body of Islamic law and theology. Yet the Abbasids were also tolerant of the many different ethnic and religious groups living within their empire. Arabs were no longer accorded privileged status and Muslims of any ethnic background could work in administrative positions.

Fragmentation

The Abbasids reached their zenith under the fifth caliph, Harun al-Rashid (786–809). After he died, civil war broke out between his sons, and the caliph's authority began to decline. As a result, the provincial emirs became more powerful and the empire began to fragment. In 861,

EMIRATE OF CÓRDOBA

The establishment of an independent Umayyad emirate in Spain, with its capital at Córdoba, marked the beginning of the Islamic empire's fragmentation. While Abd al-Rahman (reigned 756–788) was busy consolidating his hold on power, the Christian kingdom of Asturias in the north-west managed to recapture Galicia, and the Franks succeeded in retaking Narbonne. Gradually, the Emirate of Córdoba asserted control over most of Spain, which they called al-Andalus, and by 929 Abd al-Rahman III (reigned 912–961) was confident enough to declare himself caliph. The emirate reached the peak of its power in the late 10th century, with its conquest of the Maghrib (973) and a string of victories against the Christian states in the north, won by the great general Al-Mansur. However, civil war broke out in 1008 and the emirate broke into rival principalities called *taifa*. This proved disastrous for Muslim Iberia as, throughout the next four centuries, the Christian states were able to conquer the *taifa* one by one, with Granada overthrown last of all in 1492.

Above *The interior of the La Mezquita, in Córdoba – one of the best surviving examples of Moorish architecture in Spain*

the Saffarids formed an independent emirate in Persia and Afghanistan. This was followed, in 868, by the founding of a breakaway Tulunid emirate in Egypt and Palestine. The Christians of Armenia regained their independence in 886 and, in 899, the Abbasids lost the Islamic heartland of Arabia following a rebellion by the Shia Qarmatian sect.

In 905, the Abbasids managed to recover Egypt, but just nine years later the country was conquered by the Fatimids, a Shia dynasty ruling Ifriqiya. The Fatimids, claiming descent from Fatima, Muhammad's daughter, gradually extended their control over North Africa, Palestine, the Yemen and western Arabia. The Fatimid caliphate reached the height of its power in 1000, and was finally overthrown in 1171.

Buwayhids and Turks

In the 930s, a Shia dynasty called the Buwayhids, from Daylam in northern Persia, seized Persia from the Samanids (who had taken it from the Saffarids in 900).

In 945, they captured Baghdad and assumed effective control of what remained of the Abbasid Empire. The Abbasid rulers kept the title of caliph, and remained the spiritual leaders of the empire but in political terms they were mere figureheads. In the 990s, the Buwayhids found themselves challenged by Turkish forces under Mahmud of Ghazni. Mahmud established the Ghaznavid emirate, which flourished in Khorasan (north-eastern Persia), Afghanistan and northern India until 1037, when it was conquered by the Seljuks, a dynasty of Oghuz Turks from Central Asia.

TIMELINE

750	*Abbasids come to power*
756	*Establishment of independent emirate in Córdoba*
789	*Establishment of independent Shia caliphate in the Maghrib*
800	*Establishment of independent emirate in Ifriqiya*
861	*Establishment of indepdent emirate in Persia and Afghanistan*
868	*Establishment of independent emirate in Egypt and Palestine*
886	*Establishment of Christian kingdom in Armenia*
899	*Abbasids lose Arabia to the Qarmatians*
945	*Buwayhids capture Baghdad.*

THE BYZANTINE EMPIRE

629–1453

The administrative reforms carried out early in the reign of Heraclius (see page 81) strengthened the Byzantine Empire and effectively transformed it into a Hellenistic, Orthodox Christian state. His reform of the army and subsequent victory at the Battle of Nineveh in 627 saved the empire from conquest by the Sasanian Persians. Threats against the empire did not cease there, however, and it went on to suffer almost perpetual assault for the next 450 years.

Right *This map of the distribution of Turkic tribes appeared in the* Diwan ul-Lughat al-Turk, *a dictionary compiled by the Turkish linguist Mahmud al-Kashgari (1005–1102)*

Threats and invasions

In 634, still exhausted from their struggles with the Persians, the Byzantines were confronted with a new menace: Arabs, newly united under Islam, poured out of the southern desert and swiftly overran the empire's dominions. By 698, Syria, Palestine, Egypt and North Africa had fallen under Islamic domination. Constantinople itself was threatened, but withstood Arab sieges in 670–77 and again in 716–7. Over the following centuries, other powers took advantage of Byzantine weakness. The Lombards conquered Genoa in 640 and Ravenna in 751. The Bulgars, a Turkic people originally from Central Asia, gained control of much of the Balkans in 679; and the Arabs began the conquest of Sicily in 827.

Revival and decline

Under the Macedonian dynasty (867–1025), the Byzantines enjoyed a resurgence of power. Their armies recaptured many of their territories from the Arabs and the Bulgars, and restored their frontiers to the north and east. Benefiting both from the disunity of the Arab world and the decline of Bulgar power following Magyar and Rus attacks in the 10th century, the Byzantine revival reached its peak under Basil II (reigned 976–1025). However, the weak emperors that succeeded him neglected the *theme* system that lay at the heart of the empire's strength (see panel) and, once again, the Byzantines became victims of foreign incursion. The Pechenegs, a Turkic people from the Central Asian steppe, repeatedly invaded Thrace in the 11th century; the Normans completed their conquest of Italy by 1071; and in the same year, the Seljuk Turks defeated the Byzantines at the Battle of Manzikert and took control of Anatolia.

The loss of the rich territory of Anatolia dealt a death blow to the Byzantine *theme*

TIMELINE

634–698	*Muslim Arabs attack the Byzantine Empire, taking over Syria, Palestine, Egypt and North Africa*
827–963	*Arabs conquer Sicily*
1018	*Basil II conquers Bulgaria*
1071	*Normans complete conquest of Italy; Seljuk Turks occupy Anatolia*
1097	*Byzantines recover western Anatolia*
1204	*Fourth Crusade captures Constantinople.*

system and severely undermined the empire's ability to defend itself. It became dependent on expensive mercenaries just when its tax revenues were diminishing. Alexius I Comnenus (reigned 1081–1118) managed at least to recover the western districts of Anatolia, helped by the western European armies of the First Crusade (1096–1099), which restored some prestige to his empire. However, the Byzantine economy suffered a further blow in the 12th century with the loss of its trading privileges to Venice and Genoa.

Loss of Constantinople

The final collapse of Byzantine power was precipitated by the soldiers of the Fourth Crusade who, in 1204, sacked Constantinople and established a Latin empire in Constantinople. The Byzantines did manage to recapture their capital in 1261, but the restored empire was little more than a city-state surrounded by semi-independent provinces, constantly vulnerable to threats from both western Europe and the Turks.

Byzantine culture

Orthodox Christianity exerted a strong influence on Byzantine art, music and architecture. Byzantine writers produced scholarly works of history and fine poetry, including religious poems. Their artists painted images of Christ and the saints, known as icons, which stressed their sacred attributes. There was a long and heated debate about whether these could be used as aids to prayer. In 730, Emperor Leo III ordered all icons to be destroyed, and monks who revered them were persecuted. In 843, icons were once again allowed to be used for worship.

Despite the notable quality of Byzantine arts and culture, it exerted little influence on western Europe during the Middle

Ages, mainly because of the mutual animosity caused by its frequent religious schisms with the Roman Church. However, Byzantine culture strongly pervaded those regions that shared its Orthodox Christian faith; these included the Balkans, Georgia and, particularly, Russia.

Below *This plaque on a 12th-century French cross depicts the Sasanid King Khosrau II submitting to Heraclius*

THEME SYSTEM

The empire's survival between the seventh and 11th centuries, in the face of constant military threat, was due largely to the *theme* system introduced by Heraclius after the Persian war. Each *theme* (army unit) was settled in a particular region (also called a *theme*) under a governor (*strategos*) who acted as their military commander in wartime. The soldiers were given plots of land and so were able to work on their farms yet remained available to fight when required. In time, the soldiers could pass the plots onto their sons and thus perpetuate the system. It deteriorated in the 11th century, when soldiers were allowed to forgo military service by paying a tax, and civil administrators called praetors began to undermine the authority of the *strategoi*.

TURKISH EMPIRES

1037–1453

Between the 11th and 15th centuries, much of the Middle East and western Asia was dominated by various Turkish empires. The Seljuk Turks created a vast sultanate under their leader Toghril Beg, and when this broke up in the 12th century, different Turkish dynasties took control in the Levant. Turkish power in the region was temporarily broken in the 13th century by the arrival of the Mongols. But in the 14th century, the Ottoman Turks founded a powerful new empire in Anatolia and south-eastern Europe.

Above Mehmed II Enters Constantinople With His Army *by Jean-Joseph Benjamin-Constant (1845–1902)*

Rise of the Seljuk Sultanate

The Seljuks were a dynasty of Oghuz Turks from an area south-east of the Aral Sea. In the late 10th century, they converted to Sunni Islam and, in 1037, under Toghril Beg (reigned 1037–1063) they invaded the Ghaznavid emirate in Khorasan and occupied its western provinces. At this time, the Abbasid Empire was under the control of the Shia Buwayhids, while the Shia Fatimids governed North Africa and much of the Middle East. Toghril Beg wished to restore Sunni supremacy in the Islamic world. In 1055, his forces captured Baghdad and overthrew the Buwayhids. The Abbasid caliph rewarded him with the title of sultan, which would be used by all future Turkish emperors. Under Toghril's successor, Alp Arslan (reigned 1063–1072), the Seljuks conquered Syria and Armenia and destroyed the Byzantine army at Manzikert. Anatolia, now undefended, was swiftly occupied by the Turks.

Fall of the Seljuks

Arp Arslan's son and successor Malik Shah (reigned 1072–1092) completed the conquest of Anatolia, which the Turks called Rum, and overthrew the Fatimids in Palestine. In the last years of Malik Shah's reign, civil war broke out in Rum as rival Turkish warlords fought one another for territory. On the sultan's death, the civil war spread throughout the empire. The Seljuks of Rum formed an independent sultanate in 1095 and by 1100 the empire had splintered into a multitude of separate states. The Seljuks were consequently unprepared for an attack from the Byzantines and Fatimids. With help from the armies of the First Crusade, the Byzantines recovered western Anatolia in 1095; and the Fatimids reconquered Palestine in 1098. However, the Byzantine's grip on western Anatolia was greatly weakened by their fall to the Seljuks of Rum at Myriocephalum, in 1176.

Zangids, Ayyubids and Mamlukes

The Seljuk sultanate continued to decline through the 12th century, as provincial rulers rebelled against central government. The final Seljuk sultan, Togril Beg III was killed in battle in 1194. In the west, an independent emirate was founded by Zangi, the *atabeg* (governor) of the Seljuk province of Mosul (reigned 1127–1146). He united Mesopotamia and northern Syria under his rule and captured the County of Edessa, a Crusader state east of the Euphrates. In 1144, Zangi's son, Nur al-Din (reigned 1146–1174), completed the conquest of Syria and overthrew the Fatimids in Egypt, Yemen and the Hejaz (western Arabia). After the death of Nur al-Din, the governor of Egypt Salah al-Din (also known as Saladin) vanquished the Zangids and founded his own dynasty, the Ayyubids, who commanded the territory for the next 75 years. In 1250, the Ayyubids were overthrown by the Mamlukes, a class of Turkish warrior-slaves, who proclaimed their own sultan and continued to rule Egypt and Syria until 1517.

Mongols

In the early 13th century, a new Turkish empire, known as the Shahdom of Khwarizm, took control of Persia. However, it had barely settled in the region when it was invaded by a mighty army from the Central Asian steppe. The Mongols, under Genghis Khan, destroyed the Shahdom of Khwarizm in 1219. Over the next few decades, Mongol power transformed the politics of the region. By 1243, the Seljuk Sultanate of Rum had been reduced to vassal status and it broke up shortly afterwards. In 1258, the Mongols destroyed the Abbasid caliphate; and in 1260, they overthrew the Mamlukes in Syria. The Mamlukes managed to recover much of this territory in a subsequent victory over the Mongols, but the Mongols remained the dominant force in the region until 1405.

The Ottomans

The disintegration of the Sultanate of Rum and the continued weakness of the Byzantine Empire caused a power vacuum in Anatolia. This was exploited by the chief of a small Anatolian state called Osman I (reigned 1299–1326), the founder of the

TIMELINE	
1037	*Seljuks invade Ghaznavid emirate*
1055	*Seljuks conquer Baghdad and overthrow Buwayhids*
1092	*Civil war spreads through sultanate*
1144–1174	*Zangid dynasty flourishes*
1174–1250	*Ayyubid dynasty flourishes*
1194	*End of Seljuk Sultanate*
1219	*Mongols conquer Shahdom of Khwarizm*
1243	*Mongols reduce Sultanate of Rum to vassal status*
1250–1517	*Mamlukes flourish in Middle East*
1258	*Mongols destroy Abbasid caliphate*
1299	*Osman I founds Ottoman dynasty*
1361	*Ottomans conquer Adrianople*
1402	*Timur the Lame defeats Ottomans at Ankara*
1453	*Ottomans capture Constantinople.*

Ottoman Empire. Osman and his son Orhan (reigned 1326–1360) conquered large areas of Byzantine territory. By 1360 the Ottomans controlled most of north-west Anatolia and had begun to expand the conquest of Greece and the Balkans. In 1361, Murad I (reigned 1360–1389) captured Adrianople, the second city of the Byzantine Empire. The Ottomans made it their capital, renaming it Edirne. By 1400, the Ottomans had conquered Serbia, Bulgaria and most of the territory of the Byzantine Empire. The Ottomans suffered a major reverse in 1402 when their army was crushed by Mongol forces led by Timur in Anatolia, and their sultan was killed. They soon regrouped, however, and by the 1420s they had consolidated their grip on the Balkans and were challenging Venice over control of the eastern Mediterranean trade routes. In 1453, the Ottomans captured Constantinople and thus ended the Byzantine Empire.

Below Osman I, founder of the Ottoman Empire, leading his troops into battle

THE CRUSADES

1095–1291

The Crusades were a series of military expeditions made between the 11th and 13th centuries by western European Christian armies, against those they regarded as enemies of Christendom. The main goal of the Crusades was to recapture the 'Holy Land' (the lands sacred to Judaism, Christianity and Islam in Palestine) from Muslim control. Eight major campaigns were launched to achieve this aim. However, during this period there were also dozens of minor Crusades directed against Muslim Spain; the Ottoman Turks in the Balkans; the pagan Slavs of the Baltic; and heretics within western Europe, such as the Cathars.

Above *Richard I landing at Sandwich in Kent on 14 March 1194 on his return from captivity in Germany after the Third Crusade*

Background

Christian pilgrims had been visiting the Holy Land since the fifth century. This practice continued even after it fell under Arab Muslim control in the seventh century. In the 11th century, the Holy Land was conquered by the Seljuk Turks, militant Muslims who began to attack visiting pilgrims. The Seljuks also overran Anatolia and were threatening the European territories of the Byzantine Empire. In 1095, Emperor Alexius I Comnenus (reigned 1081–1118) called on western Christendom for military assistance. Following this, Pope Urban II (reigned 1088–1099) gave a powerful sermon, calling upon the armies of western Europe to put aside their differences and take up arms against the Muslims. This appealed both to the religious piety and adventurous spirit of feudal knights, who responded enthusiastically. Many were genuinely fired by the idea of defending Christendom, while others saw the expedition as an opportunity to win fame and fortune.

First Crusade

The first army to set out was an untrained and poorly armed band of peasants, including women and children. This self-proclaimed 'People's Crusade' was wiped out by the Seljuks when it reached Anatolia in 1096. A much bigger, better-organized force of mainly French and Norman knights followed. Taking advantage of Muslim disunity, the Crusaders won a major victory at Nicaea in 1097 and went on to capture the cities of Edessa and Antioch before heading south to Palestine. In 1099, they conquered Jerusalem. Four Crusader states were founded: the Kingdom of Jerusalem, the County of Edessa, the Principality of Antioch and the County of Tripoli.

Second and Third Crusades

In 1144, Zangi, founder of a powerful emirate in Mesopotamia and northern Syria (see page 124), recaptured Edessa, provoking the Second Crusade (1147–1149). This poorly organized force besieged Damascus and Jerusalem, but ultimately achieved nothing. In the 1170s, Saladin, the sultan of Egypt and Syria, emerged as a powerful new Muslim leader. In 1187, he recaptured Jerusalem, prompting the Third Crusade (1189–1192), headed by three of Europe's foremost rulers. The Holy Roman Emperor, Frederick I Barbarossa, drowned en route, but Richard I (Lion-Heart) of England and Philip II Augustus of France managed to capture the ports of Jaffa and Acre and strengthen the Crusader states. However, Richard's attempt to retake Jerusalem was unsuccessful.

Later Crusades

The Fourth Crusade (1202–1204) was launched with the intention of attacking Egypt, recognized as the centre of Muslim power in the region and the main threat to the survival of the Crusader states. However, the Crusaders were unable to pay for their crossing from Venice to Egypt, so they agreed instead to attack Venice's enemy, the Hungarian port of Zara. They were then sidetracked into supporting a claimant for the Byzantine throne who had promised to provide funds for their expedition to Egypt. When the funds failed to materialize, the Crusaders sacked Constantinople and established a Crusader state there, which lasted until 1261.

Egypt was once again the declared target during the Fifth Crusade (1217–1221), which captured Damietta, but failed to advance further due to the flooding of the Nile. Jerusalem was briefly regained through diplomacy during the Sixth

Crusade (1228–29), but was lost again in 1244. The Seventh and Eighth Crusades (1248–1254 and 1270), both also directed against Egypt, were costly failures. The survival of the Crusader states during the 13th century had less to do with the Crusades than the Mongols, who offered a far more potent threat to the Muslim world. When the Mamlukes decisively defeated the Mongols at Ain Jalut in 1260, they were able to turn their full might on the Christian strongholds. The last Crusader state fell in 1291.

Above A woodcut *from* Grand voyage de Hierusalem *(1522), showing Louis IX of France disembarking at Damietta in 1249*

TIMELINE

1095	*Pope Urban II launches the Crusades*
1096–1099	*First Crusade establishes the four Crusader states*
1147–1149	*Second Crusade ends in failure*
1189–1192	*Third Crusade strengthens the Crusader states*
1202–1204	*Fourth Crusade leads to sacking of Constantinople*
1217–1222	*Fifth Crusade captures Damietta*
1228–1229	*Sixth Crusade temporarily recaptures Jerusalem*
1248–1254	*Seventh Crusade recaptures Damietta*
1270	*Eighth Crusade, directed against Tunis as a base to attack Egypt, ends in failure.*

CRUSADER STATES

The four Christian states in the Holy Land were together known as Outremer (French for 'overseas'). They established a feudal system of government, similar to that of their homelands. They built large, well-defended castles, often garrisoned by orders such as the Knights Templar and Knights Hospitallers. The Christian settlers gradually came to adopt local customs, wearing long robes and eating eastern foods. Despite the generally high standard of living, the states struggled to attract settlers and suffered from a constant shortage of manpower.

RENAISSANCE EUROPE

1400–1500

The Renaissance was an intellectual and artistic movement that began in Italy in about 1350 and spread through most of Europe during the 15th and 16th centuries. The rediscovery of great works of literature from classical Greece and Rome, lost to Europe for a thousand years, inspired new ways of thinking and new styles of architecture, painting and sculpture. The philosophy that lay at the heart of the Renaissance was humanism, which emphasized the development of human potential in all spheres, including politics, literature, art and science. The 15th century was also a time when the dynastic rivalries that had dominated the politics of France, England and Spain were finally resolved, paving the way for the emergence of stable government under powerful monarchs.

Right Jeanne au siège d'Orléans *by Jules Lenepveu (1819–1898), painted in about 1886*

Below *Detail of a portrait of Henry VII of England by his court painter, Michael Sittow (c. 1469–1525)*

Italian city-states

At the start of the Renaissance, Italy was composed of around 250 separate states. The Holy Roman Empire exerted merely nominal control over parts of the peninsula, and the papacy ruled central Italy, while most of the country remained a patchwork of independent city-states. During the 14th and 15th centuries, a number of the major cities fell under the control of specific families. Milan was governed by the Visconti and, from 1447, by the Sforza family. Other ruling dynasties included the d'Estes in Ferrara, the Gonzagas in Mantua, and the Medici of Florence. To win status and prestige, they all patronized the arts and paid for the construction of fine buildings. Florence and Venice, in particular, became leading centres of Renaissance art.

France and England

For most of the 15th century, western Europe's rulers were too caught up in warfare and dynastic rivalries to pay much heed to the artistic and intellectual movement going on in Italy. From the late 1300s, France was split by a power struggle between the Burgundian and Armagnac familes over control of the mad king Charles VI (reigned 1380–1422). French weakness tempted Henry V of England to restart the Hundred Years' War in the hope of gaining the French throne for himself. With his victory over the French at Agincourt (1415) and subsequent marriage to Charles VI's daughter, Henry united England and France under his rule. However, French fortunes revived when the peasant girl Joan of Arc inspired victory at Orleans (1429). By 1453, the English had lost all their French territories save Calais.

The Burgundian duke Charles the Bold wished to create an independent kingdom, uniting his possessions in the Netherlands with the Duchy of Burgundy, but the Netherlands passed to the Habsburgs, rulers of the Holy Roman Empire, when Charles' successor Mary married into the Habsburg family in 1477. Louis XI (reigned 1461–1483) laid the foundations for a centralized French state when he seized the lands of the Duchy of Burgundy in 1477.

TIMELINE

1415	*England defeats France at Agincourt*
1429	*Joan of Arc defeats the English siege of Orleans*
1453	*The Hundred Years' War ends in victory for France*
1455–1485	*The Wars of the Roses take place in England*
1469	*The Houses of Castile and Aragon unite to form a single kingdom in Spain*
1477	*The Burgundians lose the Netherlands to the Habsburgs and the Duchy of Burgundy to Louis XI of France*
1485	*Henry VII of England founds the Tudor dynasty*
1487	*Portuguese sailors round the Cape of Good Hope*
1492	*Ferdinand and Isabella defeat Granada, driving the Muslims from Spain; Christopher Columbus discovers the New World.*

EASTERN EUROPE

Casimir IV (reigned 1447–1492) united Poland and Lithuania to create a vast state in eastern Europe, which lasted until its defeat by the Ottomans in 1526. However, Hungary, under King Matthias Corvinus (reigned 1458–1490) dominated the region in the later 15th century. His Italian wife imported ideas from the Renaissance, establishing Hungary as an artistic and cultural centre. By the end of the 15th century, Muscovy, which had originated as a remote outpost of Kievan Rus in the 13th century, had taken control of many surrounding Russian principalities to become a significant power. After the fall of the Byzantine Empire in 1453, Muscovy became the hub of Orthodox Christianity.

Above *An engraving by Theodore de Bry (1528–1598) showing the arrival of Christopher Columbus in the New World*

In England, defeat in the Hundred Years' War was followed by a period of weak, corrupt government and a power struggle between two branches of the royal Plantagenet family, the Houses of York and Lancaster; both of whom had a rose as their emblem (white and red respectively). The so-called Wars of the Roses lasted from 1455 to 1485 and resulted in a Lancastrian victory under Henry VII (reigned 1485–1509), founder of the Tudor dynasty. He married Elizabeth of York and restored stable, monarchical government.

Spain and Portugal

In Spain, the rival kingdoms of Castile and Aragon united in 1469 when Ferdinand of Aragon married Isabella of Castile to create a new European superpower. The combined forces of Castile and Aragon were sufficient to conquer Granada, the last Muslim stronghold in Spain, by 1492. In the same year, Isabella of Castile commissioned Christopher Columbus to seek out a western sea route to the Indies, which led to his discovery of the New World. Under Prince Henry the Navigator (reigned 1394–1460), Portugal turned its attention to Africa. The Portuguese captured Ceuta in North Africa in 1415 and, in the 1430s, began to explore the west African coast. In 1487, Portuguese navigators rounded Africa's southern tip, opening up a new trade route to East Africa and the Indies.

AFRICA

500–1500

The Middle Ages was a period of development in Africa as more advanced peoples from the north took their knowledge of agriculture and metalworking to less developed regions in the south. As a result, chiefdoms, cities, states and empires arose in sub-Saharan Africa. Most of Africa's medieval development arose due to internal migration. However, from the 10th century, Islam, introduced by Arab traders, exerted a strong influence on North, East and West Africa. By the end of the Middle Ages, coastal areas were opening up to European trade, and Christianity, introduced by the Portuguese, began to penetrate West and Central Africa.

Throughout the medieval period, Bantu-speaking peoples continued their migration from their homelands in West Africa to eastern and southern regions (see page 97). Their farming and iron-working skills spread with them and gradually replaced the hunter-gatherer cultures in many parts of sub-Saharan Africa.

North Africa

Below *The Great Mosque of Djenné in Mali stands on the site where the first mosque was built in the 13th century*

In the seventh century, Muslim Arab armies swept through North Africa from Egypt to the Maghreb, bringing their religion, laws and customs with them. These blended with native Berber traditions to create a distinct Islamic Moorish culture. Morocco became a major centre of trade flowing southward across the Sahara. In north-east Africa, the Christian kingdom of

Axum was pushed back to the Ethiopian highlands by the Muslim Arab advance and was finally destroyed in 975. However, an isolated Christian kingdom, known as Ethiopia, survived there throughout the Middle Ages. They built remarkable cross-shaped churches hewn from solid rock, such as the one at Lalibela, which survive to this day.

East Africa

During the early Middle Ages, the Great Rift Valley in East Africa was settled by Nilotic-speaking peoples (ethnic groups from modern-day southern Sudan, Uganda and Kenya) and Bantu-speakers. The highlands and savannahs were settled by Bantu-speakers, intermixing with native Cushitic-speakers. From the eighth century, Bantu-speakers settled the East African coast, founding ports such as Malindi and Mombasa, popular with Arab and Persian traders. The resulting fusion of African and Islamic cultures became known as Swahili (coastal) culture; and the Swahili language remains predominant. The first East African states arose in the Great Lakes Region between 1350 and 1500.

West Africa

West Africa experienced an increase in regional trade beginning in the sixth century. The resulting prosperity led to a rise in population and the emergence of ever-larger urban settlements. In the seventh century, many of these settlements began to converge to form small chiefdoms of between two and ten thousand people. The earliest-known West African chiefdom was Ghana, situated on

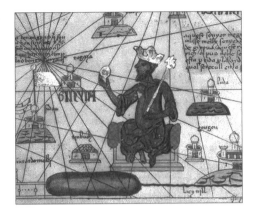

Above *Mansa Musa depicted holding a gold nugget, from the* Catalan Atlas, *produced by the Majorcan Cartographic School in 1375*

CENTRAL AND SOUTHERN AFRICA

State formation began to occur in Central Africa in the 14th and 15th centuries, when tribal federations of Bantu-speakers founded kingdoms such as Mbanza Congo and Ndongo. In the Limpopo and Zambezi River valleys in Southern Africa, a number of small chiefdoms emerged in the 11th century, including Mapungubwe, which grew wealthy from trading gold and ivory. By the 13th century, the first states began to emerge. Dominant among these was the empire of Great Zimbabwe. Its many monuments – especially the royal palace enclosure of Great Zimbabwe – were the most impressive stone structures in medieval sub-Saharan Africa. By 1450, the state of Mwenemutapa, to the north, had eclipsed Great Zimbabwe. In the late 15th century, Bantu speakers colonized the south-western tip of Africa, displacing the Khoisan peoples, indigenous hunter-gatherers of that vicinity.

the south-western edge of the Sahara, which grew rich through trading gold.

By the 13th century, Ghana had declined and the dominant state in West Africa was the empire of Mali, centered on the inland delta of the upper Niger. Mali's rise was largely a result of the increase in trans-Saharan trade by camel caravan with Muslim North Africa. Its great cities, Koubmi Saleh and Timbuktu, lay at the southern end of the caravan routes and became major centres of commerce, where slaves, ivory and gold were exchanged for salt, textiles, glass and ceramics from the north. Mali reached its zenith under Mansa Musa (reigned 1307–1352).

In the 14th century, Mali was eclipsed by the empire of Songhai, which captured Timbuktu in 1335. Songhai reached its peak under Sonni Ali (reigned 1464–1492), when Timbuktu became the main centre of Islam in West Africa. Trans-Saharan trade also encouraged the emergence of other West African states in the later Middle Ages; states such as Benin, Ife and Oyo in the West African forest and, further east, the city-states of the Hausa people, and the Kanem-Bornu empire.

TIMELINE	
c. 700	Foundation of kingdom of Ghana
c. 750	Trans-Saharan trade starts to increase
c. 800	Trading ports established on East African coast
c. 975	Pagan invaders destroy kingdom of Axum
c. 1000	Islam becomes established in West Africa
c. 1200	Construction of the palace enclosure at Great Zimbabwe
c. 1250	Mali becomes the dominant state in West Africa
1432	Portuguese begin to explore West African coast
c. 1450	Great Zimbabwe supplanted by Mwenemutapa
1464	Songhai becomes the dominant state in West Africa
1490	Portuguese convert king of Congo to Christianity.

INDIA

550–1500

The collapse of the Gupta Empire in 550 marked the end of a golden age in Indian cultural history, and the subcontinent once again fragmented into small warring kingdoms. New empires rose and fell during the Middle Ages, many of them producing fine sculpture and temple architecture. The early Middle Ages witnessed the decline of Buddhism and the revival of Hinduism, and consequently the caste system became an entrenched part of India's social order. Islam arrived on the point of a sword in the eighth century, and then even more forcefully in the 11th. By 1200, Muslim forces dominated northern India.

Above *The remains of one of the many temples at the medieval city of Hampi, in Karnataka state, India*

Central and southern India

Kingdoms ruled by various influential dynasties arose in the central and southern India during the medieval period. In the seventh century the Chalukyas dominated the Deccan in central India, while the Pallavas ruled the area around Kanchipuram and Mamallapuram from the sixth to the ninth centuries. In the far south, around Madurai, the Pandyas flourished from the sixth century to the 12th. The Hoysalas dominated the region around Dorasamudra in the 11th and 12th centuries. Their capital city, Vijayanagara, became the centre of a mighty Hindu empire that thrived from the

14th to the 16th centuries. However, the most expansionist dynasty of the era was the Cholas. Centred on Tanjore in south-east India, they built a strong navy that enabled them to trade with, and conquer, distant lands. At their height, from the 10th to the 12th centuries, the Chola sphere of influence stretched as far north as the Ganges, and included colonies in Sri Lanka, the Maldives and Indonesia. The Cholas were instrumental in carrying Hinduism into South-east Asia.

Northern India

In the early seventh century, Harsha (reigned 606–647) ascended the throne of Kanauj, the most powerful Indian kingdom. Harsha embarked on a career of conquest that united most of northern India under his rule. However, the attempt to extend his empire into the Deccan was defeated by the Chalukyas in 633. Harsha's empire disintegrated soon after his death and northern India broke up into small kingdoms. There were constant struggles between rival dynasties such as the Pratiharas and the Palas of Bihar and Bengal. The roughly equal military and economic strength of the opposing kingdoms prevented any one power from achieving dominance. This perpetual conflict and division made the north vulnerable to attack by Mongols and Turks.

The spread of Islam

India's first contact with Islam came during the early eighth century when Arab armies conquered Sind and Multan. The Arab advance was halted by the Gurjara-Pratiharas, a Rajput (warlord) dynasty who ruled the greatest kingdom in post-Harsha northern India. Islam returned in the early 11th century in the guise of the Turkish ruler, Mahmud of Ghazni, who launched no fewer than 17 invasions of India. In doing so, he broke the hold of the Gurjara-Pratiharas, conquered several kingdoms and destroyed many Hindu temples. However, Mahmud only annexed the Punjab region, leaving the other kingdoms under the control of vassals. Muslim incursions ceased following Mahmud's death and the subsequent decline of the Ghaznavid emirate. The next Islamic invader was Muhammad of Ghur (reigned 1173–1206), ruler of the Ghurid Empire. His triumph against the Rajput kings at Tarain in 1192 was decisive in breaking Hindu power in northern India. By 1200, Muhammad had won control of the Indus and Ganges plains, marking the start of six centuries of Muslim dominance.

Delhi Sultanate

Muhammad, assassinated in 1206, was succeeded by one of his generals, a former slave called Qutb-ud-Din, who seceded from the Ghurid Empire to form an independent sultanate, centred on Delhi. Qutb-ud Din's reign was constantly threatened by Hindu rebellions, but his successor, Ilutmish (reigned 1211–1236), stabilized and strengthened Muslim rule in northern India, from Sind to Bengal. A new dynasty, the Khaljis, came to power in 1290. Under its second ruler, Ala-ud Din (reigned 1296–1336), the sultanate extended its control southwards as far as the Tapti River in the Deccan.

The Delhi Sultanate reached its greatest extent under Muhammad ibn Tughluk (reigned 1325–1351), who briefly managed to conquer the Deccan. To consolidate the sultanate's hold over the south, Muhammad shifted the capital (including its entire population) from Delhi to

TIMELINE	
606–647	*Harsha unites northern India*
711	*Arabs conquer Sind in western India*
c. 850	*Foundation of Chola state*
999–1030	*Mahmud of Ghazni conquers north-west India*
1151	*Ghurids overthrow Ghaznavid Emirate*
1175–1192	*Muhammad of Ghur conquers northern India*
1206	*The Delhi Sultanate is founded*
1343	*The Hindu city of Vjayanagar is founded*
1398	*Timur sacks Delhi.*

Daulatabad in central India. However, this led to a loss of control over the north, and after just two years, Muhammad was forced to return to Delhi. He placed the Deccan under the command of a governor, Hasan Gunghu, who rebelled in 1347 and formed the Bahmani Sultanate.

Left Maharana Pratap, a 16th-century Rajput ruler, by Raja Ravi Varma (1848–1906)

Below Qutub Minar, completed in 1200, is the tallest monument in India and one of Delhi's landmarks

In the late-14th century, the Delhi Sultanate began to decline and its hold over the northern provinces slackened. In 1398, the Turko-Mongol warlord Timur invaded and sacked Delhi, further weakening the state. More Turko-Mongol invasions took place between 1414 and 1421, and by 1451 the power was reduced to Delhi and its immediate surroundings. Under the Lodis, a dynasty from Afghanistan, the sultanate regained control of much of northern India. However, the recovery was shortlived. The sultanate was finally destroyed in 1526 by the warlord Babur, founder of the Mughal Empire.

SUI AND TANG CHINA

589–907

After almost 400 years of civil war, China was reunited in 589 by Wendi (reigned 589–604), founder of the Sui dynasty. Under Wendi's autocratic but effective leadership, strong, centralized government was reestablished. He founded a new capital at Luoyang, issued a new law code, standardized coinage and promoted Buddhism. Wendi's son and successor Yang (reigned 604–617) oversaw a major expansion of the Great Wall and the construction of the Grand Canal, the longest canal in the world. These and other building projects strained the economy and the use of forced labour caused resentment. Yang's unpopularity grew after his attempt to conquer the Koguryo kingdom (611–614) in northern Korea was defeated with heavy losses. From 613, there were widespread peasant rebellions that damaged the agricultural base and took the empire to the brink of collapse.

Below *At the time of its construction the Chinese Grand Canal was the longest in the world*

In 617, a leading Sui general, Li Yuan, rose in revolt and captured the Sui capital, Luoyang. In 618, after Yang was assassinated by his own officials, Li Yuan became the first emperor of the Tang dynasty. Known posthumously as Gaozu (reigned 618–626), the emperor was preoccupied for most of his reign with defeating his rivals and trying to restore order to his realm. Gaozu was succeeded by Taizong (reigned 626–649), who succeeded to the throne after murdering his two brothers and deposing his father.

Taizong

The new emperor embarked on an ambitious programme of economic and political reform, designed to strengthen the Chinese state. He brought Chinese land under government control, and granted every male peasant an equal-sized plot. In return, the peasants were required to pay part of their crop in tax and also to serve as soldiers or labourers on building projects when required. Inspired by the Han dynasty's example, Taizong also created a professional civil service to administer the country. Promotion within the civil service depended on passing examinations. He divided the country into 15 administrative regions, each under the control of a government commissioner. Under Taizong's able rule, peace and order were restored, agricultural productivity rose and the economy flourished.

Foreign adventures

During Taizong's reign, China began to extend its control into Central Asia, defeating the western Turks and creating a military protectorate in the Tarim Basin. Under Gaozong (reigned 649–683) and his gifted empress Wu Zetian (the dominant political figure in China from 660 to 705), Furghana and Soghd were brought under

Chinese control, and Koguryo was conquered in the east. However, these conquests over-extended the empire and by 676 all three were lost. China's Central Asian empire was further undermined in 751, when it suffered defeats by the Arabs at the River Talas and by the Thai kingdom of Nan Chao at Dali. In 791, China lost the vital Ganzu Corridor to the Tibetans at Tingzhou, cutting off its passage into Central Asia.

Rebellions

After Wu Zetian, the Tang emperors proved generally ineffectual. The dynasty suffered a major crisis in 755 when An Lushan, the military governor of north-eastern China, led a rebellion. He captured the former capital of Luoyang (the Tang capital was Chang'an) and declared himself emperor of a new dynasty, the Great Yen. An Lushan was assassinated in 757, but the rebellion was continued by his sons and officers until 763. Vast numbers were killed (some sources estimate 36 million casualties) and large areas of China's most fertile lands were left depopulated. This also greatly diminished imperial authority in China, and power devolved to some 40 semi-autonomous regional governments. The weakened state suffered further rebellions, this time by peasants, in 859,

TANG CULTURE

The early Tang emperors, especially Wu Zetian, were keen promoters of Buddhism. However, Emperor Wuzong (reigned 840–846) suppressed the religion, destroying temples and expelling thousands of monks. Buddhism survived as a popular Chinese religion, but Confucianism was restored as the official state ideology. Tang China is also remembered as a golden age for the arts, especially literature. More than 48,000 poems survive from this period, the finest written during the 'High Tang' period of the eighth century. The greatest of all Chinese poets, Du Fu, lived at this time. The Tangs also presided over notable achievements in painting and tomb sculpture. Fine silks and ceramics were exported, and the first true porcelain was produced in eastern China.

Right *The influential and prolific poet Du Fu was born in 712 in Henan Province and died in a boat drifting on the Xiangjiang River in 770*

868 and 874–884. By the late ninth century, central authority had collapsed and power was seized by provincial warlords. The Tang emperors continued as figureheads until the final emperor was overthrown in 907. Whereupon, China entered another period of disunity known as the Five Dynasties and Ten Kingdoms (907–960).

TIMELINE	
589–618	*Sui dynasty*
640–659	*China expands into Central Asia*
751	*China is defeated by the Arabs and by Nan Chao*
755–763	*An Lushan rebellion leads to weakening of central authority*
791	*China loses control of Ganzu Corridor*
874–884	*Major peasant rebellion accelerates the decline of the Tang dynasty*
907	*Tang dynasty ends.*

SONG CHINA

907–1279

The Song dynasty ruled most of China between 960 and 1279. The period is split into the Northern Song (960–1126), whose capital was at Kaifeng, and the Southern Song (1127–1279), who had their capital at Hangzhou. The Song never governed the whole of China; their rule was limited to areas of ethnic Chinese settlement. Manchuria and eastern Mongolia were controlled by the kingdom of Liao (916–1124). Liao was conquered by the Jin dynasty (1124–1234), who also captured Kaifeng and drove the Song south. Both the Jin and the Southern Song were eventually brought down by the Mongols.

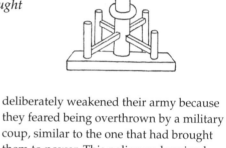

Right *An early revolving typecase using movable type characters. Movable type printing was invented in China circa 1000*

The period of disunity that began with the fall of the Tang lasted until 960. That year, a general named Zhao Kuangyin, with the support of his army, seized power from the last of the five dynasties that had ruled over most of northern China since 907 and proclaimed himself Emperor Song Taizu (reigned 960–976). Taizu then began the process of unifying China under his rule. His younger brother and successor, Song Taizong (reigned 976–997) completed the reunification. Once their grip on power had been consolidated, the Song emperors

deliberately weakened their army because they feared being overthrown by a military coup, similar to the one that had brought them to power. This policy undermined their later ability either to deal with outside threats or to expand their territory.

Liao and Xixia

Powerful kingdoms lay on Song China's northern border, occupying areas that had once been part of the Chinese empire. The Khitans, a Turko-Mongol tribe, had taken advantage of the period of disunity to settle Manchuria and eastern Mongolia. Here they formed a kingdom known as Liao, named after their ruling dynasty. Emperor Taizong tried to conquer Liao in 979, but his army was routed near Beijing. When the Khitans besieged the Song capital Kaifeng in 1004, the Song emperor was forced to buy them off with an annual tribute of silver, silk and tea.

In the north-west, the Xiazhou clan of the nomadic Tangut people had settled the Chinese provinces of Ningxia, Gansu and Shaanxi in the late 10th century. Here they founded the kingdom of Xixia. Though not

TIMELINE

960	*Song Taizu proclaimed emperor*
969	*Gunpowder rockets first used in warfare*
979	*Song Taizong completes reunification of most of China*
c. 1000	*Movable type printing is invented*
1117–1124	*Jürchen conquer Liao and establish Jin dynasty*
1127	*Jin capture Kaifeng; Song capital moves south to Hangzhou*
c. 1150	*Chinese navigators first use the magnetic compass*
1226	*Mongols conquer Xixia*
1234	*Mongols conquer Jin empire*
1279	*Mongols conquer Song empire.*

as threatening as Liao, Xixia effectively blocked any Chinese attempt to expand into Central Asia via the Ganzu Corridor. Expansion to the south was similarly blocked by the Thai kingdom of Nan Chao and the Viet kingdom of Annam.

Jin

In 1124, Liao collapsed following an invasion by the Jürchen people of Manchuria. The Jürchen set up their own kingdom in the north under the Jin dynasty. The Song government had initially supported the Jürchen action against Liao, but now found themselves faced by an even more formidable threat from the north. In 1127, the Jin captured Kaifeng and imprisoned the Song emperor. However, one of the emperor's sons escaped and fled south to Hangzhou. There, he became the first Southern Song emperor. The Jin controlled northern China until 1234, but their attempts to conquer southern China failed. Demographic shifts, originating from the mass migrations of the fourth century (see page 88), meant that for hundreds of years the south had exceeded the north both in terms of population and wealth; and

the Song had no difficulty in defending themselves from the Jin.

Mongols

At the start of the 13th century, the nomadic Mongol peoples of the Central Asian steppe were united under Genghis Khan (see pages 138–139), who proceeded to invade Xixia and Jin. The Song repeated their earlier mistake towards the Jürchen by supplying the Mongols with troops to bolster their campaign. In 1234, following the Mongol defeat of the Jin, the Song opportunistically tried to capture the Jin cities of Kaifeng and Luoyang, but this merely provoked the Mongols to attack *them*. Song resistance to the Mongols was stubborn, but broke down following the capture of their capital, Hangzhou by Kublai Khan in 1276. The final Song emperor was killed in battle three years later, and Kublai Khan founded the Yüan dynasty.

Above *Kublai Khan on a hunting expedition, painted on a silk handscroll in 1280 by the Chinese court artist Liu Guandao*

SONG ACHIEVEMENTS

The Song emperors presided over a period of economic expansion and technological innovation. Agricultural productivity was greatly improved by bringing more land under cultivation and by the introduction of new strains of rice from Vietnam, enabling double cropping (growing two crops in one season). New commercial crops were produced, including sugar, tea, bamboo and hemp. Traditional crafts such as silk making, papermaking, lacquerware and ceramics flourished. Improved roads and canals boosted internal trade, while the invention of the magnetic compass in the 12th century encouraged the Chinese to sail further and trade over much greater distances. In fact, trade increased to the point that, for the first time in Chinese history, tax revenues from commerce exceeded those from land. All this mercantile activity required a more sophisticated financial system. The Song government inaugurated the first Chinese banks, minted billions of coins annually and introduced the world's first paper money.

Above *Twelfth-century stoneware from the Northern Song Dynasty*

THE MONGOL EMPIRE

1204–1405

The Mongol Empire was the largest land empire ever created. At its peak, in the mid-13th century, it stretched from Hungary to Korea and included more than 100 million people. The Mongols had previously lived as nomadic tribespeople on the steppe lands of modern-day Mongolia, scarcely noticed by the outside world. All that was to change in the early 13th century when Temujin, a Mongol warlord, united the Mongol tribes. In recognition of his leadership, they gave him the title Genghis Khan – universal ruler.

Right *An image of Genghis Khan presiding over his Mongol Empire at its greatest extent*

Expansion east and west

The Mongols were fierce warriors with a proud tradition of horsemanship and mounted archery. Genghis Khan moulded them into a formidable army, highly disciplined and expert in the tactics of mass assault. In 1209, Genghis attacked Xixia in northern China and, in 1211, he turned on the Jin (see page 137). Meanwhile, Mongol forces were expanding westwards across the steppe, reaching the Turkish Muslim Shahdom of Khwarizm in Persia in 1219 and conquering it by 1223. Between 1223 and 1230, they overcame the eastern Turkic peoples living in the area of modern-day Kazakhstan and western China, recruiting many of them into the Mongol armies.

Genghis Khan died on campaign in China in 1227 and was succeeded by his son Ogodei (reigned 1229–1241), under whose rule the empire continued to expand. In the east, the Mongols conquered the Jin in 1234; they then turned their attention on the Southern Song. In the west, the Caucasus (the region between the Black and Caspian Seas) was conquered in the 1230s; and by 1243, Anatolia was under Mongol control. In 1237, the Mongols invaded Russia; and were victorious at Liegnitz in 1241. An even more audacious assault on eastern Europe achieved victory in Pest, Hungary, in the same year.

Yüan dynasty

The Mongol Empire was becoming too big to be ruled by one man. The last overall ruler was Mongke (reigned 1251–1259), grandson of Genghis. After his death, the empire began devolving into independent khanates. His brother, Kublai Khan (reigned 1260–1294) ruled Mongolia and China. Kublai established the Yüan dynasty and extended Mongol rule to the whole of China in 1279. Under his reign, China enjoyed a golden age of art and theatre. Large-scale construction projects were undertaken, including the building of a new capital in Daidu (present-day Beijing). Mongol rule in China lasted until 1368, when a series of popular uprisings brought down the Yüan dynasty, which was replaced by the Ming.

Above *The Pagoda of Bailin Temple in Hebei Province was built in 1330, during the Mongol rule of China*

Khanates of Central Asia and the Middle East

Further west in Central Asia, an independent khanate was founded by the descendents of Chagatai, Genghis's third son; this reached from modern eastern Kazakhstan to modern Uzbekistan and Turkmenistan. Descendents of Genghis's fourth son founded The Golden Horde, comprising the western part of the empire (including present-day Russia, Ukraine, western Kasakhstan and the Caucasus). During the 14th century, the Mongols of western Central Asia assimilated into the larger nomadic Turkish population and lost much of their original cultural identity.

Another independent Mongol state, the Ilkhanate, controlled Persia. It was founded by Hulegu (reigned 1255–1265), a brother of Mongke. Hulegu captured Baghdad in 1258 and brought down the Abbasid Caliphate. In 1260, his forces were defeated by the Mamlukes at Ayn Jalut in Palestine, thus shattering the myth of Mongol invincibility. War between the Mongols and the Mamlukes continued until 1320, but the Mongols never managed to extend their border beyond the Euphrates. In 1295, the Mongols of the Ilkhanate converted to Islam. The Golden Horde followed suit in 1313.

REFORMS OF GENGHIS KHAN

The Mongols' success in establishing such a vast and long-lasting empire was in large part due to the changes instituted by Genghis Khan. Under Genghis, the Mongols adopted a written version of their language (essential for administration and communication over such distances), as well as a system of law known as the Yasa. The Yasa decreed, for example, that military service for all males was compulsory, with promotion based strictly on merit. Genghis also promoted the idea that the Mongols had a divine mandate to conquer the world. All those who resisted this mandate should be treated ruthlessly. This philosophy may explain the extreme brutality that accompanied many Mongol conquests during their era of expansion, and later under Timur.

Timur

In the late 14th century, a Turko-Mongolian army commander from Transoxiana, named Timur (reigned 1361–1405) attempted to rebuild the Mongolian Empire. He united much of Central Asia, Persia and Mesopotamia under his rule, but did not succeed in his attempt to conquer China in 1405 and died shortly afterwards. Timur was a brutal conqueror, though once his empire was established he became a devout Muslim and patron of the arts. However, he failed to set up an efficient administration or make provision for his succession and his empire fell apart after his death.

Below *Hulagu Khan, a grandson of Genghis Khan, and his wife Dokuz, from a 14th-century history of the world by Rashid Al-Din*

TIMELINE	
1204–1206	*Temujin (Genghis Khan) unites the Mongol tribes*
1209–1234	*Mongols conquer Xixia and Jin*
1219–1223	*Mongols conquer Khwarizm Shahdom*
1234–1279	*Mongols conquer Southern Song*
1237–1241	*Mongols invade Russia and eastern Europe*
1241	*Batu founds Golden Horde*
1256	*Hulegu founds the Ilkhanate*
1361–1405	*Timur conquers a new Mongol empire*
1368	*The Mongol Yüan dynasty is overthrown in China.*

JAPAN AND KOREA

600–1500

Medieval Japan and Korea were both strongly influenced by the civilization of China, and the rulers of both tried to build centralized states on the Chinese model. By the 15th century, Korea was unified under a single authority. In Japan, however, after a promising start under the Yamato, the political system became increasingly decentralized and feudal in nature.

State building in Japan

In the early seventh century, the Yamato emperor Prince Shotoku (reigned 593–622) began the process of building a centralized state. In 604, he introduced a constitution that asserted the authority of the emperor over the nobility. Shotoku also made Buddhism the state religion to reinforce a sense of national identity. The Taika Reforms of Emperor Kotoku (reigned 645–654), introduced in 646, brought all land into state ownership and created a centralized taxation system. In 702, a new law code, the Taiho laws, was created. Finally, in 710, Empress Gemmel (reigned 707–710) built a new capital city at Heijo (near modern Nara), modelled on the Chinese capital Chang'an.

Yet despite these efforts, the imperial state was always vulnerable to factional influence. Nara was filled with Buddhist temples, whose monks came to play a significant role in court politics. To escape their influence, Emperor Kammu (reigned 781–806) moved the capital to Heian (modern Kyoto) in 794. Here, the powerful

Above Fujiwara no Fuhito, a powerful member of the medieval Japanese imperial court, drawn by Kikuchi Yosai (1781–1878)

Fujiwara clan became increasingly influential. In 858, Yoshifusa, head of the Fujiwara, was appointed regent to the boy emperor, and for the next 300 years, the Fujiwara were Japan's effective rulers.

Shoguns

The lack of a strong centralized state allowed powerful land-owning families to take control of the provinces, supported by a class of hired warriors called samurai. In the 12th century, a struggle between two rival families, the Minamoto and the Taira, resulted in the Gempei Wars (1180–1185). The Minamoto emerged victorious and in 1192 their leader Yoritomo assumed the title of shogun (meaning 'barbarian-conquering great general').

Yoritomo established a military government at Kamakura (near modern Tokyo). Yorimoto's successors lacked his abilities, and from the early 13th century the Hojo family became regents for a series of puppet shoguns from the Minamoto or imperial families. In 1333, the Hojo family were overthrown by the Emperor Go-Dago, supported by the Minamoto leader Ashikaga Takauji, and imperial rule was restored. Just three years later, Takauji rebelled, forcing the emperor to flee Heian, whereupon Takauji established the Ashikaga Shogunate. The shoguns controlled the provinces through the shugo (military constables), who gradually gained power in their own right.

In the 15th century, a dispute over shogun succession led to civil war (1467–1477). Shugo authority in the provinces passed to feudal warlords called daimyo, supported by samurai armies. The Ashikaga survived until 1573, but by 1500

TIMELINE	
604	Prince Shotoku introduces new constitution (Japan)
660–668	China conquers Koguryo and Paekche (Korea)
858	Fujiwara Yoshifusa becomes regent (Japan)
c. 900	The kingdom of Silla collapses (Korea)
926	Khitan nomads overrun Parhae (Korea)
1258	Korea becomes a Mongol vassal state
1333–1336	Go-Daigo tries to restore imperial rule (Japan)
1333–1384	Kan'ami Kiyotsugu, founder of Noh drama (Japan)
1446	Korean alphabet replaces Chinese script
1467–1477	Onin War leads to rise of daimyo and feudalism (Japan).

Japan had fragmented into some 400 independent states. Daimyo castles became the centres of political influence and many spawned large urban communities. The emperors continued to rule at Heian as powerless figureheads.

Korea

By 600, three kingdoms had emerged in Korea: Koguryo, Silla and Paekche. In 660, the Chinese Tang dynasty, in alliance with Silla, conquered Koguryo and Paekche. Silla then drove the Chinese from the peninsula in 676 and took control of Paekche and southern Koguryo. Northern Koguryo held out against Silla, and its leader Tae Cho-yong founded a new state, Parhae, in 694. During the eighth century, both Korean states cultivated strong cultural and economic links with the Chinese, and modelled their administrative and legal systems on Tang China. In 780, a power struggle between the aristocracy and the monarchy in Silla led to the break-up of the kingdom in the ninth century. A new kingdom was formed by Wang Kon (reigned 918–945), who founded the Koryo dynasty (918–1392) from which Korea gets its name. Around this time, Parhae was destroyed by Khitan nomads.

By the 11th century, Korea had constructed a fortified frontier against the Khitans on the Yalu River. In 1170, a coup destroyed the monarchy, leaving the nation leaderless until the Choe family seized power in an 1196 military coup. From 1231, the Mongols began a series of invasions, and by 1258 had reduced Korea to vassal status. A period of political instability followed the end of Mongol domination in 1356. It ended with the overthrow of the Koryo dynasty by General Yi Songgye (reigned 1392–1398), founder of the Yi dynasty, which was destined to last until 1910. The Yi expanded to the north-east and by the 15th century, Korea's modern borders were established. Under the Yi, Confucianism replaced Buddhism as the country's main ethical and philosophical system. Seoul was founded as the capital and Hangul, the new Korean script, was promoted, encouraging the development of a vernacular literature.

Above left
Minamoto no Yoritomo, the first shogun of the Kamakura shogunate, painted on a hanging scroll in 1179 by Fujiwara no Takanobu

Below *An example of Hangul script, the Korean alphabet invented in the 15th century*

SOUTH-EAST ASIA

500–1500

Several powerful kingdoms and empires emerged in South-east Asia during the Middle Ages. Heavily influenced by India, local rulers adopted Buddhism or Hinduism as a means of consolidating and legitimizing their authority. China, though less culturally influential, maintained strong trading and diplomatic links with South-east Asia. By the close of the period, Islam was overtaking Hinduism in Indonesia.

Above *The temple of Angkor Wat, Cambodia, built in the 12th century as a state temple and capital city for King Suryavarman II*

Cambodia

The modern state of Cambodia was dominated for much of the medieval period by the Khmer people. The first Khmer state was Chen-la, which emerged around 400. At first a vassal state to Funan (see page 91), by 600 it achieved independence and eventually conquered Funan. Chen-la reached its zenith in about 700 under Jayavarman I, but then declined and fragmented. In the early ninth century, the Khmer were reunited by Jayavarman II (reigned 802–850). By the 880s, they had conquered the Mon and Thai peoples to the north and west. Yasovarman I (reigned 889–910) founded a new capital at Angkor, dominated by the temple of Angkor Wat. The empire reached its height in the 11th and 12th centuries. From the 14th century, it suffered repeated assaults from the Thai kingdom of Ayutthaya, and was forced to move its capital to Phnom Penh in 1431 and to abandon Angkor in 1440.

Thailand

The earliest state formed by the Thai people was Nan Chao. It emerged in about 600, in what is now western Yunnan province in southern China. Nan Chao was conquered by the Mongols in 1253, but before that, in the 11th century, Thai people began migrating southwards into modern-day Thailand, at that time occupied by Mon and Khmer peoples. By the 12th century, small Thai principalities had formed, absorbing aspects of Khmer Hindu culture, including their royal ceremonies, dance and literature. Around 1250, a powerful Thai kingdom was founded at Sukhothai. In 1378, this was conquered by another one centred on Ayutthaya. By the 15th century, Ayutthaya had driven the Khmers from Angkor and had established itself as the most powerful kingdom in the region.

Myanmar

From around 600, Buddhist city-states were created along the Irrawaddy River valley by the Mon people in the south and the Pyu people in the north. In the early ninth century, Nan Chao launched a series of raids on Mon and Pyu cities and destroyed the Pyu capital, Halingyi. The fall of the Pyu allowed the Burmese people, centred on the city of Pagan, to emerge as the dominant power in northern Myanmar by 849. By 1057, Myanmar was unified after Pagan, under Anawrahta (reigned 1044–1077), had conquered the Mon, the coastal Arakanese and the Shan hill peoples. By the late 13th century, Pagan had declined and became a vassal state of the Mongols. The Shan, Mon and Arakanese re-emerged by the 15th century, only to be reconquered by the Burmese Toungoo dynasty in the 16th.

Vietnam

Occupied by China since the third century BC, it was only in AD939 that the Vietnamese were able to establish an independent state, called Dai Viet. By the 11th century, Vietnam was unified under a centralized government, ruled by the Ly dynasty (1009–1225) and then the Tran (1225–1400). Dai Viet clashed with the Khmer in the 12th century and resisted attempted conquest by Mongol China in the 13th. The war against the Mongols depleted Dai Viet's resources and it was conquered by Ming China in 1407. The Chinese were driven out in 1428 by Lê Loi, founder of the Lê dynasty.

Island South-east Asia

For much of the medieval era, the most powerful state in Island South-east Asia was Srivijaya in Sumatra, which had been expanding since 682. By its peak, in the ninth century, Srivijaya dominated southern Sumatra, much of Java, parts of the Malay Peninsula and western Borneo. Sea raids by the Cholas of south India in the 11th century weakened Srivijaya, and its power was further eroded in the early 13th century by the expansionist kingdom of Singhasari in east Java. Singhasari was destroyed by Mongol China in 1293 and succeeded by a new state, Majapahit. At its height, under Hayam Wuruk (reigned 1350–1389), Majapahit's influence extended from Sumatra and the Malay Peninsula in the west to New Guinea in the east, although only central and east Java were under its direct control. Its navy was used to enforce tribute payments from provincial rulers. By the early 15th century, Majapahit was in decline, and the Hindu empire was unable to control the rising influence of Islam in the region. After a series of battles with the Sultanate of Demak, Majapahit eventually collapsed in 1527.

Above The Khon dance is a centuries-old traditional Thai dance form. It can take a week to perform

TIMELINE

682	*Srivijaya starts to expand (Islands)*
802	*Khmer Empire is founded (Cambodia)*
849	*Pagan is founded (Myanmar)*
939	*Dai Viet is founded (Vietnam)*
1057	*Myanmar is unified under Pagan rule*
1280	*Srivijaya is conquered by Singhasari (Islands)*
1293	*Majapahit is founded (Islands)*
1378	*Sukhothai is conquered by Ayutthaya (Thailand)*
1407	*China conquers Dai Viet (Vietnam)*
1440	*Khmer abandon Angkor (Cambodia).*

NORTH AMERICA AND THE PACIFIC

500–1500

North America was first settled around 12,000 years ago when bands of prehistoric migrants crossed the Bering Strait into Alaska and began spreading southwards. Gradually, these Paleoindians adapted to the local environments where they settled, and by around 100BC several distinctive cultures had emerged. Although some farming had developed at this stage, wild food sources – both animal and vegetable – were so abundant that there was little incentive to abandon the nomadic hunter-gatherer lifestyle. On Pacific islands such as Hawaii and Tahiti, complex societies emerged during the medieval period.

Above The Cliff Palace is an ancient Anasazi cultural settlement in Chapin Mesa. It was built between 1190 and 1280, and was inhabited by approximately 100 people.

Hunter-gatherers

For most of North America, hunting, fishing and gathering remained the dominant mode of existence throughout the medieval period. On the Pacific coast, marine food sources were sufficiently abundant to support permanent settlements and fairly complex societies. In the sparsely populated Great Plains and sub-Arctic regions, big-game (especially buffalo) hunting was boosted by the development of the bow and arrow in the first millennium AD.

South-west

The first North American communities to adopt agriculture as their major food source lived in the deserts of the south-west. From around AD300, they began to grow maize, beans, squash and cotton close to lakes and rivers. By 900, more productive yields became possible through the use of irrigation systems. By the ninth century, three main cultures had emerged: the Anasazi, Mogollon and Hohokam. The Anasazi created multi-roomed adobe and sandstone dwellings along cliff walls. Among the best-preserved of these are at Chaco Canyon, which contained 125 villages linked by 400 km (250 miles) of roads. The Mogollon produced distinctive pottery, decorated with geometric designs and representations of animals and people. The Hohokam were skilled makers of jewellery from shell, stone and bone, and were perhaps the first culture to master acid etching. Droughts caused the decline of these cultures from around 1300.

East

The first agricultural communities in eastern North America emerged in the eighth century, growing maize and beans; and by 1000, permanent farming villages were established throughout the region. In the 12th century, farming in the Mississippi basin was productive enough to support North America's first towns. The largest, such as Cahokia, were the centres of powerful chiefdoms. These Mississippian cultures, ancestors of the Chickasaw and Choctaw tribes, followed a religion known as the Southern Cult.

They buried their rulers in mound-top tombs containing rich grave goods, and sometimes human sacrifices. Mississippian culture declined around the 15th century.

North

The continent's Arctic region remained uninhabited until 2500–1900BC, when settlers – ancestors of modern Inuits – arrived there from Siberia. Gradual adaptation to Arctic conditions led to the emergence of Thule culture on the islands of the Bering Sea, late in the first millennium BC. Thule Inuit spent the summer hunting large sea mammals, and in winter they lived in settlements of between 10 and 100 people. From the Bering Sea, Thule Inuit spread along Alaska's west and north coasts. From Point Barrow in the north, they spread east, supplanting the pre-existing Dorset culture, until they reached Greenland in the 13th century. In Greenland, the Thule Inuit traded and sometimes fought with Viking settlers. When the Viking communities died out in the 15th century, Thule Inuit replaced them.

Polynesia

By AD500, the Polynesians had voyaged south to Easter Island and north to the islands of Hawaii. In the ninth century they began the settlement of New Zealand, where they hunted 32 species of native birds to extinction. The Polynesians were highly skilled toolmakers. Their artists worked with stone, wood, shell, bone and vegetable fibres, depicting gods and ancestors. The most impressive examples of Polynesian art are the 887 stone statues erected on Easter Island between 1000 and 1600. On large islands with fertile volcanic soil, where high-yield agriculture was

NAN MADOL

To the west of Hawaii lies Pohnpei Island in Micronesia. Off its eastern shore is the ruined city of Nan Madol, constructed some time between AD500 and 1500. The city is made up of 92 small artificial islands, linked by a network of canals, giving the city its nickname, the Venice of the Pacific. Covering an area of 28 km² (11 square miles), Nan Madol probably supported a population of between 500 and 1000 people. Its builders are not known, but only a powerful, centralized state would have had the resources to construct such a city. According to legend, it was the capital of the Saudeleur dynasty, which ruled Pohnpei in the early part of the second millennium AD. The north-eastern portion of the site, known as Madol Powe, contains royal tombs and the dwellings of priests; while Madol Pah, in the south-west contains royal residences and a ceremonial centre.

possible, complex societies emerged. Strongly hierarchical chiefdoms arose, for example, on Hawaii and Tahiti. In Hawaii, commoners were not allowed to touch the clothes or shadow of the chief; and on Tahiti it was forbidden even to say the chief's name. Elsewhere, the small, low-lying coral islands supported simple fishing communities.

Below *An engraving of Hawaiian priests travelling across Kealakekua Bay for rituals on making first contact with Westerners, by John Webber, an artist on Thomas Cook's ship*

Toltecs and Aztecs

800–1520

Two peoples dominated Mesoamerica during the medieval period: the Toltecs and the Aztecs. Both were greatly influenced in terms of religion and culture by the city of Teotihuacán, which had flourished in the Valley of Mexico between 300BC and AD750.

Above *A vessel in the Toltec style, made of orange-ware clay, excavated at Teotihuacán*

Toltecs

Following the collapse of Teotihuacán in the mid-eighth century, Mexico fragmented into a number of fortified city-states, which fought each other for territory and power. One of these was Tula. The people of Tula, called Toltecs, were descended from Chichimeca and Nonoalca peoples. By 950, the Toltecs had defeated rival cities and had established themselves as the dominant power in Mexico. They were greatly influenced by the Teotihuacán culture and adopted several of their gods, including the rain god Tlalec, and a feathered serpent whom the Aztecs would later called Quetzalcóatl (the Toltec name is unknown).

Tula covered 13 km² (5 square miles) and had a population of around 50,000. At its centre was a ceremonial area with two temple pyramids, where human sacrifices may have been carried out, and two sacred ball courts. Tula also contained large stone statues of warriors, which may have been the columns of a temple, and a skull rack displaying the heads of slain enemies. The Toltecs traded with cities throughout Mesoamerica. They may have occupied the Mayan city of Chichén Itzá in the 11th

century – the striking similarities between the two cities certainly suggest that the Toltecs exerted a strong influence on Chichén Itzá.

Although little is known of Toltec history, some clues are apparent in the legends of the Aztecs, who claimed descent from them. According to Aztec tradition, a Toltec ruler called Topiltzin-Quetzalcóatl reigned in the 10th century. He soon came to be associated with the feathered serpent god Quetzalcóatl. His opposition to human sacrifice offended the god Tezcatlpoca, who overthrew him. Topiltzin-Quetzalcóatl fled eastwards overseas, promising to return one day to reclaim his kingdom. Tula was destroyed in around 1168 by unknown invaders and the city was abandoned until the rise of the Aztecs in the 14th century, when it was partly reoccupied.

Aztecs

At some point during the 12th century, a farming people called the Aztecs, possibly originating from present-day northern Mexico, migrated into the Valley of Mexico. For some 200 years they fought territorial battles with other Mesoamerican tribes before founding a permanent settlement called Tenochtitlán, on an island in Lake Texcoco in 1325. The Aztecs served as mercenaries for the city-state of Azcapotzalco, but in 1426 they sided with the city of Texcoco to destroy Azcapotzalco. In 1434, they formed an alliance with two other leading powers in the Valley of Mexico – Texcoco and Tlacopan. This Triple Alliance imposed tributary status on the other states in the region. Tenochtitlán dominated the alliance and took the bulk of the tribute. By the time of Moctezuma II (reigned 1502–1520), the Triple Alliance ruled over some ten million people.

Aztec society was based on a rigid hierarchy. At the top was the emperor, who was advised by a council of nobles. The nobles, who were relatives of the emperor, could be warriors, priests or judges. Below the nobles were the commoners, who were made up of farmers, craft workers and merchants. Below the commoners were the slaves. Each rank of society dressed in a particular way. The Aztecs were a very warlike society. Their best soldiers were known as jaguar or eagle knights. They fought with spears and javelins and aimed to take their enemies prisoner rather than kill them. Prisoners of war were sacrificed to Aztec gods.

The Aztec Empire came to a sudden end with the invasion of the Spanish conquistador Hernán Cortés in 1519–1521. The Aztecs greatly outnumbered the Spanish forces, but the Spanish had superior weaponry and armour. Also, as Cortés advanced towards Tenochtitlán, he gained numerous willing allies among the Aztecs' tributary states. Moctezuma's response was hesitant – he suspected that Cortés was the returning Quetzalcóatl of legend. He offered the Spaniards gold to pacify them, and even allowed himself to be taken prisoner. When the Aztecs turned on the Spanish forces, the Spaniards sacked Tenochtitlán, then forced the Aztecs to work for them as slaves. Many thousands of Aztecs perished from European diseases such as smallpox, to which they had no resistance.

Below Founded about AD400 and expanded some 450 years later, Chichén Itzá was a centre of religious, military and political power

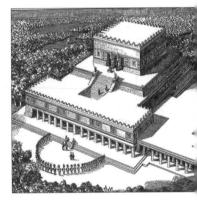

Above *A depiction of the Aztec king Moctezuma II, whose empire fell to the invading Spaniards*

MAYA

Although the classic age of the Maya ended about 800, when its lowland cities in central Yucatán were abandoned, Mayan civilization continued in northern Yucatán, where Chichén Itzá soon became the dominant city. In about 1000, Chichén Itzá may have been conquered by the Toltecs. Certainly a heavy Toltec influence is noticeable from this time. Maya chronicles state that in 1221, there was a revolt and civil war in Chichén Itzá; and from this point, power in the Yucatán shifted to the city-state of Mayapán, 100 km (60 miles) to the west. Mayapán continued to dominate until the 1440s. By the time the Spaniards arrived in 1517, the northern Yucatán contained 16 rival Mayan states with no one in overall control. The last independent state, Tayasal, did not fall until 1697.

SOUTH AMERICA AND THE INCAS

1000–1533

During the period immediately before the Spanish conquest, the dominant civilization of South America were the Incas. From around 1430, the Incas conquered a vast empire that stretched over 4,000 km (2,500 miles) along the western coast and mountains of South America. Thanks to their road network and efficient administration, the Incas maintained a powerful hold over every part of their territory. Yet the highly centralized nature of the Inca state under a single, all-powerful ruler made them vulnerable to external attack and when the Spanish conquistadors invaded in 1532, the Inca empire swiftly collapsed.

Right A Moche spouted vessel in the form of a reclining figure, showing the high degree of skill found in Moche ceramics

Chimú

Following the collapse of the Huari and Tiahuanaco empires in about 1000 (see page 95), civilization on the Pacific coast and highlands of South America fragmented into a multitude of small states. Around 1200, the state of Chimú embarked on a gradual process of expansion until, by the early 1400s, it controlled more than a thousand kilometres of the Peruvian coast. The Chimú grew out of the remnants of Moche culture, and their pottery bears some resemblance to that of the Moche. They also produced black ceramics and elaborate metalwork from copper, gold, silver and bronze. Unlike the Incas, who worshipped the sun, the Chimú worshipped the moon and regarded the sun as a destroyer.

Rise of the Incas

The Inca state was founded in about 1200 at Cuzco, in the Peruvian highlands. For over 200 years, the Incas controlled little more than Cuzco and its surrounding valley. Then, during the 15th century, it suddenly grew into the largest empire in pre-Columbian America. The Incas' remarkable expansion began in the reign of Pachacutec (1438–1471), whose name meant 'world-shaker'. Pachacutec used a mixture of bribery, diplomacy and military might to build his empire. In 1470, the Incas defeated the Chimú, their only serious rival as an imperial power. Pachacutec's policy of expansion was continued by his son Tupac Yupanqui (reigned 1471–1493) and grandson Huayna Capac (reigned 1493–1525). By the end of the latter's reign, the Inca empire had reached its practical limits – further expansion would have taken it into the Amazonian rainforest or other places unsuited to agriculture. The empire included parts of modern-day Peru, Bolivia, Ecuador, Chile, Argentina and Colombia.

TIMELINE

c. 850	Chimú capital founded at Chan Chan
c. 1200	Chimú begins to build its empire
c. 1200	Inca state founded at Cuzco by semi-legendary Manco Capac
1438	Incas begin to build their empire
1470	Incas conquer the Chimú
1525–1532	Inca civil war
1532–1533	Spanish conquistadors, led by Francisco Pizarro, conquer the Inca empire.

Inca administration

Pachacutec established a highly centralized and hierarchical system of administration for his empire. At the top was the Sapa Inca, the semi-divine emperor, who ruled from his palace at Cuzco. Beneath him were the governors of the four quarters of the empire. Below them were provincial governors, followed by district officers, local chiefs and, finally, foremen, each responsible for governing ten families. Farmers paid tax by supplying the state with part of their produce. Throughout the empire large granaries were built for storing food, and officials made sure that no one starved. In return, everyone had to spend part of the year working on public projects such as building roads, fortresses or irrigation systems, terracing steep hillsides for farmland, or serving in the army.

Inca communication

The Incas managed to run their empire very efficiently, despite the fact that they did not develop writing. What they used instead was an elaborate device involving coloured knotted strings, known as *quipu*. These were both a means of keeping records and a general system of communication. To convey messages swiftly across mountainous country, the Incas built over 32,000 km (20,000 miles) of stone-paved roads. Where roads crossed rivers, engineers built suspension bridges from ropes and matting. There was no wheeled transport, and the quipu messages were carried by a relay system of runners. By this means, news of a rebellion in the far north, for example, could reach Cuzco within six days.

Spanish conquest

Huayna Capac died in 1525 from smallpox, an outbreak that had spread south from the Spanish base in Panama – it was a sign of disasters to come. His death was followed by civil war as his sons fought over the succession. The elder son Atahualpa finally triumphed in April 1532, but barely had time to rebuild the weakened empire. Seven months later, the Spanish conquistador Francisco Pizarro, with just 168 troops, launched a surprise attack on Atahualpa and his entourage at Cajamarca, and took the emperor hostage. The following year the Spanish executed him and installed a puppet ruler. Following a rebellion in 1536, the Spanish assumed direct control, although sporadic Inca resistance continued until 1572. The Spanish were fortunate in the timing of their invasion, so soon after a bloody civil war. Also, their capture of Atahualpa effectively paralysed an empire that relied on the Sapa Inca for every important decision. As with the Aztecs, European diseases took a major toll on the Inca population.

Above *An Inca Quipu, used to record information by means of knots made in cords of different colours*

Below *The Spanish invaders attack the Inca city of Cuzco in 1533*

WORLD RELIGIONS

500–1500

Five world religions dominated the medieval era: Christianity, Judaism and Islam in the west, and Buddhism and Hinduism in the east. Christian communities existed in isolated areas in Asia and Africa, but by and large Christianity remained confined to Europe during this period. For a full discussion of Christianity in medieval Europe, see pages 110–111. Islam, born in the seventh century, was the most expansionist religion of the period, encroaching upon and affecting all the other major religions.

Above *Detail from* The Giving of the Keys to St Peter *by Pietro Perugino, a fresco painted in 1481–2 in the Sistine Chapel in Rome*

Islam

After the Prophet Muhammad established the Ummah in 622, Arab Muslim armies advanced with remarkable rapidity through Arabia and the Middle East, western Asia, North Africa and Spain. From the 11th century, Turkish Muslims carried Islam into Central Asia and India. However, only at the very beginning of its history was Islam a united force. As early as 681, the religion had split doctrinally between Sunni and Shia, and in the eighth century it began to fragment politically as the Islamic empire separated into independent emirates. A mysical movement within Islam, known as Sufism, also emerged in the eighth century.

Christianity

By 750, Islam had reduced the area under Christian domination to around half that it had been in 600. Christian communities in the Middle East, western Asia, North Africa and much of Spain found themselves living under the authority of Islamic governments. Although these communities were tolerated they were subjected to higher taxes, and there were strong financial and social incentives for Christians to convert to Islam. Many did, and so Christianity declined in these areas. The Crusades temporarily restored Christian control to the Holy Land between the 11th and 13th centuries, but Christianity was thrown firmly back on the defensive in the 15th century, when Muslim Ottoman Turks conquered the Byzantine Empire.

Judaism

By the medieval period, Jewish people were dispersed throughout Europe, North Africa, the Middle East and western Asia. There were even Jewish communities in

China and India. Jews in Christian Europe frequently faced persecution and expulsion. In 1144, the Jews of Norwich, England, were accused of using the blood of Christian children to make matzo (bread without yeast). This false accusation, the 'blood libel', spread all over Europe. In 1290, Jews were banished from England and in 1394 they were expelled from France. Jews were widely blamed for the Black Death of the 14th century and many were murdered by angry mobs. In Islamic countries, Jews were allowed to practise their faith but were forced to wear distinctive clothing and pay an annual tax. However, Jewish communities flourished under Islam. Great works of religious scholarship were written, and many Jews became successful merchants, traders and craftsmen. Jews who had prospered in Muslim Spain faced expulsion or forcible conversion after the Christian Reconquista in 1492.

Buddhism

Buddhism was severely weakened in India, the land of its birth, when many centres in the north-west were destroyed by White Huns in the sixth century. The revival of Hinduism in the seventh century (see panel) hastened its decline; but it was the series of devastating Muslim invasions, starting in the 11th century, that finally ended 1,700 years of Buddhism in mainland India. It continued to flourish in Sri Lanka and much of South-east Asia, although from the 13th century Islam became the dominant religion in Indonesia. In China, Buddhism reached a peak of popularity between the sixth and ninth centuries. Many schools developed, especially Chan (known in Japan as Zen) Buddhism and Pure Land Buddhism. Some 40,000 temples and monasteries were built during this period.

HINDUISM

Starting in the seventh century, Hinduism underwent a revival that took it away from the strict Brahmin-controlled ritual of Vedic times and helped lay the groundwork for the modern faith. Leading this revival were the so-called poet-saints of southern India, with their focus on a personal god and on practical forms of worship. They inspired the *bhakti* movements (movements of religious devotion), which soon spread north to embrace all India. Philosophers such as Shankara (*c.* 780–812) and Ramanuja (1017–1137) added strength to this revival, by incorporating popular aspects of Buddhism within Hinduism while continuing to stress the authority of the Vedic texts. After the Muslim conquest of India in the 13th and 14th centuries, many Hindus, especially those from the lower castes, converted to Islam. However, Hinduism remained India's dominant religion.

Left *In Sanskrit, 'bhakti' means 'devotion'. Bhakti movements were a form of worship dedicated to particular Hindu gods*

In the ninth century, there was a backlash against the power and wealth of the monasteries, weakening Buddhism, and in the 12th century, Confucianism (see page 101) became the official state religion of China. Buddhism was introduced to Tibet in the seventh century, where a unique form of the religion known as tantric Buddhism developed. By the 14th century, Buddhism had become the state religion of Tibet.

Dawn of a New Era

1494–1559

The end of the 15th century and the start of the 16th was a transformational time in European and world history, marking the start of what historians would later refer to as the 'early modern period'. Beginning in the 1490s, Europeans began to explore the world, opening up trade routes and colonizing new lands. Over the following centuries, different regions of the world would interact and influence each other to a greater extent than ever before. The new world powers that would dominate this era were Spain, Portugal, France, the Netherlands and England. Within Europe itself, the main themes and developments of the early modern period included the Reformation and the ensuing religious conflict, the emergence of absolute monarchies, the rise of the nation-state, the scientific revolution and the growth of capitalism and urbanization.

DOMINIONS OF THE HOUSE OF HABSBURG IN EUROPE. AT THE ABDICATION OF CHARLES V
Scale of Statute Miles

Above *A map of the Habsburg Empire following the Battle of Mühlberg in 1547*

By the 1490s, the monarchies of England, France and Spain had triumphed over internal adversaries and consolidated their positions within their realms (see pages 128–129). The old feudal bonds that had often worked to decentralize power during the medieval period were breaking down. Instead, power became concentrated at royal courts, which grew dramatically in size as kings offered positions to powerful nobles whose loyalties they wished to secure, and to lesser nobles eager for patronage and influence.

However, the image of strong kings and centralized states should not be exaggerated. Local and regional loyalties remained strong, national borders remained fluid, and the idea of the nation-state was still very new. Spain, for example, was composed of the kingdoms of Aragon, Castile and, from 1512, Navarre, which were themselves made up of smaller principalities. Political stablility in Spain depended on the monarch's willingness to respect the traditions and privileges of these component realms. France also remained fairly decentralized, with only 16 out of 25 provinces under direct royal control and with laws differing widely between regions.

The Habsburg Empire

In the early 1500s, the House of Habsburg – one of several ancient European dynasties – acquired through marriage a powerful empire that would dominate Europe for the next 200 years. The Habsburgs had ruled the Holy Roman Empire since the 13th century (see page 109). By the 16th century, the empire had been reduced to just Austria and Germany. Emperor Maximilian I (reigned 1493–1519) married into the Burgundian family and so added the Low Countries and Franche-Comté to the Habsburg dominions. Then Maximilian's son, Philip the Handsome married Joanna, heiress of Spain and its dominions, including Majorca, Sicily, Naples and the New World colonies. Thus, Philip's son, Charles V (reigned 1519–1556) inherited the largest European empire since the days of Charlemagne. Charles added Milan to his possessions in 1522 and repulsed French invasions of Naples, Florence and Piedmont, thereby confirming Habsburg dominance in Italy.

Charles V also shouldered responsibility for confronting the Ottoman threat to Christian Europe in the Mediterranean, Hungary and Austria, overcoming a siege of Vienna in 1529. In 1535 he gained a foothold in North Africa with the conquest of Tunis – lost, however, to the Ottomans in 1574. Charles ruled the Netherlands and Spain directly, while devolving responsibility for Austria to his brother Ferdinand. Through marriage, Ferdinand acquired Hungary and Bohemia in 1526, and from this time the Habsburgs split into two branches: a Spanish line descended from Charles, and an Austrian line descended from Ferdinand. The successor to the Spanish line was Philip II (reigned 1556–1598), who continued Charles' policy of developing the lucrative New World empire and using American silver to pay for military campaigns in Europe.

Italian wars

Even in this new era, monarchs remained dynasts at heart – even more so than heads of state. Thus, when the French king Charles VIII invaded Italy in 1494, he did so not for the glory of France but in pursuit of a supposed claim to the Kingdom of Naples through his paternal grandmother. The invasion turned out to be a disastrous failure, but it marked the beginning of a long series of devastating wars on the Italian peninsula that lasted until 1559 and threatened the legacy of the Renaissance. The wars involved, at various times, France, Spain, the Holy Roman Empire, England, Scotland, Switzerland, Venice, the Papal States and many of the Italian city-states. The minor dynastic dispute that gave rise to the wars was soon forgotten, and they evolved into a general struggle for power and territory among the various participants. By the time the conflict ended, Habsburg Spain had established itself as the dominant power in Italy and Europe, France was weakened, and many of the city-states of Italy had either been reduced to second-rate powers or collapsed completely.

TIMELINE

1494	*Charles VIII of France invades Italy*
1513	*The English defeat of the Scots at Flodden ensured English dominance over Scotland throughout the Tudor period*
1515	*France I of France defeats the Swiss at Marignano to control northern Italy*
1519	*Charles of Habsburg, king of Spain since 1516, is elected Holy Roman Emperor*
1525	*Francis I is captured by the Spaniards at Pavia and held for a year*
1529	*Vienna is besieged by the Ottoman Turks*
1556	*Charles V abdicates; he is succeeded by Philip II in Spain and by Ferdinand I as emperor*
1559	*Treaty of Cateau-Cambrésis ends Italian Wars.*

Above *Charles VIII, known as 'the Affable', King of France 1483–1498. He succeeded to the throne at the age of just 13*

THE AGE OF EUROPEAN EXPLORATION

1415–1600

The great era of European exploration that began in the 15th century arose primarily out of a desire to seek out new trade routes and partners. It was made possible by advances in cartography, navigation and shipbuilding. By the mid-1400s, much of the overland route between Europe and Asia was controlled by the Ottoman Turks. Muslims controlled the sea routes between Asia and the Middle East, and Venice had a monopoly on the trade in eastern goods, including spices, between Middle Eastern ports and the rest of Europe. Other European powers were eager to break into this lucrative trade by finding a direct sea route to the Indies.

Above *In this engraving by Johannes Stradanus (1523– 1605), Amerigo Vespucci holds the astrolabe which guided his course to America*

Portuguese exploration

Portugal led the way with a series of expeditions, beginning in 1415, to the west coast of Africa. In 1445, the westernmost tip of Africa was rounded. By 1460, the Portuguese had established trade links with modern-day Sierra Leone, bringing back gold, spices and slaves. In 1488, Bartholomew Dias rounded the Cape of Good Hope – Africa's southern tip – and sailed into the Indian Ocean, opening up the possibility of a sea route to India, which was finally achieved in 1497–1498 by Vasco da Gama.

Spain and Portugal in America

While the Portuguese were attempting to find an eastern sea route to the Indies, a Genoese sailor called Christopher Columbus was convinced a route lay to the west, across the Atlantic Ocean. In 1485, Columbus managed to persuade Queen Isabella of Spain to sponsor his expedition. He set out in 1492, making landfall in the Bahamas, the first European to set foot in the Americas since the Vikings in 1000. Columbus, vastly underestimating the distance between Europe and Asia, believed he had reached the Indies, and called the natives 'Indians'. He made four voyages across the Atlantic between 1492 and 1502, exploring the West Indies and the coast of Venezuela. He died in 1506, still unaware of his error.

The first man to the refer to these lands as a 'New World' was Amerigo Vespucci, an Italian navigator who explored the eastern coast of South America between 1499 and 1502. A German cartographer labelled the newly found continent 'America', a Latin version of Vespucci's first name. In 1500, two explorers, the Spaniard Vicente Yanez Pinzon and the Portuguese Pedro Alvares Cabral, independently discovered the future Portuguese colony of Brazil.

Determined to exploit their newly discovered territory, the Spaniards used their settlements on Hispaniola, Cuba and Puerto Rico as bases for expeditions of plunder and colonization. Their first mainland base was set up in Panama in 1509. The conquistador Vasco Núñez De Balboa led an expedition across the Isthmus of Panama to the Pacific Ocean in 1513 and became the first European to reach the eastern coast of the Pacific. In 1519–1521,

SHIPS AND NAVIGATION

The voyages of exploration of the 16th and 17th centuries were greatly facilitated by breakthroughs in ship design and navigation pioneered by the Portuguese. The invention of the caravel – a small, highly manoeuvrable two- or three-masted ship with a greater ability to tack than previous ship designs – enabled Portuguese sailors to make their long-distance voyages around the African coast. The art of navigation by the stars, using the quadrant and astrolabe – Arab-invented instruments – was greatly improved by the Portuguese during the 1480s. Sebastian Cabot was largely responsible for spreading these navigational techniques in England.

Hernán Cortés conquered the Aztec empire in Mexico (see page 147); and in the 1530s, Francisco Pizarro extended Spanish control over the Inca empire in Peru and Bolivia (see page 149). In 1519, the navigator Ferdinand Magellan led a Spanish-sponsored voyage around the southern tip of South America into the Pacific Ocean. Although Magellan was killed in the Philippines, one of his ships managed to complete the first circumnavigation of the globe, returning to Spain in 1522.

The Spanish also ventured to North America. In 1513 Juan Ponce de Leon explored the south-west coast of Florida. Then, in 1539, Hernando de Soto travelled through modern-day Georgia, Alabama, Mississippi and Arkansas. The following year, Francisco Vásquez de Coronado explored Arizona, New Mexico, Texas, Oklahoma and Kansas. These expeditions gave Europeans an idea of the enormity of the North American continent.

English and French in North America

The Spanish and Portuguese jealously guarded their newly established colonies and sea routes in Central and South America. So the other European maritime nations, primarily the English and French, focused their attention on North America,

always in the hope of finding a north-west passage to Asia. In 1497, John Cabot, an Italian navigator sponsored by King Henry VII of England, made landfall on the northern continent. He explored 640 km (400 miles) of the Canadian coastline between Newfoundland and Cape Breton. Cabot's son Sebastian went back there in 1509, travelling as far south as Cape Cod.

In the 1520s, France took the lead. Verrazano, sailing in the service of the French, explored further south, demonstrating that Cabot's and Columbus's discoveries were part of a single landmass. In the 1530s and early 1540s, Jacques Cartier began the exploration of Canada's interior, travelling up the St Lawrence River as far as Montreal. He was unsuccessful in his search for a north-west passage connecting the Atlantic and Pacific oceans, but helped advance French claims to the region. The English returned in the 1570s, with the voyages of Martin Frobisher and John Davis.

Above A caravel did not have much space for cargo but it was easy to manoeuvre in shallow bays

Above
Christopher Columbus (1451–1506), the sailor who discovered the New World

THE REFORMATION IN EUROPE

1517–1618

The Protestant Reformation was a powerful religious movement that swept through Europe during the 16th century, which split the Church, led to numerous wars, and vitiated papal authority. The Reformation arose in response to perceived corruption and abuses of power by the Roman Catholic Church in the late 15th and early 16th centuries, and was given added impetus by a general spirit of religious revivalism that desired a greater role for the laity in the life of the Church. The result was the translation of the Bible into the vernacular, and the founding of numerous new Churches, free of papal authority, under the general banner of Protestantism.

Left Portrait of Martin Luther *by Lucas Cranach the Elder (1472–1553), who was both his friend and acted as his unofficial portraitist*

levels had risen substantially since the European invention of printing in the 1450s. Many agreed with his criticisms and his call for a return to the original message of Christ's teachings. Both the Church and the Holy Roman Empire viewed Luther as a grave threat and he was excommunicated in 1521.

Martin Luther

The Reformation is generally considered to have begun on 31 October 1517, when a German monk named Martin Luther nailed 95 theses to the door of the castle church at Wittenburg in Saxony. Luther's theses were criticisms of indulgences – grants sold by the pope to individuals to partially remit the time they would have to spend in purgatory for their sins – one of the most notorious of the Church's corrupt practices. Luther's views quickly spread across Europe, helped by the fact that printed copies of his writings were widely circulated and that literacy

Below *Martin Luther's 95 theses, printed for him by Melchior Lotter. By the end of 1519, about 250,000 copies were in circulation*

Impact of Lutheranism

In Germany and other parts of Europe, there were widespread pro-Lutheran, anti-clerical uprisings by peasants and other members of the lower classes. Several German princes took up the popular Lutheran cause as a means of asserting their independence against both the empire and the pope. Charles V, the Holy Roman Emperor, vigorously opposed them, but could not prevent the formation of a league of Protestant estates at Schmalkalden in 1531. The emperor went to war against the league in 1546–1547, but in 1555, at the Peace of Augsburg, he was forced to grant its members the right to adopt Lutheran reform. The authority of the Church came under threat from other rulers, as well – including those with no love of Lutheranism. In 1527, Gustavus Vasa seized Church lands in Sweden, and in 1534, Henry VIII of England rejected papal authority and declared himself head of a new Church of England.

Luther's message was taken up and adapted by Church reformers elsewhere in Europe. In Switzerland, Ulrich Zwingli founded a reform movement that differed from Lutheranism over the meaning of the Eucharist. A more radical form of Protestantism was espoused by the Anabaptists, who renounced such Church practices as the swearing of oaths, tithe payments, the Mass and child baptism. However, the most influential Reformation figure after Luther was John Calvin, whose uncompromising approach to religious life dominated the Protestant movements in France (the Huguenots) by the 1540s and the Netherlands by the 1560s. In fact, Calvinism was the driving force behind the Dutch Revolt against Spanish rule (1566–1648). It was officially adopted by the Churches in Switzerland (1541), Scotland (1560s) and three German estates (1600s). In England, Elizabeth I's Settlement of 1559 finally established Protestantism as the national religion, following her sister Mary's brief reimposition of Catholicism (1553–1558). By the early 17th century, almost 40 per cent of the European population was Protestant.

Counter-Reformation

Quite early on, the Catholic Church had accepted the need for a concerted response to the Protestant challenge. The fightback, later termed the Counter-Reformation, began with the pope's adoption of the Jesuits (1540), an order devoted to preaching and charitable work, to spearhead a campaign to reform the Church from within. It was followed by the Council of Trent (1545–1563), which standardized the Mass throughout the Church and introduced various clerical reforms in the hope of tempting 'heretical' Protestants to return to the faith.

But the Counter-Reformation was about

FRENCH WARS OF RELIGION

In France, many members of the royal government and the nobility had become Huguenots, comprising a powerful political and religious force. From 1562, the Huguenots fought a series of conflicts with the monarchy, known as the French Wars of Religion. The crown's cause was helped by a surge of anti-Huguenot feeling in France, culminating in the St Bartholomew's Day Massacre of 1572 when some 30,000 Huguenots were slaughtered. The Edict of Nantes of 1598, which ended the wars, guaranteed religious toleration in France, but confirmed the Huguenots as a religious minority within a Catholic country.

more than reform and evangelism. In Philip II of Spain, the Church found a monarch willing to take military action against those countries that deserted the faith. Philip suppressed the revolt of the Moriscos (Moors who had converted to Christianity) in 1568. He attempted to put down the Dutch Revolt, recapturing most of the southern Netherlands. In 1587, when Elizabeth I executed her Catholic cousin Mary Queen of Scots, ending English Catholic hopes of a return to the faith under Mary, Philip II reacted by sending a large fleet to invade England in 1588. In this quest, he failed; his Armada were defeated as much by the weather and poor planning as by the English navy.

Below The invasion of England by the Spanish Armada was four years in the planning but the ships were not suitable for warfare at sea

EUROPE IN THE TIME OF THE THIRTY YEARS' WAR

1618–1648

For most of Europe, the first half of the 17th century was a time of religious, political and social upheaval, as well as economic hardship for many. The period was dominated by the long conflict in central Europe known as the Thirty Years' War (1618–1648). Monarchs tried to increase their power, often using religion as a means of rallying support or gaining political advantage. Religion remained a key source of tension, with the uncompromising attitudes of both the Calvinists and the Counter-Reformation Catholics frequently leading to conflict. Such a militaristic age required large, expensive armies, and increases in taxation at a time of population decline frequently risked destabilizing states.

Below *Gustavus Adolphus of Sweden lost his life leading a cavalry charge at the Battle of Lutzen in 1632*

Spain

In the early 17th century, Spain suffered an economic slump due to government overspending and a decline in American revenues. By 1609, finances were so poor that Spain was forced to agree a 12-year truce with the Netherlands, recognizing Dutch independence. In 1619, despite on-going economic difficulties, Spain provided financial support to the Austrian Habsburgs to fight the Protestants in Bohemia. Then, in 1621, Spain renewed its conflict with the Netherlands. To pay for this, the Spanish monarchy raised taxes, which sparked uprisings in Portugal (1640), Catalonia (1640–1653) and Naples (1647–1648). These rebellions, sponsored by the French, undermined Spain and marked the beginning of its decline as a world power.

France

The French king Henry IV (1589–1610) was certain that France would never be secure unless the Habsburgs, both Spanish and Austrian, were weakened, and he pursued strategies to that effect. This policy was continued under Cardinal Richelieu, France's powerful chief minister (1624–1642) and his successor Mazarin (ruled 1642–1661). The French enjoyed military success against the Habsburgs in Flanders, the Rhineland, Italy and the Pyrenees, and supported anti-Spanish revolts in Spanish territories (see above). While fighting against Catholics abroad, France fought against Protestants at home. When the Huguenots rose in revolt in 1627, Richelieu ordered the army to besiege the Huguenot stronghold of La Rochelle. The defenders held out for a year before capitulating.

Thirty Years' War

The Thirty Years' War began as a civil war between Protestants and Catholics in Bohemia (modern-day Czech Republic) in the Holy Roman Empire. Bohemian Protestants, rebelling against the Catholic emperor, threw two of the emperor's officials out of a window (the Defenestration of Prague). The rebels removed the Catholic king of Bohemia, Ferdinand, and replaced him with the Protestant prince Frederick. When Ferdinand became Holy Roman Emperor in 1619, his army decisively defeated the Bohemians and Catholicism was restored as the state religion. Alarmed by Bohemia's

BRITISH ISLES

England had struggled to control Ireland beyond a small area around Dublin (the Pale) since conquering it in the 12th century. During the English Reformation, Catholicism had become a focus for Irish opposition to English rule. James I and IV of England and Scotland (1603–1625) planted Ulster (a rebellious area in the north) with Protestant settlers in an attempt to prevent further uprisings. In England, Charles I threatened the Elizabethan Religious Settlement by introducing religious reforms that many of his subjects felt brought the Church of England too close to Roman Catholicism. His attempts to force through these reforms led to a disastrous war in Scotland (1639–1640) and a massacre of Ulster Protestants (1641). Charles' autocratic ways incurred the hostility of Parliament and sparked the English Civil War (1642–1649). The king was executed in 1649 and a Commonwealth was established under Oliver Cromwell, leader of the Parliamentary forces.

defeat, the Protestant king of Denmark, Christian IV, led an army against the Holy Roman Empire in Saxony (part of modern Germany). But the Holy League, a military alliance of German Catholic states, defeated the Danes at Lutter (1626) and Christian IV was forced to withdraw.

The Protestant king of Sweden, Gustavus Adolphus, concerned about the growing power of the Catholic emperor, intervened in the conflict in 1630. The Swedish army defeated the emperor's forces in two battles in 1631. Ferdinand's army, helped by Spanish allies, met the Swedes at Lutzen in 1632. The Swedes won, but Gustavus Adolphus was killed in battle. The Swedes fought on until their defeat at Nordlingen in 1634. By this time, the war had become less about religion and more of a general struggle for territory and power. Cardinal Richelieu of France, determined to weaken the Habsburgs, intervened on the side of the Protestants, although France was a Catholic nation. From 1635, a combined French and Swedish army won a long series of battles against the Holy Roman Empire.

In 1648, the Peace of Westphalia was signed. By this treaty, the French acquired Alsace and Lorraine; Sweden gained control of Western Pomerania, Bremen and Verden; and the Peace of Augsburg (1555) was confirmed, whereby each German prince could determine the religion of his state. For the first time, Calvinism was given legal recognition alongside Lutheranism and Catholicism. With the Peace of Westphalia, the Holy Roman Empire effectively ended as a political entity because the German states were granted almost complete sovereignty.

Above *Charles I was executed on 1 January 1649. His last words were 'I go from a corruptible to an incorruptible Crown, where no disturbance can be'*

TIMELINE

1605	*Failure of the Gunpowder Plot, a Catholic plot to assassinate James I of England*
1609	*12-year truce agreed between Spain and Netherlands*
1613–1625	*Plantation of Ulster*
1620	*Spain conquers the Lower Palatinate*
1627–1628	*Huguenot stronghold of La Rochelle is besieged and captured*
1629	*Ferdinand issues Edict of Restitution, demanding restoration of Church property to the Catholics, Catholic position in the empire*
1648	*Peace of Westphalia guarantees religious freedom to Calvinists.*

SWEDISH EXPANSION IN THE BALTIC

1521–1721

At the start of the 16th century, the Baltic region stood on the verge of great changes. Denmark, Norway and Sweden-Finland had been united under a single monarch, based at Copenhagen, since the Union of Kalmar (1397). Baltic trade – including the vitally important Northern European seaports, which handled the grain, copper, furs and naval supplies essential to the region's prosperity – had been under the control of the powerful Hanseatic League since the late 12th century. In the eastern Baltic, the Teutonic Knights, an order of German crusaders, had ruled over a region including East Prussia, Estonia, Livonia and Courland since the 13th century. The largest country in the region was Poland-Lithuania, created by a dynastic marriage in 1385.

Above *The poet Tannhäuser in the habit of the Teutonic Knights, from the* Codex Manesse, *a 14th-century illuminated manuscript*

Above *Fifteen-year-old Eric of Pomerania was crowned the first king of the Kalmar Union on 17 June 1397. The Union lasted 126 years*

Rise of Sweden

In the early 16th century, several developments began to threaten this status quo. The English and Dutch began to compete with the Hanseatic League for control of the seaports. In the east, the Teutonic Knights were in decline. In 1521, a Swedish nobleman, Gustav Vasa, supported by the Hanseatic city of Lübeck, led a successful rebellion against the Danish king Christian II, ending the Kalmar Union. Gustav Vasa became king of Sweden in 1523, initiating a period of Swedish expansionism. Under Gustav's rule, Sweden joined the English and Dutch in trying to break the Hanseatic monopoly on Baltic trade. Sweden overcame its disadvantages – a small population, poor fleet and ports that were icebound in winter – through efficient administration and strictly enforced military conscription.

In the 1520s, the eastern Baltic territories of the Teutonic Knights began to break up, leading to civil war in 1556–1557. Sweden competed with Denmark, Russia and Poland for control of these lands, and especially their ports. In the ensuing Livonian War (1557–1582), Sweden acquired Estonia, including the Hanseatic port of Reval, confirming its new status as a major power. Most of Livonia went to Poland. By the early 17th century, the Netherlands dominated most of the former Hanseatic trade network. Denmark, meanwhile, remained the principal military force in the Baltic and proved this by expelling Sweden from the North Sea port of Älvsborg in 1613. However, a disastrous military intervention in northern Germany in 1625–1629 (see pages 158–159) considerably weakened the Danish presence.

Swedish dominance

Internal turmoil in Russia, known as the Time of Troubles (1598–1613), enabled Sweden to acquire Karelia and Ingria from the Russians in 1617. Under Gustav Adolphus (reigned 1611–1632), Sweden attacked Poland, capturing Riga in 1621 and the whole of Livonia by 1625. By 1626, Sweden also controlled all the Prussian coastal ports and had now eclipsed Denmark as the leading Baltic power. The death of Gustav Adolphus at Lützen (1632) and their defeat at Nördlingen (1634) were setbacks, but Swedish military power was once again demonstrated by a successful war with Denmark (1643–1644), which handed Sweden Jämtland and Järjedalen, a 20-year lease on Halland and freedom of passage through the deep-water Sound. After a decisive victory over the imperial forces at Jankau (1645), Swedish gains at the Peace of Westphalia included West Pomerania and the ports of Stettin and Wismar.

To protect Sweden's control of its Prussian ports, Charles X (reigned 1654–1660) invaded Poland in 1655, occupying the country until 1660. Charles' success and Sweden's growing power prompted the formation of an anti-Swedish coalition of Russia, Denmark, Brandenburg and the Holy Roman Empire. The First Northern War (1655–1660) was inconclusive, although Sweden did manage to capture Denmark's possessions on the Swedish mainland.

Sweden's decline

By 1660, Sweden had reached the zenith of its power. With a population of only just over a million, finding the manpower to defend its growing empire was always likely to be a struggle. The first hint of its military vulnerability came in 1675, when a Swedish force was defeated by the Brandenburg army at Fehrbellin. In 1700, Denmark, Saxony, Poland and Russia united in a coalition against Sweden. In the Great Northern War (1700–1721), Sweden under Charles XII (1697–1718) at first enjoyed great success, defeating each of its enemies in rapid succession. In 1708, Charles invaded Russia, hoping to form an alliance with the Ukrainian Cossacks. He was lured south by the retreating Russians and, in 1709, the exhausted Swedes were defeated at Poltava by a force led by Tsar Peter I. Swedish hopes of imperial domination ended there. In the 1721 Treaty of Nystadt, Sweden surrendered Livonia and Estonia to Russia and handed part of Western Pomerania to Prussia.

Below Jan Chryzostom Pasek, Polish nobleman and soldier, painted in battle at Lachowicze in 1660 by Juliusz Kossak (1824–1899)

COLLAPSE OF POLAND

Poland had been a large and powerful state between the 14th and 16th centuries. However, rivalries among its nobles and a series of ineffective rulers sent it into decline, while costly wars ruined its economy. Starting in the latter half of the 17th century, the Polish state suffered increasingly from the expansionism of surrounding powers. Greatly weakened by the Swedish occupation (1655–1660), Poland lost the eastern Ukraine and Smolensk to Russia in 1667. By 1717, it had become a Russian protectorate. Then, between 1772 and 1795, Poland was divided among Russia, Prussia and Austria, and ceased to exist as an independent country.

THE EXPANSION OF RUSSIA

1492–1783

In the mid-15th century, the Russian state of Muscovy was a small, isolated principality in north-eastern Europe, paying tribute to the Tatars, descendants of the Turko-Mongols of the Golden Horde. Since the fall of Constantinople to the Ottomans (1453), this little state remained the only significant centre of Orthodox Christianity. Under Ivan III (reigned 1462–1505), it embarked on a campaign of expansion, annexing Ryazan and Yaroslavl (1463), Rostov (1474), Tver (1485) and its major rival, the Hanseatic member Novgorod (1478). Ivan completed the project in 1480 by liberating Muscovy from Tatar domination. By the end of Ivan's reign, Muscovy had grown into a nation: Russia.

Ivan the Terrible

Below *Detail of Tsar Ivan the Terrible by Viktor Vasnetsov, painted in 1897*

Vasily III (reigned 1505–1533) completed the annexation of Russian territories, absorbing Pskov (1510) and Ryazan (1521), and began to encroach on the Polish-Lithuanian territory, taking Smolensk in 1514. His son, Ivan IV 'the Terrible' (reigned 1533–1584) was a sickly three-year-old on his accession. A regency government introduced major military and administrative reforms, strengthening the state. In the 1550s, Russian forces conquered the Tatar khanates of Kazan and Astrakhan, vastly expanding Russian territory and opening trade routes to the Caspian Sea and Central Asia. Ivan took control of the government in the late 1550s and reversed many of the regency's reforms. He replaced trained administrators with cronies and sycophants and created the *oprichnina,* a collection of territories under his personal control that he could tax to fund his lavish court lifestyle. In the *oprichnina,* the semi-independent boyars (upper nobility) were forcibly removed from their estates, provoking rebellion. During the resulting civil war, a Crimean Tatar army sacked Moscow. Ivan's disastrous handling of the Livonian War (see page 160) cost Russia Estonia and Livonia. By the end of Ivan's appalling reign, the Russian state was close to collapse.

'Time of Troubles' — and after

The political instability that followed Ivan IV culminated in the 'Time of Troubles' (1604–1613), a period of chaos and civil war during which no one was in overall control. A Polish force opportunistically took over Moscow in 1610, but was ousted in 1612 by a coalition of boyars. A new tsar, Michael (reigned 1613–1645), was installed, the founder of the Romanov dynasty. Russia had been so weakened that it could not prevent the loss of Ingria and Karelia to Sweden in 1617, and of Smolensk and Chernigov to Poland in 1618. However, in the latter part of the century, it did become strong enough to reverse this trend. In the 1650s, while Poland was under Swedish occupation, Russia annexed the Ukraine; then, between 1667 and 1689, it regained Smolensk and Chernigov.

Expansion into Asia

During the late 16th and 17th centuries, Russian merchants and adventurers, together with Cossacks (frontier people), began to explore and settle the lands to the east of the Urals. In 1581 they conquered the Khanate of Sibir; and went on to build *ostrogs* (fortified trading posts) along the Irtysh and Ob, which ensured control of the lower reaches of both rivers by 1592. The country's frontier continued to expand eastwards in the 17th century. Settlers

fact-finding mission to Europe in 1697–1698. Back home, he promoted Russian industries such as mining, armaments and shipbuilding, although this attempt at industrialization had little effect upon Russia's largely rural economy or upon the living standards of peasants.

In the Great Northern War (1700–1721), Russia broke the power of Sweden, its mightiest rival in the Baltic, winning back Estonia, Livonia, Ingria and Karelia, and the coastal ports of Vyborg, Reval and Riga. Peter founded a new capital, St Petersburg, on the Baltic, to which he attracted French culture and English and Dutch trade. He also managed to open the Black Sea to Russian trade with the capture of the port of Azov from the Crimean Tatars in 1696. It was lost again in 1711, but regained under Anna (reigned 1730–1740) in 1739.

Peter the Great died in 1725, having laid the foundations for Russia's emergence as a great power and major player on the European stage – a process that was completed later in the century under Catherine II (reigned 1762–1796). Russia went on to play a part in European wars, almost destroying Prussia in the Seven Years' War (1756–1763) and partaking in the partition of Poland in 1772. Between 1768 and 1783, Russia expanded southwards, driving the Ottoman Turks from the lands surrounding the Black Sea.

Left This 17th-century book illustration shows a crowd at the Ipatiev Monastery begging Mikhail Romanov's mother to let him become their tsar

Below *Peter the Great, painted in 1838 by the French artist Paul Delaroche*

Above *Catherine II, Empress of all the Russias, shown in her coronation robes by Alexey Petrovich Antropov*

imposed Russian rule on the native populations of the new territories, enforced by garrisoned *ostrogs*. The Lena river was reached in 1632, the Indigirka in 1639 and the Kolyma in 1644. Russian explorers arrived at the Pacific coast by 1637, the Bering Strait in 1648 and Kamchatka by 1679. By 1800, they had established settlements in Alaska.

Peter the Great

By the time Peter I (later 'the Great') came to power in 1689, Russia had trebled its size in just one century by expanding right across northern Asia. Peter's main concern, however, was with the west. Determined to introduce western culture, ideas and technology to his country, Peter went on a

TIMELINE	
1480	*Muscovy wins independence from Tatars*
1565	*Ivan IV establishes oprichnina, bringing him into conflict with the boyars*
1571	*Moscow is sacked by Crimean Tatars*
1581	*Russia begins conquest of Siberia*
1613	*Founding of Romanov dynasty*
1637	*Russian explorers reach the Pacific coast of Siberia*
1655	*Russian ostrogs built along the Amur River*
1700–1721	*Great Northern War*
1768–1783	*Russian victories over the Ottoman Turks lead to conquests around the Black Sea.*

EUROPE IN THE AGE OF ABSOLUTE MONARCHS

1648–1715

The Peace of Westphalia (1648) that concluded the Thirty Years' War did much to settle the religious conflicts that had engulfed Europe since the Reformation. In most of the continent, the religious extremism that had threatened to destabilize states was largely vanquished. The nobility had evolved from power-hungry territorial magnates to tame courtiers, and the second half of the 17th century saw an expansion of royal power and the emergence of absolute monarchy.

Right The Protestant Dutch prince William of Orange became William III of England and Ireland and William II of Scotland

Britain

An exception to the trend towards absolute monarchy were the kingdoms of the British Isles. Here, the religious extremists – the Puritans – won their battle against the Crown (the English Civil War) and took power in the 1650s. When the Commonwealth collapsed in 1660, it was not replaced by an all-powerful king – hard-won rights and freedoms would not be so easily relinquished – but by a monarch constrained by a constitution. This constitutional settlement, and England and Scotland's status as Protestant countries, were threatened by the Catholic king James II (reigned 1685–1688). Protestant rebels invited the king's son-in-law, the Protestant ruler of the Netherlands, William of Orange, to invade. James fled, and William became king of England, Scotland and Ireland. In 1707, Scotland and England were united to form Great Britain.

Franco-Spanish War

The conflict between France and Habsburg Spain did not end with the Peace of Westphalia. The French had been weakened by the Fronde (1648–1653), a series of civil wars caused by Mazarin's increases in taxation to pay for the war. Spain took

advantage and won a string of victories in 1654–1656. France, helped by England, defeated the Spanish in Flanders and Dunkirk and won valuable territories in the subsequent Peace of the Pyrenees (1659). However, Spain, with territories in Italy and the Netherlands, remained the largest state in western Europe.

Louis XIV

The monarch who most personified absolutism was Louis XIV (reigned 1643–1715). He came to the throne aged four and did not assume power until Mazarin's death in 1661. Louis was a charismatic figure, who established good relations with

WAR OF THE SPANISH SUCCESSION (1701–1714)

When Charles ll of Spain died childless in 1700, he declared in his will that the crown should pass to Philip of Anjou, grandson of Louis XIV. The other European powers feared that France would now annex the Spanish Empire. In 1701, a Grand Alliance was formed to prevent Philip's succession, including Habsburg Austria, England, the Netherlands, Portugal and several German states. The Grand Alliance won a string of victories against the French between 1704 and 1708, yet French military strength was such that it was able to continue fighting effectively on a number of fronts. The situation changed in 1711 when the Archduke Charles – the allies' candidate for the Spanish throne – became Holy Roman Emperor and ruler of Austria. Austria's allies feared the prospect of Charles ruling both Spain and Austria and began to negotiate with France. In 1713, the Treaty of Utrecht confirmed Philip's succession to the Spanish throne while handing Spain's Italian and Dutch territories to Charles. Thus, the territories of the now-extinct Spanish Habsburgs were divided between the Bourbons (the French royal house) and the Austrian Habsburgs, maintaining a balance of power in Europe.

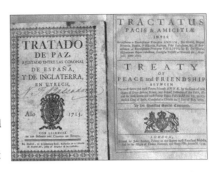

Above *A first edition of the Treaty of Utrecht, printed in 1713 in English, Spanish and Latin. The treaty marked the end of the War of Spanish Succession*

the nobility, bringing political stability to France. He was a great patron of the arts, and his military achievements were glorified in numerous paintings. In foreign policy, Louis was determined to win back lands formerly under French rule and to supplant Habsburg Spain as Europe's foremost power. This was not an unrealistic hope. France was western Europe's most populous state, with all the military potential that implied, and Louis immediately set about strengthening the army.

In the War of Devolution (1667–1668), France invaded the Spanish Netherlands and captured Lille. In the Dutch War (1672–1679), it invaded the Netherlands. The French army was halted when the Dutch opened the dykes. Louis was abandoned by his English allies and made enemies of several German princes, but France managed to acquire Franche-Comté, Freiburg and more of the Spanish Netherlands. Further territorial gains in the 1680s, and a programme of fortress construction, strengthened France's frontiers. However, Louis' aggression provoked other powers to form alliances against him. By 1690, France was at war with Austria, Bavaria, Britain, the Netherlands, Spain and Savoy-Piedmont, Italy's leading power. Although the country held its own in this conflict and in the subsequent War of the Spanish Succession (see panel), the pressure of a generation of almost constant warfare took its toll. By the time Louis died in 1715, France was exhausted and economically depleted.

Below *Louis XIV was known as the Sun King, an autocratic monarch around whom France and the court revolved like the planets round the sun*

18TH-CENTURY EUROPE

1715–1783

By the end of the War of the Spanish Succession (see page 165), a new order had become apparent in Europe. Spain, once Europe's pre-eminent state, had been reduced to little more than a battleground for the ambitions of others. France, exhausted by so many wars, had been weakened, but remained a leading player. The Netherlands, badly over-extended by the wars, would never regain the economic and political power of its 17th-century golden age. Britain, however, had proved itself a potent economic and military power; and Austria, as inheritor of the Spanish Habsburg territories in the Netherlands and Italy, had emerged as a new force in central Europe. From 1740, a power struggle between Austria and Prussia would dominate the lands of the Holy Roman Empire.

TIMELINE

1717–1720	War of the Quadruple Alliance
1721	Robert Walpole, Britain's first prime minister, ushers in a period of economic growth
1733–1738	War of the Polish Succession
1740–1748	War of the Austrian Succession
1756–1763	Seven Years' War.

Above *Philip V of Spain with his second wife, Elisabetta Farnese, and his family, painted by Louis-Michel van Loo*

After 1714, the new concept of a 'balance of power' ensured that no state could dominate Europe, as Spain had done in the 16th century and France in the 17th. Thus when Philip V, the Bourbon king of Spain seized Sardinia from Austria and Sicily from Savoy in 1717–1718, a Quadruple Alliance of Britain, Austria, France and the Netherlands formed against him, forcing Spain to relinquish these gains in 1720.

Wars of succession

In an echo of the dynastic power struggles of previous ages, the War of the Polish Succession (1733–1738) saw the Bourbons and Habsburgs doing battle for control of Poland. When Augustus II, king of Poland, died in 1733, Polish nobles elected Stanislas Leszczynski, father-in-law of Louis XV of France, as their new monarch. This was supported by France, who hoped a Bourbon Franco-Polish alliance would balance Austrian and Russian power. For the same reason, the succession was opposed by Russia and Austria, who forced Poland to accept Augustus, Elector of Saxony, as king instead. France and Spain went to war against Austria, Russia and several German states. France won most of the battles and acquired territories in Germany and Italy from Austria, but at the Treaty of Vienna (1738), Augustus remained the Polish king. The war exposed Poland's impotence in the new European order, confirmed by the First Partition of 1772, when the country was carved up by Russia, Austria and Prussia.

The War of the Austrian Succession (1740–1748) was caused by the death of Charles VI, ruler of Austria, who was succeeded by his daughter Maria Theresa. Because German law required a male successor, her claim was disputed and Austria soon came under attack from Frederick II of Prussia, who conquered Silesia. France, Spain, Bavaria and Sardinia joined the assault, but Austria, under Maria's courageous leadership and with support from Britain and the Netherlands, held out and was able to retain most of its territories, apart from Silesia.

Seven Years' War

In her determination to recover Silesia, Maria Theresa of Austria formed an anti-Prussian alliance with tsarina Elizabeth of Russia and, through clever diplomacy, with France. Frederick II, expecting an Austrian attack, negotiated an alliance with Britain. In 1756, he launched a pre-emptive strike against Saxony, Austria's ally, starting the Seven Years' War (1756–1763). Despite this conquest, Frederick's prospects appeared bleak, as Austria, France, Russia, Sweden and most of the German states aligned themselves against him. The Prussian king moved decisively, knowing speed was his only hope. In 1757, his troops routed the French at Rossbach, Saxony, then crushed the Austrians at Leuthen, Silesia. The following year, Britain inflicted further defeats on the French. The Prussians had

overreached themselves, however, and were now close to exhaustion. Fortunately for them, their enemies did not coordinate their attacks. In 1762, the tsarina died and was succeeded by Peter III, an enthusiastic admirer of Frederick, who concluded a separate peace with him. This turn of fate saved Prussia and by the terms of the 1763 treaty, it retained Silesia.

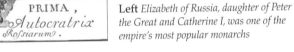

ELISABETA ∫*Imperatrix et* *Omnium* **PRIMA,** *Autocratrix* *Rossiarum.*

Above *Maria Theresa of Austria married Francis I, Holy Roman Emperor, and had 16 children. Her youngest daughter was Marie Antoinette, future wife of Louis XIV of France*

Left *Elizabeth of Russia, daughter of Peter the Great and Catherine I, was one of the empire's most popular monarchs*

RISE OF PRUSSIA

One of the most significant and unlikely developments of the 18th century was the rise of Prussia to major power status. Brandenburg-Prussia was a collection of territories dispersed across northern Europe; it included eastern Pomerania, Brandenburg and East Prussia, ruled over by the Hohenzollern dynasty. It had a small population and few natural resources, yet its rulers, Frederick I (reigned 1713–1740) and Frederick II 'the Great' (reigned 1740–1786) proved able and ambitious administrators. They built a government based on discipline and authority, whose first priority was to support the Prussian army, enabling Prussia to perform well above expectations on European battlefields. The rest of Europe woke up to Prussia's military might when it seized Silesia from Austria in 1740, then managed to hold onto it against a powerful coalition during the subsequent Seven Years' War.

THE RISE OF EUROPEAN CAPITALISM

1492–1775

The dramatic rise of Europe during the early modern period to a position of global economic dominance can be explained by two factors: firstly, European exploration, which led to the discovery of new lands to the west and trade routes to the east; and secondly, the growth of merchant capitalism. This early, pre-industrial form of capitalism developed in European cities such as Venice, Antwerp, Genoa, Amsterdam and London, where sophisticated banking and credit systems were established, providing finance for long-distance trade, as well as for kings and governments. By the late 18th century, with the development of industrial methods of production and the arrival of factories, merchant capitalism gave way to modern, industrial capitalism.

Antwerp

In 1492, Europe's dominant economic powers were Venice and the Hanseatic League, each controlling a network of trade routes. This changed in the early 1500s when Portuguese ships began arriving in the Flemish city of Antwerp, bringing spices from the East Indies, and thereby breaking the Venetian monopoly of the spice trade. At the same time, Hanseatic merchants started to face serious competition from their Flemish and English counterparts over control of the lucrative Baltic grain trade. In the first half of the 16th century, Antwerp became the centre of international trade. The city was packed with merchants and financiers, and cargo from all over the world would pass through its port: Spanish ships bearing American silver; Portuguese vessels laden with pepper and cinnamon; and Dutch and Flemish ships carrying Baltic grain to southern Europe.

Below Pirates Attacking a British Navy Ship, *by Willem van de Velde the Younger (1633-1707)*

Dutch 'Golden Age'

In 1557, Antwerp's banking system was damaged by Spain's bankruptcy, and over the next few decades the city became engulfed in the religious wars of the Netherlands. Genoa took Antwerp's place as Europe's leading financial centre. Then, in the early 1600s, Genoa itself was supplanted by Amsterdam. The fall of Antwerp in 1585 had led to a massive migration of merchants and bankers to the port of Amsterdam, where a stable and flexible banking system soon developed. This, combined with Dutch seafaring skills, the largest merchant fleet in Europe, and an abundance of cheap energy from windmills and peat, enabled Amsterdam and the Netherlands to dominate European and Asian trade for the rest of the century.

Trading rivalries

During the second half of the 17th century, with the decline of Spain and Portugal, a growing commercial rivalry developed between Europe's leading economic powers, England and the Netherlands, sharpened by their governments' willingness to adopt mercantilist policies (a form of protectionism designed to keep all wealth derived from the colonies within their own borders). This resulted in three Anglo-Dutch wars between 1652 and 1674. The Dutch emerged victorious in the second and third conflicts, confirming their status as Europe's strongest naval power.

France, too, tried to compete for economic supremacy, but its efforts were hampered by its late arrival to the race for colonial territory and trade; and also by its inability to commercialize its agricultural and manufacturing sectors. During the 17th century, the English and Dutch were able to improve agricultural productivity, and thereby release labour for manufacturing, by the enclosure of common land, improved crop rotation and animal husbandry techniques, and the drainage of marshland. French peasant traditions, however, proved strongly resistant to such reforms.

English efforts to supplant the Netherlands finally began to take effect in the 1680s. As the Dutch economy started to stagnate, the English, with their stable banking model and established system of national debt, benefited from huge overseas investment, much of it from the Dutch themselves. A further boost came in 1685 when Louis XIV revoked the Edict of Nantes, prompting a flood of Huguenot refugees to southern England; these immigrants brought with them expertise in brewing, papermaking, glass making, ceramics and silk weaving.

TIMELINE

1501	*First Portuguese ships laden with East Indies spices arrive at Antwerp*
1535	*Antwerp becomes the distribution centre for Spanish-American silver*
1585	*Antwerp is sacked by Spain. Its merchants and bankers move to Amsterdam*
1627	*A second Spanish bankruptcy damages Genoa's banking system*
1693	*The British National Debt is established*
1769	*Richard Arkwright invents the spinning frame*
1776	*James Watt's improvements to the steam engine lead to the industrialization of weaving and milling production.*

SLAVE TRADE

The economies of the European empires established in the Americas between the 16th and 18th centuries were highly dependent on slave labour. Many of the native population died from European diseases, so the Spanish and the Portuguese began importing slaves from West Africa. In the 17th century, as the British, Dutch and French acquired colonies in North America, they sought labour for their coffee, cotton and tobacco plantations, and so the African slave trade expanded enormously. Between the mid-16th and mid-19th centuries, Europeans shipped more than 12 million black slaves from Africa to the Americas. It is estimated that some two million died en route.

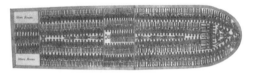

Right *The infamous plan of how to carry the maximum number of slaves on a ship*

Industrialization

Whereas the Netherlands was able to triumph in the age of merchant capitalism, it lacked the population and natural resources to compete in the era of industrialization. Throughout the 18th century, Britain's exploitation of coal produced a new and plentiful form of energy at a time when Dutch peat sources were becoming exhausted. The British development of the steam engine as a source of mechanical power, and the mechanization of the textile industry in the 1770s, gave rise to the first factories, heralding a new age of industrialized production.

Below *The development of the steam engine transformed the progress of industrialization*

THE EUROPEAN ENLIGHTENMENT

1650–1800

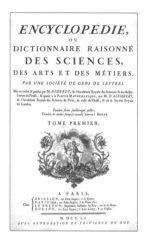

Above *The* Encyclopédie, *published in France 1751–1772, encompassed 35 volumes*

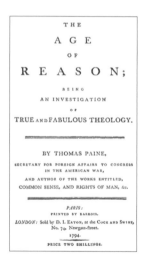

Above *Thomas Paine's* Age of Reason *(1793–1794) challenged Christian doctrines*

The religious wars of the 17th century, and the devastation they wrought, prompted many of Europe's intellectuals to begin questioning the notion that blind faith was the best route to wisdom and a contented life. Inspired by the remarkable discoveries in science, or 'natural philosophy' as it was then known, educated people began to conclude that perhaps the scientific method, with its emphasis on the use of reason, could offer a surer path to knowledge, as well as to a more peaceful and harmonious existence. The idea that reason should be the principal guide in human affairs formed the basis of a movement known as the Enlightenment, which dominated European thought from the late 17th century until around 1800.

The power of reason, philosophers argued, was unique to humans, and the key to human advancement. Reason could be applied to beneficial effect not just to the sciences but to philosophy, social organization, politics, education, law and the arts. They contrasted reason with the ignorance, dogma, superstition and unquestioning acceptance of authority that characterized the Middle Ages. The use of reason, they argued, was seen at its most effective in the field of mathematics.

Mathematics

Enlightenment thinkers were very influenced by mathematics, which they saw as the model for all scientific enquiry. By the late 16th century, mathematics had become a major discipline in most European universities. Italian Renaissance painters and architects used the principles of geometry to represent perspective. In the physical sciences, the Italian Galileo Galilei (1584–

1642) used mathematics to reveal the law of falling bodies; as did the Englishman Isaac Newton (1643–1727) when he formulated the laws of gravitation and motion. Philosophers began to view the universe as a mathematical construction. They concluded that mathematics – a process that begins with an axiom, or self-evident truth, then moves through a series of self-evident steps to a conclusion – should drive progress in all the sciences so that, ultimately, the mysteries of nature would lie revealed as a simple set of laws.

Networks of scholarship

By the mid-17th century, developments in print and paper production and the growth of literacy and learning were bringing information and ideas to ever larger numbers, particularly in the cities. This broadened the influence of the Enlightenment. As well as universities like Cambridge, the royal courts of Germany and Italy became centres of scientific innovation, as did institutions such as the Accademia dei Lincei in Rome and the Royal Society in England. Important advances were made in anatomy, astronomy, chemistry and physics.

TECHNOLOGY

The scientific advances of the Enlightenment period were made possible by the development of more sophisticated instruments with which to observe and manipulate natural phenomena. The invention of the microscope in the early 17th century furthered the studies of zoology and botany; while the invention of the telescope around the same time transformed the study of astronomy. The development of pumps in the 1640s, for moving fluids from lower to higher pressure, proved to scientists that a vacuum was possible, contrary to the views of the ancient Greek thinker Aristotle. Pump designers such as Denis Papin were influential in the early history of the steam engine. The Englishman Thomas Newcomen invented the first practical steam engine in 1712, which was used to drain water from mine workings.

Above *The invention of the microscope made biological discoveries possible*

Networks of correspondence linked scholars in different cities, and many of these learned letters were printed in philosophical journals, which first appeared in the 1660s.

In the *Encyclopédie*, published in France between 1751 and 1766, leading Enlightenment scholars collaborated to produce a vast work encapsulating the current state of human knowledge. The editors hoped the encyclopedia would help in the process of banishing medieval dogma and superstition and replace it with the Enlightenment ideals of tolerance and rationalism. The work even went so far as to define religion as a branch of philosophy and not the ultimate source of knowledge, leading the French government to place it under an official but ineffectual ban for many years.

Political ideas

Enlightenment thinkers such as Voltaire and Montesquieu wished to apply the principles of reason to society and politics. Voltaire campaigned for causes that seem unexceptional today but were radical at the time; they included freedom of worship, civil liberties, the right to a fair trial and the abolition of judicial torture, censorship and serfdom. Montesquieu believed that human nature was subject to scientific laws, just like the rest of the universe. He speculated that climate had an influence on human temperament and that a nation's ideal government depended on its climate. Cooler climates favoured democracy, while the only workable government in hot countries, he concluded, was despotism. Montesquieu's absolute faith in reason was typical of Enlightenment thought. The ideas of Enlightenment thinkers such as Voltaire, Denis Diderot, Jean-Jacques Rousseau, John Locke and Thomas Hobbes were to have an important influence on the leaders of the American and French Revolutions (see pages 196–197 and 198–199).

Above *Voltaire was known for his wit as well as his pursuit of social reform and freedom of worship*

THE RISE OF THE OTTOMAN EMPIRE

1492–1640

The Ottoman dynasty was founded by Osman I, a Turkish Muslim warrior based in Anatolia in the early 1300s. Over the next 200 years the Ottomans built one of the world's most powerful empires. At its height, in the 16th century, the empire controlled much of south-western Asia, the Middle East, south-eastern Europe and North Africa. Ottoman military dominance during this period was due to superior artillery, a powerful navy and an effective system of recruitment and training. Particularly feared were the Janissary regiments – the children of Balkan Christians, surrendered as tribute, trained under strict discipline and fiercely loyal to the sultan.

Above *This painting by the Turkish miniaturist Mohammed Bey shows the Turkish attack on Belgrade on 4 July 1456 under the leadership of Mehmet II*

Ottoman expansion

The Ottoman conquest of Constantinople in 1453 ended the Byzantine Empire and secured the Ottoman Empire's status as the dominant power in south-eastern Europe and the eastern Mediterranean. This marked the beginning of an era of expansion in which the empire extended its borders deep into Europe, the Middle East and North Africa. The empire prospered under a series of effective sultans, including Mehmet II (reigned 1451–1481) and Selim I (reigned 1512–1520). In 1516 Selim attacked and destroyed the Mamluke Sultanate, leading to the annexation of Syria, Palestine, Egypt and the two holy cities of Islam, Mecca and Medina. This was enough to persuade the *sharif* of Mecca to declare the Ottoman sultan caliph.

Below *The Emperor Suleiman the Magnificent, in a portrait believed to have been painted by Titian in about 1530*

Suleiman the Magnificent

The Ottomans reached the height of their power under Suleiman the Magnificent (reigned 1520–1566). Suleiman personally led the Ottoman armies in their wide-ranging conquests, capturing Belgrade (1521), Rhodes (1522) and large parts of North Africa. His victory at Mohács in 1526 reduced Hungary to vassal status. Transylvania, Wallachia and Moldavia also became tributary states during Suleiman's reign. In 1529, Suleiman even laid siege to Vienna, although over-extended supply lines and a severe winter forced an Ottoman retreat. Under Suleiman, the Ottomans became a powerful naval force. Their domination of much of the Mediterranean allowed them to conquer Algeria (1541), Tunis (briefly in 1535 and then again 1574), Nice (1543) and Cyprus (1571). Suleiman was also an accomplished poet and a great supporter of the arts. Under his patronage, Ottoman architecture reached its zenith.

The Ottoman conquests in the Levant placed them at the hub of a vast network of overland trade routes. From the east came spices, silks and porcelain; from Africa, gold dust, slaves and precious stones; and from Europe, textiles, glass and timber. Control of this network made the Ottomans enormously wealthy and won them political leverage in Europe, especially from the Venetians, who were eager for a share of trade with the east.

Ottomans in Europe

By the 1540s, the Ottomans had become significant players on the European stage, joining France, England and the Netherlands in a military alliance against Habsburg Spain and Austria. Major campaigns were conducted against Austria in the 1540s and 1560s. However, after 1568, the Ottoman-Habsburg frontier on the Danube stabilized and would barely change until the 19th century. In 1571, an alliance of Christian European states achieved a decisive naval victory against the Ottoman fleet at Lepanto. Although the Ottomans rebuilt their fleet within six months, the loss of so many experienced sailors at Lepanto had damaged their fighting effectiveness and prevented further Ottoman expansion in the Mediterranean.

Suleiman's reign was the high-water mark of Ottoman military dominance, even though it remained a major expansionist power until 1683. From the later 16th century, the Ottomans began to fall behind Europe in terms of naval strength and battlefield technology. The development of alternative sea routes to Asia by Portugal,

WARS WITH THE SAFAVIDS

Europe was saved from further Ottoman expansion largely because, for most of the 16th and early 17th centuries, the empire was preoccupied in a protracted conflict with the Safavid Empire of Persia – a Shia empire and therefore a natural rival to the Sunni Ottomans. Under Selim I, the Ottomans won a major victory over the Safavids at Chaldiran in 1514, which gave them control of Kurdistan. Then, in 1535, Suleiman the Magnificent captured Baghdad, annexing Mesopotamia and awarding the Ottomans access to the Persian Gulf. These advances were reversed in a debilitating war between 1602 and 1618, when the Safavids reconquered Mesopotamia and Kurdistan. Murad IV (reigned 1623–1640), the last sultan to lead his forces from the front, led a revival, recapturing Yerevan in 1635 and Baghdad in 1639.

Spain, France, the Netherlands and England also undermined the Ottoman economy. The Ottomans were further weakened by a series of rebellions in Anatolia, the Jelali revolts; these occured in the late 16th and early 17th centuries, and again in the 1650s. A further problem was caused by the Janissaries, the sultan's elite troop who, by the 17th century, had become over-powerful in Ottoman politics and frequently rebelled against sultans they disapproved of.

Above *The Knights of St John defending Rhodes from the Ottoman armies, 1522*

TIMELINE

1514	*Selim I beats Safavids at Chaldiran*
1516	*Selim I beats Mamlukes at Marj Dabiq*
1533	*Suleiman makes peace with Ferdinand of Habsburg*
1574	*Ottomans recapture Tunis, completing conquest of North African coast*
1622	*Sultan Osman II is murdered by Janissaries*
1639	*Treaty of Qasr-I Shirin establishes a permanent border between Ottoman and Safavid Empires*
1639	*Murad attempts to reduce Janissary power by abolishing the Christian children tribute system (devshirme).*

THE DECLINE OF THE OTTOMAN EMPIRE

1640–1783

The decline of the Ottoman Empire was a very gradual process, punctuated by frequent revivals, and was almost imperceptible at first. The empire's agriculture-based economy remained strong and self-sufficient, and under effective leaders such as the Köprülü dynasty of grand viziers, the Ottomans were still a formidable force on the world stage. Slowly, however, institutional problems within the empire, and its dwindling status as a centre of international trade, made the Ottoman decline increasingly apparent.

Above *Roxelana, or Khourrem, once a Polish captive in Suleiman the Magnificent's harem, became his legal wife and the mother of his heir*

Rebellions

Between 1640 and 1656, the empire suffered a succession of internal crises: rebellion in the provinces; discontent in the army as inflation caused soldiers' wages to decline; and problems of succession due to a lack of mature candidates for the sultanate. Ottoman naval weakness was exposed by its failed attempt to capture Crete from Venice in 1645 and the subsequent blockade of the Dardenelles by the Venetian fleet, threatening Constantinople itself. These years were part of a period known as the 'Sultanate of Women', when the 'regent mothers' in the sultan's harem became politically powerful.

Male authority was restored in 1656 with the accession of Mehmet Köprülü to the office of Grand Vizier (chief minister to the sultan). In his brief five-year term, the vizier rooted out corruption, sacked incompetent officials, put down several rebellions, strengthened the empire's defences against Austria and brought the Cretan campaign to a successful conclusion. Mehmet was succeeded by his son, Köprülü Fazil Ahmed (ruled 1661–1676), under whom the Ottomans captured Podolia in the Ukraine from Poland and completed the conquest of Crete.

Revival and retreat

This evidence of revival emboldened Fazil Ahmed's successor, Kara Mustafa Pasha (ruled 1676–1683), to launch another attack on Vienna. However, the siege of 1683 was poorly planned and the Ottoman army was routed by a combined German and Polish force. It proved to be the last Ottoman assault on Christian Europe. Following Kara Mustafa's death by execution, the empire suffered a further spell of poor leadership, corruption and internal division. Military defeats mounted. Between 1684 and 1690, Austrian armies overran Hungary and Transylvania, capturing Belgrade in 1688, while the Venetians occupied the Peloponnese and Russia threatened Azov.

A brief Ottoman revival began under Grand Vizier Mustafa Köprülü in 1690. He led a counter-offensive that drove the Austrians out of Transylvania and Hungary and back across the Danube. However, the following year Mustafa was killed in a major Ottoman defeat at Slankamen. In 1696, Peter the Great (of Russia) took Azov, and the following year an Ottoman army was ambushed by the Austrians at Zenta in northern Serbia, causing great losses. In a peace treaty two years later, the chastened Ottoman empire was forced to surrender long-held territory, including Hungary and Transylvania to Austria, and Podolia to Poland. This marked the beginning of a gradual Ottoman retreat from the Balkans.

Institutional and economic problems

By the early 18th century, the Ottoman Empire was beset by internal problems. Tax revenues from the provinces had declined, as thousands left the countryside for towns and cities. Short of cash, the sultans sold the right to collect taxes from state-owned lands to private entrepreneurs. For many, this was a licence to rob. Banditry became common in the provinces and the government struggled to maintain order. As military conquests dried up, the system of recruiting Janissaries, the devshirme (which involved taking the children of conquered peoples) began to collapse. The Janissary corps grew increasingly powerful and corrupt, preferring the luxuries of court life to the rigours of campaigning. In addition, the empire faced a painful economic decline. Ottoman trade routes to the east, via the Red Sea and Persian Gulf,

were increasingly bypassed as ever more Asian goods were transported round the Cape of Good Hope to Amsterdam or London. And Russia's eastward expansion had opened up an alternative trans-Siberian trade route to China, bypassing the traditional Ottoman and Safavid caravan routes.

Left *Kara Mustafa Pasha, a Grand Vizier and military leader who fought to maintain Ottoman dominance*

Ottoman defeat

Despite these difficulties, the Ottomans remained a considerable fighting force. With their victory over Tsar Peter the Great at Prut River in 1711, they recovered Azov and stalled – for the time being, at least – Russia's bid to dominate the Black Sea area. From 1714, the Ottomans once again went on the offensive in Europe, capturing the Peloponnese from Austria, then Belgrade in 1739 (having lost it in 1717). However, these achievements proved ephemeral, disguising the reality that the Ottoman Empire was falling seriously behind its rivals in terms of military tactics and technology; a fact brutally demonstrated in a crushing defeat delivered by the Russians in 1770, resulting in the destruction of the Ottoman navy and the final loss of the Crimea. By the end of the 18th century, most Ottoman territories beyond the empire's heartland in Anatolia and the Middle East were effectively independent.

Below *The Janissary corps were the powerful professional soldiers of the Ottoman Empire*

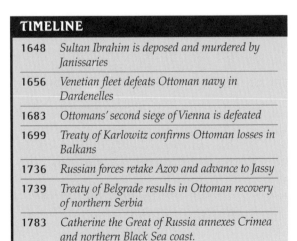

TIMELINE	
1648	*Sultan Ibrahim is deposed and murdered by Janissaries*
1656	*Venetian fleet defeats Ottoman navy in Dardenelles*
1683	*Ottomans' second siege of Vienna is defeated*
1699	*Treaty of Karlowitz confirms Ottoman losses in Balkans*
1736	*Russian forces retake Azov and advance to Jassy*
1739	*Treaty of Belgrade results in Ottoman recovery of northern Serbia*
1783	*Catherine the Great of Russia annexes Crimea and northern Black Sea coast.*

SAFAVID PERSIA AND THE RISE OF MUGHAL INDIA

1500–1779

During the 16th century, powerful states emerged in Persia and India. The Safavid Empire of Persia grew rapidly after its establishment by Shah Ismail, but encountered more than its match in the mighty Ottoman Empire to the west. A combination of weak leadership and foreign invasion ended Safavid Persia in 1722. The Mughals, a Turkic people from Ferghana, invaded northern India in the early 1500s, where they founded a powerful empire that would endure until the late 18th century.

Rise of Safavid Persia

During the 15th century, Persia was a divided land, with rival dynasties ruling over its different regions. One of these dynasties, based in the north-west, was that of the Safavids, founded by Shaikh Safi of Ardabil in the early 14th century. His descendent, Ismail I (reigned 1501–1524) conquered the city of Tabriz, then the rest of Persia – the first time it had been unified as an independent state since the seventh century. Ismail took the title *shah* (king) and ruled the country from Tabriz.

Under Ismail's rule, Persia expanded to the north-east, capturing Khorasan from the Uzbeks (a Turkic people from Central Asia) and, to the west, occupying the area between the Caspian Sea and the Persian Gulf, bringing the Safavids into direct confrontation with the Ottoman Empire. Ismail established Shia Islam as the state religion and stressed religious differences with the Sunni Ottomans as a motive for going to war with them. In fact, the ensuing 150-year long conflict was over control of territory, particularly the fertile plains of Mesopotamia. In a seesawing of military fortunes, the Safavids won Mesopotamia in 1509, lost it in 1534, won it back in 1623, then lost it permanently in 1638.

Above *A detail of a fresco showing a courtly scene dating from the era of Safavid ruler Shah Abbas*

Decline of the Safavids

The Safavid Empire reached its cultural and territorial height under Shah Abbas I (reigned 1588–1629). During this period, the Safavids won back many of the lands they had lost to the Ottomans, captured Kandahar from the Mughals and inflicted a decisive defeat on the restive Uzbeks in Khorasan. Abbas created a new Safavid capital at Esfahan, which he adorned with numerous mosques, palaces, schools, roads and bridges. He promoted local industry – carpet-making and silk-weaving – and encouraged trade with England and the Netherlands.

After the reign of Abbas II (1642–1666), the Safavid Empire slid into decline. A series of ineffective shahs funded their luxurious personal lifestyles by raising taxes and nurturing a culture of sycophancy and corruption. When Shah Sultan Hosain (reigned 1694–1722) attempted forcibly to convert the Afghans in eastern Persia to Shia Islam, it provoked an uprising. An Afghan army descended on Esfahan, capturing and executing the shah and ending Safavid rule in Persia. Persia suffered a period of foreign occupation and internal division until the rise of a military leader, Nadir Shah, in the late 1720s. He managed to expel the Afghans in 1729 and in 1732, he drove the Ottomans from Mesopotamia. By 1738, he had conquered Afghanistan, and the following year he captured Delhi from the Mughals. His empire, briefly powerful, disintegrated just as rapidly after his assassination in 1747. Persia remained divided until the rise of the Qajar dynasty in 1779.

Rise of Mughal India

In the late 15th and early 16th centuries, Uzbeks moved eastward into Ferghana, homeland of the Mughals, descendants of Timur's Mongols. The Mughals, driven out of Ferghana, moved southwards. Under their leader Babur (reigned 1501–1530), a direct descendent of Genghis Khan and Timur, the Mughals conquered Kabul in 1504. They used the city as a base for a series of raids on India starting in 1519. Then, in 1526, they launched a full-scale invasion.

At the time, India was a patchwork of warring Hindu and Muslim states. The most powerful were the Muslim Delhi Sultanate, ruled by the Lodi dynasty, which dominated the north; and the Hindu empire of Vijayanagara, which controlled a large area of the south. Babur's Mughals defeated Ibrahim Lodi of the Delhi Sultanate at Panipat in 1526 and occupied the Lodi capital at Agra. Babur went on to conquer much of the rest of northern India; however, he died before he could consolidate his empire.

Babur's son Humayun (reigned 1530–1540; 1555–1556) captured the fortress of Champanir in Gujarat in 1535, but suffered defeat by the Afghan leader Sher Khan Sur in 1540, which nearly brought the fledgling Mughal Empire to an end. The Surs occupied Delhi and the Gangetic plain, forcing Humayun into exile in Persia and Kabul. In 1555, one year before his death, Humayun re-emerged to conquer Hindustan. His son Akbar (reigned 1556–1605) not only rebuilt the empire, but expanded its frontiers right across northern India. Akbar's conquest of Gujarat, with its seaports, in 1572, followed by rich, fertile Bengal in 1576, laid the foundations for the empire's long-term economic strength.

Above *A miniature portrait of Babur, under whom much of northern India came under Mughal rule*

TIMELINE

1504	*Uzbeks drive the Mughals out of Ferghana*
1510	*Shah Ismail drives Uzbeks from Khorasan*
1539	*Afghan Surs reconquer much of Mughal territory*
1556	*Mughals under Akbar rout Sur army at Panipat*
1576	*Mughals complete conquest of Bengal*
1603–1623	*Shah Abbas conquers most of Mesopotamia*
1722	*Afghans overthrow Safavid dynasty*
1729	*Nadir Shah retakes Isfahan from the Afghans.*

MUGHAL INDIA

1605–1765

The Mughal Empire continued to expand under Akbar's successors. When Aurangzeb, the sixth Mughal emperor, died in 1707, almost the entire subcontinent had fallen under Mughal control. However, by this time, the seeds of its demise had also been sown, and within 50 years Mughal authority had all but collapsed in India.

Mughal rule

During the reigns of Akbar's son Jahangir (1605–1627) and grandson Shah Jahan (1628–1658), the Mughals expanded into the Deccan Plateau, pacifying the Rajputs through a combination of military force and dynastic intermarriage. Although they lost Kandahar to Persia, and suffered Uzbek attacks on their north-western border, the story for much of the 17th

Below *Emperor Aurangzeb seated on a golden throne in the durbar, or Mughal court*

century was one of steady expansion. The empire achieved its greatest extent under Aurangzeb (reigned 1658–1707), who conquered Bijapur in 1686 and Golconda in 1687.

From Akbar's time, the empire was divided into provinces called *subahs.* These were administered by public officials known as *mansabdars,* recruited from India's ruling class. Each *mansabdar* was given a rank, defining his status, pay and obligations. Taxes were collected from the peasantry by *zamindars,* local Hindu landowners, who paid it into the treasury after keeping a proportion for themselves.

Although a devout Muslim, Akbar, like his father and grandfather before him, had pursued a policy of religious toleration, helping to legitimize Mughal rule over India's Hindu majority. This situation changed under Akbar's successors, especially Aurangzeb, who adhered to a very strict form of Sunni Islam. Aurangzeb tried to introduce Sharia law (Islamic law) throughout the empire. He replaced Hindu temples with mosques and imposed a special tax on non-Muslims.

Challenges to Mughal rule

In the 1670s, Aurangzeb's policies provoked a series of rebellions by the Jat people of northern India, and the Sikhs in the north-west. More seriously, the Marathas, a Hindu people from the Western Ghats, inflicted one defeat after another on Mughal armies from the 1660s, sacking the major port of Surat (1664) and launching raids across the Deccan Plateau. By 1707 the Marathas had attained their independence from the empire.

Challenges to Mughal authority grew more serious in the 18th century. In 1739, the Persian leader Nadir Shah defeated a Mughal army at Karnal and sacked Delhi. The following year, the Marathas invaded the Carnatic and defeated the Mughals at Damalcherry. Under a succession of weak emperors, the empire's administrative system started to collapse. *Mansabdars,* frustrated at being denied inherited wealth (all wealth reverted to the emperor at death) allied with *zamindars* (landowners) to carve out local power bases. In many parts of India, semi-independent principalities began to spring up.

MUGHAL ART

The Mughals presided over one of the most glorious eras in Indian art and architecture. A new school emerged, blending traditional Indian with Persian styles. Among the most impressive works of architecture were the Taj Mahal, built as a mausoleum for the wife of Shah Jahan; the forts at Agra and Delhi; and the Jami Masjid (Great Mosque) in Fatehpur Sikri. Mughal art found its greatest expression in illuminated manuscripts and miniature paintings. Decorative arts included inlay work, carpets of intricate design, and painted glassware.

European influence

European economic interest in India rose dramatically after Vasco da Gama's discovery of a sea route to Asia in 1497. In the early 1500s, the Portuguese began establishing trading bases at Goa, Daman and Diu. For the most part, the arrival of the Europeans was welcomed by local merchants and traders, and trading links with European companies became increasingly important to the economy of the Mughal Empire.

During the 17th century, the Portuguese were displaced by the Dutch and British East India Companies, and by the 18th century the Dutch company had been supplanted by its French equivalent. These companies had been given charters by their respective governments to acquire territory if necessary, where they could act as quasi-governments, introducing legislation, administering justice, issuing currency, negotiating treaties and even waging war. However, their activities in India remained largely commercial until Mughal authority began to break down in the 18th century.

In the 1740s, the French and British East India Companies became drawn into the conflict between the Marathas and the semi-independent Nizam (Administrator) of Hyderabad. The French, siding with the Nizam, gained control of Mughal south India in exchange for military support.

The British company supported the Marathas, helping them to victory over the French and their allies in 1752. The British capture of Pondicherry in 1761 ended French power in India. In 1756, the British company clashed with Siraj ud-Daulah, an independent Mughal viceroy in Bengal. The company's victory in 1756 led to its takeover of Bengal, its first territorial acquisition on the subcontinent.

The Marathas' ambition to replace the Mughal Empire was dashed in 1761 when its army was routed at Panipat by an invading Afghan force under Ahmad Shah Durrani. Ahmad Shah's army withdrew after the victory, leaving the British East India Company well placed to benefit from the power vacuum. Over the next two decades, the company began to acquire increasing amounts of territory, laying the foundations of British rule in India.

Above *More than three centuries after it was built, the Taj Mahal remains one of the most beautiful and romantic sights in the world*

TIMELINE	
1608	*British East India Company receives its first trading concessions in India*
1632	*Shah Jahan begins Mughal conquest of Deccan*
1669–1678	*Religious persecution prompts rebellions by Jats and Sikhs*
1707	*Death of Aurangzeb marks beginning of decline of the Mughal Empire*
1757	*Marathas end Mughal authority in Gujarat*
1765	*East India Company acquires Bengal and Bihar.*

MING CHINA

1368–1644

In the dying decades of Yüan rule, Chinese peasants suffered crop failure and famine on top of harsh taxation and land confiscations. There were uprisings in almost every province, and by the 1350s several powerful rebel leaders had emerged. One of these was Zhu Yuanzhang, based in the Yangtze Valley. In 1368, Zhu marched north and captured the Yüan capital near Beijing. Zhu proclaimed himself emperor, founding the Ming dynasty. He established his capital at Nanjing on the Yangtze River. Zhu Yuanzhang was the first commoner to become emperor for 1,500 years. He reigned as Hongwu Emperor (reigned 1368–1398) and proved to be one of China's most autocratic rulers, removing numerous advisors, including the post of prime minister, and concentrating power in his own hands.

Above *The Yongle Emperor commissioned the* Yongle Encyclopedia, *which was compiled by 2000 scholars and comprised 400 volumes*

Shortly after the death of Hongwu, his son Zhu Di, known as the Yongle Emperor (reigned 1402–1424), came to power. He led five military campaigns against the Mongols, winning large amounts territory from them. In order to oversee these new lands, he moved the capital north to Beijing in 1421. Here he built an elaborate palace complex known as the Forbidden City.

Exploration to isolation

Yongle sent the admiral Zheng He on several long-distance voyages to the South China Sea, the Indian Ocean and the Persian Gulf. Zheng He collected tribute from vassal states and established trade links as far away as the east coast of Africa. After Zheng He's death in 1433, maritime expeditions ceased and China turned inward. Government economic policy became geared towards domestic self-sufficiency rather than external trade. The Ming emperors that followed Yongle were mostly weak, and the government became infected by factionalism and power struggles between the imperial eunuchs and the Confucian scholar-officials.

Foreign contacts and incursions

In the 16th century, an era of peace and stability brought a steady increase in population and a return to international trade. A thriving textile industry emerged in northern China. Chinese cotton, tea and silk were sold to Japan in exchange for metals and spices, and were taken to Europe in exchange for American silver. In 1557, the Portuguese built a trading post at Macao, the first permanent European base on mainland China. The Dutch followed suit in 1622 with a fortified base on Taiwan.

In the 1540s, China suffered a further bout of Mongol attacks on its northern frontier, despite the Great Wall (see panel). The Mongol leader Altan Khan (reigned 1543–1583) invaded China twice, laying siege to Beijing in 1550, and only departed after being granted special trading privileges. At around the same time,

GREAT WALL OF CHINA

To defend against attacks on China's northern frontier, the Ming decided to join up numerous pre-existing defensive walls to create the Great Wall of China. Unlike earlier walls of rammed earth, the Ming construction used bricks and stone. Begun in 1475, intermittent work continued on the Wall right through the Ming dynasty. By the time it was finished, in the mid-17th century, the Wall was (and remains) the world's longest human-made structure, stretching over 6,400 km (4,000 miles). It has been estimated that between two and three million men died during its construction. Many were buried inside the wall.

China's south-eastern coast suffered raids by Japanese pirate-traders known as *wako*. Attacks from *wako* only ceased in the 1580s, when Toyotomi Hideoyoshi unified Japan under his rule and destroyed the *wako* bases in the south. In 1592, Hideoyoshi changed from being a friend of the Ming to an enemy, when he launched a full-scale invasion of their tributary state of Korea. The Japanese force comprised some 200,000 soldiers. The Ming responded by sending an army of around a million men in support of Korea.

Demise

Although the Ming succeeded in their objective of driving the Japanese from Korea, the seven-year war left them exhausted and depleted of funds. Harsh tax rises were imposed, which coincided with plagues and crop failures in the countryside. Corruption among government bureaucrats fuelled popular resentment. Peasant uprisings soon spread to the cities, and by 1627 there were armed rebellions all over north China. Ming authority crumbled as the death toll mounted. A rival power, the Manchus, took control of Liaodong, the territories north of the Great Wall, and Korea. From 1641, rebel leaders Li Zucheng and Zhang Xianzhong founded kingdoms within north and west China. In 1644, Li Zucheng seized Beijing, the day after the suicide of Chongzen, the last Ming emperor. Within a year, Li Zucheng had been driven from Beijing by the Manchus, led by Dorgun (reigned 1628–1650), who then established their own Qing dynasty.

Left Toyotomi Hideyoshi leads an assault on the castle on Inaba Mountain, from One Hundred Aspects of the Moon by Tsukioka Yoshitoshi (1839–1892)

TIMELINE	
1405–1433	*Zheng He undertakes a series of seven maritime expeditions*
1520–1521	*Portuguese expedition establishes first European trade contact with China*
1556	*An earthquake in Shanxi province kills 850,000*
1552–1555	*Wako attack China, besieging Nanjing*
1592–1598	*Ming armies repel two Japanese invasions of Korea*
1627	*Open insurrection breaks out in northern China, heralding the demise of the Ming.*

THE RISE OF MANCHU QING CHINA

1644–1783

The Manchus, who came to power following the collapse of the Ming dynasty, were a federation of Jürchen tribes. The Jürchens were originally a nomadic people from an area north of Korea. In the early 17th century, a number of the tribes were united under the leadership of Nurhachi (reigned 1586–1626), who organized his people by introducing political and military institutions. In 1616, he took the title Jin Khan to imply continuity with the Jürchen Jin, who had ruled northern China in the 12th and early 13th centuries (see page 137). As Ming authority crumbled in the 1620s and 1630s, Nuhachi's people took advantage of the power vacuum to seize the lands to the north of the Great Wall, the Liaodong basin, and China's vassal state, Korea.

Above *While the Manchus allowed subjugated peoples to maintain their own culture in other respects, they had to wear their hair in the Manchu style*

In the 1630s, Nurhachi's son Dorgun (reigned 1628–1644) renamed his people the Manchus and proclaimed a new dynasty, the Qing. In 1644, Dorgun conquered Beijing, which became the capital of Qing China. Dorgun took the role of regent to his young nephew Shunzi (reigned 1644–1661), who became the first Qing emperor. Over the next 15 years, the Manchus gradually imposed their authority throughout China. The most serious rebellion against their rule occurred in southern China in 1674. Wu Sangui, governor of Yunnan and Guizhou, supported by Shang Zhixin of Guangdon and Geng Jingzhong of Fujian, led a popular revolt that was put down only after five years of fighting.

Qing rule

By the end of the 17th century, all rebellions had been quashed and Qing control over China was absolute. Just one further uprising (of non-Chinese tribal peoples in Yunnan, in 1726–1729) interrupted over a century of internal peace and stability. Although they were foreign conquerors and maintained their own traditions and identity, the Manchus did not try to change native (Han) Chinese customs – the only exception being their insistence that all Chinese men adopt the Manchu hairstyle with its shaved front and long, plaited ponytail, or 'queue', at the back.

TIMELINE

1645–1659	*Manchu armies complete conquest of China*
1674–1681	*Wu Sangui rebels in the south*
1683	*Taiwan falls under Chinese control*
1689	*Russia exchange Amur region for trade with China*
1751	*Tibet falls under Chinese control*
1755–1759	*Dzungaria and Kashgaria fall under Chinese control*
1765–1769	*Burma becomes a vassal state of China.*

The Manchus retained many elements of the Ming administrative structure. However, they strengthened central control by introducing a Grand Council to manage political and military affairs under the direct supervision of the emperor. The main government departments in Beijing had both a Manchu and a Han Chinese head. Mindful of the dangers of rebellion in the provinces, military garrisons were placed in the larger provincial cities. Han Chinese provincial governors were answerable to Manchu governor-generals.

Qianlong era

The Qing dynasty reached its height under the Qianlong Emperor (reigned 1735–1796), who presided over an era of peace and prosperity, as well as enormous territorial expansion. Aggressive military campaigns to the north and west won China the largest Asian empire since the time of the Mongols. By the end of the 18th century, Manchuria, Mongolia, Xinjian, Tibet and Taiwan had all been brought under Qing control; while vassal status was imposed on Burma (modern Myanmar), the Ryukyu Islands (part of modern Japan), Korea and northern Vietnam. For the first time in 2,000 years, the Chinese had no need to fear the nomad threat on their northern frontier.

Such a long period of peace had a demographic impact on China. By the end of the 18th century, the population had risen to 300 million (from around 100 million at the end of the Ming period). Over-population in the Yangtze Valley and south-east led to large-scale migrations to the west and south-west, causing tensions between migrants and existing communities.

European contacts

The Manchus were reluctant to engage in trade with Europe. Commerce was restricted to the port of Guangzhou on the South China Sea, and Kyakhta in the north. Britain, China's main European trading partner, bought tea in exchange for money in the form of silver. The British, chafing at these Qing-imposed restrictions, tried to find ways of increasing their level of trade with China. In 1793, a British envoy named Sir George Macartney travelled to Beijing to show the emperor samples of British goods. Qianlong was unimpressed and refused to make concessions. However, despite the emperor's isolationist stance, the British had already found a means of forcing their way into a trading relationship that would prove extremely disadvantageous to the Chinese. As early as the 1720s, British merchants had begun smuggling opium into China. By 1800, the opium trade was thriving.

Above *The Qianlong Emperor, painted the year after he came to power by Giuseppe Castiglione*

Left *A portrait of Sir George Macartney, British envoy to the Qianlong Emperor*

ARTS AND SCHOLARSHIP

The arts flourished during the Qianlong era. The emperor himself was a prolific poet, as well as a collector of ceramics. Qianlong encouraged traditional scholarship and commissioned a vast collection of all the important works on Chinese culture. Produced in 36,000 volumes, it contained around 3,450 complete items, handwritten by some 15,000 copyists. The collection, entitled *Siku Quanshu*, preserved many works, but was also used as a way of rooting out and suppressing those that criticized either the Qing or other previous non-Chinese dynasties. Qianlong oversaw an expansion of education and a rise in literacy levels, with schools opening in many rural areas.

JAPAN

1500–1800

The Ashikaga shogunate, founded by Ashikaga Takauji in 1336, continued until 1573. However, following the civil war of 1467–1477, central authority collapsed and the Japanese polity dissolved into a multitude of independent warring states, ruled by local lords called daimyo. The emperor and his shogun (military commander) held only nominal authority in the land. Buddhist monasteries became centres of resistance to daimyo rule, as monks united peasant farmers in rebellion. Despite the chaos and disunity, Japanese economic and cultural life continued. The more powerful daimyo became patrons of the arts, supporting poetry, painting and Noh theatre, a form of musical drama that developed in the 14th century.

Above *Maria-Kannon figurines were objects of secret Christian worship in Japan*

The first daimyo with the power and ambition to attempt reunification was Oda Nobunaga, who built up a large domain in central Japan in the mid-16th century. In 1568, he seized control of the imperial capital Kyoto, and five years later he deposed the last Ashikaga shogun. By 1580, Nobunaga had destroyed the rebellious Buddhist monasteries and established his authority throughout central Japan. Before he could extend his rule further, he was assassinated by one of his vassals.

Reunification

Nobunaga was succeeded by Toyotomi Hideyoshi, one of his most talented generals, who continued the policy of reunification. By the early 1590s, Hideyoshi had succeeded in bringing the whole of Japan under his control. He introduced policies to consolidate his position. Peasants were disarmed and samurai were confined to castle towns (to prevent them

from supporting peasant insurrections). Customs borders were abolished and trade was brought under government control. In the 1590s, Hideyoshi led two invasions of Korea, both unsuccessfully (see page 181). He was succeeded by his rival Tokugawa Ieyasu (reigned 1603–1605), who founded the Tokugawa shogunate.

Bakuhan

The Tokugawa shoguns did not attempt to reimpose a centralized monarchy on Japan, but shared power with the local daimyo in a system known as *bakuhan*. The shoguns exerted direct control over around a quarter of the land, while the 250 to 300 daimyo remained sovereign within their own domains, with the power to raise armies, levy taxes, pass laws and administer justice. In return for these privileges, the daimyo were expected to pledge their loyalty to the shogun; spend half their time at the Tokugawa capital at Edo (modern Tokyo); provide support for the construction of public works; and obtain the Shogun's permission before building new castles or making dynastic marriages with other daimyo families. If a daimyo breached these rules, the shogun could confiscate his lands.

Foreign contacts

Japan's first contact with Europeans came in 1543, when Portuguese traders landed at Tanegashima, an island off Kyushu. The Portuguese introduced the Japanese to firearms, which had a dramatic impact on Japanese warfare, rendering their mounted warriors obsolete. Roman Catholicism, first introduced to Japan by the Spanish Jesuit missionary Francis Xavier in 1549, won many converts, including some daimyo. The Tokugawa shoguns, fearful that Christianity would undermine Japan's native culture, banned the religion and persecuted converts. This culminated in a massacre of 37,000 Japanese Christians at Hara castle in 1638, which practically eradicated the faith in Japan. The desire to suppress Christianity led the government to place a ban on European traders, keeping Japan in a state of virtual isolation from Western influences until the mid-19th century.

Social and cultural changes

The 17th century proved to be an era of peace. As a result, the samurai were no longer needed to serve as warriors for the daimyo. So they gave up their swords for pens and became an urbanized class, working as bureaucrats for shogun or daimyo governments. They retained their separate identity, however, by cleaving to traditional samurai values such as courage, loyalty, piety and self-control; known collectively as *bushido*.

Peace also brought economic prosperity. The population swelled to 30 million and a prosperous new merchant class emerged in Japan's major cities and castle towns. Many became creditors to the samurai and daimyo, undermining the traditional hierarchies of Japanese society. This affluent urban elite patronized new forms of entertainment, including *kabuki* (stylized drama) and *bunraku* (puppet theatre). Merchants and commoners alike loved to buy *ukiyo-e* ('pictures of the floating world'), coloured woodblock prints showing scenes of urban life. Poets developed a new, highly concise form of poetry called the *haiku*.

Threats from within and without

The good times, however, were not felt by all. A growing gap between rich and poor led to social tensions during the 18th century. Many of the landed gentry had grown wealthy through activities such as moneylending, while the peasants, afflicted by poor harvests, natural disasters and government corruption, grew poorer. From 1760, peasant riots were increasingly frequent. The Tokugawa shoguns, while reeling from chaos in the countryside, also faced a new external threat. From the 1790s, Russian, British and French ships began appearing in Japanese harbours, hoping to breach Tokugawa isolationism and establish trading links.

TIMELINE	
1568	*Oda Nobunaga captures Kyoto*
1571–1582	*Hideyoshi conquers lands in western and eastern Japan for Nobunaga*
1590	*Hideyoshi unifies Japan under his rule*
1603	*Ieyasu founds Tokugawa shogunate*
1609	*Dutch trading base established on Hirado Island*
1637–1641	*Portuguese traders are expelled from Japan*
1703	*Edo is badly damaged by earthquake and fire*
1745	*Under Ieshige, Tokugawa shogunate begins to slide into corruption*
1760	*Widespread peasant rebellions begin.*

Above *The samurai Hasekura Rokuemon Tsunenaga led a diplomatic visit to Rome, where he was painted in 1615 by Claude Deruet*

SOUTH-EAST ASIA

1500–1800

The early modern period witnessed a growing European influence within South-east Asia. Most of the mainland states were strong enough to maintain their independence, although by the 18th century, western powers were becoming increasingly involved in the internal politics of these kingdoms. In Island South-east Asia, European incursions faced determined resistance from existing Islamic trading networks.

Right *Ruins at Ava, or Innwa, the capital of Burma 1364–1841. Founded on an artificial island, it was abandoned following an earthquake*

Cambodia

Following the abandonment of Angkor in 1440, Cambodia entered a long period of economic, social and cultural stagnation. It was increasingly dominated by its Thai and Vietnamese neighbours, almost to the point of losing its own ethnic and cultural identity. The Khmer ceased building monuments and their Hindu faith was supplanted by Thai-influenced Theravada Buddhism. In the 16th century, the Khmer established a new capital at Lovek. Its access (via the Mekong Delta) to international trade routes made the Khmer more open to outside influences and more dependent on maritime trade than in earlier periods. The Cambodian monarchy was already dominated by Spanish and Portuguese merchant-adventurers when Lovek was conquered by the Thai in 1594. Cambodia remained under either Thai or Vietnamese control until the establishment of a French protectorate there in 1863.

Thailand

Thailand was dominated by the kingdom of Ayutthaya, but was actually a patchwork of self-governing principalities ruled by members of the king of Ayutthaya's family. Sometimes, these princes would combine against the king or ally themselves with a foreign power. In 1569, rebel princes helped Burmese forces conquer Ayutthaya. Thai independence was restored by Naresuan (reigned 1590–1605), who drove out the Burmese in 1593. Europeans arrived in the 1500s and were given permission to trade. However, as western influence grew under the cosmopolitan Narai (reigned 1657–1688), it aroused the resentment of Thai nobles and Buddhist clergy. Under Phetracha (reigned 1688–1693), Europeans were expelled, and for the next 150 years, the Thais insulated themselves from western influence. The kingdom of Ayutthaya was destroyed in 1767 by invading Burmese armies. The Burmese were driven out a year later and Thailand was re-established as Siam under Taksin (reigned 1768–1782). He reunited the country and reinstated Thai rule on the Malay Peninsula and in Laos.

Myanmar

In the 16th century, the Burmese kingdom of Taungoo, under Tabinshwehti (reigned 1531–1551), conquered the Mon kingdom centred on Bago. By 1540, Lower Burma was reunified under Taungoo. Tabinshwehti's successor Bayinnaung (reigned 1551–1581) went on to conquer Upper Burma (1555), Manipur (1556), the Shan states (1557), Chiang Mai (1557), Ayutthaya (1569) and Lan Xang (1574), uniting most of western South-east Asia under his rule. However, Bayinnaung's empire disintegrated soon after his death. The Thais drove the Burmese from Ayutthaya in 1593. In 1599, Bago, the Taungoo capital, was sacked by the Rakhine (from southern Burma), with the help of the Portuguese. The Portuguese promptly took Thanlynin, Burma's most important seaport. Anaukpetlun (reigned 1605–1628) drove out the Portuguese in 1611 and re-established Taungoo rule. The Mons, with French and Thai help, destroyed Taungoo in 1752, and afterwards formed an independent state in Lower Burma and Ava. Burma was reunified under Alaungpaya (reigned 1752–1760), the founder of the Konbaung dynasty.

Vietnam

Between 1428 and 1788, Vietnam was ruled by the Lê dynasty, with only one brief interruption (1527–1533) when the Mac dynasty seized the throne. After 1533, Vietnam was divided: with the deposed Mac dynasty continuing to rule in the north from Hanoi; and an alliance of two clans, the Nguyen and the Trinh, ruling in the south, with the Lê emperors acting merely as figureheads. In 1592, Hanoi was captured by the Trinh, and the Mac emperor was executed. The Trinh now controlled the north and the Nguyen controlled the south; both claiming to rule

ISLAND SOUTH-EAST ASIA

From the early-16th century, European powers sought ways of bypassing the Muslim merchants who controlled the spice trade between Indonesia and Europe. In 1511, the Portuguese captured the port city of Malacca from the Sultanate of Malacca. Further east, they established fortified trading bases in Ternate, Amboina, Solor and Kupang, to manage the production of cloves and sandalwood, but found they were unable to break existing Muslim trading networks there. The Europeans were equally unsuccessful at breaking the Muslim stranglehold over the Sumatran and West Javan pepper trade. The aggressive Dutch East India Company took control of Amboina (1606), Jakarta (1619), the nutmeg-producing Banda Islands (1621), Malacca (1641) and the clove-producing Moluccas (1650s). Later, in the 18th century, the Dutch company directed its energies towards control of coffee and sugar in Java, but its network was taken over after 1770 by more powerful trading concerns from Britain, France, the USA and China.

in the name of the Lê emperor, and all the while (from 1627) fighting each other for domination of the whole country. In 1788, both were defeated by a peasant uprising led by the Tay Son brothers. The Tay Son were subsequently overthrown, with help from the French, by the Nguyen, who reunited the country under their rule.

Above The Dutch *drove the British out of Jayakarta in 1619, renamed it Batavia and established a trading post there*

AFRICAN KINGDOMS

1500–1800

The first Europeans arrived in sub-Saharan Africa in the mid-1400s, and thereafter Western influence grew rapidly, especially for states situated on or near the coast. The most significant and catastrophic impact of European involvement in Africa during the early modern period was undoubtedly the transatlantic slave trade. Nevertheless, for most of the many thousands of states and polities of pre-colonial Africa, the European influence was minimal, and age-old lifestyles and cultures continued much as before.

Above *The tomb of the Askia dynasty at Gao in Mali, capital of the Songhai empire from 1493. Built of mudbrick, it is more than 10 m (33 ft) high*

East Africa

In the early 16th century, Portugal created a chain of trading bases along the East African coast, from Socotra (off the Horn of Africa) in the north to Delagoa Bay in the south, then proceeded to dominate Indian Ocean trade. In the 1520s, the Portuguese were drawn into a conflict in the Horn of Africa, supporting the Christian kingdom of Ethiopia

when it was invaded by Adal, which was an alliance of Islamic states, united under the leadership of an imam called Ahmed Gran. The Ethiopians and Portuguese defeated Adal in 1543, after a 15-year conflict. In the later 17th century, Portugal went to war with the Dutch in a trade dispute. Distracted by this, the Portuguese were unable to prevent Oman, a semi-independent Ottoman sultanate, from occupying most of their northern bases and usurping their commerce with India. To the north, a nomadic tribe of cattle herders, known as the Funj, conquered the Islamic state of Nubia in the early 16th century, then set up their own kingdom centred on the city of Sennar. In 1523, the Funj monarch converted to Islam. Funj remained an independent kingdom until 1821, when it was absorbed by the Ottoman Empire.

West Africa

The most powerful African empire of the early modern period was Songhai, centred on eastern Mali. Founded in the early 15th century, Songhai rose to prominence under Sonni Ali (reigned 1464–1492) and reached its zenith under Muhammad Ture (reigned 1492–1538). The empire grew wealthy by trading gold, ivory and slaves in exchange for salt, glass and other luxuries. Its greatest city, Timbuktu, became an important centre of Islamic culture. Weakened by a civil war of succession, Songhai came to an end in 1591 following defeat by a Moroccan army at the Battle of Tondibi. Finding themselves unable to govern such a vast territory, the Moroccans withdrew, allowing it to splinter into small independent kingdoms.

Several other West African empires

KANEM-BORNU

European influence was mainly confined to the coastal regions from the 16th to 18th centuries, and had little impact on inland regions. The most important external influence on the state of Kanem-Bornu in the central-southern Sahara during the period was the Ottoman Empire. Under Idris Aluma (reigned 1571–1603), Kanem-Bornu emerged as a regional power, mainly due to the importation of Ottoman firearms. Known for his piety, Aluma imposed Sharia law on Kanem-Bornu, turning it into a fundamentalist Islamic state. He exported his Islamic ideals to the neighbouring pagan states of Wadai and Bagirmi.

flourished during this period, trading with each other along the Niger and other river routes. These included Mossi (modern Burkina Faso), Oyo (modern western Nigeria), Asante (modern Ghana) and Dahomey (modern Benin). Portuguese navigators started establishing trading bases on the West African coast from the mid-15th century, followed by the Dutch and English. The slave trade began in the 16th century, but developed fully in the 17th, significantly distorting the economies and demographics of West Africa. States such as the Bambara Empire and Dahomey came to rely on exchanging slaves for European firearms, which were then used to capture more slaves. The Gold Coast-Benin area was the hub of the West African trade; in the 18th century, 35,000 slaves a year were transported from here.

Central and Southern Africa

Portuguese navigators first arrived on the Central African coast in 1482. Here they encountered the powerful kingdom of Congo, which had grown rich from trading in ivory, copperware, ironware, raffia cloth and pottery. Portuguese missionaries converted Congo's king and nobles to Christianity in 1491, marking the beginning of a gradual Westernization of the kingdom. In the 16th century, Congo became an important source of slaves for European traders. In the 1570s, the Portuguese established an important slave-trading colony in Angola, a region that bordered Congo and the neighbouring states of Ndongo and Lunda. However, European expansion in the area was halted in 1622 when a Portuguese invasion of southern Congo was driven back. Anti-Portuguese riots then broke out across the kingdom, threatening their merchant community. A further Portuguese defeat in 1670 ended their ambitions in Congo until the late 1800s. During the 17th and 18th centuries, the Dutch became increasingly influential in central and southern Africa. By 1783, their colony in the Cape region, on the tip of southern Africa, had become the largest European settlement on the continent.

Above *Nzinga a Nkuwu, ruler of Congo 1470–1509, converted to Christianity and took the name João I in honour of the Portuguese king João II*

TIMELINE	
1492–1538	*Songhai Empire enjoys its 'golden age'*
1523	*Funj converts to Islam*
1528–1543	*Ethiopian-Portuguese force defeats Adal*
1591	*Songhai Empire is overthrown by Morocco*
1592	*British begin participation in transatlantic slave trade*
1598	*Portuguese begin Jesuit missions to Ethiopia*
1626	*French colonization of Madagascar begins*
1652	*Cape Town is founded by Dutchman Jan van Riebeck*
1701	*Kingdom of Asante emerges*
1747	*Dahomey is conquered by Oyo.*

SPANISH COLONIZATION OF THE AMERICAS

1550–1783

At its height, Spain's American empire extended from Alaska in the north to southern Chile and Patagonia in the south and included modern-day western USA, Mexico, Central America, Venezuela, Colombia, Ecuador, Peru, Bolivia and Argentina. The colonization of these areas and the exploitation of their gold and silver deposits won Spain great wealth and power. It was also catastrophic for native peoples, because it destroyed numerous ancient cultures and wiped out huge numbers through exposure to diseases from Europe.

Right *On board the* Golden Hind, *Francis Drake attacked Spanish ships and returned to England with their treasures*

Colonial rule

Following the discoveries and conquests of the early 16th century (see pages 154–155), Spanish rule of the new territories was quickly consolidated. The empire was organized into two viceroyalties, under the authority of government-appointed viceroys: New Spain (comprising Mexico, Central America and the Caribbean) and Peru (comprising Panama and Spanish South America). The Roman Catholic Church played a key role in the colonies. Priests and friars taught the natives about Christianity and European customs. While some clergymen dismissed indigenous culture as primitive, many made efforts to defend and preserve it, studying the people's customs, learning their languages and recording their histories.

Colonial economy

Colonists built their settlements on or near existing towns. They introduced new crops such as sugar and cotton, and farmed cattle. But above all, the wealth of the new empire was built on Mexican and Peruvian gold and silver, which the colonists mined in vast quantities. By the 1550s, there were around 250 Spanish towns in the Americas. From this time, small-scale farming shifted to a system of large estates, or plantations, called *haciendas*. Because so many of the native population had died from disease, thousands of African slaves were shipped in to work on the haciendas or in the mines.

Fleets of Spanish cargo ships, with naval escorts, regularly plied the routes between Seville and Veracruz (on the east coast of

TIMELINE	
1534	The first African slaves land in Brazil
1538	Spain takes control of Colombia
1565–1567	Rio de Janeiro is founded by Portuguese colonists
1569	Spain establishes a stable government in Peru
1577–80	English sailor Francis Drake raids Spanish settlements on the Pacific coast
1655	An English expedition captures Jamaica during Oliver Cromwell's war against Spain
1680	Portugal bans the enslavement of native Brazilians
1761	Spain occupies part of modern Texas
1780–1781	Spanish forces recapture west Florida and the Bahamas from Britain.

Mexico), and Peru and the west coast of the Central American isthmus. In the 17th century, rival European powers began to target Spanish-American interests. English, French and Dutch ships raided Caribbean ports or attacked Spanish ships carrying treasure back from the colonies. In 1632, the English occupied Belize in Central America, and in 1655 they took control of Jamaica, a major centre of sugar production.

Colonial culture

In the early 17th century, revenue from the New World began to decline, weakening Spain's economy. By the 1650s, following numerous exhausting and expensive wars, Spain was forced to reduce contact with its American colonies. Consequently, colonists felt less of a connection with Spain and began to develop a separate identity. With time, increasing numbers of Creoles (people of Spanish descent who were born in the Americas) and *mestizos* (people of mixed Spanish and indigenous descent) helped to create a new culture that blended indigenous and Spanish traditions. In the 18th century, as the Spanish-American population expanded, colonists began to establish settlements and missions in modern-day New Mexico, Texas, California and Arizona. As well as precious metals, exports included animal hides, sugar, tobacco, cocoa beans, cotton and indigo.

BRAZIL

In 1500, Portuguese navigator Pedro Alvares Cabral made landfall on the Brazilian coast (see page 154). Settlement of the new colony began in earnest in the 1530s, with colonists growing sugar and raising cattle. Plantation agriculture, relying on slave labour, began in the 1550s. In the 1620s, as part of a wider war with Spain and Portugal, the Dutch attacked Brazil, but were driven back by the Portuguese with the help of native Brazilians. The discovery of gold in the late 17th century led to an expansion of Brazil's borders, deeper into the continental interior. Gold revitalized the colony's economy and led to a rapid rise in population. By the 18th century, some 80 per cent of European gold came from Brazil.

Decline of Spain

For one year, in 1762, during the Seven Years' War (1756–1762), Britain occupied Havana in Cuba, and Spain only regained control there by ceding Florida. However, the same war brought an end to France's American empire, and Spain was able to acquire the vast territory of Louisiana. Spain recovered Florida following Britain's defeat in the American War of Independence (1775–1783). But these acquisitions did not prevent a general decline in Spanish control of its empire in the latter part of the 18th century. Increasingly, the British and other European powers began to trade directly with Spanish colonies. Goods exported by Spain to the New World were often manufactured by other nations and carried on English ships. The colonists themselves became increasingly independent-minded and resentful of the Spanish demands on their natural resources. The stage was set for the independence movements of the following century.

Above *Following a siege lasting two months, Havana was seized by the Royal Navy on 30 July 1762*

Left *Cocoa beans were a valuable crop, from which came chocolate. It was introduced to Europe by the Spanish*

EUROPEAN EXPLORATION OF NORTH AMERICA

1500–1700

For a long period after John Cabot's arrival in North America in 1497, the true nature and scope of the continent he had discovered remained shrouded in mystery. After Florentine navigator Giovanni Verrazzano had traced the Atlantic seaboard in 1524, a sense emerged of North America's enormous length, if not its even vaster breadth. Early ventures inland encountered dense woodland and hostile natives. Unlike Central and South America, there seemed little prospect of an immediate return for investors in terms of gold or silver, and it was only in the 1670s that the continent's rich agricultural interior was revealed. The first European explorers of North America made only sporadic attempts at establishing colonies there. They were driven more by the hope of finding a passage around or through the continent to Asia.

Above right
A portrait of Sir Martin Frobisher (c. 1535–1594), one of the English navigators who explored the Canadian Arctic

Seeking a north-west passage

In the late 16th and early 17th centuries, English navigators Henry Hudson, Martin Frobisher, John Davis and William Baffin probed the inlets and bays of the Canadian Arctic in vain attempts to find a route around the continent into the Pacific. The French focused on trying to find a way through the interior. They were also motivated by profits to be made from the fur trade, and developing trading links with Native American tribes. Jacques Cartier explored the St Lawrence River in three voyages between 1534 and 1542. Samuel de Champlain founded a fur trading post in 1608, which grew into the city of Québec; he also explored modern-day northern New York state.

French exploration continued until the 1750s. Jesuit missionaries (seeking Native American converts), explorers and fur trappers travelled further along the St Lawrence River and opened up new territory in the Great Lakes region, still hoping to discover the fabled route to the Pacific. Their dreams of finding it were destined to founder in the vastness of the Great Plains that lay beyond Lake Manitoba, but the failed quest at least began the process of opening up the continent's interior, and provided a basis for French claims to the region.

The French did, however, discover a north-south passage. Nine years after Jacques Marquette and Louis Joliet explored the upper Mississippi River in 1673, René-Robert Cavelier, sieur de La Salle managed to navigate the Mississippi from its junction with the Ohio River to the Gulf of Mexico. He claimed all the land drained by the river for France, naming it Louisiana after Louis XIV.

TIMELINE

1513	*Juan Ponce de Léon begins Spanish exploration of Florida*
1584–1590	*Raleigh's Roanoke colony fails*
1608	*Champlain founds Québec and explores the area around Lake Champlain*
1613–1615	*First French fur trading route opens*
1620	*Pilgrim Fathers found a colony at Cape Cod*
1630–1670	*French Jesuits explore the Great Lakes*
1671	*English explorers are first Europeans to cross the Appalachians.*

Spanish exploration

While the French were beginning their exploration of Canada in the 1540s, the Spanish were venturing into the southern areas of North America from their bases in Mexico and the Caribbean. Fired by rumours of gold and great cities ripe for conquest, Hernando de Soto and Francisco Vásquez de Coronado led military expeditions into Florida, New Mexico, and what would become the southern United States. They returned exhausted and empty-handed; their pioneering achievements as the first Europeans to visit these lands were not recognized until many decades later. Florida was colonized in 1565 and became an important Spanish possession, protecting the treasure fleets en route to Europe. The west coast was only settled in the 17th century, with a string of fortified bases and missions founded in New Mexico and along the Californian coast.

Colonization

English explorers Humphrey Gilbert and Walter Raleigh failed in their attempts to found colonies in North America in the 1580s. The first successful English colony was Jamestown, Virginia, in 1607, followed by Plymouth Colony, founded in 1620 at Cape Cod Bay. The English then began a steady colonization of the Atlantic seaboard from French Acadia to Spanish Florida. The sole Dutch colony, New Netherland, founded in 1621, was taken over by the English in 1664 and renamed New York.

Unlike French settlements in North America, whose primary purpose was fur trading and establishing missions, from the start, the English colonies were intent on establishing an agricultural economy based on the acquisition of land. This hunger for land led to numerous bloody

conflicts with the Native Americans. The Appalachian mountains presented another major obstacle to expansion, and it was not until the 1670s (by which time the natives had been weakened through exposure to European diseases), that the first English traders and explorers were able to cross the Appalachians and penetrate the lands to the west, along the Ohio River valley.

By the 1690s, most of eastern North America, from Canada to the Mexican Gulf, had been colonized by the French and English. The French colonies were widely spaced, with the largest settlements around the St Lawrence River, the Great Lakes region in the north, and the mouth of the Mississippi River in the south. A string of trading and military posts connected the two regions. The English colonial empire consisted of 12 colonies along the Atlantic seaboard. A 13th, Georgia, was founded in 1733.

Above This painting by William H. Powell shows Hernando DeSoto in 1541, as the first European to view the Mississippi

Below Sir Walter Raleigh's ventures in the New World came to nothing and eventually he was beheaded at the Tower of London

COLONIAL NORTH AMERICA

1650–1775

From the mid-17th century, North America increasingly became a battleground for the global rivalries of the major European powers, and wars in Europe often spilled over into the western hemisphere. Thus, during a period of Franco-Dutch enmity in 1655, the Netherlands took possession of the American colony of France's ally Sweden, in modern-day Delaware. And in 1664, during an Anglo-Dutch war, Britain annexed the colony of New Netherland. However, the rivalry that dominated the latter end of the 17th century, and most of the 18th, was between Britain and France.

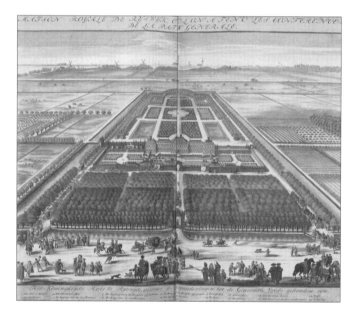

Above *The Treaty of Ryswick was negotiated at the Huis ter Nieuwburg in Ryswick, a palace belonging to Stadtholder Frederik Hendrik*

Between 1689 and 1763, Britain fought a series of wars with France for control of the North American continent. As well as international prestige, important economic prizes were at stake, not least the lucrative fur trade on the mainland, and the sugar industry in the Caribbean. During these wars, French and British troops were frequently aided by Native American allies.

King William's War

The first of the four conflicts was King William's War (1689–1697), known in Europe as the War of the League of Augsburg. English colonists and their Native American allies, the Iroquois, fought French colonists and their allies, the Huron, in Canada and on the northern frontier of New England. The French sacked English trading forts on Hudson Bay, while the English captured Port Royal, the capital of French Acadia. The Treaty of Ryswick, which ended the war, returned Port Royal to the French and left the rivalry unresolved.

Queen Anne's and King George's Wars

The next conflict, Queen Anne's War (1702–1713), was an extension of the War of the Spanish Succession in Europe. It was fought by Britain and the Netherlands against France and Spain. The northern New England frontier again provided the setting for numerous battles between the French and British. The British failed in their attempt to capture Québec in 1710–1711, but their victories in Europe won them significant North American concessions in the Peace of Utrecht (1713–1714). From France, Britain acquired Newfoundland, Acadia (renamed Nova Scotia) and Hudson Bay, as well as greater access to the fur trade. From the French ally, Spain, Britain obtained trading concessions in Spanish America.

A generation later, in 1739, Spain attempted to block trade between its North American colonies and Britain. The ensuing conflict coincided with – and became mixed up with – the War of Austrian Succession in Europe (1740–1748).

Ticonderoga. The conquest of Québec in September 1759 by General James Wolfe was a fatal blow for the French, although they struggled on until the fall of Montreal in 1760. Under the Treaty of Paris (1763), Britain acquired almost all French territory in Canada, and all their settlements east of the Mississippi River. Britain also received Florida from Spain (France's ally since 1762), which handed Britain control of the entire continent east of the Mississippi. French territories west of the Mississippi had already passed to Spain in 1762.

In North America the war was known as King George's War (1744–1748). There were no significant exchanges of territory in this conflict.

French and Indian War

The final and decisive war in the 100-year rivalry between France and Britain was the French and Indian War (1754–1763). This time, the fighting began in America and then spread to Europe, where it was called the Seven Years' War (1756–1763). After King George's War, territorial rivalries between Britain and France intensified as their respective colonies expanded. In the 1740s, the Iroquois Indians allowed, for the first time, some British settlement in the Ohio River valley. The French, fearing the loss of the Ohio fur trade, decided to establish a military presence in the area. In 1753 they built a chain of forts along the Allegheny River, at the eastern end of the valley. This land was also claimed by the British colony of Virginia. War broke out in 1754.

The French fiercely resisted British attempts to seize the disputed territory, and their success continued into 1756 with the taking of Britain's Fort Oswego and the destruction of Fort William Henry. The tide turned in 1758–1759, when British forces captured Louisbourg and Crown Point, and Forts Frontenac, Duquesne, Niagara and

NATIVE AMERICANS

The indigenous tribes of North America initially prospered from the arrival of European settlers. From French explorers seeking food and furs, the Iroquois and Algonquian peoples of Canada obtained firearms, blankets, metal and cloth. In the Great Lakes region, the Huron people's alliance with the French in the 1650s saved them from annihilation by the Iroquois. In the south-west, buffalo-hunting by the Plains peoples was transformed by the acquisition of horses from the Spanish. However, as time went on, the negative effects of European colonization became increasingly apparent. The native population dwindled as so many succumbed to European diseases. They also suffered a steady loss of their lands, particularly at the hands of English colonists. The Powhatan Confederacy was driven from Virginia in the 1650s; and the Tuscarora and Yamasee lost their territories in the Carolinas in the 1710s. From 1730 to 1755, the Shawnee and Delaware were forced to flee west down the Ohio River.

THE AMERICAN REVOLUTION

1763–1783

The United States was forged out of a conflict between Britain and its colonies in North America, known as the American Revolution. This revolution came about for a variety of reasons. During the 18th century, the colonies underwent profound demographic and economic changes, which altered their relationship with their mother country and made the colonists more independent-minded. The short-term catalyst for the revolution was a growing resentment at British policy: starting in 1763, Britain enacted a series of measures designed to limit the colonists' political freedom; to halt their territorial expansion; and to increase Britain's income from the colonies.

Left *Arrested in Britain for his Quaker beliefs, William Penn left for America, where he founded Pennsylvania*

Furthermore, many of the immigrants were non-British. Some 30 per cent arrived from Germany, Scotland and Ireland; and about one-fifth were slaves of African descent. There was also great religious diversity, with large numbers of Roman Catholics, Presbyterians, Lutherans, Mennonites and Quakers, as well as Anglicans. Such diversity of nationality, ethnicity and religion made it far harder for Britain to command the loyalty of the colonies.

Economic changes also contributed to the movement for independence. Britain maintained a mercantilist policy towards its colonies. In other words, the colonies were there purely to serve British economic interests, providing it with raw materials unavailable at home, in exchange for British-manufactured goods. The policy discouraged any colonial trade except with Britain, and from the 1650s Britain imposed laws to tax any external trade. The emergence of a dynamic agricultural and commercial economy in the colonies during the 18th century undermined British mercantilism. By the 1750s, the colonial economy had come to depend on non-British trade.

Demographic and economic changes

The 13 British colonies experienced a major population growth during the 18th century. In 1700, their combined population stood at around 250,000. By 1775, thanks to a rising birthrate and large-scale immigration from Europe, there was ten times that number.

TIMELINE

1765	*Stamp Act imposes first direct taxation on American colonies*
1766	*Declaratory Act gives Britain the right to pass laws in the colonies*
1770	*The Boston Massacre: five colonists are killed by British soldiers during a riot*
1773	*Boston Tea Party*
1775	*The War of Independence begins*
1776	*Congress adopts the Declaration of Independence*
1778	*France enters the war on the side of the Americans*
1779	*Spain declares war on Britain and retakes Florida*
1782	*British defeat French at Les Saintes in the West Indies, saving British colonies there*
1783	*The Treaty of Paris.*

Rising resentment

For a long period, Britain overlooked the growing economic independence of its colonies; it did not enforce its mercantilist laws because those same colonies continued to make the home-country very wealthy. However, the French and Indian War of 1754 to 1763 (see page 195) saddled Britain with severe debts. The government looked for means of generating more income from the colonies, as well as bringing them more firmly under British control. The colonists were soon confronted by a steady stream of new legislation. The Royal Proclamation (1763) restricted colonial expansion to a line east of the Appalachian mountains; this was due to Britain's fear of new and costly conflicts with native tribes. The Sugar Act (1764) imposed taxes on imported sugar; and the Quartering Act (1765) obliged the colonies to provide barracks and supplies for British troops. The Stamp Act (1765) was the first direct tax imposed on the colonists.

These measures were greatly resented by the colonists, especially the Stamp Act, which provoked riots and widespread civil disobedience. After the colonies united in demanding its repeal, the Stamp Act was replaced by the Townshend Acts, which imposed a duty, or indirect tax, on imported goods such as glass, lead, paper and tea. In protest, Americans refused to buy British goods. As tensions escalated, a group of colonists raided British ships in Boston harbour and threw their cargo of tea overboard. Britain punished the so-called 'Boston Tea Party' by passing a series of laws known in America as the Intolerable Acts (1774). One closed Boston Harbour until the lost tea was paid for. Another reduced the power of the Massachusetts legislature and handed extra powers to the colony's British-appointed governor. In response, representatives of 12

of the colonies met at the First Continental Congress, where they voted to cut off trade with Britain unless certain laws and taxes were repealed.

American War of Independence

Fighting broke out in early 1775, when Britain refused to back down. British forces suffered early defeats, but their superior numbers and naval capability soon began to tell. On 4 July 1776, the Second Continental Congress adopted the Declaration of Independence, proclaiming the colonies to be free and independent states. The USA was born – if only as an idea. Many colonists were either ambivalent about independence or remained loyal to Britain. The Patriots (supporters of independence) were a minority and their armies had fewer troops and were less organized than the British. Yet they fought on familiar terrain, had young, daring leaders, and did not suffer the British problem of stretched supply lines. The decisive factor in the war was the entry of France on the side of the colonists in 1778, which forced Britain to scatter its forces to defend other parts of its empire. In 1781, American and French forces achieved a crushing victory over the British at Yorktown, all but ending the war. The 1783 Treaty of Paris confirmed the independence of the new United States of America.

Above The Boston Tea Party, *in a lithograph from 1846. The colonists disguised themselves as Narragansett Indians to take the British by surprise*

THE FRENCH REVOLUTION

1789–1799

The French Revolution was a watershed in the history of continental Europe, marking the moment when the absolute monarchies of the early modern period began to crumble, and modern nation states, dominated by the middle classes, started to emerge. The Ancien Régime in France had been under attack by Enlightenment thinkers since the mid-18th century. They called for an end to absolutist rule and the introduction of a more representative system of government. Angered by poverty and food shortages and inspired by the success of the American revolt against the British, the mood of the middle and lower classes in France during the 1780s was increasingly incendiary.

Above *Having sent thousands to the guillotine, Robespierre eventually met the same fate himself*

Right *The Bastille prison was a symbol of tyranny – but the crowd found only seven prisoners within it to release*

National Assembly

By 1788 the French government was in severe debt, thanks to recent costly wars – not least France's support for the American Revolution. To avoid bankruptcy, Louis XVI decided to raise taxes. The Parlement of Paris insisted that Louis gain the approval of the Estates-General, an assembly of representatives from the three 'estates', or social classes – clergy, nobility and commoners (comprising the lower and middle classes). In June 1789, the Third Estate withdrew from the Estates-General to form a National Assembly, pledging to write a new constitution.

Storming the Bastille

The people of Paris feared the king would attack the National Assembly, so on 14 July a huge crowd stormed the Bastille fortress, a symbol of Ancien Régime despotism. Peasant uprisings broke out all over the countryside, causing many nobles to flee France. In August, the National Assembly published its *Declaration of the Rights of Man*, proclaiming that sovereign power resided in the nation, not the king. It abolished the tax advantages of the clergy and nobles and guaranteed the same basic rights to all. The right to vote and hold office was extended to citizens who paid a certain level of taxes. The Assembly seized and redistributed Church property, using the money to pay off the national debt.

National Convention

As foreign armies invaded France in support of Louis, the Parisian mob stormed the royal palace and took the king prisoner. With the king's removal, the moderate reformist revolution, supporting a constitutional monarchy, gave way to a more radical, democratic revolution.

A National Convention was formed, which declared France a republic under the slogan 'Liberty, Equality, Fraternity'. The king was beheaded in January 1793. A radical faction called the Jacobins took control of the Convention, and its leaders, notably Maximilien Robespierre, became the new rulers of France.

Reign of Terror

The Jacobins presided over the bloodiest period of the Revolution, known as the Reign of Terror. Hundreds of thousands of 'counter-revolutionaries' were jailed, including royalists, nobles, and anyone who disagreed with Jacobin policy. Some 18,000 were executed by guillotine. The Jacobins planned radical reforms – an extension of the franchise, free education, social welfare, income tax and the abolition of slavery – but did not rule long enough to carry these through. The most significant Jacobin achievement was its reorganization of the army, introducing mass conscription and replacing aristocratic officers with younger, patriotic soldiers. This helped to turn the tide of the Revolutionary Wars in France's favour (see panel).

Directoire

Military victory and the end of any threat to France's borders removed the justification for the Reign of Terror, yet the killing frenzy continued, alienating many former supporters of the revolution. By 1794, the Jacobins began to fight amongst themselves. In July, Robespierre's enemies removed him and he and his supporters were guillotined. In 1795 the National Convention issued a new constitution, preserving the early revolutionary achievements while discarding Jacobin extremism.

FRENCH REVOLUTIONARY WARS

The rulers of other parts of Europe were greatly alarmed by the democratic ideals of the French Revolution. In 1792, several of them formed an anti-revolutionary alliance called the First Coalition. In April, Austria and Prussia launched a joint invasion of France with the aim of restoring royal power. In 1794–1795, following Jacobin reforms, a revitalized revolutionary army drove out the invading armies and crossed into the Netherlands, Germany and Italy. In 1796, the French general Napoleon Bonaparte conquered northern Italy. When he invaded Austria in 1797, the Austrian government sued for peace, conceding Belgium to France. In 1798, Bonaparte occupied Egypt and gained control of Switzerland and Rome. In 1799, a Second Coalition was formed, inflicting a series of defeats on France in Italy and driving them back to the Alps. By the end of the French Revolutionary Wars, in 1802, France had won back northern Italy, but lost Egypt.

France remained a republic, but once again only citizens who paid a certain amount of taxes could vote.

The government formed under the new constitution was called the Directoire and consisted of a five-man executive and a two-house legislature. During its four-year reign, the Directoire was troubled both by continuing economic problems and opposition from royalists and Jacobins. In October 1799, rebel leaders plotted to overthrow the Directoire. Needing support from the army, they turned to the most talented of France's new crop of military leaders, Napoleon Bonaparte. In November, Bonaparte seized control of the government and installed himself as military dictator, ending the revolution.

Above The Battle of Varoux, *by Adam Victor-Jean, painted in 1837 – a commemoration of a French victory over the Austrians in November 1792*

Left *Once a lawyer who opposed the death penalty, Robespierre became a revolutionary who demanded the death of the king*

NAPOLEONIC EUROPE

1800–1815

Napoleon Bonaparte, or Emperor Napoleon I as he became, was an outstanding military commander and the dominant figure of his age. A man of extraordinary energy and vision, he built an empire that covered most of Western and central Europe. Although Napoleon's autocratic style ran counter to the democratic principles of the French Revolution, in other ways he embodied its ideals. His Napoleonic Code helped to abolish the last vestiges of feudalism and promoted equality, liberty and the rule of law throughout the territories he ruled. Ultimately, his own ambition, as well as rising nationalism in the countries he conquered, led to his downfall.

Below *A portrait of Napoleon Bonaparte by Jean Auguste Dominique Ingres*

Rise of Napoleonic France

In 1799, Napoleon was named First Consul of France. The following year he defeated the Austrians at Marengo, reimposing French rule in northern Italy. In 1801 Napoleon's army was thrown out of Egypt by the British. The 1802 Treaty of Amiens brought peace to Europe, but it proved a brief respite. The following year, Napoleon began preparations for an invasion of Britain. His Grand Army, assembled on the coast of northern France, prompted the British to form a defensive alliance, the Third Coalition, with Austria, Russia and Sweden.

On learning of this, Napoleon changed his plans and marched against Austria, defeating them at Ulm in October 1805. Shortly afterwards, Britain's Royal Navy, led by its most talented admiral Horatio Nelson, defeated a combined French and Spanish fleet at Trafalgar. Nelson was killed, but the French navy was crippled, ending all prospect of an invasion of Britain. In December of that year, the Grand Army defeated Austrian and Russian forces at Austerlitz, despite being outnumbered. Under the Treaty of Pressburg, France and its allies gained further territories in Italy and Germany.

Confederation of the Rhine

In July 1806, Napoleon dissolved the Holy Roman Empire, uniting all the German states except Prussia under French rule in a Confederation of the Rhine. In response, Prussia formed an alliance with Russia, but before the Russian army arrived, Napoleon smashed Prussian forces at Jena and Auerstadt. His victory over Russia at Friedland in June 1807 forced the Tsar to make peace with France. Napoleon was now at the height of his power, confirmed by the Treaty of Tilsit, which broke the Third Coalition and won France and its German allies a third of Prussian territory.

However, by 1809, French control of the Confederation of the Rhine was being undermined by rising German nationalism. When Austrian troops attacked French forces in Bavaria, Napoleon invaded Austria, capturing Vienna in May and defeating an Austrian army at Wagram in July. Under the Treaty of Schonbrunn, Austria handed over much of its territory to France.

Invasion of Russia

With the Russian economy suffering the effects of the Continental System (see panel), in 1810, Tsar Alexander decided to resume trade with Britain. Napoleon assembled an army of 600,000 and, in 1812, marched on Russia, capturing Moscow in September. However, the harsh Russian winter and the need for supplies, forced him to withdraw. Thousands of French troops died from cold and starvation during the retreat. Many others were killed by bands of mounted Russian Cossacks. Of the original army, just 100,000 survived.

TIMELINE

1802	*Treaty of Amiens between Britain and France*
1805	*British victory at Trafalgar; French victory over Russia and Austria at Austerlitz*
1806	*French victory over Prussia at Jena*
1807	*Treaty of Tilsit marks zenith of Napoleon's power*
1812	*French Retreat from Moscow*
1813	*France is defeated at Leipzig*
1815	*Napoleon suffers his final defeat at Waterloo.*

Downfall

In 1813, before Napoleon could rebuild his forces, Prussia and Russia jointly declared war on France. Napoleon managed to defeat them at Lutzen and Bautzen, but the exhaustion of his troops compelled him to make peace. A Fourth Coalition formed against France, this time including all of Europe's major powers. The French won a further victory at Dresden in August 1813, but the losses in Russia and the sheer weight of forces ranged against them finally proved decisive. At the 'Battle of the Nations' at Leipzig, Napoleon suffered his first major defeat and was forced to withdraw from Germany. The allies invaded France and, despite a brilliant rearguard action by Napoleon, captured Paris in March 1814. Napoleon abdicated and was exiled to Elba in the Mediterranean. The Treaty of Paris forced France to give up almost all of its conquered territories.

Hundred Days

In an unexpected coda to his remarkable career, Napoleon escaped Elba in March 1815 and returned to France with some 1,000 supporters. Troops sent to stop him flocked to his banner instead. As he approached Paris, Louis XVIII, the newly installed Bourbon monarch, fled, and Napoleon resumed control. The allies,

who had been busy redrawing the map of Europe at the Congress of Vienna, hastily formed a new military coalition. Napoleon defeated the Prussians at Ligny before attacking a British army led by the Duke of Wellington at Waterloo. Wellington, with belated Prussian help, prevailed, and Napoleon was forced once again to abdicate. Under the second Treaty of Paris, France had to pay war damages and return to its 1790 borders.

Above *Though the British won the Battle of Trafalgar, Admiral Nelson was mortally wounded*

PENINSULAR WAR

Lacking the naval power to defeat Britain militarily, Napoleon attacked the British economy. His Continental System, established in 1807, banned trade between Britain and the countries under his control. When Portugal ignored the boycott, Napoleon sent French troops through Spain to occupy Lisbon. This sparked an uprising in Spain, formerly an ally of France. Meanwhile, a British army under the Duke of Wellington established a base in Portugal. Napoleon sent an army to occupy Madrid in December 1808. The ensuing Peninsular War was long and bloody. British, Portuguese and Spanish troops finally defeated the French in 1813.

The Industrial Revolution

1770–1914

The Industrial Revolution began in Britain in the latter half of the 18th century and spread to mainland Europe in the early 19th. Over the following century, Europe's nations were transformed from traditional agricultural economies into modern industrial ones. The Industrial Revolution was caused by the widespread adoption of capitalism, allied to the invention of power-driven machinery and the development of the factory system.

Above *The spinning jenny was a multiple-spool spinning wheel that dramatically increased productivity*

Methods of production

Before the Industrial Revolution, most goods were produced by hand in rural homes or urban workshops. Merchants, known as entrepreneurs, distributed the raw materials to workers, collected the finished products, paid for the work, then sold it. Growing demand for consumer products, together with a shortage of labour, placed pressure on entrepreneurs to find new, more efficient methods of production. With the development of power-driven machines, it made economic sense to bring workers, materials and machines together in one place, giving rise to the first factories. For added efficiency, the production process was broken down into basic individual tasks that a worker could specialize in, a system known as the division of labour.

'Workshop of the world'

Britain was uniquely placed to be the birthplace of the Industrial Revolution. It had abundant reserves of coal to power the new machines and iron ore to create tools, machine parts, bridges, ships and trains. Also, Britain's political stability and its government's free-market, laissez-faire approach to economic policy encouraged entrepreneurs to invest in new business ventures. As the world's leading colonial power, Britain also had access to raw materials from many parts of the globe, as well as markets in which to sell its products.

The move towards mass production began with the textile industry in northern England. New machines, starting with James Hargreaves' spinning jenny (1764), improved the speed and efficiency of spinning and weaving. By the 1780s, Britain had some 120 textile mills producing high-quality cloth at unprecedented rates. James Watts' improvement of the steam engine and Henry Cort's enhancement of the ironmaking process in the 1780s were other milestones in the mechanization of industry. A good transport infrastructure was needed to move

TIMELINE

1774–1779	*Samuel Crompton of Britain develops the spinning mule*
1783–1784	*A new purifying process makes iron-smelting more efficient*
1825	*The Stockton and Darlington Railway opens*
1831	*Michael Faraday builds the first electric motor and generator*
1835	*The first German railway opens in Bavaria*
1856	*Britain's Henry Bessemer pioneers the manufacture of steel from iron ore*
1885	*Germans, Daimler and Benz develop the automobile*
1909	*Bakelite, the first plastic, is patented.*

raw materials and finished goods over long distances, and during the 18th century British engineers constructed a network of canals to link cities and connect coal fields to rivers. By 1815, Britain was producing more coal, pig-iron and textiles than the rest of Europe combined, and had become known as the 'workshop of the world'.

The revolution spreads

Belgium was the second country to industrialize. From 1830, helped by government subsidies and fuelled by Belgian coal, the cities of Ghent, Liege and Verviers became major textile-manufacturing centres. In the German states, coal production doubled between 1830 and 1850, and iron ore mining increased sharply after 1850. Industrialization in France was held back by revolution, war and a poor transport system. Although there was some industrialization, France remained a largely agricultural economy for much of the 19th century.

The first rail networks were built in the 1820s, ushering in a new era of rapid transportation of goods and raw materials; and by the 1890s, all major railway routes in Europe had been established. The Industrial Revolution gained further momentum in the mid-19th century as European countries began to adopt free-trade policies; abolishing the import duties they had imposed to protect local producers from external competition. In 1846, Britain dropped its import tariff on corn. France, Belgium and the Zollverein (a Prussian-led customs union of the German states) reduced import taxes in the 1860s.

A REVOLUTION IN FINANCE

With the growth of manufacturing industry during the 19th century came a corresponding growth in the finance industry, to handle the increased flow of money. Banks and private investors played a crucial role in the Industrial Revolution by providing loans to industrialists, to allow them to buy new equipment and improve and expand their factories. Individual investors made fortunes in this way, but there were also many spectacular bankruptcies. A less risky method of funding capital projects was developed, especially in continental Europe, involving joint-stock companies: instead of loaning money directly to an industrialist, investors could buy shares in a limited liability company (in which their financial liability, in the case of bankruptcy, was limited to a certain sum) that would provide industrialists with credit.

Between 1865 and 1914, a so-called 'Second Industrial Revolution' occurred. The development of steel and the newly discovered power source of electricity boosted productivity, and mechanization spread to other industries, including food, drink, clothing, transport and entertainment. A new consumerist culture encouraged the mass production of goods such as bicycles, cars, radios and gramophones.

Above *Newly invented lathes speeded up the manufacture of many items*

Left *The arrival of the steam locomotive brought faster mobility for both people and goods*

Consequences of the Industrial Revolution

1800–1914

The Industrial Revolution had far-reaching social and political consequences for Europe. It marked the emergence of a new ruling elite of middle-class industrialists, supplanting the landed nobility. It also gave rise to an entirely new social division – the industrial working class – as millions of rural labourers migrated to the towns, to take up jobs in the factories. In the rapidly expanding industrial cities, workers were often forced to live in cramped, unsanitary conditions, and outbreaks of disease were common. To protect themselves against exploitative employers, workers organized themselves into trade unions. This frequently led to confrontation with factory owners and the government. New ideas circulated on how to create a fairer society. Some argued for a more equal distribution of wealth, while others attempted to incite a workers' revolution. Fear of social breakdown led many governments to alleviate the worst effects of rampant capitalism, and conditions in some areas improved in the later 19th century.

Right *The leader of the Luddites, as shown in an engraving first published in May 1812*

Working and living conditions

Conditions in factories were generally harsh and, with so many workers, the traditionally close bonds between employer and employee were no longer possible. People laboured 12 to 14 hours a day, six days a week, for very low wages. The machines set the pace, forcing people to perform repetitive tasks rapidly with little rest. Employers frequently hired women and children too, as cheap, unskilled labour. The children were often younger than ten years old; some were deformed by their work or suffered injuries from the machinery.

Cities could not keep up with the demand for housing as workers continued to arrive from the countryside; and many were obliged to live in the severely overcrowded slums that grew up around

the factories. Open sewers and a lack of clean drinking water often led to epidemics of typhoid and cholera. In the 1830s, the life expectancy of men in Birmingham, England, was slightly over 40 years. The natural environment also suffered, as factory smoke polluted the atmosphere in the cities.

Workers' responses

The mechanization of industry caused some traditional skills to become obsolete and cost many craft workers their livelihoods. Some unemployed English workers turned their resentment on the machines that had taken their jobs and began attacking

factories and machinery. They became known as Luddites, after the legendary character Ned Ludd. The first recorded Luddite attacks occurred in 1811.

Workers began to form trade unions in the late 1700s. Unions were strongly opposed by governments and industrialists and banned in England between 1799 and 1824; nevertheless, the movement grew. Trade unions often organized strikes for higher wages or better working conditions. In the 1830s and 1840s, a British working-class movement, called the Chartists, campaigned for political equality and social justice, but its demands were ignored by Parliament. A Chartist-organized general strike in 1842, involving half a million workers, succeeded in stopping production across Britain.

Middle classes

The great beneficiaries of the Industrial Revolution were the middle classes – business and professional people – who enjoyed a general improvement in living standards and better diets and health care, leading to a huge increase in population. Industrialization made available many new products, and provided unprecedented comforts and convenience to those who could afford them. The revolution also gave more political power to the middle classes,

with business interests often dictating government policy. The application of steam power to the printing industry led to a dramatic growth in newspaper and popular book publishing, which in turn encouraged literacy and greater political participation. The new industries required engineers, clerical and professional workers, thus expanding employment opportunities.

Despite these benefits, many middle-class people felt uncomfortable about the hardships suffered by workers, and the rising inequalities in wealth caused by the Industrial Revolution. Some, such as the German thinker Karl Marx, argued that capitalism would soon be overthrown in a workers' revolution, to be replaced by a socialist system in which private property was abolished and the means of production were owned collectively. Others, called social democrats, preferred to see the worst effects of capitalism ameliorated through progressive taxation and the nationalization of key industries.

Under pressure from campaigners for social reform, as well as trade unions, many European governments introduced legislation to make life better for workers. From around the 1840s, working hours in factories and mines were cut and wages rose. Housing was gradually improved. Child labour was banned and compulsory free state education was instituted throughout much of Europe.

Above The provision of compulsory free state education for all brought literacy to the masses

TIMELINE

1799–1824	*Trade unions are banned in Britain*
1833	*Britain's Factory Act restricts the use of children in factories*
1846	*Repeal of the Corn Law in Britain ushers in an era of free trade*
1880–1889	*A social welfare system is introduced in Germany*
1909–1910	*National strikes by rail and postal workers in France.*

THE GROWTH OF NATIONALISM IN EUROPE

1815–1849

In the wake of Napoleon's defeat, the victorious allies met in Vienna with the aim of restoring the old order. Yet the return of familiar empires and dynastic rulers could not disguise the fact that Europe had fundamentally altered. Powerful new movements had been unleashed by the French Revolution and the Napoleonic Wars. Middle-class liberals, heirs of the Enlightenment, campaigned for democratic constitutional government and a free-market economy. Utopian socialists argued for restructuring society along egalitarian lines. But the ideology that exercised the most powerful grip on the European imagination, and presented the greatest challenge to the political establishment in the decades after 1815, was nationalism.

Above *A scene from the Greek war of independence (1821–1832) by a contemporary painter, Panagiotis Zografos*

Concert of Europe

The dominant figure at the Congress of Vienna (1814–1815) was the conservative Austrian foreign minister, Prince Klemens von Metternich. Under his leadership, the Congress restored Bourbon rule to France and Habsburg control to southern Germany, northern Italy and much of Central Europe. Metternich hoped the restoration of these dynasties would give political legitimacy to the new order. To maintain a balance of power, stronger new kingdoms were created by merging Norway with Sweden and the Netherlands with Belgium. Metternich established the 'Concert of Europe': regular conferences between the great powers to resolve any disputes that threatened the peace.

Nationalist struggles

Metternich and the other European leaders were very quickly confronted by the new force of nationalism that had begun to emerge in Europe during the late 18th century. Increasingly, people wished to live in states with a common ethnic and linguistic identity and – inspired by the

French Revolution – under constitutions that guaranteed their rights as citizens. As a concession to nationalism, the Congress of Vienna granted independence to Switzerland in 1815, but ignored the nationalist aspirations of many other peoples. When uprisings broke out in southern Italy (1820) and Spain (1822), the Congresses of Troppau and Verona, respectively, approved firm action to suppress them.

1830 revolutions

In 1830–1831, a series of revolutions threatened to overwhelm the Concert of Europe. It began in France with the overthrow of the repressive regime of Charles X. The more radical revolutionaries wished to establish a republic, but the upper-middle-class Orléanist faction engineered the succession of the 'citizen king' Louis-Philippe as a moderate constitutional monarch. Liberals and nationalists throughout Europe were inspired to launch revolutions of their own. Uprisings in Modena, Parma, the Papal States, Poland and some parts of Germany were all suppressed. However, an uprising against Dutch rule in Belgium met with a divided response from the European powers. The French, under Louis-Philippe, supported Belgian independence. Russia, Prussia, Austria and Britain were opposed, although none were prepared to commit troops in support of the Netherlands, and so an independent Belgium was achieved in 1839.

Nationalism in the Ottoman states

Nationalist struggles were generally containable by strong states – less so in the declining Turkish Ottoman Empire. After an uprising in Serbia in 1815, the Ottoman sultan was forced to offer the Serbs some autonomy. A similar measure of self-rule was conceded by the Ottomans to Moldavia and Wallachia in 1829. In 1821, a nationalist revolt broke out against Ottoman rule in Greece. By early 1822 the Greeks had won control of the Peloponnese. Turkish forces, with Egyptian support, invaded in 1825. They recaptured towns and ravaged much of the Peloponnese, but failed to suppress the uprising. The European powers, alarmed by the chaos and disruption to trade, and impressed by the conservative character of the Greek leaders, intervened on the side of the nationalists. In 1827, a British, French and Russian naval force destroyed the Ottoman-Egyptian fleet at Navarino. The Ottomans accepted Greek independence in 1832.

'Year of Revolutions'

In the year 1848, another spate of revolutions swept through Europe, this time coming very close to overturning the existing order. France was, once again, the catalyst. Demonstrations against Louis-Philippe's regime resulted in the king's abdication and the establishment of a Second Republic. Unrest quickly spread to Hungary, Croatia and the Czech lands, where nationalists

TIMELINE	
1815	*The Congress of Vienna reshapes post-Napoleonic Europe*
1815–1817	*Serbians gain limited independence from the Ottoman Turks*
1821–1832	*Greek War of Independence*
1822–1823	*Congress of Verona authorizes France to invade Spain to restore Spanish monarchy*
1830	*Louis-Philippe is elected 'King of the French' after the July Revolution*
1839	*The Dutch recognize Belgian independence*
1848	*Liberal nationalist revolutions sweep through Europe, ushering in short-lived republics*
1867	*Hungarian nationalists force the Habsburg rulers of Austria to establish a dual monarchy, thereafter known as Austria-Hungary.*

overturned Austrian rule and set up liberal governments with democratic constitutions. Metternich was forced to resign and flee abroad. In northern Italy, Austrian rulers were deposed and republics proclaimed. Many of the German states sent representatives to a newly created parliament at Frankfurt, with the aim of uniting Germany.

The revolutionaries were fatally divided over their aims, however, allowing conservative forces to reassert control. In France, Louis Napoleon Bonaparte, who had been elected president, declared himself emperor in 1852 and brutally suppressed workers' protests. The Habsburgs crushed the rebels in their territories, regaining control over Austria, Italy and Hungary. The Frankfurt assembly broke up under pressure from Prussia.

Right *Louis Napoleon Bonaparte, the Emperor Napoleon III, was the last monarch of France*

GERMAN AND ITALIAN UNIFICATION

1815–1871

Arguably the most significant outcome of 19th-century European nationalism, in terms of the future history of the continent, was the emergence, by 1871, of unified nation-states in Italy and Germany. Neither of these eventualities looked likely in 1848–1849, when nationalist uprisings were crushed and the status quo was forcibly reimposed. As it happened, neither Italy nor Germany would be unified through popular insurrection, but through a combination of political manoeuvring and military force.

Italian nationalism

The Congress of Vienna restored Austrian domination over much of northern Italy. The rest was divided into kingdoms ruled by absolute monarchs. At this time, only a small section of the nobility and the middle class indulged in dreams of a united, independent republic of Italy. Some Italian nationalists formed secret societies, the largest of which was the Carbonari. An important early champion of Italian unification was

Above *Giuseppe Garibaldi, whose fight for Italian independence made him a hero*

Guiseppe Mazzini (1805–1872), who created the organization 'Young Italy', to awaken ordinary Italians to the ideas of nationalism and republicanism.

The Carbonari organized nationalist uprisings in 1820, in Sicily and Sardinia-Piedmont; and in 1831, in the Papal States, Parma and Modena. All were put down by Austrian forces. In 1848, the wave of nationalist revolt that spread through Italy was forcefully suppressed by the Austrians and the French. Conservatism was not wholly triumphant, however. In Sardinia-Piedmont, a constitutional government survived, and in 1852 its new nationalist prime minister, Count Camillo di Cavour (1810–1861) began the process that would lead to Italian unification ten years later.

Risorgimento

Cavour's first aim was to gain independence from Austria. To this end, he negotiated a secret alliance with France. Then, in 1859, he engineered a war with Austria. With French help, Sardinia-Piedmont defeated Austria, forcing the Austrians to cede Lombardy (via France) to the Piedmontese king, Victor Emmanuel. In a series of elections in 1859–1860, all the northern Italian states, except Austrian-controlled Venetia, voted to join Sardinia-Piedmont.

Meanwhile, an Italian nationalist revolutionary leader called Guiseppe Garibaldi (1807–1882) invaded Italy from the south with a small army of followers. He conquered Sicily and Naples, then handed both over to Victor Emmanuel. Next, Cavour moved his forces into the Papal States, forcing elections there. All but Rome voted to join Sardinia-Piedmont. By March 1861, the whole of Italy, apart from Rome

TIMELINE	
1833	*Guiseppe Mazzini founds 'Young Italy'*
1848–1849	*Italian revolts against Austrian rule fail*
1849	*Victor Emmanuel becomes king of Sardinia*
1859	*Piedmont, supported by France, expels Austria from northern Italy*
1860	*Garibaldi invades Sicily and captures most of southern Italy*
1863–1864	*Prussian-Austrian force expels Denmark from Schleswig-Holstein. Prussia gains Schleswig; Austria gains Holstein*
1866	*Prussia defeats Austria in Seven Weeks War; Austria loses Venetia and Holstein*
1870	*Prussia triumphs in Franco-Prussian War*
1871	*Wilhelm I proclaimed kaiser (emperor) of a united Germany.*

and Venetia, was united under the rule of Victor Emmanuel. Venetia joined in 1866 – Prussia promised Venetia to Italy in return for Italian support in Prussia's war against Austria (see below). Finally, Italy annexed Rome in 1870.

German nationalism

In 1849, the idea of a unified German nation seemed even more farfetched than a united Italy. Germany had never existed as a single entity, being composed of many small states, each proud of their own separate identity. Furthermore, Habsburg Austria was keen to maintain a status quo that allowed it to dominate central Europe. Nevertheless, powerful forces within German society saw advantages in unification. These included intellectuals, proud of the common heritage of the German-speaking peoples; Protestants, wishing to create a large state to balance Catholic Austria; liberals seeking a modern, centralized nation with a representative government; and businessmen desiring the larger markets of a united country.

Bismarck

Surprisingly, the main architect of German unification was a conservative Prussian statesman named Otto von Bismarck. Appointed prime minister in 1862, Bismarck was no German nationalist, but a realist, who viewed the liberal-nationalist forces within Germany as irresistible and believed the best compromise would be to create a united country on Prussian terms. Bismarck was a subtle, flexible politician, consistently underestimated by his rivals both inside and outside Germany.

Bismarck's immediate goal was to remove Austrian influence over northern Germany. In 1865, he persuaded France to accept Prussian dominance in northern Germany. He then won over liberal-nationalist opinion

by creating a new confederation of north German states, with a parliament elected by universal male suffrage – the most democratic assembly in Europe at that time. In response, Austria coaxed support from German states including Bavaria and Saxony, suspicious of Prussian power. In the ensuing Seven Weeks' War (June–July 1866), Prussia quickly defeated Austria and Saxony and gained the territories of Hanover, Saxony and Holstein, confirming its domination of the North German Confederation. Bismarck set about modernizing and liberalizing the confederation, offering a unified law code, religious freedom, and postal and telegraph services, in the hope of encouraging the southern German states to join.

Above *Left to right: Otto von Bismarck with Minister of War Albrecht von Roon and Chief of Staff Helmuth von Moltke*

German Empire

The catalyst for the final stage of unification was France. In 1870, the French emperor Napoleon III forced a war with Prussia by refusing to allow the Prussian king's Hohenzollern relative to become king of Spain. The Prussian army routed the French, capturing both their emperor and their capital. Bismarck took advantage of the victory to press the remaining German states of Baden Württemberg and Bavaria to join the confederation. Encouraged by guarantees of significant autonomy, they agreed; and in January 1871, the German Empire was proclaimed, with Wilhelm I of Prussia its first emperor.

Below *Otto von Bismarck and Napoleon III after the Battle of Sedan, fought on 1 September, 1870, during which the French emperor was captured*

THE RUSSIAN EMPIRE

1783–1917

Under Catherine the Great (reigned 1762–1796), Russia became a major world power, although it remained economically underdeveloped compared with Western Europe. Russian peasants were bound to the land as serfs, paying rent to local landlords, a system that had disappeared from Western Europe in the Middle Ages. Yet, with a very small middle class, the Russian state depended for its revenue on maintaining serfdom.

Nicholas I

Many among the Russian elite were infected by the liberal ideas that swept Europe in the post-Napoleonic era. Some younger members of the aristocracy formed a revolutionary group called the Decembrists, which revolted in 1825. The revolt was quickly suppressed, but so alarmed Tsar Nicholas I (reigned 1825–1855) that he introduced a number of repressive measures: replacing aristocratic military officers with professionals; censoring the press; restricting travel outside Russia; banning political organizations; and establishing a secret police force.

In 1828–9, Russia won a war against the Ottoman Empire, thereby gaining territory around the Black Sea and control of the Dardenelles, which allowed it to move its merchant ships between the Black Sea and the Mediterranean. This brought Russia into conflict with Britain and France, who objected to Russian expansion in the Black Sea region. Russia lost the subsequent Crimean War (1853–1856) and was forced to give up some of its newly acquired territory.

Alexander II

Alexander II (reigned 1855–1881) saw this defeat as symptomatic of Russia's continuing backwardness compared with the rest of Europe. Realizing that Russia's economic reliance on serfdom was holding it back, he emancipated the serfs in 1861 and redistributed land among them; then began moving Russia towards the

Below A Bashkir switchman on the Trans-Siberian railway in the Ural Mountains, photographed in 1910 by Sergei Prokudin-Gorskii

EXPANSION IN ASIA

From the mid-1800s, Russia expanded further into Asia. In 1858 China agreed to cede Russia lands north of the Amur River and east of the Ussuri River. In a series of military campaigns between 1865 and 1876, against the khanates in Bukhara, Khiva and Tashkent, the whole of Western Central Asia was brought under Russian rule. In 1867, Russia sold its American territory (which would later be renamed Alaska) to the United States for $7,200,000. In the 1880s, the Russians began building the Trans-Siberian railway to help them exploit Siberian mineral wealth. Entrepreneurs' attempts to engage in trade with Manchuria and Korea brought Russia into conflict with Japan. Japan defeated Russian forces in 1904–1905, and Russia was forced to give up the southern half of the island of Sakhalin and control of the southern Manchurian railways.

adoption of a capitalist economy. He also reformed education and the judiciary along Western lines; introduced a railway network; lifted restrictions on the press; devolved more power to local civic authorities; and modernized the armed forces. Liberal reformers wanted to go further, desiring a constitutional monarchy, or even a republic. Some secret groups plotted to overthrow the tsar and establish a liberal democratic or socialist state. In 1881, a revolutionary group called the People's Will assassinated Alexander.

Alexander III

Alexander III (reigned 1881–1894) abandoned his father's reform programme and introduced repressive policies reminiscent of his grandfather, Nicholas I. He censored the press, restricted academic freedom and centralized political power. His 'Russification' programme imposed Russian language and education on non-Russian communities within the empire. Alexander's policies held Russia's revolutionary forces in check until the 1890s, when a series of bad harvests caused famine in the countryside. This coincided with increasing discontent among the middle and working classes in the rapidly industrializing cities. By the accession of Nicholas II (reigned 1894–1917), the mood in Russia had become dangerously volatile.

Nicholas II

Many people wished to topple the tsar's regime, but there was disagreement about what kind of government should take its place. Liberals favoured a Western-style parliamentary government; socialists wished to foment simultaneous revolutions by the peasants and the urban workers; Marxists – orthodox followers of the German philosopher Karl Marx –

wished to promote revolution among the industrial working class.

Between 1899 and 1904, there were frequent workers' strikes and anti-government protests. In January 1905, government troops fired on striking workers in St Petersburg, igniting an uprising that quickly spread through Russia. The liberal leaders of the 1905 revolution demanded constitutional reforms, which Nicholas was forced to agree to, including the establishment of an elected assembly, the Duma. The Duma functioned intermittently between 1906 and 1914. Its more radical proposals were quashed by Nicholas, but working with prime minister Pyotr Stolypin (1862–1911), significant reforms were enacted, such as providing peasants with loans to buy land.

Above *Alexander III was an autocratic Tsar under whose rule Russia moved ever closer to revolution*

Collapse

Despite these attempts to restore his political authority by working with the reform movement, Nicholas was rapidly running out of time. In 1914, World War I erupted and Russia found itself simultaneously at war with Germany, Austria and the Ottoman Empire. With its armies fighting on three fronts, and the economy in virtual collapse, the regime was ill-prepared to defend itself when revolution broke out in 1917. Within a very short time, Tsarist Russia had collapsed.

THE EUROPEAN ALLIANCE SYSTEM

1871–1914

The emergence of a powerful, unified Germany in 1871 threatened the European balance of power that had been nurtured by Metternich and his successors since 1815. However, Bismarck was not interested in expanding German power or territory, merely in maintaining its current dominant position and preserving peace on the continent.

Three Emperors' League

Bismarck was aware that the most serious threat to peace came from France, which nursed powerful grievances against Germany for the loss of Alsace and part of Lorraine, following its defeat in the Franco-Prussian War. He sought to isolate France, firstly by forming the Three Emperors' League with Austria-Hungary and Russia in 1873. This was not a straightforward achievement, since Austria-Hungary and Russia had rival ambitions in the Balkan lands of the declining Ottoman Empire.

Below *A map of Europe on the eve of World War I, from the* New Age History Readers, *published in 1921*

Triple Alliance

Realizing that the alliance between Austria and Russia was probably unsustainable in the long run, Bismarck secured a secret agreement with Austria-Hungary and Italy in 1882, called the Triple Alliance. He maintained friendly relations with France by encouraging its colonial expansion in North Africa. When the Three Emperors' League expired in 1887, Bismarck replaced it with a Reinsurance Treaty with Russia, in which Germany recognized the Balkans as being within the Russian sphere of influence. It also pledged German neutrality in the event of a war between Austria-Hungary and Russia; and similarly, Russian neutrality in the case of a war between Germany and France. Bismarck also informally agreed with Britain that Germany would neither compete for colonial territory in Africa and Asia, nor construct a large fleet to challenge Britain's naval supremacy.

Franco-Russian alliance

All this careful diplomatic work began to unravel in 1890, with the accession of the hot-headed new German emperor, Kaiser Wilhelm II. The emperor's incautious approach to foreign affairs brought him into conflict with Bismarck and prompted the latter's resignation. When Wilhelm refused to renew the Reinsurance Treaty with Russia, the door was opened to a Franco-Russian alliance, duly signed in 1894. Under this agreement, each country pledged its support to the other in the event of a war with Germany. Now Germany was faced with the prospect of having to fight a war on two fronts.

Triple Entente

While Bismarck had been content with maintaining Germany as the dominant power on the European continent, Wilhelm had more global ambitions. Under his direction, Germany began an aggressive campaign of colonial expansion, directly competing with British economic interests in southern Africa. Wilhelm further alarmed Britain by embarking on a massive programme of naval construction. Britain had previously adopted a stance of 'splendid isolation' from European affairs, but in 1904 the British government concluded an agreement with the French in the common interest of reining in Germany. In 1907, a similar agreement was reached with Russia, and the Triple Entente was formed.

Chain reaction

Thus an alliance system evolved, in which the Triple Alliance of Germany, Austria-Hungary and Italy was ranged against the Triple Entente of Britain, France and Russia. With each country guaranteed the support of its allies in the event of conflict with a member of the opposing alliance, there now existed the danger of a chain reaction leading to a Europe-wide war. The alliance system was tested numerous times between 1907 and 1914. In the Agadir Crisis of 1911, Germany, with colonial ambitions in North Africa, sent a gunboat to the Moroccan port of Agadir, nearly sparking a war with France.

Balkan tensions

However, the most likely flashpoint for a conflict was the Balkans. The region seethed with nationalist sentiment, with its many small states desiring self-

determination. Austria opposed these causes, fearing they might inspire independence movements among the minority groups within its own empire. In 1908, Austria decided to make a show of power in the Balkans by annexing the provinces of Bosnia and Herzegovina. This outraged Serbia, which had its own designs on Bosnia, due to the many Serbs living there. Russia sided with Serbia, and Germany supported Austria. War looked likely until Russia, still recovering from defeat to Japan, backed down. Tensions rose once again with the Balkan Wars of 1912–1913, a conflict between several Balkan states from which Serbia emerged strengthened and enlarged, alarming Austria and Germany, which viewed Serbia as a satellite of Russia.

PREPARING FOR WAR

In the years before 1914, all the major powers believed war was likely and made suitable preparations. Each country enlarged its army through conscription and worked on rapid mobilization plans. Germany developed the Schlieffen Plan to enable it to fight a war on two fronts. Advances in military technology increased the destructive power of armed forces. Machine guns and artillery could fire more rapidly and accurately than ever before. Railways could be used to speed up the movement of troops and supplies to the front. In 1906, Britain perfected the Dreadnought, the first modern battleship. Heavily armoured, steam-driven and with greater firepower than any contemporary ship, its launch marked the beginning of a naval arms race with Germany.

Left In this Russian poster from 1914, the figures represent the Triple Entente allies France, Russia and Britain

Below The arrival at Agadir of the gunboat Panther *aroused anxiety about German intentions in both Britain and France*

THE DEMISE OF THE OTTOMAN EMPIRE

1783–1923

Evidence of Ottoman military weakness grew ever more apparent as the 18th century drew to a close. The Turkish empire was defeated in two wars against Russia (1768–1774 and 1787–1792), resulting in further territorial losses. Napoleon's 1798 invasion of Egypt was another forewarning of European ambitions to take over Ottoman lands. Attempts to modernize the armed forces under Selim III (reigned 1789–1807) were obstructed by conservative interests, particularly the Janissary corps. By this time, the Janissaries had become lazy and parasitic, extorting money from the state, attempting to influence policy and deposing or killing any sultan who threatened their status.

Mahmud II

The Janissary corps met with a violent end in 1826, when thousands of them were massacred on the orders of the Sultan Mahmud II (reigned 1808–1839). Mahmud proved an effective ruler. As well as abolishing the Janissaries, he strengthened central authority; weakened the power of provincial lords; and attempted to reassert control over the empire's periphery. In this final task he failed. He was forced to surrender to nationalist forces in Serbia in 1829, granting it autonomy, in return for annual tribute payments. After Britain, France and Russia intervened decisively on behalf of the Greek nationalists, Mahmud was obliged to concede Greece in 1832.

Above *Selim III was a patron of the arts and a notable musician as well as a reformist ruler*

Trouble in Egypt

In Egypt, the Ottoman viceroy Mehmet Ali, originally sent to resist Napoleon's invasion, became effective ruler from 1805. The Ottoman government tolerated the situation – because Mehmet proved an effective ally – until 1831, when he and his son Ibrahim

Pasha seized control of Ottoman Syria. Ottoman attempts to retake Syria failed when Ibrahim Pasha crushed Turkish forces at Konya (1832) and later at Nizib (1839). These defeats brought the Ottoman Empire to the brink of collapse, and it was only saved by Austria and Britain, who feared that a power vacuum in the region would threaten their trade links with India.

Tanzimat

In the interests of propping up the Ottomans, Britain encouraged the empire to modernize. Mahmud's successor Abd al-Madjid (reigned 1839–1861) adopted a reform programme known as the Tanzimat (reorganization), introducing Western-style changes in education, finance, government and the military. One condition of British support for the Ottomans against Russia in the Crimean War (1853–1856), was continuation of the Tanzimat. However, by the 1870s, as the Ottomans reeled from successive financial and foreign policy crises, the reform programme ground to a halt.

San Stefano and Berlin

In 1876, Abd al-Hamid II (reigned 1876–1909) introduced the first Ottoman constitution and tried to restore stability, but was hit the following year by a Russian invasion. The Russians swiftly overran Ottoman territory, almost as far as Constantinople. Under the 1878 Treaty of San Stefano, the Ottomans were forced to cede most of their European possessions, including a pro-Russian Bulgaria, enlarged to contain Macedonia and Thrace. The other European powers, concerned at Russian expansionism, convened the Congress of

Berlin where they managed to revise San Stefano: the Ottomans regained Eastern Rumelia and Macedonia; Russia received territory in eastern Anatolia; Britain gained Cyprus; Serbia and Montenegro became independent; and Austria-Hungary took de facto control of Bosnia and Herzegovina (although, officially, they remained Ottoman possessions).

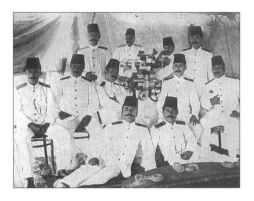

Left The Young Turks originated among military students, but their progressive and nationalistic views spread throughout society

Further losses

During the 1880s, European powers sought increasingly interventionist solutions to the so-called 'Eastern Question', that was the instability caused by Ottoman weakness. Tunisia was lost to the French (1881); Egypt to the British (1882); and Eastern Rumelia to Bulgaria (1885). To achieve a stronger grip on what remained of his empire, Abd al-Hamid adopted a raft of autocratic measures. He suspended the constitution, centralized political authority and established a spy network. He also pursued a policy of friendship with Germany, inviting in their officials to reorganize Ottoman finances and armed forces.

Young Turks

Abd al-Hamid's repressive measures provoked opposition in many quarters. A coalition of nationalist anti-government groups, known collectively as the Young Turks, organized a coup in 1908, forcing the sultan to restore the constitution and introduce parliamentary government. When the sultan's conservative supporters rebelled in 1909, Abd al-Hamid was deposed and banished. The Young Turks, under their leader Enver Pasha, took full control of the empire. The Young Turks introduced liberal reforms, but were unable to stem the haemorrhage of Ottoman power and territory. In 1911, Italy occupied Tripolitana, and in the Balkan Wars (1912–1913) the Ottomans lost all their Balkan lands except eastern Thrace. In 1914, Enver Pasha concluded a secret pact with Germany, believing it to be the only country capable of protecting Ottoman interests.

The end

World War I was a catastrophe for the Ottomans. Russia invaded Anatolia and a British-supported Arab revolt defeated Turkish forces in the Middle East. Under the Treaty of Sèvres (1920), the empire was reduced to Turkey alone. In the Turkish War of Independence (1919–23), nationalists drove non-Turkish forces from Anatolia. In 1923 the Republic of Turkey was founded, ending over 600 years of Ottoman rule.

TIMELINE	
1787–1792	*Catherine II wages war against the Ottoman Empire*
1828–1829	*The Ottomans lose control of the easten Black Sea ports*
1832	*The Ottomans lose Greece following War of Independence*
1840	*Austria and Britain intervene to save the Ottoman Empire during Ottoman war with Egypt*
1878	*Montenegro, Romania and Serbia win independence*
1895	*Turkish nationalists form the Young Turks*
1908	*The Young Turk rebellion breaks out in Thessalonica*
1914	*Russia, Britain and France declare war on the Ottoman Empire*
1919–1923	*War of Independence leads to establishment of Republic of Turkey.*

THE WESTWARD EXPANSION OF THE UNITED STATES

1783–1910

In 1783, the newly formed United States of America was a small nation, consisting of just 13 former colonies clustered around the Atlantic seaboard and extending no further west than the Mississippi River. During the following century, the young country would expand inexorably westward across the North American continent, vastly increasing its territory, population and economic might.

Initially, expansion was limited by French possession of lands beyond the Mississippi. However, this obstacle was removed in 1803 with the Louisiana Purchase, the acquisition by the USA of a great swathe of the midwest from the French emperor Napoleon. This vast territory, consisting of around 530 million acres, was bought for just 15 million dollars, or three cents per acre.

Gradually, transcontinental USA began to take shape as more territories were acquired through a combination of purchase, diplomacy and military conquest. West Florida was annexed from Spain in 1813. In 1819 Spain also ceded East Florida and all its lands in the northwest, including the present-day states of Washington, Oregon and Idaho. Later, in the 1830s and 1840s, the USA won large territories in the south-west from Mexico, including Texas and California. Finally, in 1867, the US government purchased Alaska from Russia.

The pathfinders

Before these newly acquired territories could be settled, they needed to be explored and mapped. In 1804, an expedition was commissioned by President Thomas Jefferson to explore the Western regions of the continent. The expedition, headed by Meriwether Lewis and William Clark, lasted for two and a half years and covered around 8,000 miles. Lewis and Clark established a route between the Mississippi River and the west coast and brought back encouraging news about the natural wealth of the West, inspiring a new era of exploration.

Government-sponsored expeditions led by Zebulon Pike (1804–1807) and Stephen Long (1817–1823) explored Colorado and New Mexico and the lands near the Red and Arkansas Rivers. Traders and fur trappers such as Jedediah Smith opened up the Santa Fe Trail between Missouri and New Mexico in 1821. And from about 1810, hunters and trappers known as 'mountain men' explored the Rockies. This golden age of exploration produced a number of famous frontiersmen whose daring feats became the stuff of legend. They included Davy Crockett, renowned for his bear hunting, and his death in defence of Texan independence at the Battle of the Alamo; James Bowie, pioneer, explorer and

Below *The Lewis and Clark expedition, illustrated in the children's book* The Story of Our Country *by E. Boyd Smith (1920)*

inventor of the Bowie Knife; and Kit Carson, mountain man, army scout and buffalo hunter.

Pioneers and settlers

The Americans who migrated west into the newly explored territories did so for a variety of reasons. Some, leaving the crowded cities of the north-east, were attracted by tales of the vast open spaces of the interior, with its fertile soil and abundant game. Others, such as the Mormons who settled Utah, came to escape religious persecution. Some had fled the great southern plantations in desperation, displaced by the slave labour forces purchased by their owners. Many came out of a sense of 'manifest destiny'; a belief that America was destined by God and history to expand across the entire continent. The government added a further incentive to settlers by offering free land, so long as it was occupied and farmed.

From 1843, pioneers set off each spring in long wagon trains along the 'Oregon Trail', which stretched 3,500 km (2,170 miles) from Missouri to the Pacific coast. The steady flow of migrants became a torrent after the discovery of gold in California in 1848. Over 100,000 'Forty-Niners' swept into California, infected with 'gold fever' and hoping to strike it rich. Few found gold, but many ended up settling there as farmers and traders.

While the Oregon Trail and the gold rush helped develop the far West during the 1840s, much of the interior of the West remained unsettled during this period. It was

THE NATIVE AMERICANS

The westward expansion of the USA came at a terrible cost to the native inhabitants of the continent. As the pioneers blazed their trails westward, they ruthlessly occupied Native American lands. The pioneers were given military assistance in this endeavour by federal troops, who fought many battles against the natives in the so-called Indian Wars (1861–68 and 1875–90). White settlers were also responsible for the indiscriminate slaughter of huge numbers of buffalo, the main food source of the Plains people. Many native peoples, including the Cherokee, Delaware and Wichita, were forcibly removed from their ancestral homelands and placed on reservations, to make way for settlers.

not until the 1860s that ranchers and farmers began to occupy the Great Plains west of the Mississippi. This settlement was greatly helped in that decade by the arrival of the railroads and telegraphic communication.

By the early 20th century, the USA had grown into a major industrial nation, spanning the entire width of the North American continent. It had settled a territory almost the size of Europe, despite formidable physical and geographical challenges. And it had done so largely through the adventurousness and tenacity of its pioneering people.

Above It was at Sutter's Mill in Coloma that flakes of gold were first found, precipitating the California gold rush

TIMELINE	
1803	*France sells its North American territory to the USA in the Louisiana Purchase*
1804–1806	*Lewis and Clark's expedition charts an overland route west to the Pacific*
1843	*The settlement of Oregon begins with the establishment of the Oregon Trail*
1848–1849	*The discovery of gold in California sparks the Gold Rush*
1861	*The first transcontinental telegraph line is completed*
1862	*The Homestead Act grants free family farms to settlers*
1869	*The transcontinental railroad is completed.*

THE AMERICAN CIVIL WAR

1861–1865

The American Civil War was a conflict between the Northern states of the USA (the Union), who wished to maintain the United States as one nation, and the Southern states (the Confederacy), who had seceded from the union. The war lasted four years and cost more than 600,000 lives. There were many reasons for the conflict, including growing cultural differences and economic disparities between North and South and arguments over the division of power between federal and state governments. However, the most important cause was the longstanding disagreement over slavery.

Above *Abraham Lincoln, 16th president of the United States, photographed in November 1863*

Right *An illustration of the first Confederate Cabinet; Jefferson Davis is third from the right*

A nation divided

The economy of the 11 Southern states depended on slavery. Southerners used slave labour to produce their crops, especially cotton, and some four million slaves of African descent worked on their farms and plantations, and in their towns and cities. From the early 19th century, a small yet vocal lobby had emerged in the North calling for the abolition of slavery. Already illegal in the North, the abolitionists managed, in the 1820 'Missouri Compromise', to extend the ban to the new states of the Louisiana Purchase (except Missouri). For many, this seemed to settle the issue, but it flared up again with the annexation of new territories from Mexico in the west. Abolitionists demanded slavery be banned there also; while Southerners, keen to expand into these areas, pressed government to permit it. An 1850 compromise declared California a free state, while allowing the other territories to decide on the issue for themselves.

Further decisions chipped away at the Missouri Compromise, thereby extending the rights of slave-holders. The 1854 Kansas-Nebraska Act permitted slavery in those two states; and in the 1857 Dred Scott case, the Supreme Court ruled that Congress could not, after all, prevent slavery in the territories. Outraged abolitionists formed the Republican Party in order to further their cause. Abraham Lincoln, Republican candidate in the 1860 presidential election, was opposed to slavery and against its extension to new territories. On his election, seven Southern states immediately seceded from the Union, forming themselves into the Confederate States of America and electing Jefferson Davis as their president. The four remaining 'slave states' joined them when the Civil War started.

Progress of the war

War broke out on 12 April 1861 when Confederate forces attacked Fort Sumter, a federal army post in South Carolina. Lincoln, who viewed the secession as illegal and the preservation of the Union as his duty, took this as a declaration of war. He was aware that the South depended on

European imports, so one of his strategies was to blockade its coastline, hoping to starve the Southern states into submission. He also wished to take the Confederate capital, Richmond, Virginia. The Confederate generals, notably Robert E. Lee, proved superior to their Union counterparts, however, and the South won several victories in 1861–1862, preventing Union forces from capturing Richmond and the key town of Fredericksburg.

In September 1862, the Confederates went on the offensive with an invasion of Maryland, but were forced to retreat at the Battle of Antietam (Sharpsburg). This first Union victory encouraged Lincoln to issue his Emancipation Proclamation, freeing all slaves in the Confederacy. The Proclamation gave a moral focus to the Union cause and encouraged the recruitment of African American soldiers. By the war's end, 186,000 of them had served in Union armies. It was only gradually that Southern slaves felt the Proclamation's impact, as Northern armies moved southwards. Meanwhile, Confederate armies, under Robert E. Lee, continued to be successful, winning the Battle of Fredericksburg (December 1862) and Chancellorsville (April 1863). In June, Lee's army swung north into Pennsylvania. At Gettysburg, it suffered its first major defeat, a battle that proved the turning point of the war.

Victory for the North

By 1863, the North's greater manpower and economic resources were beginning to tell. The South never fully recovered from its losses at Gettysburg, and it proved its last major offensive. To make matters worse, in 1862 Union armies under Ulysses Grant had seized control of the Mississippi River, splitting the Southern forces in two. As 1863 progressed, Confederate forces were driven out of Tennessee, back into Georgia. In 1864,

TIMELINE	
1854	*The Kansas-Nebraska Act repeals the Missouri Compromise and sparks a war between abolitionists and pro-slavers*
1857	*The Dred Scott decision outlaws restrictions on slavery in the territories*
Jan 1861	*Abraham Lincoln becomes US president*
Apr 1863	*The Civil War begins*
Jan 1863	*The Emancipation Proclamation is signed, liberating slaves in the Confederacy*
July 1863	*The Union army defeats the Confederate army at Gettysburg*
Apr 1865	*Richmond falls; the Confederates surrender at Appotamox*
1865	*The Thirteenth Amendment to the US Constitution abolishes slavery.*

bloody campaigns in Virginia, Georgia and the Carolinas further depleted the South's human and material resources, and caused great devastation and famine in the region. On 9 April 1865, the South surrendered.

Lincoln was assassinated five days later, yet his place in history was already assured: he had preserved the United States as one nation and freed the slaves. Shortly afterwards, Congress passed constitutional amendments abolishing slavery and giving African Americans US citizenship. The cultural divide between North and South remained, however, and the Civil War had added an extra legacy of bitterness. Furthermore, racial discrimination continued, and the civil rights of African Americans would not be fully recognized for another 100 years.

Below A print showing The Battle of Gettysburg, a turning point in the American civil war

THE INDUSTRIAL EXPANSION OF THE UNITED STATES

1800–1914

During the 19th century, the United States underwent a dramatic transformation from a simple agricultural economy into an industrial superpower. The first phase of this transformation, which lasted from 1800 until the Civil War, witnessed developments in transportation and manufacturing, and the emergence of a vibrant capitalist economy. In the post-Civil War phase, the United States experienced rapid industrialization, population growth and urbanization.

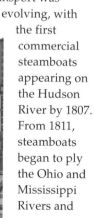

Below *New York's Woolworth Building was completed in 1913 and at 57 storeys was the tallest building in the world until 1930*

Transportation

The sheer size of the United States presented a challenge to early 19th-century entrepreneurs. Urban centres and rural settlements were widely dispersed, making markets difficult and expensive to reach. An effective transportation network was therefore crucial to economic growth. The process began with the construction of roads called 'turnpikes', mainly in New England and the mid-Atlantic states. Between 1790 and 1820, known as the 'turnpike era', over 3,200 km (2,000 miles) of roads were constructed. By the 1830s, roads extended westwards as far as Illinois. At the same time, river and canal transport was evolving, with the first commercial steamboats appearing on the Hudson River by 1807. From 1811, steamboats began to ply the Ohio and Mississippi Rivers and their tributaries, stimulating growth in the Midwest and South by providing access to markets in the north and east. Between 1816 and 1840, a network of over 5,000 km (3,000 miles) of canals were built, linking the Atlantic seaboard with the Midwest and the Great Lakes.

However, the most transformational and iconic transport system in 19th-century America was the railroad. The first, between Baltimore and Ohio, opened in 1830. Other cities quickly saw the benefits, and in just 10 years, 5,324 km (3,307 miles) of track had been laid. By 1850 this had grown to over 15,000 km (around 10,000 miles). The First Transcontinental Railroad, opened in 1869, completed the rail network; rendering the wagon trains of previous decades obsolete and helping to spread the fruits of eastern economic prosperity to the American West. Transcontinental communications were further improved by the introduction of the telegraph in 1837. By 1861 there were 80,000 km (almost 50,000 miles) of telegraph cable in the United States.

Industrialization

Improvements in transport encouraged the first stage of industrialization in the early 1800s. Another stimulus was the shortage of imports during the War of 1812 against Britain, which provided the impetus for a domestic manufacturing industry. The textile industry led the way with the first North American mill, founded in 1813. Until the Civil War, industrialization was gradual and sporadic, despite the country's vast natural resources and steadily expanding population (31.5 million by 1861).

After the Civil War ended in 1865, there came a huge surge in industrialization as speculators – both foreign and American – rushed to invest in what they perceived as a nation with a bright future. Railroad builders, spurred by federal land grants, drove economic growth. As more urban centres and rural areas were linked by rail, new markets opened up for the rapidly industrializing north-east, further stimulating production. Technological innovation and improved factory methods made it possible to produce goods faster, in greater quantity and more cheaply than ever before. From the 1870s, the United States led the way in a second industrial revolution, becoming a world leader in steel production and a pioneer of the new power source of electricity. By 1901, the Carnegie Steel Company in Pennsylvania was producing more steel than the whole of Britain.

The unregulated nature of the American economy allowed entrepreneurs to flourish and businesses to grow at astonishing rates, but it also encouraged ruthless, sometimes anti-competitive, practices. Some achieved monopolistic domination of their industry, and a class of super-rich business magnates emerged, including John D. Rockefeller (oil), Philip D. Armour (meatpacking), J. Pierpoint Morgan (finance) and Andrew Carnegie (steel).

Population and urban growth

More than 25 million European immigrants – especially from Germany, Scandinavia, Britain, Ireland, Italy and Eastern Europe – entered the United States between 1870 and 1916 to help fill the growing demand for cheap labour in the rapidly expanding industrial sector. Cities such as New York, Chicago, Pittsburgh, Cleveland, Milwaukee, Cincinnatti and St Louis grew enormously. By 1910, the

INVENTING THE MODERN WORLD

A spirit of technological innovation infected the United States in the later 19th century, and American inventors pioneered a host of remarkable new devices, including the typewriter (1867), the mimeograph (1875), the telephone, microphone and phonograph (1877), electric light (1879) and the camera (1888). In 1908, the mechanic Henry Ford launched the first affordable automobile, the Model T, thus revolutionizing American transport.

population stood at 92 million, over half of whom lived in towns and cities. Worker exploitation was common, and employees organized themselves into labor unions, often striking over pay and job losses. One general strike in 1877 spread to six cities and eventually had to be suppressed by federal troops. Yet, whatever the social problems caused by industrialization, its economic impact on the nation as a whole was extraordinary. By 1914, American had overtaken Britain as the world's leading industrial power, with more telephones, telegraphs, electric lights and motor cars than any other country.

Above Henry Ford supplied the public with affordable motorized transport that rapidly replaced the horse and trap

THE DEVELOPMENT OF CANADA

1763–1914

By the 18th century, the area now known as Canada was composed of two territories: the French province of New France, or Canada, on the St Lawrence River, and British Nova Scotia on the Atlantic seaboard. After its victory over France in the Seven Years' War (1756–1763), Britain took control of Canada, which it renamed the Province of Quebec. Quebec's 6,500-strong population of French-speaking Roman Catholics were understandably fearful that Britain would force them to change their ways. To reassure them, the British parliament passed the Quebec Act (1774), which guaranteed freedom of worship and allowed Quebec to maintain the French legal system. The act also significantly enlarged Quebec territory to include lands south of the Great Lakes. Thus, Canadian loyalty was secured at a time of increasing rebelliousness by the 13 British colonies. This proved invaluable to the British during the American Revolution (1775–1783), when American forces besieging Quebec City found little support for their cause.

Quebec divided

Below *The bombardment by the British fleet of Fort McHenry during the Battle of Baltimore, 13 September 1814*

When the Americans won their independence, Britain was forced to surrender all of its lands south of the Great Lakes to the newly formed USA, greatly reducing Quebec's territory. Quebec also changed demographically as some 50,000 American colonists, who had remained loyal to Britain during the conflict, fled northwards to Quebec and Nova Scotia – the ancestors of much of modern-day Canada's English-speaking community. Determined not to repeat the mistake it had made with the 13 colonies, Britain decided on a more sensitive approach to its administration of Quebec. The Constitutional Act of 1791 was an acknowledgement of the colony's bicultural nature, and the desire of the English-speakers to live under English and Protestant laws and institutions. The act divided Quebec into two parts – English-speaking Upper Canada (modern Ontario) and French-speaking Lower Canada (modern Québec) – under the authority of a British governor and an appointed legislative council.

Expansion

Between 1775 and 1821, the Hudson's Bay Company (HBC), which owned much of north-east Canada, and the North West Company (NWC) of Montréal, fought for control of Canada's fur trade. The competition spurred on exploration of Canada's west, as rival traders searched for new routes and suppliers. NWC fur traders Alexander McKenzie, Simon Fraser and David Thompson explored and

WAR OF 1812

In the War of 1812 between the USA and Britain, the USA invaded Canada, briefly threatening the survival of Upper Canada before its forces were driven back. The war strengthened Canadian patriotism and reinforced the belief that Canada should remain independent and separate from the USA. It was the last aggressive act between the two countries. Further border changes were agreed peaceably and by 1846, the US-Canadian frontier had become permanently established.

mapped the Western territories as far as the Pacific and the Arctic Oceans.

Between 1815 and 1850, huge numbers of English, Scots and Irish immigrants flooded into British North America. By the 1840s, the population had reached around 1.5 million, and – except in Lower Canada – was now vastly more British than French. Most settled in established colonies, but new ones were also founded. Scottish philanthropist Lord Selkirk set up the Red River Colony in 1812 in the central region; and in the far west, Vancouver Island (founded 1849) and British Columbia (founded 1858) formed a single colony (British Columbia) in 1866.

Rebellion

In 1837, French-speaking revolutionaries in Lower Canada tried to overthrow British authority. In the same year, radicals in Upper Canada took up arms against British monarchical rule, demanding representative government. Both rebellions were quelled, but demonstrated the urgent need for constitutional reform. To promote assimilation between the two communities, the Act of Union (1840) united Upper and Lower Canada into a single Province of Canada. In 1848, an elected legislature was established, although its allocation of seats between French and English-speaking parts became a further focus of discontent.

Union

During the 1860s, Canadians suffered frequent border raids by Fenians (Irish Americans demanding Irish independence from Britain). They also felt threatened by the growing power of the USA to their south, and its rapid westward expansion. The British and Canadians agreed that a federal union, in the interests of security, was the best answer and in 1867, the

British North America Act was passed. This united Nova Scotia, New Brunswick, Québec and Ontario (the latter pair having reacquired their former names) into the Dominion of Canada, with a constitution based on the British parliamentary system.

The founders aimed to unite all the remaining British colonies to create a transcontinental nation. The purchase of Rupert's Land from the HBC in 1870 vastly extended Canadian territory in the north-east, and a new province of Manitoba was created there. By 1873, Manitoba, British Columbia and Prince Edward Island had joined the new federation. The Canadian Pacific Railway, completed in 1885, played a crucial role in unification, linking British Columbia and the east, and promoting human settlement along its route. Canada's expansion continued into the 20th century, as new settlers poured in from eastern Europe and the USA. The provinces of Alberta and Saskatchewan were created in 1905, and in 1912 the remaining lands of the HBC were added to Québec, Ontario and Manitoba.

Above A cartoon in the London magazine Punch, *dated 11 June 1870, shows a Canadian kicking out an Irish Fenian*

INDEPENDENCE IN LATIN AMERICA

1783–1830

In the 18th century, Spain's Bourbon monarchs sought ways of increasing the flow of revenue from their American colonies. Spain needed more money to defend its empire from European rivals, particularly Britain and France. Pressure was placed on the colonies to increase production in agriculture and mining; and equally to reduce administration and defence costs, and expand frontiers. This led to discontent among the creole population (those of Spanish descent, born in the colonies), made worse by Spain's attempts to monopolize commerce with European and American markets at the expense of creole traders, and by increasing creole exclusion from positions within the colonial administration in favour of peninsulares (Spanish-born Spaniards).

Above *The slave revolt in the French colony of Saint-Domingue in 1791, which ended in the establishment of the republic of Haiti*

By the late 18th century, many creoles had grown resentful of Spanish authority. Influenced by the ideas of the Enlightenment and the American and French Revolutions, they began to desire independence from Spain. However, few creoles rebelled because of fear that without Spanish protection, they would be unable to defend themselves from uprisings by the African, indigenous and mixed-race communities, which together comprised some 80 per cent of Spanish America's population. Their fear was reinforced by two events: the 1780 Inca uprising in Peru, led by Tupac Amaru; and the 1791 slave revolt in the French Caribbean colony of Saint Domingue, which led to the foundation of the African-

Below *This statue of Simón Bolívar stands at the Sixth Avenue entrance to Central Park in New York*

Caribbean republic of Haiti in 1804.

The event that changed creole attitudes and accelerated moves towards independence was Napoleon's invasion of Spain in 1808. Napoleon replaced the Spanish Bourbon king Ferdinand with his own older brother, Joseph Bonaparte, causing a major conflict of loyalties throughout Spanish America. Did they recognize the new king, pledge allegience to Ferdinand, or form self-ruling governments? In most cases, creoles preferred the third option – as a temporary measure at least – until Bourbon rule was restored.

Mexico and Central America

A war of independence began in Mexico in 1810, led by the priest Miguel Hidalgo. After Hidalgo's execution the following year, the movement was led by the military commander Agustín de Iturbide. By 1822, Iturbide had driven the Spanish royalists from the country and founded the Mexican Empire, with himself as emperor. Around this time, Spain's Central American colonies also declared their independence, forming themselves into the United Provinces of Central America. The union lasted until 1838, when it separated into the independent states of today.

Spanish South America

Two figures dominated the story of South American independence. In the north, Simón Bolívar led the struggle to free present-day Venezuela, Colombia, Ecuador, Peru and Bolivia. In the south, José de San Martín, fought for independence for Argentina, Chile, Bolivia and Peru. Bolívar began his fight against Spanish royalist forces in 1811. After many fierce battles, he established the independent republic of Gran Colombia in 1822. In 1830–1831, Gran Colombia separated to form Venezuela, Ecuador and New Granada.

In 1816, Argentina declared its independence from Spain. José de San Martín realized that if Argentina was to remain a free state, the rest of the continent would have to be liberated as well. In 1817 he invaded Peru over the high Andean passes, surprising royalists and defeating them at the Battle of Chacabuco. Inspired by San Martín's example, Chilean patriot Bernado O'Higgins invaded Chile in 1818, defeating the royalists at the Battle of Maipú and securing the country's independence. By 1821, San Martín had taken Peru's capital Lima and proclaimed independence, although most of the countryside and highlands remained under royalist control. San Martín asked Simón Bolívar to complete the liberation of Peru, which he and his general Antonio José de Sucre achieved at the Battles of Junin and Ayacucho in 1824-1825. Upper Peru, which declared its independence in 1825, renamed itself Bolivia, in honour of Bolívar.

BRAZIL

As in the case of Spanish America, the catalyst for independence in Brazil was Napoleon's 1808 invasion of the Iberian Peninsula. The French occupation of Portugal prompted the Portuguese prince regent, later Joào VI, to flee to Brazil. When the French were driven out of Portugal in 1814, Joào elected to remain in Brazil, raising it to the status of a kingdom equal to Portugal. However, when his government tried to return Brazil to colonial status in 1820, the army decided to lead a revolution in 1822, declaring Brazil an independent constitutional monarchy under Joào's son Pedro I (reigned 1822–1830).

Above *Pedro I was independent Brazil's first Emperor. After political and economic crises he abdicated in favour of his five-year-old son, Pedro II*

Paraguay, in northern Argentina, achieved liberation in 1811. In Uruguay, which lay between Brazil and Argentina, independence was proclaimed in 1816, but the country was then occupied by Brazil in 1820 and only managed to liberate itself in 1828. By 1826, the last royalists had been driven out of South America, and the once-mighty Spanish-American Empire consisted merely of Cuba and Puerto Rico. The US government's Monroe Doctrine of 1823, which declared US hostility to any European attempts to recolonize the Americas, guaranteed the continued independence of Central and South America.

TIMELINE

1808	*The Braganzas (Portuguese royal family) flee to Brazil*
1810–1811	*Miguel Hidalgo begins Mexico's War of Independence*
1810–1814	*Independence movement in Chile is defeated*
1819	*Simón Bolívar founds Republic of Gran Colombia*
1823	*The USA recognizes newly independent states and proclaims the Monroe Doctrine.*

LATIN AMERICA POST-INDEPENDENCE

1830–1910

Independence did not bring peace to Latin America; the new nations faced formidable challenges. War had wrought devastation across the region, destroying farms, factories, mines and infrastructure. The colonial rulers had raided public funds before they fled, leaving little money available for reconstruction. National boundaries, based on colonial administrative divisions, were not clear-cut, and many battles were fought throughout Latin America during the 19th century in defence of territory.

Right *The rule of Juan Manuel de Rosas was brutal. After he was overthrown in 1852 he spent the rest of his life as a farmer in Britain*

Wars

In the War of the Triple Alliance (1865–1870), Argentina, Brazil and Uruguay fought Paraguay. As a result, Paraguay lost at least a fifth of its population and Argentina and Brazil gained large chunks of Paraguayan territory. Chile defeated Bolivia and Peru in the War of the Pacific (1879–1883) over control of the mineral-rich Atacama Desert. Bolivia's loss of this territory left it a landlocked country.

There were also frequent interventions in the region by foreign powers. In pursuit of its goal of a coast-to-coast nation, the

Above *A detail from a painting by Cándido López of the Battle of Tuyuti on 24 May 1866, at which the Paraguayan forces were routed*

United States attacked Mexico in 1846. Mexico lost, and was forced to cede California, Nevada, Utah, most of Arizona and New Mexico, and parts of Colorado and Wyoming. Spain suppressed Cuban independence in two wars (1868–1878 and 1895–1898). The US became drawn into the conflict, which led to the Spanish-American War (1898) and Spain's surrender of Cuba and Puerto Rico to the US. In 1901, Cuba became independent, on the proviso that the US could intervene in its internal affairs.

Political struggles

There were also power struggles *within* each country, between conservatives and liberals. Conservatives wished to retain many aspects of colonial life, including a politically powerful Catholic Church; and many favoured constitutional monarchy. Liberals, influenced by Enlightenment ideas, supported the establishment of republics with representative governments; more equal treatment of non-European and mixed-race communities; private property; public education; and a weaker Church.

In the 1850s and 1860s, liberal governments came to power throughout most of Latin America. In Mexico; liberal reforms led to a civil war with the conservatives (1858–1860), which the liberals won. Mexican conservatives then persuaded France to invade Mexico. In 1864, the French installed an Austro-Hungarian archduke, Maximilian von Habsburg, as Mexico's emperor. He ruled until 1867, when the liberals regained power.

In some countries, local leaders called

caudillos fought for power against liberal leaders. The *caudillos* were backed by rural militias who were unwilling to see their countries ruled by urban elites. In Argentina, a *caudillo* called Juan Manuel de Rosas (ruled 1829–1852) used a combination of bribes and brutality to unite other Argentine *caudillos* under his authority.

Social changes

Liberal policies that promoted equality often left American Indians worse off than they had been under colonial rule, when they had at least enjoyed protection against Spanish encroachment on their lands. Liberal governments, especially in Mexico, forcibly redistributed these collectively owned lands, turning the Amerindians into smallholders or wage-earners.

Slavery was abolished in Central America in 1824, in Chile in 1825, and in the British West Indies in 1834. The other Latin American republics abolished slavery during the 1850s and 60s. Many former slaves, although officially free, had little choice but to continue working for their former masters on extremely low wages. Slavery clung on in Brazil, where powerful plantation owners dominated the weak government of Emperor Pedro II (reigned 1840–1889). In 1888, Pedro finally abolished slavery, freeing around 750,000 slaves. The following year, the army, supported by the plantation owners, forced Pedro from power, and Brazil became a republic.

Economic development

Impoverished by war and plundered by former colonial rulers, the newly independent nations of Latin America lacked the resources to build self-sufficient economies. Consequently, in the post-independence period, their economies were based on the export of raw materials and import of manufactured goods. Attempts at home-grown manufacturing industries in Mexico, Colombia and Brazil in the 1830s and 40s all failed, owing to competition from European and American imports.

The Industrial Revolution did, however, benefit Latin America by expanding global demand for its raw materials and reducing the price of imported goods. From the 1860s, the Latin American economies grew rapidly and wealth flooded into the region. Foreign investors, especially from the US, put their capital into fruit companies, mines, and rail and harbour construction.

The population of many Latin American countries more than doubled between 1820 and 1880, as immigrants arrived from Europe – a million coming to Brazil in 1898 alone – and a sizeable middle class of business people, professionals and bureaucrats emerged. By 1914, the region was producing 18 per cent of the world's cereals, 38 per cent of its sugar and 62 per cent of its coffee, cocoa and tea.

Below *The Panama Canal opened in 1914, but at a cost; some 30,000 workers are estimated to have died during its construction*

TIMELINE	
1836	*Texas secedes from Mexico after the Battle of San Jacinto*
1836–1839	*Bolivia and Peru form a brief union*
1846–1848	*Mexican-American War*
1865–1870	*War of the Triple Alliance*
1879–1883	*War of the Pacific*
1889	*The Republic of the United States of Brazil is founded*
1903	*Panama wins its independence from Colombia*
1904–1914	*US engineers build the Panama Canal.*

THE BRITISH IN INDIA

1765–1905

During the second half of the 18th century, the British East India Company steadily expanded its dominions on the Indian subcontinent. At this stage it had no plans for the conquest of India, but viewed its role as primarily commercial. Territories were only annexed to protect the company's commercial interests. For example, when Tipu Sahib of Mysore invaded the British protectorate of Travancore in 1789, Lord Cornwallis, the governor-general, declared war and ended up taking control of half Tipu's territory.

Expansion

The threat of an invasion of India by Napoleon prompted a more proactive British policy. Mysore was defeated in 1799 (annexed in 1831) and the Maratha Confederacy was conquered in 1818. Annexed territories included Kumaon and Ceylon (both 1815), Peishwa's Lands (1818) and Chota Nagpur (1833). Independent states such as Hyderabad (1800), Rajputana (1818) and Kashmir (1846) were reduced to dependencies, with British troops garrisoned on their territory. From 1848, Lord Dalhousie, the governor-general, followed the policy of 'lapse': when a Hindu prince died without heir, his lands automatically passed to the Company.

The British acquired several new territories in the course of military campaigns to protect India's borders to the north-west and east. To secure the north-west

Right *Lord Dalhousie was Governor-General of India from 1848 to 1856*

Above *The Kabul expeditionary force on the march in November 1878, sketched by Lieutenant C. Pulley of the 3rd Gurkhas*

frontier from the possibility of Russian incursion, the Company twice attempted to take control of Afghanistan. In both the First and Second Afghan Wars (1839–1842 and 1878–1880), the British occupied Kabul but failed to dominate the rest of the country. The north-west frontier of British

India was, however, extended with the conquest of Sind (1843) and – after two wars with the Sikhs – the Punjab (1849). In response to a threat from Burma in the east, the Company took over Assam, Arakan and Tenasserim (1824–1826). Burma was brought under full British control in 1886.

The Indian Mutiny

The East India Company was successful in defending India from external threats, but was often less sure-footed in its dealings with India's people. The prohibition of local customs and traditions under Lord Bentinck (governor-general 1828–1835), the practice of Christian conversion, and the insistence on English as the language of education and commerce, all contributed to growing discontent among Indians. This flared into a full-scale rebellion known as the Indian Mutiny, in 1857. The uprising began in one of the Company's native armies, the Bengal *sepoys*, who were stationed in Meerut, near Delhi. A rumour spread among Hindu and Muslim soldiers that the rifle cartridges (which they had to bite to open) had been greased with pork and beef fat, which would have violated the dietary laws of both religions. The rebellion spread quickly through northern and central India. Delhi was captured and two other cities besieged. However, the rebels were poorly organized with few weapons, and by 1859 they had been defeated.

Nevertheless the rebellion sent shockwaves through British India, and caused widespread changes. The first and most noticeable change came in 1858: the East India Company was dissolved and the British government began to rule India directly. There were also other, less overt changes. A mutual distrust tinged relations between the rulers and the indigenous population from that time on. The Anglo-Indian community became more insular and disconnected from the native population. Gurkha and Sikh troops, who had remained loyal during the rebellion, formed the core of the reformed British Indian army.

The Raj

The period in which India was ruled directly by the British government is known as the Raj. In the administration of its territories, the East India Company had already introduced British-style institutions, including a British judicial system. The process of Westernization gathered pace during the Raj. Railway, telephone and telegraph networks were constructed; irrigation schemes expanded; and universities established. Indians were educated in the principles of a competitive market economy and Protestant values.

However, in many ways Britain's economic interests would not have been well served by transforming India into a fully Westernized nation. In fact, the British did little to promote industrialization on the subcontinent, aware that India's primary purpose was to supply raw materials for British manufacturers – particularly cotton for the textile industry – and to provide a captive market for British goods. The other resource that India had in abundance was people; thousands of Indian men served as soldiers, defending the British Empire around the world.

TIMELINE

1803–1818	Second Maratha War ends in defeat of Maratha Confederacy
1813	Christian missionaries are licensed to preach in India
1835	English is made the language of education
1836	A major road-building programme begins
1853	The first railway in India opens in Bombay
1876	Queen Victoria is given the title Empress of India
1876–1878	Five million die from famine in the central and southern provinces
1909	The Morley-Minto constitutional reforms introduce a measure of democratic government, but Indians are still denied true political representation.

Indian nationalism

After the Indian Mutiny, Indians were increasingly denied a role in the administration of their country. Many began to desire a more representative form of government. The Indian National Congress was founded in 1885, initially to promote the cause of Indians within the empire. However, by the early 1900s it had emerged as the major voice of Indian nationalist aspirations, calling for a government and constitution that reflected the will of the entire population. Soon this demand would evolve into a movement to end British rule in India.

Below *A train pulls into a railway station near Calcutta in 1867, part of the expanding rail network*

THE DECLINE OF MANCHU QING CHINA

1783–1911

During the 18th century, Qing dynasty China wished to keep contact with the outside world to a minimum. They restricted European merchants to the port of Guangzhou and – while happy enough to sell them tea, silk and porcelain in exchange for silver – showed little interest in buying European goods. Consequently, Europe suffered a large trade deficit with China. Britain, one of the biggest customers for Chinese goods, was determined to find ways of reversing the deficit. From the 1780s, British merchants began smuggling large quantities of the addictive drug opium into the country. By the early 1800s, despite Qing attempts to ban opium imports, it had become a huge business, shifting the balance of trade in favour of Britain.

Above *Britain's refusal to halt the smuggling of opium on merchant ships in spite of Chinese protestations led to the Opium Wars*

Opium Wars

Opium addiction destroyed countless Chinese lives, caused a huge drain on silver, and encouraged corruption among government officials. In 1839, the Qing used force in an attempt to put an end to the trade, seizing stores and threatening British merchants. The British sent a naval force and occupied several Chinese ports, forcing the Qing to negotiate. The Treaty of Nanjing (1842) handed the island of Hong Kong to Britain and sanctioned the British to trade through five 'treaty ports'.

The treaty was greatly resented by the Chinese, who were slow to implement it. British merchants grew impatient and in 1856 the Second Opium War broke out.

Once again the British prevailed. Under the Convention of Beijing (1860), restrictions on foreign travel and missionary work in China were lifted and the opium trade was legalized. The Opium Wars and the resulting treaties weakened the Qing dynasty politically and increased the West's control of China's economy. They also encouraged other powers, including Russia, Japan and the USA, to demand similar treaties, further reducing Chinese sovereignty.

Territorial losses

Qing military weakness, exposed in the Opium Wars, led to a steady loss of territory during the second half of the 19th century. In 1854, Russian forces annexed the Ili region in the north-west, then moved into Xinjiang, which they occupied until 1881, when the Qing paid them to leave. Russia also took control of Amur (1858) and Ussuri (1860) in eastern Siberia, in order to acquire an ice-free coastline on the Sea of Japan. From 1875, China began to lose control of its tributary states. By 1880, Japan had taken control of the Ryukyu Islands and weakened China's grip on Korea. By 1886, Britain had annexed Burma, and France had completed its conquest of Indochina and established a protectorate over Tongking. In 1895, China lost Taiwan and the Pescadores to Japan.

Rebellions

The steady loss of Chinese territory and sovereignty to foreign powers eroded Qing authority. The perception of Qing weakness, as well as official corruption, high taxation and the tensions caused by internal migration, provoked rebellion against their rule. The rebellions grew more serious after 1850, and at times threatened the very survival of the dynasty. There were indigenous uprisings in Taiwan; Muslim revolts in Xinjiang and Yunnan; peasant insurrections in Henan; and tribal unrest in Guizhou.

The Taiping Rebellion (1851–1864), led by Hong Xiuquan, proclaimed the end of Qing rule and the founding of Taiping Tianguo (Heavenly Kingdom of Great Peace). The rebellion spread across 16 provinces. In 1853, Hong Xiuquan and his supporters captured Nanjing and in 1860 were threatening Shanghai. The rebellion eventually spread to 16 provinces and was only suppressed at a cost of some 20 million lives.

Boxer Uprising

Battered by foreign encroachment and internal dissent, Qing rulers turned to the scholar official Li Hongzhang to introduce reforms. He attempted to transform China into a modern military and industrial state along Western lines, but his efforts were blocked by conservative forces close to the powerful dowager empress Cixi (reigned 1862–1908).

The anti-Western attitudes of Cixi and her court in Beijing were shared by a growing number of Chinese. Nationalist and xenophobic sentiments lay behind the Boxer Uprising of 1900–1901. It was begun by the Yihetuan, a secret Chinese society known in the West as the Boxers, who wished to exclude all foreigners from China. They attacked Christian missionaries in the north-eastern provinces and foreigners in Beijing. Cixi supported the rebellion with imperial troops, which besieged foreign legations in Beijing. The rebellion ended only when an international force occupied the capital.

TIMELINE	
1839	Imperial commissioner Lin Zexu sent to Guangzhou to stop opium trade
1844	France and USA sign trade agreements with China
1851–1864	Taiping Rebellion
1855–1857	The Miao tribal rebellion in Guizhou
1863–1873	Muslim uprisings in Gansu, Qinghai and Shanxi
1894–1895	China is defeated in Sino-Japanese War, and loses Taiwan and Pescadores
1896	Chinese reformist scholar-official permits Russia to build a railroad across Manchuria
1900–1901	The Boxer Uprising
1908	Dowager Empress Cixi dies
1911–1912	Chinese revolution leads to the establishment of a republican government.

Under the International Protocol (1901) the Qing was ordered to pay an enormous indemnity payment and offer further trade concessions. Russia increased its influence in Manchuria, supplanted by Japan in 1905.

Revolution

Since 1894, the nationalist revolutionary leader Sun Yat-Sen had been plotting the overthrow of the Qing and the establishment of a republican government. In October 1911, Sun Yat-Sen's followers rose up in armed rebellion. The revolution began in the city of Hankou and quickly spread across south-east and central China. The Qing ordered their most senior general Yuan Shikai to confront the rebels, but instead he negotiated with them, offering to arrange the abdication of the Qing emperor in exchange for the presidency of the new government. The revolutionaries agreed and in February 1912, Yuan became the first President of the Republic of China, ending 2,000 years of imperial rule.

Above *Sun Yat-Sen, father of the Republic of China, based his idea of revolution on the three principles of nationalism, democracy and equalization*

THE MODERNIZATION OF JAPAN

1800–1914

The feudal bakuhan *system, established in the early 1600s by the Tokugawa shogunate, continued to operate in Japan until the mid-19th century. Under this system, the shoguns, based in Edo (modern Tokyo), ruled with the support of local daimyo, who were sovereign in their own territories. The emperor, based in Kyoto, remained a semi-divine, ceremonial figurehead.*

Above right
Samurai from the Satsuma clan, which was instrumental in restoring imperial rule to Japan

Foreign contact

The Tokugawa shoguns tried to limit contact with foreigners, concerned about threats to their culture and sovereignty. However, from the late 1700s, foreign powers began to apply increasing pressure on Japan to open itself to trade. The shoguns continued to rebuff these advances until 1853, when a US gunboat expedition, led by Commodore Matthew Perry, arrived. The presence of US warships in Japanese waters was sufficient to persuade the shogunate to grant the first concessions to a Western power, permitting trade through two ports. Under American pressure, more Japanese ports were soon opened to international trade.

In the 1860s, a growing xenophobia infected many young samurai, and attacks were carried out against foreign traders and their vessels. The anti-foreign movement was particularly strong in Western Japan, where it evolved into an organized rebellion against the shogunate, who were blamed for allowing the foreigners in. In 1867, leaders of two Western domains, Choshu and Satsuma, organized a coup by bringing to power the young emperor Meiji. Choshu-Satsuma forces defeated the shogunate army in a brief civil war. By 1869, the revolution, known as the Meiji Restoration, was complete.

Meiji reforms

Although the Meiji Restoration implied a return to imperial rule, in fact the emperor's main role in the new government was to confer legitimacy and act as a unifying symbol in a divided nation. The government, based at Edo – now renamed Tokyo – was dominated by young samurai from Choshu and Satsuma. All of them believed in the need to strengthen Japan and resist foreign incursion, but were divided over how to achieve this. Conservatives wished to preserve the traditional social order, while radicals believed modernization was the answer. The radicals prevailed. Before Japan could modernize, however, it had to unite under a single centralized authority. In 1871, the feudal *bakuhan* system was abolished and daimyo domains were replaced by prefectures administered by government-appointed officials. The traditional Japanese social hierarchy was abandoned and citizens were given equal status regardless of background. This angered many samurai, but their rebellions were all swiftly crushed by the new, conscripted army.

Japan became more pragmatic about the question of foreign influence, accepting the need to learn from the West as a means of strengthening itself. During the 1870s, Meiji leaders travelled to Western countries, to study their laws and institutions. This inspired widespread reforms in Japanese education, the armed forces, and the tax system; and was followed in the 1880s by political reforms, including the introduction of a limited form of representative government. Japan imported Western plant and materials, including steam engines, cotton-spinning mills and steel, to fast-track its own industrialization. By the 1890s, Japanese factory production was already having a major impact on the economy, reducing reliance on foreign imports.

Expansion

By the mid-1890s, Japan was sufficiently self-assured to persuade the Western powers to renegotiate the treaties signed by the Tokugawa shogunate and provide more favourable terms for Japan. The Meiji leaders were now determined to develop a colonial empire, partly as a defensive buffer and partly for international prestige. The first expansionist moves had been made in the 1870s, when Japan took advantage of Qing China's weakness to acquire the Ryukyu Islands and increase their influence over Korea.

China remained the key obstacle to Japanese expansion in the region, and in 1894 Japan launched a surprise attack on Chinese forces in Korea. Japan's newly modernized armed forces defeated the Chinese in nine months. Under the subsequent Treaty of Shimonoseki (1895), China recognized Korean independence and ceded Taiwan, the Pescadores and the Liaodong Peninsula in southern Manchuria to Japan. Concerned over Japan's growing dominance in East Asia, the Western powers then forced a revision to the treaty, making Japan forfeit Liaodong.

TIMELINE	
1853	A US naval force under Commodore Perry forces Japan to open its ports to US trade
1863–1864	Western forces attack Kagoshima and Shimonoseki after attacks on Westerners by Satsuma and Choshu rebels
1867	Choshu-Satsuma samurai rebel against shogunate
1868	The Meiji Restoration
1877	Samurai rise up in protest against Meiji reforms (the Satsuma Rebellion)
1889	The Meiji constitution is introduced
1894–1895	Sino-Japanese War
1902	The Anglo-Japanese alliance recognizes East Asia as being within Japan's sphere of influence
1904–1905	Russo-Japanese War
1910	Japan annexes Korea.

Russo-Japanese War

When Russia began to increase its own influence in Korea and southern Manchuria in the late 1890s, it stirred resentment in Japan. In February 1904, the Japanese navy attacked the Russian fleet at Port Arthur in the Liaodong Peninsula. The ensuing war lasted until May 1905, when the Japanese wiped out the Russian fleet at the Battle of Tsushima, forcing them to surrender. Japan's victory shocked the world and marked its arrival as a global power.

Under the Treaty of Portsmouth (1905), Russia handed control of the Liaodong Peninsula and the southern half of Karafuto to Japan and acknowledged Japanese influence in Korea. That influence gradually increased, and in 1910 Japan formally annexed Korea. Japan now had a defensive buffer zone stretching from Karafuto in the north through Korea in the west to Taiwan in the south, and a major sphere of power in East Asia.

Above *The Meiji Emperor in military dress in 1872. This image became the official imperial portrait*

COLONIALISM IN SOUTH-EAST ASIA

1790–1914

In the final decade of the 18th century, Western intervention in South-east Asia began to intensify, reaching a peak between 1870 and 1914, during which time almost the whole region was subjected to European or American rule. Siam (modern Thailand), ruled by the Chakri dynasty, remained the only independent state. In the early years of the 20th century, colonial rule in South-east Asia began to come under threat from nascent nationalist movements and the rise of Japan.

Above *The Malacca Straits in 1831 – a vital trade route for the British at the time and still one of the most important sea lanes in the world*

Malacca Straits

British interest in South-east Asia was driven partly by a desire to exploit the region's natural resources and partly to safeguard Britain's trade route with China, which had to pass through the Malacca Straits between Sumatra and the Malay Peninsula. The first step to securing the Straits was the purchase of the island of Penang in the Malacca Straits in 1786. In 1795, British naval forces used Penang as a base to capture Malacca from the Dutch. The British captured Singapore in 1819, which soon became established as the major centre of trade in the region. In 1824, Britain ceded the pepper-trading centre of Benkulen in Sumatra (which they had established in 1685) as well as all claims to Sumatra, in exchange for Dutch recognition of British control over Penang, Port Wellesley, Singapore and Malacca, collectively known as the Straits

Settlements. Britain's sea lanes were now well protected.

Malay Peninsula

From the 1870s, Britain also began acquiring territory on the Malay Peninsula. In 1896, these became the Federated Malay States and emerged as a major centre of rubber and tin production in the early 1900s. Five more peninsula states were acquired from Siam in 1909, comprising the Unfederated Malay States.

Sumatra and Java

Following their territorial losses to the British, the Dutch faced severe challenges to their rule of the East Indies from the indigenous peoples.

On Java, rebel forces, led by Prince Dipo Negora, fought a bitter war against the Dutch from 1825 to 1829. Dutch attempts to extend their territory on Sumatra met determined resistance from Muslim militants in Minangkabau, finally overcome after a 17-year struggle in 1838. After this, the Dutch gradually extended their control northwards along both coasts, but attempts to take the north of the island were thwarted for 30 years (1873–1903) by the powerful Sultanate of Acèh. In the early 1900s, a new Western-educated elite among the indigenous population of Java, started to clamour for independence.

North Borneo

In 1841, the sultan of Brunei rewarded the British adventurer James Brooke with a territory in North Borneo called Sarawak, for his help in putting down a revolt there. In 1881, a royal charter was granted to the newly established British North Borneo Company, to administer Sarawak and exploit it for commercial purposes. Further territory was acquired, and in 1889 North Borneo became a British protectorate.

Burma

Britain's concern to protect the eastern frontier of India, including opium-producing Bengal, led to the gradual annexation of neighbouring Burma. Following a war in 1824–1826, sparked by Burma's invasion of Bengal, Britain won control of Arakan and Tenasserim in Lower Burma. The rest of Lower Burma was secured after a second war (1852–1853), and Upper Burma was gained in a third (1885–1856). Thereafter, Burma was absorbed into British India.

New Guinea

The first colonial claim on New Guinea came when the Dutch took possession of the Western half of the island in 1828. Germany, a latecomer to the colonial scramble for territory, competed with Britain for the eastern half. In 1884, it was agreed that Germany could occupy the north-east and adjacent island chain (renamed the Bismarck Archipelago) and Britain the south-east. British New Guinea became an Australian territory in 1906.

FRENCH INDOCHINA

French missions and trading bases had existed in Vietnam since the 17th century. However, the first concerted effort at colonization did not occur until the late 1850s, on the instigation of the glory-seeking Napoleon III. In 1858, a French expeditionary force captured Saigon and Da Nang. Further gains were made in the Mekong Delta and by 1863, France had established a protectorate over Cambodia. Between 1883–1885, France battled with China for control of the surrounding territory. By 1887, the French had won control of Cochin China, Annam and Tongking, which they merged with Cambodia to form French Indochina. In 1893, the colony was extended to include Laos. In 1896, Britain and France agreed that Siam should remain independent to act as a buffer state between their territories in Burma and Indochina. In the early 1900s, Vietnamese student nationalists began to advocate violence against the French colonial authorities.

Philippines

During the 1890s, the USA encouraged Filipino nationalists to fight for independence against the Spanish, who had ruled the Philippines since 1565. The Filipinos therefore felt betrayed when the US took control of the islands in 1898, following their victory over Spain in the Spanish-American War. The nationalists continued their struggle against the new occupiers until 1905 without success, but at the cost of over 100,000 Filipino lives.

Below The Submission of Prince Dipo Negoro to General De Kock *by Nicolaas Pieneman, painted a year after the war ended*

COLONIALISM IN AUSTRALIA AND NEW ZEALAND

1788–1914

The first European contacts with Australia occurred in the 17th century, when Dutch explorers charted the continent's Western and northern coasts. In 1642, Abel Tasman sighted Tasmania and followed part of the New Zealand coastline. In 1769–1770, British navigator James Cook charted the New Zealand coast and landed in eastern Australia, which he claimed for Britain. European settlement began in 1788 when the British government founded a penal colony there. Some 750 convicts and 200 soldiers landed at Botany Bay before being transferred to Port Jackson (modern Sydney). Over the next 80 years, a further 160,000 convicts were shipped to penal colonies founded on Australia's eastern, southern and Western coasts.

First settlers

Settlers initially lived off whaling, fishing and sealing, as well as supplies shipped from England. Gradually, discharged soldiers and freed convicts began cultivating small areas of land. The land surrounding Sydney was not suitable for agriculture, but in the 1820s, an inland route was developed to reveal vast plains suitable for pastoral farming. Free settlers turned to sheep rearing, and wool exports to Britain soon became a key part of Australia's economy.

The need for more pasture led to conflicts with local Aboriginal inhabitants. When Aboriginals tried to resist the seizure of their lands and water resources, settlers carried out revenge attacks, and occasional massacres. Because of this, and exposure to European diseases such as smallpox, the Aboriginal population declined drastically. By 1900, the population had fallen to about half of its 1788 total.

Gold fever

From the 1830s, the British government began encouraging the immigration of free settlers to the Australian colonies. The free population grew dramatically after 1851, with the discovery of gold at a number of sites. The population grew from 405,000 in 1850 to four million in 1900. Gold fever gripped the colonies as prospectors converged on the mines at Bathurst, Ballarat, Bendigo and Kalgoorlie, to try and make their fortunes. Thousands of Chinese and Asian miners were shipped in as indentured labourers. The Chinese became the targets of fierce racism and this led to stricter immigration laws.

Gold mining transformed Australia's economy and society. It also had an impact on its political development. Each miner had to purchase a license before he could dig for gold. Miners at Ballarat were strongly opposed to the license fee and established a reform movement, which also demanded the right to vote. Their protests led to a massacre in 1854. The following year, the license fee was abolished and miners gained the vote.

Self-government

As the population increased, so colonists' demands for independence from Britain grew more insistent. The British government conceded this right in principle in 1850, and New South Wales,

Above A portrait of Captain James Cook, painted by Nathaniel Dance in 1775. He is shown wearing a captain's full dress uniform of the period

Above *The Fimiston Open Pit, known as the Super Pit, off the Goldfields Highway at Kalgoorlie-Boulder – Australia's largest open-cut gold mine*

Victoria and Tasmania became self-governing by 1856; followed by South Australia (1857); Queensland (founded 1859); and Western Australia (1870). All the states opted for representative goverments with universal male suffrage. Then in 1894, women in South Australia were among the first in history to be given the vote. In 1901, the Commonwealth of Australia was established, promoting inter-state trade and facilitating a common defence policy.

Exploration

The navigator and mapmaker Matthew Flinders was the first to circumnavigate Australia in 1802–1803, but inhospitable conditions inhibited exploration of the continent's interior for several more decades. Edward Eyre crossed South Australia, east to west, in 1839–1841, and Ludwig Leichardt trekked north-west from Moreton Bay to Port Essington in 1844–1845. Burke and Wills were the first to traverse the entire continent, crossing south to north in 1860–1861. John Stuart found the continent's geographical centre during his crossing in 1860. Further expeditions in the 1870s focused on Western Australia, opening up Pilbara and Kimberley regions for grazing. Transcontinental

NEW ZEALAND

The first European settlers were seal hunters from New South Wales, who landed in the Bay of Islands in 1792. They gave muskets to the indigenous Maoris in exchange for land, which led to the 'Musket Wars' between rival Maori groups from 1818. Australian whalers and sealers also founded settlements on South Island. Warfare between settlers and Maori tribes became common. The lawless conditions prompted the British government to intervene. In 1840, British representatives and Maori leaders signed the Treaty of Waitangi, under which the Maori gave up control of their land in exchange for property ownership, citizenship rights and protection. Misunderstandings over the terms of the treaty led to further clashes and a war in 1859–1863. Maori resistance continued until 1872, and a formal peace was agreed in 1881. An 1861 gold strike at Otago stimulated immigration to New Zealand, and gold soon replaced wool as New Zealand's main export. In 1907, New Zealand became a self-governing dominion within the British Empire.

communications were helped by the establishment of a telegraph system in 1872, and the completion of the Trans-Australia Railway in 1917.

Above *The Maori chief Hone Wiremu Heke Poka, with his wife Hariata to his left and uncle Kawiti on the right*

TIMELINE

1788	*The first British settlers land in Australia*
1803	*A penal colony is established on Van Diemen's Land*
1827	*Perth is established in Western Australia*
1830	*The Aboriginal population on Van Diemen's Land is virtually wiped out by this time*
1840	*500 Maori chiefs sign the Treaty of Waitangi*
1851	*Gold is discovered at Bathurst*
1854	*The miners' uprising at the Eureka Stockade, Ballarat*
1859	*Queensland is established as a separate colony*
1865	*The New Zealand capital moves from Auckland to Wellington*
1901	*The Commonwealth of Australia is proclaimed*
1907	*New Zealand is granted dominion status.*

AFRICA

1800–1880

By the early 1800s, there were European colonies dotted all around the coastline of Africa, yet Europeans had little or no knowledge of the interior of the continent. The harsh conditions and hostility of native peoples, such as the Asante of West Africa, deterred exploration. The largest European presence was at Cape Colony in Southern Africa, and from here European settlements had expanded as far north as the Limpopo by the mid-19th century. Apart from European incursions, traditional African cultures were affected by Islamic expansionism emanating from Egypt and the Sokoto Caliphate; and furthermore by mass migrations caused by Zulu conquests in the south. The slave trade continued to have a major impact on Africa's economy and society.

Above right
Parts of East Africa in the 19th century had a thriving trade with the Middle East and Britain, and some could afford finery and other luxuries

The slave trade was abolished by most European countries and the USA in the early 19th century; consequently, the focus turned to trading other commodities, such as ivory, palm oil, gold and rubber. Despite Britain's attempts to enforce the ban on slave trading with its Royal Navy, some three million slaves were taken from Africa during the 19th century.

North Africa

In the early 19th century, the Ottoman viceroy of Egypt, Mehmet Ali, transformed the province into an independent state in all but name. Ali invaded Sudan to the south in 1820–1822 to gain control of this valuable source of gold and slaves. In 1830, France invaded Algeria – a militarily weak state, dependent on the declining Ottoman Empire – and gained control of its northern area. The French governed it as part of France, extending French citizenship to its inhabitants. But the colonial rulers gave large amounts of land to European settlers, inciting a rebellion that was finally defeated in 1847.

East Africa

The Indian Ocean ports of Malindi, Mombasa, Tanga and Kilwa, controlled by the Sultanate of Zanzibar, were busy centres of trade in the 19th century, where Swahili-speaking Africans did business with Omani Arabs and Indians. Slaves were exported from here to the Middle East and Asia until 1873, when Britain managed to persuade the sultan to close the slave market. The Muslim traders of Zanzibar forged strong links with many inland kingdoms in East and Central Africa, including Urambo,

TIMELINE	
1804	*Usman dan Fodio begins his jihad*
1822	*Liberia is founded for freed American slaves*
1835–6	*The Boers' Great Trek leaves Cape Colony*
1852–1856	*David Livingstone explores the African interior and becomes the first European to see the Mosi-oa-Tunya (the smoke that thunders), which he renames the Victoria Falls*
1875	*Egypt invades the Horn of Africa.*

Ukimbu and the Sultanate of Utetera, whose prosperity was based on the sale of slaves and ivory. To the north, the ancient kingdom of Ethiopia, which had splintered into small kingdoms during the 16th century, reunited in the 1870s under John IV, and began to expand. It was the only African state to avoid colonial occupation during the 'scramble' (see pages 240–241).

West Africa

In West Africa, the Islamic leader Usman dan Fodio (1754–1816) established the Sokoto Caliphate and, in 1804, launched a 'jihad' (holy war) against the Hausa kingdoms to the north. Usman's advance caused the destruction of some long-established kingdoms, including Oyo and Segu. By the 1850s, the Sokoto Caliphate dominated the region, uniting much of Hausaland under its authority. Britain's annexation of Lagos in 1861 marked the beginning of the decline of Sokoto. The caliphate survived until 1903.

Southern Africa

The largest European settlement in Africa was in the south. In the early 19th century, the Afrikaner (Dutch) and British settlers were clustered in Cape Colony on the southern tip. The British began to dominate, culminating in Britain's formal annexation of the colony in 1814, prompting the Cape Boers (Afrikaners) to embark on a Great Trek to the Natal. When Britain annexed Natal in 1843, the Boers moved on once more, founding the Orange Free State and Transvaal. Britain recognized these Boer republics in the 1850s. The discovery of diamonds in Griqualand in 1871, and gold in Witwatersrand in 1886, sparked a rush of European immigrants and transformed the economy and society of southern Africa.

Among the indigenous cultures of southern Africa, the most significant

EUROPEAN EXPLORATION

Starting in the 1820s, European explorers, whether motivated by scientific interest, missionary zeal or simply a sense of adventure, began to journey into Africa's interior. In 1827–1828, Frenchman René-Auguste Caillé travelled through West Africa, dressed as an Arab, and was probably the first European to reach Timbuktu. In the 1850s, Scottish explorer David Livingstone journeyed through Central and Southern Africa and fought to end the slave trade. His discoveries inspired other expeditions, exploring the sources of the Nile, Congo, Zambezi and Niger. The charting of Africa played an important role in establishing colonial boundaries after 1880.

development of the period was the rise and expansion of the Zulu kingdom in the 1820s under King Shaka (reigned 1816–1828). Shaka was a great military tactician who won a string of victories against neighbouring kingdoms, which were then absorbed into a Zulu confederacy. Zulu expansionism led to large-scale migrations throughout the region, known as *mfecane*, which in turn gave rise to new kingdoms, including Lesotho, Swazi and Ndebele. Zulus clashed with Boers in Natal during the 1830s. The most spectacular of these encounters was the Battle of Blood River in 1838 in which 470 Boers defeated some 10,000 Zulus.

Below *An illustration of the Battle of Blood River by R.C. Woodville from Harper's Monthly, 1897; the battle ended in Zulu defeat by the Boers*

THE SCRAMBLE FOR AFRICA

1880–1914

Between 1880 and 1914, virtually the entire continent of Africa was colonized by European powers, with only Liberia and Ethiopia remaining independent. The partitioning of the continent, known as the Scramble for Africa, occurred at a bewildering speed; in fact, most of the process was completed in just ten years following 1880. The Scramble arose for a variety of reasons, including a desire to exploit Africa as a source of raw materials and a market for manufactured goods, as well as the prestige that comes with possession of an overseas empire. The late 19th and early 20th century was a time of increasing nationalistic rivalry between European nations, and the Scramble was one important manifestation of this.

Above *This Punch cartoon by Edward Linley Sambourne, published on 10 December 1892, caricatured Cecil Rhodes as a Colossus bestriding Africa*

Berlin Conference

The basis for the partitioning of Africa was agreed at the Berlin Conference of 1884–1885. Here, representatives of 15 European nations met to  settle rival colonial claims. The sphere of influence of each power was defined as the hinterland of any coastline controlled by that power. To prevent nations from establishing colonies in name only, the 'principle of effectivity' was introduced: powers had to fly their flag there; draw up treaties with local chiefs; administer and police the territory; and make economic use of it. If a power did not do these things, another one could legally take over the territory. The principle of effectivity accelerated the process of colonization as nations rushed to establish their claims on territories ahead of their rivals.

Colonization

Colonization was, in certain cases, facilitated by African rulers, several of whom hoped to enlist Europeans as allies in their struggles against traditional enemies. The Bugandans, for example, helped the British conquer territory to form Uganda in 1903. Others were tempted by the notion of partnership in commercial enterprises. Once Europeans were invited in, however, they proved impossible to remove.

In many cases, colonization was carried out by corporate entities such as the British South Africa Company, the Royal Niger Company, the German South West and East Africa Companies and the Portuguese Niassa Company. The companies generally took a forceful approach to colonization, by abolishing existing currencies and trade patterns, levying taxes and conquering territory without clearance from their governments.

Colonization transformed the society and culture of Africa in fundamental ways. To pay taxes, many were forced to take up wage labour for the first time. Thousands of unskilled labourers were recruited to work on rubber, sugar and cocoa estates, in mining operations or to build railways. Railway networks linked the interior with coastal ports; thereby stimulating trade, the growth of cities and the emergence of an African merchant class.

Colonization caused terrible suffering for some indigenous populations. Indentured labourers on the cocao plantations of Portuguese São Tomé and Príncipe lived and worked in inhuman conditions. Leopold II of Belgium ran the Congo as a private, commercial fiefdom, using millions of Congolese as forced labour for ivory and rubber extraction.

Responses

Colonization, especially in its crueller manifestations, frequently caused resentment among the indigenous population. This was expressed in various forms of resistance, ranging from non-payment of taxes and avoidance of labour to armed insurrection. There were uprisings in 1892 by the Ijebu, a former Yoruba people in modern-day Nigeria; by the Matabele people, a branch of the Zulus, in 1896; and by the Mandinka of West Africa, in 1898.

Most rebellions were quickly suppressed, however, owing to superior Western weaponry. One exception was the Asante in West Africa, who resisted colonization by the British in four wars, fought between 1823 and 1896. Their kingdom was eventually incorporated into the Gold Coast colony in 1900. Another was the Mahdist Revolt, a Sudanese Islamic rebellion under Muhammad Ahmad, which managed to overthrow Anglo-Egyptian rule in Sudan between 1885 and 1898. Due to its establishment as a 'freed slave state' and the unofficial support of the USA, Liberia retained its independence during the scramble, although it lost some territory. Ethiopia was the only African state to resist European colonization by military means, with its decisive victory over Italian forces at the Battle of Adowa in 1896.

Many Africans tolerated colonization and were happy to embrace its beneficial aspects. Education offered a means of social advancement and the possibility of jobs in the colonial administration. The spread of literacy led to the development of a politicized class from which nationalist movements would eventually emerge. Christianity spread quickly through the indigenous populations, often blending with traditional African creeds, and soon became the majority faith in East, Central and Southern Africa.

Above *An inhabitant of Bulawayo in Matabeleland, photographed in about 1890*

Below *Boer guerrillas photographed during the Boer War, 1899–1902*

THE BOER WAR

Rival claims to the land and valuable mineral resources of Southern Africa led to the Boer War of 1899 to 1901 between Britain and the Boer republics of Transvaal and the Orange Free State. Following British attempts to annex the Transvaal, Boer forces besieged the towns of Mafeking, Kimberley and Ladysmith, and won battles at Magersfontein, Colenso and Stormberg. British reinforcements under General Kitchener lifted the sieges and invaded the republics. Thereafter the Boers switched to guerrilla tactics. Kitchener destroyed Boer farms and interned families in concentration camps. These ruthless tactics, together with the British use of African troops, forced the Boers to surrender.

SCIENCE AND TECHNOLOGY

1783–1900

During the 19th century, science divided into specialized fields such as physics, chemistry and biology. Key advances were made in all these areas, particularly by researchers working in Germany, Britain, France, Russia and the USA. Science helped to transform practices in agriculture, industry and daily life with the development of new materials, sources of power and forms of communication. Scientific discoveries also offered an enhanced understanding of the universe, the Earth and the evolution of life.

Right *Scientists test the phonograph, invented by Thomas Edison (1847–1931)*

Physics

Major advances were made in the course of the 19th century in the understanding of electricity and magnetism. Britain's Michael Faraday used experiments to demonstrate in 1831 that a moving magnet could induce an electric current, the principle behind electric generators and dynamos. In 1864, another British scientist, James Clerk Maxwell, developed four mathematical equations to show that electricity and magnetism were simply alternative expressions of the same phenomenon, electromagnetism. His equations demonstrated the principles behind electromagnetic waves, and proved that light itself was a form of electromagnetic energy. Maxwell's belief that the electromagnetic spectrum must include other forms of wave was proved correct by German scientist Heinrich Hertz, who discovered radio waves in 1888, and his compatriot Wilhelm Roentgen, who discovered X-rays in 1895. The discoveries in physics led to many new inventions, including the telephone, phonograph, radio, radar and television.

Chemistry

In 1803, British scientist John Dalton founded modern chemistry with his theory that all matter is made up of tiny particles called atoms. Dalton demonstrated how each atom has a unique mass and that atoms remain unchanged when they

TIMELINE

1800	*Alessandro Volta describes the electric battery*
1803	*John Dalton demonstrates his atomic theory*
1828	*Friedrich Wöhler synthesizes the organic compound urea*
1838	*Matthias Schleiden shows that all plants are made of cells*
1843	*James Prescott Joule proves that heat is a form of energy and advances the theory that energy cannot be created or destroyed, but only changed in form*
1846	*Morton and Long invent anaesthesia*
1848	*Lord Kelvin develops the scale of absolute temperature*
1859	*Charles Darwin publishes* On the Origin of Species
1866	*Gregor Mendel publishes his principles of heredity*
1869	*Dmitri Mendeleev publishes his Periodic Table of the Elements*
1873	*James Clerk Maxwell publishes his theory of electromagnetism*
1896	*Henri Becquerel discovers radioactivity.*

combine with other atoms to form compounds. Dalton's belief that atoms were the smallest units of matter was disproved by Joseph Thomson's 1897 discovery of a subatomic particle, the electron. Dmitri Mendeleyev of Russia brought order to the field by organizing the chemical elements in his periodic table (1870). From his 1828 study of urea, German chemist Friedrich Wöhler was able to prove that organic compounds could be synthesized from inorganic ingredients. By the end of the 19th century, hundreds of organic materials had been created in the laboratory, from synthetic dyes to aspirin. Chemists also discovered other important materials, including the first synthetic fertilizer (1842) and the explosive, nitrocellulose (1846).

Life sciences

In his book *On the Origin of Species* (1859), English naturalist Charles Darwin demonstrated that plant and animal species changed, or evolved, over time. He suggested that this process occurs through natural selection: life forms best suited to a particular environment are most likely to survive and reproduce. Darwin's theory of evolution provoked fierce opposition from Church leaders, particularly his theory that humans had evolved from apelike ancestors, because it conflicted with the Biblical account of the Creation. However, by the late 19th century, most biologists accepted that evolution occurred, though not all agreed that natural selection was the mechanism. An Austrian monk-scientist named Gregor Mendel spent ten years (1856–1866) studying pea plants in order to understand the laws that governed how characteristics are passed on from one generation to the next. Mendel's principles of heredity laid the foundations of the science of genetics,

GEOLOGY AND ASTRONOMY

In the 19th century, scientists began to argue that the Earth was far older than the 6,000 years that the Biblical scriptures implied. Estimates of the Earth's age ranged from 100,000 to millions of years. Some, such as James Hutton of Scotland, believed that rock layers could be dated by the fossils they contained. Theories were developed about mountain-building, earthquakes, volcanoes and ice ages. Astronomers spotted the first asteroid (1801) and the planet Neptune (1846). In the 1840s, Irish stargazer William Parsons was the first to see a galaxy beyond our own Milky Way.

although his work would not be recognized until 1900.

Medicine

During the 19th century, great progress was also made in the diagnosis and treatment of disease. German physician Rudolf Virchow, a pioneer of pathology (the scientific study of disease), showed that all diseases arise from disorders in cells, the basic units of body tissue. French physiologist, Claude Bernard made important discoveries about the pancreas, liver and nervous system. And Russian physiologist, Ivan Pavlov developed the theory of the conditioned reflex. Two Americans, Crawford Long and William Morton discovered that ether could safely put patients to sleep during surgery; it was the first effective anaesthetic.

In the 1870s, Louis Pasteur established the germ theory, revealing the causes of age-old diseases such as anthrax, diphtheria, tuberculosis, leprosy and plague. Pasteur developed a vaccine for rabies in 1885. Vaccines for diphtheria and tetanus followed in the 1890s. Pasteur's work on bacteria inspired English surgeon Joseph Lister to use carbolic acid to sterilize surgical wounds, greatly reducing the mortality rate of those undergoing surgery.

Above *Charles Darwin lived to the age of 73 and was honoured with burial at Westminster Abbey*

Below *The discoveries made by Louis Pasteur saved the lives of millions*

WORLD WAR I

1914–1918

World War I arose as a conflict between European powers, but bonds of empire and traditional allegiences with nations in other parts of the world helped to turn it into the first global war. It was also the first total war: the participating nations mobilized their entire populations and economic resources to achieve victory, and the civilians on the 'home front' became directly involved in the war effort. It was the most destructive conflict in history to that date, with more than 10 million killed and over 20 million wounded.

The European alliance system (see pages 212–213) had divided the continent into two hostile blocs of power: Germany, Austria-Hungary and the Ottoman Empire (later called the Central powers) on one side, with Britain, France and Russia (later called the Allied powers) on the other. From the 1890s, Germany, Europe's newest and fastest-growing state, raised tensions with its undisguised imperialist ambitions. All nations armed themselves for a war that many believed inevitable.

The spark that ignited the conflict occurred, predictably, in the unstable Balkans, where Austria-Hungary and Russia competed for influence. In July 1914 a Serb nationalist assassinated the Austrian archduke Franz Ferdinand. Austria-Hungary declared war on Serbia. Russia, Serbia's ally, began to mobilize. Germany, fearing a simultaneous attack by France and Russia,

Below *Archduke Ferdinand and his wife Sophie in Sarajevo on the day they were assassinated by Serb nationalist Gavrilo Princip*

enacted its Schlieffen Plan. The plan required Germany to launch a knock-out blow against France by attacking through Belgium before transporting troops east to fight Russia. However, the plan failed when German forces were halted at the Marne, 80 km (50 miles) short of Paris. Stalemate followed on the Western Front.

The Western Front

Both sides quickly realized that the only way of holding a defensive line against modern machine guns and artillery was to dig trenches. By winter 1914, a continuous line of trenches stretched from the Swiss border to the Belgian coast. The Western Front barely moved for the next three and a half years. Attempts to break the deadlock with new weapons such as poison gas and flame throwers, and tactics like tunnelling beneath opposing trenches to blow them up, had little impact. In 1916, both sides launched major offensives. In the Battle of Verdun, France eventually managed to resist German attempts to capture the city, but at terrible cost in casualties on both sides. The British led an offensive at the Somme in July. By September the Allies had advanced around 11 km (7 miles) at a cost of 600,000 lives. The Germans lost a similar number.

The Eastern Front

The Russian army invaded eastern Germany in late August 1914, but was defeated by German forces at the Battle of Tannenberg. A second Russian army invaded the Austro-Hungarian territory of Galicia, controlling almost all of it by the end of 1914. Austria-Hungary invaded Serbia three times in 1914 and was driven back each time. In May

1915, the Central powers broke through Russian lines at Galicia and advanced some 300 km (less than 190 miles). A Russian counter-offensive in June 1916 nearly knocked Austria-Hungary out of the war, but also exhausted Russia. Both sides lost around a million men. By November, the Central powers, with Bulgaria's help, had overrun Serbia.

Other fronts

World War I was ultimately decided by the fighting on the eastern and Western fronts, but significant battles also took place elsewhere. Although an ally of Germany and Austria-Hungary, Italy only joined the war in May 1915, and then on the side of the Allies. Italy fought Austria-Hungary for two years along the Isonzo River, gaining little territory but suffering enormous casualties before its defeat in October 1917. Another front opened in February 1915 when Allied warships attacked Turkish forces guarding the Dardanelles, hoping to open a supply route to Russia. When the attack failed, the Allies landed troops (mainly Australian and New Zealand forces) on the Gallipoli Peninsula on the strait's Western shore. The assault was another costly failure.

Allied victory

When tsarist Russia collapsed in 1917 and the revolutionary Bolshevik government withdrew from the war in early 1918, German ambitions to expand into eastern Europe seemed about to be realized. However, British financial might, and its ability to replenish forces and supplies from its empire, was beginning to make a difference in the west. The deployment of German submarines had prompted the USA to join the war on the Allied side in April 1917. The Allies blockaded German ports, adding to Germany's worsening economic situation. Germany launched a

series of offensives in the west in early 1918, but by August they were thrown onto the defensive by an Allied army bolstered by American forces. In September, Bulgaria surrendered, followed soon afterwards by the Ottoman Empire and Austria-Hungary. On 11 November 1918, Germany signed an armistice agreeing to Allied terms. At 11 am that day, the fighting stopped. World War I was over.

Above A ration party of the Royal Irish Rifles at the Somme in July 1916

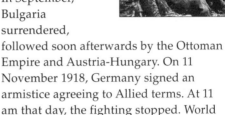

TIMELINE	
28 June 1914	*Archduke Franz Ferdinand is assassinated*
28 July 1914	*Austria-Hungary declares war on Serbia; World War I begins*
August 1914	*Germany defeats Russia at Battle of Tannenberg*
Sept 1914	*German advance stopped by the French at Battle of the Marne; the start of trench warfare*
7 May 1915	*A German U-boat sinks the US liner* Lusitania, *helping to sway American opinion in favour of the Allies*
Feb–Dec 1916	*Battle of Verdun*
June 1916	*Arabs revolt against the Ottoman Empire*
July–Nov 1916	*British offensive on the Somme*
Sept 1916	*Tanks are used for the first time in battle*
6 April 1917	*The USA declares war on Germany*
3 March 1918	*Treaty of Brest-Litovsk imposed by Germany on Bolshevik Russia deprives Russia of vast areas of eastern Europe*
August 1918	*Allied forces launch a successful offensive at Amiens*
11 Nov 1918	*Germany signs an armistice with the Western Allies after the Kaiser flees to the Netherlands*
18 Jan 1919	*Paris peace conference opens*
28 June 1919	*Treaty of Versailles ends World War I.*

THE RUSSIAN REVOLUTION AND THE SOVIET UNION

1917–1939

Above *This Russian poster from the time of the Revolution reads 'Still Not a Member of the Cooperative – Sign Up Immediately!'*

World War I placed enormous economic and social strains on Russia. There were severe shortages of food, fuel and essential items, and many blamed Tsar Nicholas II for the situation. In March 1917 there was a popular revolt in the capital, Petrograd. Nicholas tried to order in the troops and override the Duma (parliament) but his political authority had collapsed and he was forced to resign. The Duma established a provisional government, while soviets – democratically elected committees representing workers and soldiers – formed throughout Russia. They were dominated by socialist parties, including the Bolsheviks, led by Vladimir Ilych Lenin. When the moderates in the government decided to continue with the war, popular support shifted to the more radical soviets. In November 1917 (October in the old Russian calendar), the Bolsheviks seized power.

Civil war

The Bolsheviks immediately withdrew from World War I and began talks with Germany, resulting in the Treaty of Brest-Litovsk (March 1918) under which Russia agreed to give up the Baltic states, Finland, Poland and the Ukraine. The fledgling regime was almost immediately caught up in a civil war, as anti-communists, known as the Whites, fought to overthrow them. The Whites were a mix of anti-Bolshevik socialists, liberals, aristocrats, nationalist-separatists and peasants. They were supported by Britain, France, Japan and the USA. However, the White forces were poorly organized and lacked coherent leadership and by 1920 the Bolsheviks' Red Army had defeated them. Following the civil war, the Red Army recaptured the Ukraine, Georgia and eastern Armenia and suppressed nationalist-separatist movements in Byelorussia (modern Belarus) and Central Asia. In 1921 the Red Army was defeated by a Franco-Polish force and ceded the Western parts of Byelorussia and Ukraine to Poland.

Establishing control

When the Bolsheviks took power, much of Russia was in turmoil. Peasants had seized farmland from Russian nobles, and workers had taken control of many factories. At first Lenin supported these seizures, but after the civil war broke out, the government tightened its grip, taking over factories and forcing peasants to hand over most of their produce to feed the army and the urban population, in a policy known as 'war communism'. This provoked widespread revolts in 1920–1922 and led to a famine in the Volga region that killed five million. Lenin was forced to compromise his socialist principles with the 'new economic policy' (NEP), introduced in 1921, which permitted small businesses and farms to engage in free trade while the government retained control of banking and heavy industry. During the 1920s, the economy steadily grew. In 1922 the Bolsheviks, now renamed the Communist Party, established the Union of Soviet Socialist Republics (USSR), or Soviet Union. Byelorussia, Transcaucasia and Ukraine joined Russia to form the union's first four republics. Eventually 15 republics made up the Soviet Union.

Industrialization

When Lenin died in 1924, a power struggle developed among members of the Politburo (executive committee of the Communist Party). One leading figure, Joseph Stalin, used his position as General Secretary to create a power base within the Party, and defeated his rivals one by one. By 1928 Stalin had achieved absolute control. Determined to make the Soviet Union a global power on a par with the West, he launched a programme of rapid industrialization. The first Five Year Plan was adopted in 1928. The Plan's over-optimistic targets led to tremendous inefficiency and waste, yet remarkable progress was made. Vast new mineral extraction plants, factories and power stations were established in the Urals, the Volga area and Siberia, and railways were built to link the new industrial hubs. The population of the big cities nearly doubled between 1928 and 1933.

Collectivization

To feed the expanding population of urban workers, Stalin had to radically reorganize the countryside. In 1929, he ordered the collectivization of agriculture. Private holdings were abolished and peasants were forced to work on giant collective farms. Wealthy peasant farmers, known as *kulaks*, were deported to the *gulag* (the prison camp system). Many peasants responded by slaughtering their livestock and only planting enough for themselves. This was forcibly requisitioned, causing famine. By 1933, some 14.5 million people had died, either from famine or in the gulag.

The Great Purge

The failures of industrialization and

TIMELINE	
March 1917	*Tsar Nicholas abdicates and a provisional government is set up*
Nov 1917	*The Bolsheviks seize power*
Mar 1918	*Treaty of Brest-Litovsk*
1918–1921	*Civil War between the 'Whites' and the 'Reds'*
1920	*The Red Army invades Poland*
1921	*The new economic policy is introduced*
1922	*Formation of the Soviet Union*
1928	*The first Five Year Plan is announced*
1929	*The collectivization of agriculture is announced*
1932–1933	*Famine in the Ukraine and Central Asia kills 5 to 7 million*
1933	*The second Five Year Plan is announced*
1934–1938	*The Great Purge.*

collectivization to achieve the targets of the Plan, as well as Stalin's own increasing paranoia, led him to embark on the 'Great Purge' in 1934. Many former Bolsheviks and senior Party members underwent show trials where they were forced to confess to long lists of crimes before being shot. The NKVD (secret police) arrested millions for subversive activities and sent them to the gulag. Most were never seen again. People were encouraged to spy on their neighbours, and even family members, as fear spread throughout the country. The purge greatly weakened the Party and the bureaucracy, and in 1938 it spread to the armed forces, where hundreds of senior officers were arrested and imprisoned. This was poor timing as only three years later, the Soviet Union would be at war with Germany.

Above *Joseph Stalin projected himself as the wise father of the nation but in fact was responsible for the deaths of millions of citizens*

EUROPE BETWEEN THE WARS

1918–1939

World War I destroyed Europe's old order. Dynasties like the Romanovs, Hohenzollerns and Habsburgs all fell. The peace treaties that ended the war fundamentally altered the political map. Austria-Hungary was divided into several countries. US President, Woodrow Wilson hoped to end nationalism as a cause of conflict by giving ethnic peoples their own nations. Four new ethnically homogenous states emerged: Czechoslovakia, Estonia, Latvia and Lithuania, But many nationalist groups were frustrated to find themselves minorities within multi-ethnic states, such as the reconstituted Poland and the newly created Kingdom of Serbs, Croats and Slovenes (which became Yugoslavia). Under the Treaty of Versailles, Germany was obliged to accept full responsibility for the war. It lost Alsace-Lorraine to France, additional territory to Poland, and all its overseas colonies. Its armed forces were reduced and it was forced to pay heavy reparations to the victorious Allies. Three million ethnic Germans now lived outside Germany.

Below *In 1930 thousands of the unemployed marched on London in protest*

The peace treaties failed to establish a lasting settlement and, by creating political instability and resentment, they sowed the seeds of future conflict. Following the war, extremist movements sprang up across Central Europe. Several cities fell to communist revolutions and a widespread fear that a Russian-style revolution could sweep through Europe encouraged the emergence of a reactionary, authoritarian and ultra-nationalist ideology: fascism.

Rise of fascism

Italy, disappointed not to have been awarded territory in Dalmatia – which had been promised to it by France and Britain for its part in the war – seized it by force. Exploiting popular discontent and fear of communism, Benito Mussolini's Fascist Party came to power in 1922. By the mid-1920s, fascist-type parties had formed in most European countries.

The Treaty of Versailles caused outrage in Germany and many regarded those who signed it as traitors. When Germany reneged on its reparation payments in 1923, France occupied the industrial Ruhr region, provoking mass strikes. The German government printed more money to pay the workers. The resulting hyperinflation, as well as lingering resentment over Versailles and fear of communism, fuelled the rise of fascist parties, including Adolf Hitler's Nazi (Nationalsozialistische) Party.

Prosperity returns

The war had left Europe economically weakened. In the later 1920s, the situation improved, thanks to American loans. Britain and France realized that an impoverished and resentful Germany was a destabilizing influence, and agreed to reduce the reparations. The 1925 Locarno Pact significantly eased tensions between the Western Allies and Germany: Allied troops were withdrawn from the Rhineland; and Germany was admitted into the League of Nations, an organization formed after World War I, in 1919, to promote world peace.

The Great Depression

Europe's brief spell of prosperity and

stability ended in the early 1930s. Following the Wall Street Crash of 1929, American loans were withdrawn and Europe fell into a major economic depression. Unemployment and homelessness soared. In Germany, the number of unemployed had reached six million by 1932. In Britain, millions suffered from malnutrition and hunger marches attempted to attract attention to their plight.

Spanish Civil War

Extremism flourished once again and recently established democracies came under threat as huge numbers switched their support to either communism or fascism. By the late 1930s, right-wing dictatorships were established across most of Central Europe. In Spain, Francisco Franco's fascists, supported by the Catholic Church and the army – armed by Italy and Germany – fought a civil war (1936–1939) against the Republican government, supported by the Soviet Union. Following his victory, Franco imposed a harsh, right-wing dictatorship that lasted until his death in 1975.

Nazi Germany

Riding a wave of mass discontent, the Nazi Party gained power in 1933. The regime abolished Germany's democratic institutions and took control of its industries, trade unions and media. They eliminated unemployment through massive public works programmes. Hitler aimed to re-establish German dominance in Europe. He believed in the supremacy of the German race and its right to conquer territories to the east for greater 'living space'. He began a major programme of rearmament, in defiance of the Versailles Treaty.

Build-up to war

The League of Nations proved incapable of halting German expansionism. Britain and France hoped to appease Germany by conceding small territorial claims. Thus, Hitler was able to remilitarize the Rhineland in 1936, and absorb Austria and the Sudetenland into the Reich (German state) in 1938, without provoking a war. His subsequent demands for Polish territory did arouse strong complaint from Britain and France, who threatened war if Poland was invaded. Hitler signed the Pact of Steel with Italy in May 1939, then surprised everyone by signing a Non-Aggression Pact in August with his ideological enemy the Soviet Union. Confident that Britain would remain neutral, Hitler invaded Poland on 1 September 1939. Two days later, Britain and France declared war on Germany. World War II had begun.

Above *Troops parade past Adolf Hitler at the Nuremberg rally of 9 November 1935*

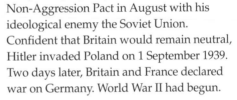

TIMELINE	
1919–1920	*Treaties of Versailles, St Germain, Neuilly and Trianon create the post-war settlement in Europe*
1921	*Following a war with Irish Republican Army, Britain agrees to grant independence to 26 of Ireland's 32 counties, which form the Irish Free State*
1924	*The Dawes Plan reduces German reparations*
1925	*The Locarno Pact guarantees German borders*
1926	*A general strike paralyzes Britain*
1929	*The Great Depression begins*
1932	*German reparations are abolished*
1936–1939	*Spanish Civil War*
Feb 1938	*German Anschluss with Austria*
1938	*Britain signs the Munich agreement with Germany, accepting German occupation of the Sudetenland*
1939	*The Nazi-Soviet Pact is signed.*

USA AND CANADA

1914–1945

Between 1900 and 1917, a 'progressive movement' swept the USA, aiming to: end political corruption; make government more responsive to the people;, improve living conditions for the poor; and regulate big business. President Woodrow Wilson (1912–1918) was a progressive, who enacted measures and oversaw amendments to the US Constitution designed to achieve some of these goals.

World War 1

Right A flapper dancing the Charlston sums up the careless hedonism of the Roaring Twenties which followed the hardships of war

The Wilson administration adopted a neutral stance on the outbreak of World War I. However, German aggression, including U-boat attacks on US merchant ships, eventually convinced Wilson to join the war against Germany in April 1917. Some two million Americans subsequently saw action. Wilson viewed the Paris Peace Conference of 1919 as a chance to establish a lasting settlement in Europe. His Fourteen Points included provisions for arms reduction and the settlement of rival territorial claims. Several of his proposals were adopted in the Versailles Treaty, including the establishment of a League of Nations to help maintain peace. However, the US Senate rejected US participation in the League.

The Roaring Twenties

In the 1920s, many young Americans reacted to the horrors of the previous decade by turning their backs on traditional ways and focusing instead on having a good time. A conservative backlash to this youthful hedonism resulted in Prohibition: a ban on alcohol that lasted from 1920 to 1933. So young Americans took to visiting 'speak-easies', these were bars run by gangsters, where they drank illegal alcohol and listened to jazz. Young women, known as 'flappers', adopted very short skirts, 'bobbed' their hair and smoked in public. The Roaring Twenties, as the decade is called, was an era of spectacular economic prosperity for many Americans. Large numbers moved to the cities, so that in 1920, urban dwellers outnumbered the rural population for the first time. Affluence fed consumerism, and modern conveniences such as radios, telephones, refrigerators, washing machines and automobiles appeared in many American households.

CANADA

As a dominion of the British Empire, Canada entered World War 1 alongside Britain in 1914. Over 600,000 Canadians served in the war and some 60,000 died. Canadians won a famous victory against German forces at Vimy Ridge in April 1917. Canada's contribution to the war effort encouraged many Canadians to demand greater independence from Britain, especially in foreign affairs. In 1926, Prime Minister William King successfully negotiated Canadian independence, officially recognized in 1931. The worldwide depression during the 1930s hurt demand for Canadian exports, including food, minerals and timber. Thousands of Canadian factories, coal mines and shops closed, and hundreds of thousands lost their jobs. Relief camps were established and aid given to the poor, but strikers and protestors were harshly treated. Canada entered World War ll in September 1939. Over a million Canadians served, and some 90,000 were killed or wounded.

Stock market crash

The Roaring Twenties came to an abrupt and dramatic end in late October 1929 when the New York stock market on Wall Street crashed. Stock prices, inflated by a prolonged period of speculation, suddenly plummeted in a frenzy of panic selling. By the end of the year, around $40 billion had been wiped off share values. The immediate victims of the Wall Street Crash were the speculators – banks, businesses and individuals. As America's chief wealth-creators, their losses soon affected the whole economy. Banks reduced loans to businesses, and businesses decreased production.

Great Depression

Demand fell as consumers felt the pinch, leading to hundreds of factory and shop closures. Thousands lost their life savings as banks closed across the country. Unemployment soared, and by 1933 some 13 million Americans were out of work. Many lost their homes and soon shanty towns, known as Hoovervilles (after President Herbert Hoover, who opposed relief payments to the poor), began to appear on the outskirts of cities. Thousands were forced to queue for food from soup kitchens run by charities. Over 750,000 farmers lost their land due to sharp reductions in income and a terrible drought on the Great Plains from 1934 to 1936, known as the Dust Bowl.

The New Deal

President Roosevelt (1932–1944) introduced the New Deal, a programme of government initiatives designed to lift the country out of depression. It included public works projects to provide jobs; the provision of low-cost housing for the homeless; relief payments to farmers; and a reform of the banking system. The New

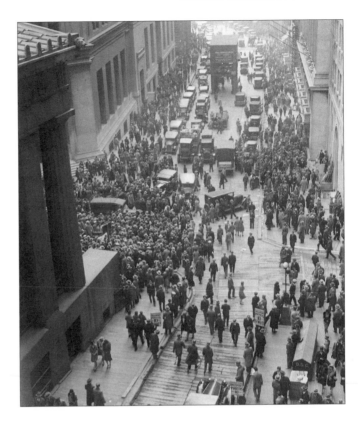

Deal brought relief to millions, but economic recovery was painfully slow and the depression did not fully end until 1941, when arms production for World War II stimulated the economy.

Above Wall Street, *seen on 1 January 1929; by the end of the year it was a scene of financial chaos*

The home front

The USA entered World War II after the Japanese attack on the US military base at Pearl Harbor, Hawaii, in December 1941. Some 15 million men and 338,000 women served in the US armed forces. Across the country, factories making consumer goods were converted to produce planes, ships, weapons and other military supplies. Because so many men were serving in the armed forces, millions of women were recruited to take their places in the factories. By 1943 the US was outproducing all the enemy nations combined.

WORLD WAR II IN EUROPE

1939–1945

Germany defeated Poland in a matter of weeks. Its new method of warfare, the blitzkrieg *(lightning war), involved the simultaneous use of tanks and dive-bombers, which threw the Polish army into confusion. Soviet forces invaded Poland from the east and, as agreed in their 1939 pact, Germany and the Soviet Union divided Poland between them. The Soviet Union then began occupying the Baltic states, but failed to defeat Finland in the Winter War of 1939–1940.*

Above *From a rooftop in central London, an air raid warden watches the Battle of Britain in progress*

Blitzkrieg

To forestall British attempts to cut off Germany's supplies of iron ore from Scandinavia, German forces invaded Denmark and Norway in April 1940. Allied efforts to help Norway were driven back, and both countries were defeated by June. Hitler's primary objective remained the conquest of the Soviet Union, but first he needed to neutralize his enemies in the west. In May, he launched a blitzkrieg against Belgium, Luxembourg and the Netherlands, defeating them in 18 days. Germany invaded France on 5 June. French defences crumbled before the blitzkrieg and German forces occupied Paris on the 14th. After the French surrender, Germany occupied northern France, while a German puppet regime (Vichy France) governed the south.

Battles with Britain

Hitler believed Britain would offer peace terms following the fall of France, but the British under Prime Minister Winston Churchill decided to fight on. German forces prepared to invade Britain, but first attempted to achieve air supremacy over the Channel. In the Battle of Britain (July–September 1940), Britain's Royal Air Force prevailed over Germany's Luftwaffe. The Germans switched to bombing British cities, but civilian morale held up, and by May 1941 Hitler had abandoned his invasion plans. Instead, Germany's U-boat fleet attempted to cut off Britain's supplies from North America. At first Germany appeared to be winning the Battle of the Atlantic, sinking thousands of tons of Allied shipping each month, but by mid-1943 the combined use of radar, sonar and aerial bombers managed to defeat the U-boat threat.

Invasion of the Soviet Union

By 1940, Italy, Bulgaria, Hungary and Romania had joined the war on Germany's side (an alliance known as the Axis). To secure Germany's southern flank prior to the planned invasion of the Soviet Union, Axis forces invaded Greece and Yugoslavia in April 1941, defeating both within weeks. On 22 June, Hitler launched Operation Barbarossa, a full-scale invasion of the Soviet Union. The attack took Stalin by surprise, and Axis forces advanced rapidly, their tanks and dive-bombers smashing through Soviet battle lines. With limited access to raw materials, Hitler needed a quick victory. He ignored advice to capture Moscow and pressed ahead on three fronts, overstretching his forces. In the autumn, as Stalin brought in fresh troops, the German advance slowed. By December, German forces had surrounded

Leningrad and reached the outskirts of Moscow, but progress was stalled by the severe winter. Germany launched fresh offensives in 1942, overrunning the Crimea and advancing on the Caucasus, but Stalin's mobilization of the Soviet Union's vast army and resources made a knock-out blow now impossible. By the end of 1942, the tide was turning against Germany. The German defeat at Stalingrad in January 1943 was devastating to morale and halted its eastward advance.

North Africa and Italy

Axis forces tried to cut off British oil supplies from the Middle East and seize control of the Suez Canal by attacking the Allies in Africa. By May 1942, German forces under Rommel were just 320 km (198 miles) from the canal, but a British army under Montgomery defeated them at El Alamein in October. By May 1943, Axis forces had been driven from North Africa. In July, the Allies, including American forces (the USA had entered the war in December 1941), invaded Sicily. Mussolini fell from power and was imprisoned (only to be later rescued by German commandos). Italy surrendered in September.

Battles in the west

On 6 June 1944, known as D-Day, the Allies launched a major seaborne invasion of northern France from Britain. German resistance was fierce but in July, the Allies punched a hole in the enemy lines and began a rapid advance on three fronts towards the German border. Paris was liberated in August. In December, Hitler attempted a final desperate assault through the Ardennes Forest in Belgium and Luxembourg, but was halted by American forces within two weeks.

TIMELINE	
Sept 1939	*Germany and the Soviet Union invade Poland*
June 1940	*Italy declares war on Britain and France*
June 1941	*Germany invades the Soviet Union*
Dec 1941	*Germany declares war on the USA*
Aug 1942	*USA begins bombing raids over occupied Europe*
Sept 1942–Jan 1943	*Siege of Stalingrad ends in German defeat*
Nov 1942	*Germans occupy southern France*
Nov 1943	*Soviet forces retake Kiev*
Apr 1944	*Red Army recaptures the Crimea*
July 1944	*Red Army enters Warsaw, sparking a Polish uprising against German occupiers*
Mar 1945	*Allied forces cross the Rhine*
May 1945	*Germany surrenders.*

Allied victory

After the victory at Stalingrad, Soviet forces slowly drove the Germans back. A German attack at Kursk in July 1943 was defeated in one of the greatest tank battles in history. In January 1944, a Soviet offensive lifted the siege of Leningrad. Stalin's armies advanced on all fronts. By July, they had occupied Romania and Bulgaria. Poland fell in January 1945 and Hungary in February. Meanwhile, the Allies began their final assault on Germany, occupying the Rhineland in March. Hitler ordered his forces to fight to the death but each day, large numbers surrendered. On 30 April, with Soviet forces besieging his capital, Berlin, Hitler committed suicide. A provisional German government signed an unconditional surrender on 7 May.

Below *Field Marshal Bernard Montgomery led the Eighth Army to victory over the Germans in North Africa*

THE HOLOCAUST

1942–1945

Between 1941 and 1945, the Nazis attempted the systematic extermination of the Jewish population of Europe, an event later termed the Holocaust. From all over occupied Europe, Jews were deported to death camps in Poland, where they were gassed and their bodies then burned on an industrial scale. By the end of World War II, around six million Jews had been killed, more than two-thirds of the Jewish population of Europe. Throughout much of eastern Europe, Jewish culture had been wiped out forever.

Anti-Semitism, or hatred of Jews, had existed in many parts of Europe since ancient times and Jews had frequently been the victims of persecution. Adolf Hitler blamed the Jews for Germany's defeat in World War I and the depression of the 1930s. When the Nazis achieved power, anti-semitism became government policy. They enacted a series of laws designed to exclude Jews from German public life. Jews were banned from the civil service, education, universities, medicine and journalism. The 1935 Nuremburg laws deprived Jews of their citizenship and prevented them from marrying non-Jews. On

Below *The gates at Auschwitz concentration camp bore the words 'Arbeit macht frei', meaning 'work makes one free' – a Nazi lie*

the night of 9 November 1938, known as *Kristallnacht*, or the 'night of broken glass', the Nazis launched an organized assault against Jewish shops, businesses and temples. Dozens of Jews were killed and thousands were arrested and sent to concentration camps.

The Final Solution

Germany's conquests in Europe after 1939 brought millions more Jews under Nazi control. Many were confined in run-down areas called ghettos. Around the middle of 1941, Nazi policy towards Jews changed. Instead of imprisoning them or placing them in ghettos, they started killing them – a policy they called the Final Solution of the Jewish Question. Special squads of SS (Schutzstaffel) troops followed the advancing German army into the Soviet Union. When they reached a village, they would round up the Jewish residents, march them into the countryside and shoot them. Nazi leaders soon sought a more efficient method of mass slaughter, and a method less disturbing for the killers. They began locking captured Jews inside sealed vans and suffocating them on the exhaust fumes as the van was driven to the burial site. By spring 1942, over a million Jews had been killed.

Death camps

In January 1942, senior Nazi officials gathered at Wannsee in Berlin to discuss ways of turning the extermination of the Jews into a more systematic operation. As a result, death camps were built in German-occupied Poland at Belzec, Sobibor, Majdanek, Chelmno, Auschwitz and Treblinka. Here they installed gas chambers disguised as showers. Each camp was capable of killing 15,000 to 25,000 people per day.

Throughout occupied Europe, Jews were taken from the ghettos on freight trains to the camps. On arrival, they were examined by an SS doctor, who singled out the able-bodied. The others – some 80 per cent – were stripped of their personal belongings and sent immediately to the gas chambers. Once the prisoners were dead, guards

removed any gold teeth from their mouths, then burned their bodies in crematoria. The able-bodied had their heads shaved and belongings confiscated. They were known thereafter by a number tattooed on their arm and were forced to work until too weak to continue, whereupon they were killed or left to die.

Towards the end of the war, as Allied forces advanced through Europe, the Nazis hurriedly closed many of the camps to remove evidence of their crimes. Vast numbers of malnourished prisoners were forced to walk hundreds of kilometres to camps inside German territory. Thousands died on these 'death marches'.

Survival and resistance

Jews found different ways of evading capture or fighting back against the Nazis. Some joined resistance movements in France, Poland and the Soviet Union. Others tried to flee, although this became increasingly difficult as the Nazi reach extended across Europe. A great number went into hiding, and there were many examples of non-Jews risking their lives by offering shelter to Jewish families. Individuals such as Oskar Schindler, a German businessman, and Raoul Wallenburg, a Swedish diplomat, were able to save thousands of Jewish lives by bribing or deceiving Nazi officials. Some Jewish partisan groups, such as Bielski Otriad in Belarus, rescued many Jews from the ghettos.

There were rebellions in several Polish ghettos, including Tuczyn and Marcinkonis. The most significant uprising took place at Warsaw in April–May 1943. There were also uprisings at Treblinka and Sobibor death camps in 1943; and in 1944 prisoners rioted at Auschwitz and set fire to the crematorium. These were mostly desperate acts by people who knew they were doomed. Although

some managed to escape, the great majority of those who took part were killed.

Other victims

Besides the death camps, the Nazis operated hundreds of prison camps in Germany and the occupied territories. Conditions in all of them were uniformly harsh and many hundreds of thousands of inmates died of starvation, disease or overwork. In some camps, prisoners died after undergoing cruel medical experiments carried out by Nazi doctors. The Jews were not the only victims of the Holocaust. The Nazis were determined to kill or enslave any they regarded as racially inferior or politically dangerous, including gypsies, Slavs (especially Poles and Soviet prisoners of war), communists and homosexuals.

Above Prisoners transported by train from Hungary arrive at Auschwitz in Poland in the spring of 1945

TIMELINE	
1935	*Nuremburg laws deny German citizenship to Jews*
1938	Kristallnacht
Nov 1939	*All Jews in Nazi-occupied Europe are obliged to wear a yellow Star of David*
Sep 1941	*Experiments on the gassing of prisoners begin*
Jan 1941	*Wannsee Conference confirms plans for the mass slaughter of Jews*
May 1941	*Large-scale gassing begins at Auschwitz*
July 1944	*A Polish resistance group occupies Majdaned before Soviet troops enter the camp*
Oct 1944	*Gassings at Auschwitz come to an end*
Jan 1945	*Soviet troops reach Auschwitz.*

JAPAN

1914–1941

Japan joined World War I on the side of the Allies. In the course of the conflict, it occupied several German territories, including Jiaozhou in north-eastern China and some islands in the Western Pacific, most of which it was allowed to retain at the war's end. The war brought economic prosperity to Japan, with an enormous boost in munitions exports, creating a large industrial labour force. Inspired by the growth of democracy in the West, many Japanese began to demand political reform. In 1925, the Japanese Imperial Diet (parliament) expanded the suffrage to include all adult males.

Above right
On 1 September 1923 the Great Kantō Earthquake struck, destroying all of Yokohama and most of Tokyo

In foreign affairs, Japan became noticeably more pacific after the war, in keeping with the global mood. In 1920, it joined the League of Nations and in 1928, Japan was one of 14 countries that signed the somewhat idealistic Kellogg-Briand Pact, which renounced war as a means of solving international disputes.

Hard times

Japan's wartime boom ended in 1920. The economy suffered a series of recessions through the 1920s; it was made worse by the Great Kantō Earthquake of 1923, which devastated Tokyo and Yokohama and caused up to 140,000 deaths. When the worldwide depression struck in late 1929, Japan's already faltering economic situation deteriorated even further. Factories laid off workers, prompting a new wave of strikes. Farmers suffered as agricultural prices plunged. Public opinion turned against the party leaders and the political establishment. Many regarded Western influences, including democratic government, as part of the problem, and wished for a return to traditional Japanese ways.

Such conservative, nationalist views, found a violent outlet with the formation of several extreme right-wing terrorist organizations. One of these groups, supported by elements within the military, assassinated Prime Minister Inukai Tsuyoshi in 1932, ending Japan's brief flirtation with democracy. The major parties voted to dissolve themselves and form a single party, the Imperial Rule Assistance Association. The IRAA, which was dominated by military and bureaucratic figures and claimed to stand

TIMELINE

1918–1922	Japanese troops invade Siberia as part of anti-Bolshevik Allied expeditionary force
1919	Japan's wartime territorial gains are confirmed by the Treaty of Versailles
1932	Japan establishes puppet state of Manchukuo in Manchuria
1933	Japan withdraws from the League of Nations
1937	Second Sino-Japanese War begins
1938	Japanese and Soviet forces clash on Manchukuo-Soviet border
1940	Japan extends its control over the whole of Indochina.

above party politics, continued to rule Japan until 1945.

Invasion of Manchuria

There were several reasons for Japan's invasion of Manchuria. The vast areas of undeveloped land and abundant natural resources were ripe for exploitation. More urgently, Japan's existing economic interests in Manchuria were under threat from Chinese nationalists, who were hoping to drive out foreign-owned businesses from China. In September 1931, Japan engineered a crisis in Manchuria as a pretext for an invasion. A Japanese force moved in and asserted control. Manchuria was renamed Manchukuo and a puppet government was installed there under Emperor Henry Pu Yi. Japanese forces occupied the Chinese province of Jehol to create a buffer zone, and threatened Beijing. Denunciations of Japanese aggression at the League of Nations were not matched by action, and in May 1933 China agreed a truce that accepted Japanese control of Manchuria.

War with China

The Second Sino-Japanese War broke out on 7 July 1937, when Chinese and Japanese troops clashed near Marco Polo Bridge on the outskirts of Beijing. By the end of the year, Japanese forces had captured Beijing, Shanghai and the Chinese capital Nanjing and were in control of most of northern China. Japan's aerial bombardment of the cities, and the massacres it carried out in the capital, known as the Rape of Nanjing, were internationally condemned. The Chinese government retreated to the inland province of Sichuan, refusing to negotiate. By the end of 1938, the Japanese had progressed along the lower Yangtze River valley beyond Hankou and had won control of several ports in southern China.

However the war had reached a stalemate. The Chinese adoption of guerrilla tactics, scorched earth and sabotage effectively stalled the Japanese advance.

World War II

With the fall of France and the Low Countries to Germany in 1940, Japan saw opportunities to expand its influence within Europe's South-east Asian colonies. Japan's war machine relied on plentiful supplies of oil and rubber, which the region had in abundance. In July, the Japanese government announced the formation of a 'Greater East Asia Co-Prosperity Sphere', an economic and political alliance of East and South-east Asian countries under Japanese leadership. In September, Japan formed the Axis Pact with Germany and Italy and received permission from the Nazi-allied Vichy regime in France to occupy northern French Indochina.

Despite these moves, Japan remained greatly dependant on the USA for vital materials, including oil, steel and heavy machinery. The US government, alarmed by Japanese expansionism, began placing embargoes on these goods. Japan's leaders knew that they could not sustain their war effort in the long term without US oil, so agreed to negotiate in April 1941. However, when Japanese troops occupied southern Indochina in July, the US responded by placing a complete embargo on oil. In October, Prime Minister Konoe resigned, having failed to reach a diplomatic resolution to the problem. Konoe was replaced by the hawkish General Hideki Tojo, who began preparations for war with the United States.

Below Prime Minister Inukai Tsuyoshi, who was assassinated on 15 May 1932

WORLD WAR II IN THE PACIFIC

1941–1945

The Pacific War (1941–1945) was fought primarily between Japan and the USA. It was caused by Japanese expansionism in East and South-east Asia and took place over a vast area stretching from Burma in the west to Hawaii in the east, and New Guinea in the south to Manchuria in the north. It was marked by military innovations, including the prominent deployment of aircraft carriers and the American use of the atomic bomb. The conflict had profound consequences for East and South-east Asia, hastening the decline of European influence and the rise of nationalism in the region.

Right *American troops fighting in Guadalcanal found their tanks hard to manoeuvre in jungle terrain*

Below *General Hideki Tojo, Japanese prime minister 1941– 1944, was executed as a war criminal in 1948*

Japanese victories

Prime Minister Hideki Tojo realized that only the United States stood in the way of Japan's plans to build an empire in Asia. On 7 December 1941, he ordered an aerial assault on the US Pacific Fleet at Pearl Harbor, Hawaii. The surprise attack killed some 3,000 sailors, and destroyed and disabled many ships and aircraft. The following day, the USA, Canada and Britain declared war on Japan. Pearl Harbor was one of a series of coordinated attacks aimed at securing Japanese regional hegemony. Thailand fell on 8 December, and Japanese forces advanced into Malaya and Burma. By Christmas, they had won control of the British colony of Hong Kong. By February 1942, Japan completed its conquest of the Malay archipelago by taking Singapore. The Dutch East Indies fell in early March. By May, Japan had conquered the Philippines and driven British forces from Burma. Japan's rapid series of victories shocked the Allies. In just a few months, Japan had become master of South-east Asia and was now within striking range of Australia and India.

The tide turns

Following a US bombing raid on Tokyo and other cities in April 1942, the Japanese decided to expand their defensive perimeter to ensure no further attacks could take place. In May, a Japanese fleet was sent to capture the Australian base at Port Moresby on New Guinea, but was intercepted by US warships. The ensuing Battle of the Coral Sea prevented the attack on Port Moresby, ending the immediate threat to Australia. The Japanese opted instead for an invasion of Hawaii. As a first step, they planned to capture the island of Midway. Having recently cracked Japan's naval cipher, the US fleet was prepared and inflicted its first decisive defeat on the Japanese navy at the Battle of Midway (June 1942).

In August, the Allies went on the offensive in the islands of the South Pacific, determined to check Japanese expansion there. The battles were hard-fought amid inhospitable jungle conditions. Japanese soldiers equated surrender with disgrace and were rarely captured alive. In New Guinea, Allied forces gradually drove the Japanese westwards, back across the mountains. Fighting continued there until mid-1944. An Allied invasion and naval blockade of Guadalcanal in the Solomon Islands, beginning in August 1942, finally led to a Japanese withdrawal in February 1943. The remaining Solomon Islands fell during 1943. Small Japanese forces clung on tenaciously on each island and required overwhelming force to defeat.

Island hopping

The Allies soon realized that they did not need to capture the strongest Japanese bases, but could progress across the Pacific by targeting the more vulnerable islands, bypassing the Japanese strongholds and thereby save time and lives. Using this 'leapfrogging' strategy, Allied forces captured one island after another across the Central Pacific, with each island used as a base from which to attack the next. After taking Tarawa in the Gilbert Islands (November 1943), they took two of the Marshall Islands (February 1944). During the fight for the Mariana Islands (June 1944), the US routed the Japanese navy in the Battle of the Philippine Sea. The US air force was able to use the Marianas as a base for bombing raids on Japan.

Allied victory

In October 1944, the Allies assembled an enormous force to retake the Philippines. The Battle of Leyte Gulf, the largest naval engagement in history, saw the first use of Japanese 'kamikaze' suicide pilots, but they could not prevent another crushing defeat for their country. In the early months of 1945, American planes firebombed Japanese cities, including Tokyo, causing huge casualties. Although defeat was inevitable,

the Japanese chose to continue fighting, forcing the Allies to commit ever more troops and resources to the struggle. Two more brutal and bloody campaigns secured the islands of Iwo Jima (February–March 1945) and Okinawa (April–June 1945).

An invasion of the Japanese mainland would undoubtedly have caused hundreds of thousands more Allied casualties. To avoid this, the US government tried to force a Japanese surrender by means of a new invention. On 6 August 1945, an atomic bomb was dropped on the Japanese city of Hiroshima, killing around 100,000. Three days later, another was dropped on Nagasaki, killing 40,000. On 8 August, the Soviet Union declared war on Japan and invaded Manchuria. These events finally persuaded Japan's Emperor Hirohito to urge his government to surrender, which they did on 14 August.

Above *The atomic bomb was dropped on Hiroshima on 6 August 1945, devastating the city and causing massive loss of life*

TIMELINE	
Dec 1941	*Japan attacks Pearl Harbor, the Philippines, Hong Kong, Malaya and Burma*
Feb 1942	*British forces in Singapore surrender to Japan*
Mar 1942	*Dutch East Indies surrender to Japan*
May 1942	*British forces withdraw from Burma*
June 1942	*US defeats the Japanese navy at Midway*
Feb 1943	*US take Guadalcanal after a six-month campaign*
Nov 1943	*Tarawa in Central Pacific captured by US forces*
Oct 1944	*Japanese navy is destroyed at the Battle of Leyte Gulf*
Aug 1945	*Atomics bombs are dropped on Hiroshima and Nagasaki*
2 Sept 1945	*Japan signs formal statement of surrender.*

THE REPUBLIC OF CHINA

1911–1949

For most of its history as a republic, China was in a state of chaos and disunity, with different forces competing for control. At first, there were signs that China might develop into a modern democratic state. The revolutionaries who had engineered the downfall of the Qing formed themselves into a political party called, the Kuomintang (KMT), and the new president, Yuan Shikai, issued a constitution. But Yuan soon moved to expand his personal power, dismissing the parliament and outlawing the KMT.

Above *Yuan Shikai, a military leader during the Qing dynasty, briefly became Emperor of China in 1916*

World War l

While Europe was preoccupied with the Great War, Japan seized the opportunity to expand its influence in China. In 1915, President Yuan permitted, among other concessions, the transfer of German territories in Shandong to Japan. After Yuan's death in 1916, central authority crumbled and, although presidents continued to hold office in Beijing, for the next decade real power devolved to warlords in the provinces. In 1917, the Beijing government, under the control of northern warlords, entered World War I on the side of the Allies, hoping to win influence at the peace talks and check Japanese expansionism. But the Treaty of Versailles (May 1919) confirmed Japanese control of Shandong, causing widespread student demonstrations against the government and Japan.

Nationalists and Communists

The demonstrations evolved into a national awakening known as the May Fourth Movement. This was part of a broader intellectual movement that had been building since the early 1910s. Thousands of young Chinese had become influenced by Western culture and ideas and were now determined to reform China. The May Fourth Movement contributed greatly to the growth of Chinese nationalism. Many of its supporters were recruited into Sun Yat-Sen's nationalist KMT, which in 1917 had set up a rival government in Guangzhou, supported by southern warlords.

Other student activists were attracted to communism, inspired by the Russian Revolution of 1917. In 1921, the Chinese Communist Party (CCP) was founded in Shanghai. In 1923, the Soviet Union persuaded the CCP to join with the KMT, as it believed the latter had the best chance of taking and holding onto power in China. The alliance was an uncomfortable one, because the KMT drew much of its backing from rich landowners and the CCP supported redistribution of wealth.

Sun Yat-Sen died in 1925 and leadership of the KMT passed to its military commander Chiang Kai-shek. In 1926, the KMT, supported by the CCP, launched an attack on the northern warlords. The following year, Chiang turned on his CCP allies, killing labour union members and communists. CCP survivors took refuge in Jiangxi in southern China. In 1928, Chiang's forces captured Beijing and reunified most of China under KMT rule.

KMT rule

Chiang's KMT attempted some modernizing reforms, but most of the government's energies were directed at establishing its authority throughout China, parts of which still remained under the control of warlords, Japan and the communists. By 1931, the CCP had set up a number of bases in Jianxi and had organized a peasant army. In 1934, KMT attacks forced the communists to evacuate their bases and embark on the 'Long March' 15,445 km (9,600 miles) north to the city of Yan'an in Shaanxi. Of the 100,000 communists who began the march, just a few thousand survived. Among them was Mao Zedong, who emerged as the new leader of the CCP.

In 1931 Japan occupied Manchuria. Chiang, unprepared to fight both Japan and the communists, did not resist the occupation and accepted Japanese demands to extend their influence in northern China. Chiang's appeasement provoked protests by students and opposition within the military. When Manchurian forces kidnapped Chiang in 1936, he reluctantly agreed to join with the communists to fight the Japanese.

War with Japan

In 1937, Japan launched a major offensive against China, capturing Beijing, Shanghai and Nanjing. By 1938, they controlled most of north-eastern China and the KMT was forced to withdraw inland to Chongqing in Sichuan. After the USA entered World War II, in December 1941, Americans sent aid and advisors to China and Chiang was able to build a modern army. However, he left most of the struggle against Japan to the USA, concentrating instead on preparing the ground for a post-war showdown with the CCP. The CCP, meanwhile, focused on building up their membership and their 'Red Army', recruiting mainly from peasants in the Japanese-occupied north and east. By 1945 they had over a million members, and were receiving arms from the Soviet Union.

Civil war

Civil war between the KMT and CCP broke out shortly after Japan's surrender. The KMT was now weaker. Rampant inflation,

TIMELINE	
1912	*The Republic of China is proclaimed*
1917	*Sun Yat-sen establishes his base in Guangzhou*
1921	*The CCP is founded in Shanghai*
1925	*Sun Yat-sen dies*
1926–1928	*The KMT's Northern Expedition against the warlords*
1930–1931	*The CCP survives three KMT attacks*
1931	*Japan occupies Manchuria*
1934–1935	*The CCP undertakes the Long March to Yan'an*
1937–1945	*The Second Sino-Japanese War*
1949–1950	*Chiang Kai-shek flees to Taiwan and establishes his Republic of Nationalist China government there.*

Left *The communist People's Liberation Army entered Beijing in June 1949, led by Mao Zedong*

food shortages and official corruption had made it unpopular, and damaged morale among its forces. Despite receiving arms from the USA, the KMT was never able to gain a military advantage against the well-organized CCP, who had mass support among the peasantry. By 1948, the momentum had passed to the communists. In January 1949, the communist PLA (People's Liberation Army) captured Beijing and the following October, Mao Zedong announced the establishment of the People's Republic of China. In December, Chiang and his followers fled to the island of Taiwan.

INDEPENDENCE IN INDIA

1905–1949

By the early 20th century, many Indians were calling for a greater say in the running of their country. During the 1920s, the Indian National Congress, the largest nationalist organization, became a mass movement under the leadership of Mohandas (Mahatma) Gandhi, with the stated goal of winning complete independence from Britain.

Partition of Bengal

The Indian National Congress protested when George Curzon, viceroy of India, partitioned the province of Bengal into separate Hindu and Muslim sections in 1905. A boycott of British goods was organized, while extremists began a campaign of bombings and assassinations of British officials. Many Muslims, already hostile to the Hindu-dominated Congress, were sufficiently alarmed by the protests to form a separate All-India Muslim League (later the Muslim League) in 1906. The League lobbied to give Muslims their own separate voice in India's political affairs. To placate the nationalists, the British introduced the Morley-Minto Reforms in 1909. These reforms allowed Indians to elect representatives to provincial legislative assemblies. Bengal was reunited in 1911.

Civil disobedience

India, as an imperial dominion, was a major source of manpower and resources for the British war effort during World War I. Some 750,000 Indian men served and over 36,000 gave their lives. In return for India's support and sacrifices, Britain promised further reforms, but could not prevent continuous nationalist protests. In 1916, Mohandas Gandhi, a rising star within the Congress, forged a pact with Mohammed Ali Jinnah, leader of the Muslim League, to campaign jointly for independence. In 1919, Britain introduced the Rowlatt Acts, restricting the civil liberties of Indians and increasing government emergency powers in order to control protests. Gandhi organized a series of non-violent protests against the Rowlatt Acts, including general strikes and demonstrations. At one protest at Amritsar, British troops opened fire on a peaceful crowd, killing nearly 400. The Amritsar Massacre caused deep public anger and stirred widespread popular sympathy for the nationalist movement.

The Montagu-Chelmsford Reforms, passed in late 1919, increased the powers of Indian-dominated provincial legislative councils and boosted Indian representation on the central legislative council. Nevertheless, real political power remained with the viceroy and the governors. The

TIMELINE

1905	*Bengal is partitioned, sparking protests*
1906	*The All-India Muslim League (later the Muslim League) is founded*
1909	*The Morley-Minto Reforms are introduced*
1919	*The Rowlatt Acts restrict Indian civil liberties, including the right to a trial by jury*
1920–1922	*Gandhi's campaign of non-violent disobedience*
1929	*The Congress issues its Declaration of Independence*
1935	*The Government of India Act creates a new constitution for India*
1937	*Following national elections, the Congress forms governments in many provinces of India*
1940	*Jinnah demands an independent state of Pakistan*
1942	*Gandhi launches his Quit India movement*
1946	*British government announces its intention of granting independence to India*
1947	*Pakistan and India become independent.*

nationalists were unimpressed and in 1920, Gandhi, now leader of the Congress, began an organized campaign of non-violent disobedience, calling on Indians to boycott British goods and government services, and to refuse to pay their taxes. Many Indians gave up their jobs and risked fines and imprisonment to take part. Gandhi's campaign mobilized nationwide support, turning the Congress into a mass movement.

New constitution

In 1929, the Congress officially declared its goal of complete independence. The following year, Gandhi led thousands of followers on a 386 km (240 miles) march to the Arabian Sea, where they extracted salt from evaporated seawater. The salt march was a protest against taxes, particularly the tax on salt. Gandhi and other Congress leaders were jailed, but the momentum was now with the nationalists. Gandhi was summoned to London for talks. The outcome was the Government of India Act (1935). This created a new constitution that increased the representation of Indians in government. Yet, crucially, the viceroy and the governors retained the power of veto and control of finances, which left the nationalists frustrated.

Many Indian Muslims feared the prospect of being governed by the Hindu-dominated Congress in an independent India. In 1940, Mohammed Ali Jinnah of the Muslim League demanded a separate state to be called Pakistan, situated in the Muslim-majority areas of the north-west, centred on Punjab; and also in the east, centred on Bengal. The Congress opposed Jinnah's plan to partition India.

World War II

In 1939, Britain declared India to be at war with Germany, without consulting Indian leaders. The provincial Congress

governments resigned in protest. In 1942, Gandhi launched the Quit India movement, calling on Britain to withdraw from India or face nationwide civil disobedience. Gandhi and other Congress leaders were imprisoned, sparking violent protests. Jinnah's Muslim League cooperated with Britain, however, in the hope of securing British support for the creation of Pakistan.

Independence and partition

In 1946, Britain announced its intention of granting India independence no later than June 1948. Intensive negotiations began over how India would be governed. On 16 August 1946 the Muslim League organized demonstrations across the country, calling for the establishment of Pakistan. Violent clashes between Hindus and Muslims spread throughout India. The continuing violence persuaded British and Indian leaders that partition was the only solution.

On 14–15 August 1947, Pakistan and India became independent nations. Partition was accompanied by bloodshed and slaughter on a massive scale. Over seven million Hindu and Sikh refugees fled from Pakistan to India and a similar number of Muslims in India fled to Pakistan. Between 500,000 and a million were killed. Gandhi, who had protested against partition and done his best to prevent the ensuing violence, was assassinated by a Hindu extremist on 30 January 1948. Jawaharlal Nehru, a friend of Gandhi, became India's first prime minister.

Above *Mahatma Gandhi leaving 10 Downing Street in 1931, following negotiations on independence for India*

Below *Gandhi and Jawaharlal Nehru in August 1942, when the All-India Congress Committee called for the immediate dissolution of British rule*

THE COLD WAR

1945–1989

By early 1945, Soviet forces had driven the Nazis out of most of Eastern Europe. Determined to establish a sphere of influence there and a buffer against future aggressors, Stalin did not withdraw his forces, but proceeded to install communist, pro-Soviet governments throughout the region. This expansionism, in defiance of earlier agreements, angered the USSR's wartime allies, Britain and the USA; their relations with the Soviet Union sharply deteriorated. This marked the beginning of the Cold War, a state of non-violent conflict between the Soviet Union and the USA and their respective allies that would continue for the next 45 years.

Post-War tensions

In 1947, US President Truman developed his 'containment policy', offering financial and military aid to countries to help them resist communist expansion. In 1949, the USA, Canada and the Western European nations set up the North Atlantic Treaty Organization (NATO), a military alliance aimed at preventing further Soviet expansion in Europe. An equivalent alliance of communist states, called the Warsaw Pact, was established in 1955. In April 1949, the nuclear arms race began when the Soviet Union tested an atomic bomb; the USA was no longer the only nuclear-armed nation.

The first major Cold War clash occurred in the German city of Berlin, which lay inside the Soviet occupation zone. Following the post-war settlement, the

Above *An aerial view of the medium-range ballistic missile launch site number 2 at San Cristobal, Cuba, photographed by the US Air Force in November 1962*

Western side of the city was controlled by the Western Allies and the eastern side by Soviet forces. In June 1948, Soviet troops blockaded West Berlin to persuade the Allies to abandon the city. The Allies responded with the Berlin Airlift, supplying West Berliners with food and fuel by air. The siege was lifted in May 1949.

1950s

In the early 1950s, the West fought its first 'hot war' against communism. In June 1950, the Communist state of North Korea invaded South Korea. The United Nations (UN), an organization set up after World War II to promote world peace, voted to send a US-led force to help South Korea. Communist forces were eventually driven back and an armistice was signed in July 1953.

The death of Stalin in March 1953 brought a slight thaw in East-West relations. The new Soviet leader, Khrushchev, urged 'peaceful coexistence' with the West. His 'destalinization' policy encouraged Eastern European nations to push for more freedom from Soviet rule. After strikes and riots in Poland in 1956, Khrushchev agreed some liberal reforms there. However, a similar uprising in Hungary later that year was brutally crushed by Soviet forces.

The nuclear arms race continued throughout the 1950s. The USA tested its first hydrogen bomb in 1952, followed by the USSR in 1955. Two years later, the Soviets tested an intercontinental ballistic missile; nuclear attack on American cities became a real possibility. By 1958, both sides had achieved a 'balance of terror'.

1960s

The thaw in the Cold War ended in May 1960 when an American U-2 spy plane was shot down over the USSR, considerably raising hostility between the superpowers. Meanwhile, the USA was growing concerned about the increasingly friendly relations between the Cuban government of Fidel Castro and the Soviet Union. In October 1962, the US discovered Soviet missile bases on Cuba. President John Kennedy demanded the removal of the missiles and set up a naval blockade of the island. The Cuban Missile Crisis was the closest the superpowers came to all-out war. After a week of talks, Khrushchev agreed to withdraw the missiles in exchange for the removal of US missiles from Turkey.

Eastern Europe remained a major source of tension. As increasing numbers of East Germans fled to the more liberal West, via Berlin, the East German communists decided in 1961 to build a wall across the city to prevent further defections. The Berlin Wall became a symbol of communist repression. In 1968, the Czechoslovakian government's introduction of more liberal laws prompted an invasion by Warsaw Pact forces, crushing any hope of Western-style freedom in that country.

During the late 1960s, the USA became increasingly embroiled in Vietnam, supporting the South Vietnamese against the Communist Viet Cong of North Vietnam, who were backed by China and the Soviet Union.

1970s and 1980s

In the 1970s, the Cold War entered another period of thaw, known as 'détente'. American and Soviet leaders signed arms limitation treaties in attempts to stop the hugely expensive and destabilizing nuclear arms race. But the Soviet invasion of Afghanistan in 1979 effectively ended détente. In the early 1980s, the US embarked on a massive build-up of nuclear weapons.

Soviet policy underwent a dramatic shift in the mid-1980s with the accession of Mikhail Gorbachev. Aware that the economically declining USSR was no longer able to compete in an arms race with the USA, he agreed with US President Ronald Reagan a sharp reduction in nuclear weapons. Gorbachev's policy of greater freedom and openness in Soviet society soon spread to Eastern Europe.

In late 1989, border controls were relaxed and people were able to pass freely between East and West. In Berlin, East Germans began to tear down the hated wall. Communist governments swiftly collapsed across Eastern Europe. In December, Gorbachev and US President George Bush declared the Cold War officially over.

TIMELINE	
Feb 1946	*Winston Churchill declares that an 'iron curtain' has descended across Europe*
1948–1949	*The Berlin blockade*
1949	*NATO is established; the USSR tests its first atomic bomb*
1950–1953	*Korean War*
1955	*Warsaw Pact is established*
1956	*Soviet forces crush Hungarian uprising*
1961	*The Berlin Wall is built*
Oct 1962	*The Cuban Missile Crisis*
1968	*Warsaw Pact forces crush Prague Spring*
1979	*Soviet Union intervenes in Afghanistan*
Nov 1989	*Berlin Wall is dismantled*
Dec 1989	*The Cold War is officially declared to be over.*

Above *Amicable relations between Ronald Reagan and Mikhail Gorbachev helped to bring the Cold War to an end*

THE USA AND CANADA

1945 ONWARDS

Following World War II, the USA experienced unprecedented economic growth and a major population boom. Prosperity and technological advances transformed American life. Millions moved to newly built suburbs, watched television and used automatic dishwashers. Car ownership dramatically expanded, as did the road network; and out-of-town shopping malls, motels, fast-food restaurants and gas stations sprang up to serve the motoring community. Prosperity was not shared by all, however, and millions remained in poverty, including a high proportion of African Americans.

Right *F-14A Tomcat aircraft re-fuelling on patrol during the First Gulf War in 1991*

McCarthyism

The spread of communism in many areas of the globe caused deep unease in 1950s America. Senator Joseph McCarthy exploited this fear with his allegations, mostly unsubstantiated, that communists had infiltrated the government, the movie industry and other areas of American life. Between 1950 and 1954, McCarthy and his allies conducted numerous hearings in which the accused were encouraged to confess their links with communism and name other suspects. Many viewed McCarthy's campaign as a witch-hunt.

Civil rights movement

Since the abolition of slavery in 1865, African Americans had continued to suffer discrimination in jobs, housing, education, transport and other areas. A movement to extend civil rights to blacks gathered pace after World War II. In 1954, the movement gained a significant victory when the Supreme Court ruled compulsory segregation in schools illegal. In the early 1960s, the movement, now led by a charismatic Baptist minister Martin Luther King, organized demonstrations, including a mass 'March on Washington' in 1963. President Lyndon Johnson sympathized and his administration pushed through

several acts between 1965 and 1968, ending race-based discrimination in the USA.

Vietnam War

President Johnson also presided over a large increase in America's military involvement in Vietnam, supporting South Vietnam in its fight against the communist North. Most Americans approved the war at first, but TV images of atrocities and the steady accumulation of American casualties caused attitudes to shift. By the late 1960s, many were arguing that the USA had no right to intervene in Vietnam. Throughout the country, students and others demonstrated against the war. Johnson's successor Richard Nixon finally managed to end US involvement in 1973.

Watergate

Nixon was engulfed in a major political scandal that dominated the latter part of his presidency. In 1972, staff on his re-election committee burgled the political headquarters of the Democratic Party in the Watergate building in Washington, D.C.

Below *Martin Luther King led the civil rights movement in the early 1960s and his assassination caused rioting in several cities across the USA*

The evidence showed that Nixon covered up the burglary among other illegal acts. To avoid impeachment, Nixon resigned in 1974, the first president to do so.

The New Right

In the late 1970s, the US experienced economic decline and a series of foreign policy failures, notably the 14-month seizure of American hostages in Iran. Many Americans were dissatisfied with what they believed to be progressive policies pursued by governments since the 1960s. Various right-wing groups, including conservative evangelical Christians, coalesced to form the New Right movement. With New Right support, Ronald Reagan won the presidency in 1980. Reagan lowered taxes; reduced the role of government; promoted business interests; and expanded American military forces.

Post-Cold War America

Following the demise of the Soviet Union in 1991, the USA became the world's most powerful nation with the strongest military and largest economy. It used its influence to counter Iraqi expansionism in the First Gulf War (1991) and Serb aggression in the Balkan conflicts of 1992–1995 and 1999.

On 11 September 2001, the USA suffered the worst terrorist attack in its history, (see also page 289) when three hijacked airliners were deliberately crashed into the World Trade Center, New York, and the Pentagon Building near Washington, D.C., killing around 3,000. The attack changed American foreign policy. President George W. Bush called for a 'War on Terror' and the US led an international force in an attack on Afghanistan, whose government had harboured the terrorists responsible. The 2003 invasion of Iraq by the US and its allies – justified as part of the war on terrorism – was opposed by many Americans.

Credit Crunch

In 2007, bad debt in the US housing market triggered an economic crisis. Banks were revealed to have huge capital deficits and many global financial institutions suffered crippling losses. In 2009, under Barack Obama, America's first black president, the Federal Reserve injected money into the economy to boost bank lending, but it couldn't prevent recession. Popular anger at the inequalities of the global financial system sparked the Occupy movement. This protest movement began in New York City in September 2011. By October it had spread to 951 cities in 82 countries.

Below French president Charles de Gaulle, speaking in Montreal on 24 July 1967, gives his support for an independent Quebec

CANADA

Like the USA, Canada enjoyed a post-war economic boom. Consecutive Liberal governments promoted social welfare. In 1949, Newfoundland, which had reverted to colonial status in 1934, rejoined Canada. In the 1960s, Quebec nationalists began a campaign to make their province a separate nation. Prime Minister Pierre Trudeau (1968–1979, 1980–1984) negotiated the 'patriation' of the (originally British-created) Canadian constitution in 1982.

This was rejected by Quebec, which was granted special status in 1987, antagonizing the other provinces. In 1994, Quebec citizens voted to remain part of Canada, and in 2011 the separatist representation in Parliament was reduced from 47 to four. In 1999 Canada gained a new territory, Nunavut, separated from the Northwest Territories, to give greater autonomy to the majority Inuit population.

The Soviet Union and Post-Soviet Russia

1945 ONWARDS

Some 27 million Soviet troops and civilians died in World War II. The nation bore the brunt of the Nazi onslaught and many of its cities were reduced to ruins. Stalin's response was to move his forces into Eastern Europe and formerly Japanese-occupied Manchuria, to fortify the USSR against future aggression. Soviet troops soon withdrew from Manchuria, but Soviet-style satellite states were formed in Eastern Europe. All contacts with the West were forcibly ended as the Cold War began. The Soviet economy was rapidly rebuilt under new five-year plans, expanding heavy industry at the expense of consumer goods. After Stalin's death in 1953, he was replaced by a collective leadership.

Above *A Soviet poster from about 1968, glorifying the roles of farmer and steelworker*

Khrushchev

After a prolonged power struggle, Nikita Khrushchev emerged as the new leader of the Soviet Union. In 1956, Khrushchev openly criticized Stalin and began a programme known as de-Stalinization, removing portraits and statues of the former dictator. He ended arbitrary arrests and relaxed curbs on free speech, although this was never enshrined in law. He improved relations with the West with his policy of 'peaceful coexistence', believing that the communist system would ultimately triumph without the need for a destructive war. Khrushchev initiated a major space programme, and in 1957 the Soviet Union launched the first satellite, Sputnik I, followed in 1961 by the launch of the first

spaceman, Yuri Gagarin. However, Khrushchev attracted criticism for his blustering, impulsive leadership style and policy failures; these included a damaging split with China; the Cuban Missile Crisis; and a decline in agricultural output that forced the USSR to buy grain from the West. In 1964, he was overthrown by a triumvirate of Politburo members, including Leonid Brezhnev and Aleksei Kosygin.

Brezhnev

Brezhnev gradually accumulated power at Kosygin's expense, and was the dominant figure by the mid-1970s. After the disruptive and chaotic Khrushchev era, Brezhnev deliberately pursued a path of stability and continuity and was intolerant of radical change. The result was a stagnation of institutions, policies and ideas. The Soviet economy continued to decline, and Brezhnev fostered relations with the West (détente) mainly in order to import Western food and technology. However, along with Western goods came Western ideas, encouraging Soviet intellectuals to protest against their government's human rights violations. Many were imprisoned for their audacity. In late 1979, to worldwide condemnation, the Soviet Union sent its forces into Afghanistan in support of the faltering communist government there.

Gorbachev

Brezhnev died in 1982 and the Soviet Union was led in turn by two elderly, conservative figures, Yuri Andropov and Konstantin Chernenko, before the accession of a relatively youthful reformist leader, Mikhail Gorbachev in 1985. Gorbachev introduced *perestroika* (restructuring), legalizing entrepreneurship to stimulate economic growth. The policy actually made matters worse by disrupting (rather than ending) the state-dominated economy, causing shortages, inflation and strikes. Gorbachev's most dramatic reform was *glasnost* (openness), which permitted freedom of expression in the media and the arts.

Faced with resistance to his policies from the Soviet Communist Party, Gorbachev reduced its power by permitting the creation of non-communist political parties in 1990. By this time, Gorbachev was losing control of the forces he had unleashed. Separatist movements in several Soviet republics demanded independence. Gorbachev offered them some autonomy but was unable to prevent the break-up of the Soviet Union. In December 1991, the leaders of the 15 republics agreed to form a new loose confederaton called the Commonwealth of Independent States (CIS).

Yeltsin

Russia remained easily the largest and most powerful state in the CIS. President Boris Yeltsin enacted free market reforms, ending price controls and boosting private ownership of industry. Prices soared, effectively impoverishing many Russians, while a small number of wealthy Russians (oligarchs) took control of Russia's biggest companies. Yeltsin faced growing opposition in the State Duma. Economic turmoil and the rise of organized crime led many to long for a return to Soviet days. In the 1995 parliamentary elections, the Communist Party won a majority. In 1994, Russia had become embroiled in a bloody conflict against separatists in Chechnya, a region in the south-west. A full-scale invasion of Chechnya in 1999 attracted international condemnation. In December 1999, Yeltsin resigned and was replaced by his prime minister, Vladimir Putin.

TIMELINE	
1953	*Stalin dies*
1956	*Khrushchev denounces Stalin at his 'secret speech' at the 20th Party Congress*
1964	*Khrushchev is deposed*
1977	*Brezhnev becomes president*
1979	*Soviet invasion of Afghanistan*
1985	*Gorbachev becomes Soviet leader*
1986	*Chernobyl nuclear power plant blows up*
1989	*Soviet Union withdraws from Afghanistan*
1991	*Gorbachev resigns following an attempted coup by conservative elements; the USSR is dissolved*
1994–2006	*Russia's war with Chechnya*
2000	*Putin is elected president of Russia*
2004	*Beslan School hostage crisis*
2008	*Medvedev becomes president*
2012	*Putin reelected as president.*

Putin

Putin won his own popular mandate in March 2000. Under his rule, Russia's economy improved dramatically, crime rates fell, and Russia regained control over Chechnya. He was rewarded with re-election in 2004. Some observers argued that his popularity was assisted by the tight control he exerted over the media, and by 2003 his government had become increasingly autocratic. Putin clashed with Russia's powerful oligarchs, and he imprisoned potential rival Mikhail Khodorkovsky, head of Yukos Oil, on charges of tax evasion. Constitutionally barred from serving a third term as president, Putin was succeeded by Dimitry Medvedev in 2008, but took over as prime minister. In March 2012, Putin was reelected president amid allegations of election fraud. Thousands took to the streets of Moscow in protest.

Below Putin became acting president of the Russian Federation after Yeltsin's resignation in 1999, then won the presidential elections in 2000 and 2012

EUROPE

1945 ONWARDS

Above *The circle of 12 gold stars on the flag of the European Union symbolizes harmony and solidarity between its peoples*

Some 40 million Europeans lost their lives in World War II, and millions more were left destitute. European power, which had shaped and dominated world affairs for so long, was now eclipsed by that of the United States and the Soviet Union. As Soviet-sponsored dictators seized control in Eastern Europe, so the impoverished nations in Western Europe turned for economic help and military protection to the United States. A military alliance, the North Atlantic Treaty Organization (NATO), established in 1949, ensured that the US would come to the defence of any Western European nation attacked by the USSR.

The US government believed that the best way of preventing further Soviet expansion in Europe was to strengthen Western Europe economically. To this end, the US government set up a major aid programme called the European Recovery Program, or Marshall Plan, in 1948. By the early 1950s, the Western European economies were more productive than they had been before the war.

Eastern Europe

By 1948, Europe was a completely divided continent. The Soviet Union banned all communications, travel and trade between the communist east and the democratic west. Eastern Europeans were not allowed to accept Marshall Plan aid. Instead the USSR set up an economic organization called Comecon to promote trade and economic cooperation in the Eastern Bloc.

The Eastern Europeans sometimes resisted Soviet authority. Yugoslavia, under

Josip Tito (ruled 1945–1980), managed in 1948 to assert its independence from the Soviet Union, while remaining Communist. In 1953, there were uprisings in East Germany, and in 1956 the Hungarians took a stand for greater freedom, soon crushed by Soviet military force. In 1968, the Czech government attempted liberal reforms, but again the Soviets and their allies ruthlessly ended this experiment.

Western Europe

The devastation caused by World War II had convinced many Western European leaders of the need for greater economic cooperation between their nations to ensure future peace. They also believed a European trading bloc would restore their economic independence and allow Europe to compete successfully with the USA and Comecon. The European Coal and Steel Community was established in 1951 to unify those industries in the Low Countries, France, West Germany and Italy. In 1957, the same six countries formed the European Economic Community (EEC), creating a single market for goods, services, workers and capital. Some saw this as the start of a process towards closer political union between their nations.

The EEC gradually expanded its membership. Britain, Denmark and Ireland joined in 1973, followed by Greece (1981) and Portugal and Spain (1986). In 1992, the EEC was renamed the European Union (EU) and cooperation between members was extended into other areas, including defence, law and order, and immigration. A European Central Bank was established and, in 1999, several EU countries adopted a single currency, the euro. Between 2010 and 2012 some European countries were revealed to have unsustainable levels of government debt, creating alarm in financial markets and threatening the stability of the euro. The Eurozone countries and the IMF approved rescue packages worth hundreds of billions of euros for the worst affected countries, Greece, Portugal and the Irish Republic.

Post-Cold War Europe

In late 1989, Gorbachev ended Soviet control over Eastern Europe. The borders between East and West reopened; the Berlin Wall was torn down; communist dictators were toppled; and free elections were held throughout the region. Eastern European nations were able to share in the rights and freedoms of their Western counterparts, including the free market. In 1990, West and East Germany reunited. Czechoslovakia broke up peacefully into the more ethnically homogenous Czech Republic and Slovakia.

Yugoslavia also broke up, but at the cost of a prolonged and bloody civil war. Rivalries which had been suppressed under communism flared up between the different ethnic groups. Four of the country's six republics, including Bosnia and Croatia, declared their independence. Serbia, one of the remaining republics, fought to keep control of those parts of Bosnia and Croatia that contained ethnic Serbs. Serb forces drove non-Serbs from territories they wished to retain, a policy known as ethnic cleansing. NATO pressure on Serbia finally brought peace to Bosnia and Croatia in 1995, but a new conflict broke out in 1998 in the Serbian province of Kosovo. Again, Serb forces engaged in extensive ethnic cleansing, which only ceased following NATO air strikes.

European expansion

Following the collapse of communism, many Eastern European countries applied to join the EU. By 2007, EU membership had expanded to 27 nations, making it the largest single market in the world. The 2009 Treaty of Lisbon increased the power of the European Parliament and created a long-term president of the European Council and a European representative for foreign affairs. In 2010, the Eurozone crisis, triggered by the economic slump of 2008, resulted in the imposition of harsh austerity measures which sparked civil unrest in many cities across the EU. In 2013, Croatia acceded to the Union, with other Balkan states scheduled to follow.

Above *A youth celebrates from the top of the Berlin Wall in 1989 after the East German regime announced that visits to West Germany would be allowed*

TIMELINE

1948	Marshall Plan gives aid to Western Europe
1949	NATO is established
1955	Allies end occupation of West Germany and Austria
1957	The Treaty of Rome sets up the EEC
1966	France withdraws from NATO
1968	Students riot in Paris and other European cities
1974	Turkey invades northern Cyprus
1977	Spain has its first post-war elections following the 1975 death of Franco
1989–1990	Fall of communist regimes in Eastern Europe
1992	Maastricht Treaty creates the EU single market
1992–1995	Bosnian War
1998–1999	Kosovo War
2003	British troops join US-led invasion of Iraq; France and Germany, among others, oppose the invasion
2007	Northern Ireland agrees a power-sharing coalition
2009	France announces its return to NATO
2010	Eurozone crisis begins.

THE PEOPLE'S REPUBLIC OF CHINA

1949 ONWARDS

During the first few years of its rule, the CCP, under Mao Zedong, consolidated its hold over China. Lost territories, including Tibet and Xinjiang in Western China, were reclaimed. Chinese troops supported Communist North Korea in its war against South Korea and the UN (1950–1953) and aided communist insurgents in their struggle against France in Indochina (1946–1954). At home, the CCP attacked or expelled any vested interests that might present a threat to its authority, including the remnants of the KMT, foreign businesses, and missionaries. The government seized privately owned farms and redistributed the land to the peasants. Thousands of landlords were killed by vengeful mobs. Under the first five-year plan (1953–1958), big businesses were taken into government control and peasants were forced to combine their holdings into large agricultural cooperatives. Rapid expansion of heavy industry ensued, although farm output increased only slowly.

Above *This image of Mao Zedong appeared on posters in 1967 with the slogan 'Long Life to Our Great Leader, Chairman Mao'*

In 1956, Mao expressed concern that revolutionary zeal had degenerated into simple authoritarianism, and encouraged Chinese intellectuals to criticize the party under the slogan 'Let a Hundred Flowers Bloom'. The policy may have been a political trap, for the following year Mao launched the Antirightist campaign, during which some half a million intellectuals lost their jobs or were imprisoned, usually for the criticisms they had made.

Great Leap Forward

The second five-year plan was termed the 'Great Leap Forward'. It was intended as proof of Mao's belief that human willpower alone could overcome such shortcomings as a lack of capital and modern technology. The rapid development of China's agricultural and industrial sectors would occur simultaneously, and, Mao predicted, within 15 years China's industrial output would surpass that of the UK. Steel was produced using thousands of backyard furnaces, workers were mobilized to work longer hours, and agricultural cooperatives were combined into vast communes to improve

efficiency. The Great Leap Forward, poorly planned and badly led, was a disaster. Industrial production halved between 1959 and 1962; grain was forcibly requisitioned from the countryside to feed the workers, creating a famine in which more than 20 million died. By 1962, the government was forced to abandon the policy.

Break with the USSR

The Soviet Union had been a friend and supporter of the People's Republic since its establishment, but by the early 1960s relations had become strained. In 1956, China criticized the Soviet policy of 'peaceful coexistence' with the West as a betrayal of communist ideals. In 1960, the Soviet Union ceased granting aid to China. When the USSR signed a nuclear test ban treaty with the USA in 1963, China broke off relations with the Soviets.

Cultural Revolution

In the wake of the catastrophic Great Leap Forward, Mao resigned as leader, though he remained Chairman of the CCP. Liu Shaoqi and Deng Xiaoping became China's new rulers. Both pursued moderate, pragmatic policies to rebuild China's economy. In 1966, Mao attempted to regain power when he launched his 'Great Proletarian Cultural Revolution', a campaign to recapture the revolutionary zeal of the early days and purge the party of its 'liberal bourgeousie' elements.

At Mao's urging, students all over China formed themselves into militias called Red Guards and began denouncing intellectuals, college professors, teachers, journalists, bureaucrats, factory managers and party officials – essentially anyone in authority who they regarded as insufficiently revolutionary. Universities closed and the demonstrations became increasingly violent as Red Guard units were reinforced by workers and peasants. Senior party officials were forcibly expelled, while many others were imprisoned and tortured. By 1968, Red Guard factions had begun fighting each other and many areas descended into lawlessness. The army was called in and Red Guard units were disbanded. By 1970, the government and the country had begun to function normally again.

Modernization

In the early 1970s, the People's Republic established diplomatic relations with a number of advanced nations, including the USA and Japan, and was admitted to the UN. Mao died in 1976, sparking a power struggle between radicals and moderates within the Party. The moderates, led by Deng Xiaoping, triumphed, and in 1978 they began a process of economic modernization. China expanded its cultural and commercial contacts with the West and imported foreign technology to improve its industry. Limited forms of private enterprise were introduced and the agricultural communes were disbanded. The reforms set in motion a remarkable economic boom that continued unabated into the 21st century.

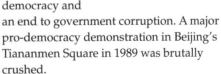

TIMELINE	
1956	*The 'Let a Hundred Flowers Bloom' campaign*
1958–1962	*The Great Leap Forward*
1966–1970	*The Cultural Revolution causes widespread upheaval in China*
1971	*China is admitted to the United Nations*
1972	*Richard Nixon visits the People's Republic, paving the way for normal diplomatic relations*
1976	*Death of Mao Zedong*
1989	*Chinese troops put down uprisings against Chinese rule in Tibet*
1989	*Chinese troops open fire on pro-democracy demonstrators in Tiananmen Square*
1997	*Britain's lease on Hong Kong expires and it reverts to Chinese control*
1999	*Macau is restored to China from Portugal*
2001	*China joins the World Trade Organization and launches its space programme.*

However, unlike the Soviet Union, the CCP did not relax its political grip on the country. In the late 1980s, students all over China began calling for greater democracy and an end to government corruption. A major pro-democracy demonstration in Beijing's Tiananmen Square in 1989 was brutally crushed.

During the 1990s and 2000s, China continued its phenomenal economic growth, fuelled by the export of manufactured goods. In 2011 it overtook Japan to become the world's second largest economy.

Above *Student protests in Tiananmen Square ended in bloodshed when the People's Liberation Army opened fire on the crowd and brought in tanks to destroy the blockades*

JAPAN AND KOREA

1945 ONWARDS

Following Japan's surrender in September 1945, the country was placed under the control of an American army of occupation. The American occupiers imposed fundamental reforms on Japan, designed to rid the country of its militaristic culture and transform it into a peaceful democratic nation. Pluralism was at first encouraged by the US administration, extending even to the development of a Japanese Communist Party, but with the onset of the Cold War, priorities changed: Japan was needed as a strong American ally in the Far East. Great efforts were made to rebuild the economy, and the communist movement was suppressed. In 1952, full sovereignty was restored.

Above right
The Shibuya area of Tokyo is popular for shopping and is the birthplace of many trends in fashion and entertainment

Economic miracle

Most Japanese were enthusiastic about the post-war reforms and eagerly set to work rebuilding their nation. By 1955, the major industries had achieved their pre-war production levels. Thereafter, the Japanese economy began to take off at an astonishing rate. Between 1955 and 1973, Japan's GDP grew at an average yearly rate of 9 per cent; faster than any other nation at that time. By 1968, it had the third largest economy in the world. There were many reasons for Japan's 'economic miracle', including a stable, business-friendly government (the conservative Liberal Democratic Party, or LDP, remained in power from 1955 to 1993); the Japanese emphasis on developing a loyal, highly skilled labour force, disinclined to strike; and, not least, the endless appetite of Japanese people for consumer goods such as cars, gadgets and household appliances.

Rapid growth had social repercussions, including large-scale urbanization and a proportionate shrinkage of the rural workforce (to just 5 per cent in the 2000s). In such a small country, these changes caused massive overcrowding in cities and brought other related problems: pollution, and over-stretched public transport and waste disposal systems. Nevertheless, a large and prosperous middle class emerged, and Japan suffered less poverty than most other industrial nations.

Economic slowdown

The long-term boom ended in the early 1970s, due mainly to a rise in the yen, which hit exports. Following economic reforms, growth resumed, but at a slower rate. In the late 1980s, Japan experienced a speculative frenzy, as millions tried to make money in stocks and shares. Japanese businesses

TIMELINE

1945–1952	*US occupation of Japan*
1948	*The states of North and South Korea are established*
1950–1953	*Korean War*
1968	*Japan becomes the world's third largest economy*
1987	*South Korea gains a democratic constitution*
1990	*Japan's speculative bubble bursts, sparking a 15-year recession*
1994	*Kim Il Sung dies*
2011	*Kim Jong Il dies and is succeeded by Kim Jong-un.*

rushed to invest overseas in South-east Asia and the USA. In 1990 the bubble burst, ushering in a long recession.

In the late 1980s and early 1990s, the ruling LDP was accused of corruption and the party fell from power. Japanese politics became highly factional, with a succession of short-lived coalition governments, making it difficult for any administration to solve their economic problems.

In March 2011, a major earthquake and tsunami struck Japan, causing nuclear meltdowns and releases of radiation from its Fukushima Nuclear Power Plant. Nearly 16,000 died in the tsunami. The clean-up operation at Fukushima is expected to take around 40 years.

Korean War

Following its defeat in 1945, Japan was forced to end its 35-year occupation of Korea. The USA and USSR agreed to divide Korea at the 38th parallel, with the Soviets controlling the north and the USA the south. In the north, the USSR supported the rise to power of the communist leader Kim Il Sung; while in the south, the USA promoted the nationalist Syngman Rhee. In June 1950, North Korean forces invaded South Korea, hoping to reunify the country under communism. A US-led United Nations force counter-attacked. The goal of liberating South Korea was quickly achieved, but the victory emboldened UN forces to seek to reunify Korea under Rhee. In October, just as victory for the south looked likely, China entered the war on the side of the north and UN forces were pushed back. By autumn 1951, the war had reached stalemate. In July 1953, a ceasefire was agreed and the border was set near the 38th parallel, as before.

Post-war relations

In the ensuing decades, north and south remained mutually hostile, and there were frequent cross-border skirmishes. In 1991, the two countries finally agreed to recognize each other and begin trading. Since 2000 there has been an easing of cross-border travel and employment restrictions. However, tensions escalated again in 2010 when North Korea shelled a South Korean island.

North Korea

Following the Korean War, Kim Il Sung established a communist dictatorship on the Soviet model. His government organized the countryside into large collective farms. Economic development focused on heavy industry and the military, at the expense of consumer goods, and living standards fell. Kim Il Sung died in 1994 and was succeeded by his son Kim Jong Il. North Korea suffered a severe famine in the mid-1990s and hundreds of thousands perished. In 2002, North Korea disclosed that it had developed a nuclear weapons programme. It is believed to have carried out at least two underground nuclear tests.

South Korea

The partition and the war left South Korea weak. Rhee's government fell in 1960, and was replaced by a military government under Park Chung Hee. The economy grew rapidly under Park, but his government became increasingly autocratic. After Park's assassination in 1979, the new government ended some of the restrictions on free speech. In 1987, a democratic constitution was introduced, guaranteeing Western-style political freedoms for all.

Above *North Korean soldiers carry a portrait of the late North Korean leader Kim Il Sung at a military parade in April 2007*

Below *South Korean leader Park Chung Hee seized power in a military coup on 16 May 1961*

SOUTH-EAST ASIA

1914 ONWARDS

By 1914, Thailand was the only state in South-east Asia not under Western rule. However, colonial authority in the region was far from secure, with nationalist movements already emerging in many countries. Over the following decades, two major developments would together prove fatal to Western dominance in the region: first, the Japanese military occupation of South-east Asia in 1941–1945; and, second, the indigenous struggles for self-determination.

Right *The Prince of Malaya and Prince William, son of the Duke of Gloucester, at the ceremony for Malaysian Independence in September 1957*

Decolonization

World War I left the colonial powers severely weakened and less capable of enforcing their rule overseas, which encouraged indigenous movements to push for independence. Britain, while defending its right to an empire in public, privately began to explore ways of handing back power to its Asian dominions. In the early 1920s, the Burmese felt encouraged by the progress of the nationalist movement in neighbouring India to push for similar concessions, and were granted limited powers of self-rule. The USA, never a natural imperial power, actually drove the decolonization process in the Philippines, promising in 1935 full independence within ten years; it was actually granted in 1946. Other Western powers were less willing to give up their possessions. In French Indochina and the Dutch East Indies, nationalist and communist uprisings in the 1920s and 1930s were ruthlessly suppressed by the colonial regimes.

Japan began its takeover of the region in 1939. Its rapid conquests shattered the myth of Western military supremacy and added further fuel to the nationalist fire. The Japanese occupiers exploited the desire for

TIMELINE	
1926–1927	*Communist uprising in the Dutch East Indies*
1929	*Kingdom of Siam is renamed Thailand*
1941–1945	*Japanese occupation of South-east Asia*
1946	*The Philippines is granted independence*
1948	*Burma achieves independence*
1956	*Indonesia's last links with the Dutch crown are severed*
1965	*Federation of Malaysia established, including Malaya, North Borneo, Sabah and Sarawak, Singapore (to 1965)*
1976	*Indonesia annexes Portuguese East Timor*
1986	*Pro-democracy campaigner Corazon Aquino takes over from the dictator Ferdinand Marcos in the Philippines*
1988	*A military junta (SLORC) takes power in Myanmar*
2002	*East Timor achieves independence*
2004	*An Indian Ocean tsunami devastates much of coastal South and South-east Asia, killing around 283,000.*

self-determination by promising the indigenous populations a level of independence and following the Japanese surrender in 1945, the colonial powers faced strong resistance in their attempts to reimpose their authority in the region. Britain chose the path of peaceful negotiation, granting Burma independence in 1948. Withdrawal from Malaya took longer as British and Commonwealth forces became caught up in a prolonged battle with communist guerrillas. Independence was eventually achieved in 1957 when the colonial regime handed power to anti-communist nationalists. The communists were finally defeated in 1960.

Following the war, nationalist leaders in the Dutch East Indies unilaterally declared independence, renaming the state the Republic of Indonesia. The Dutch fought to regain control of their former colony until 1949, when they withdrew under UN pressure. The longest and most bitter conflict, however, occurred in French Indochina (see pages 278–279).

Economic boom

Beginning in the mid-1960s, much of South-east Asia experienced a remarkable, 30-year period of economic growth. East Asian, European and American multinational companies were eager to exploit the plentiful supply of cheap labour in the region. As a result, countries such as Thailand, Malaysia, Singapore and Indonesia – formerly known for exporting agricultural produce and minerals – developed large industrial bases and began exporting manufactured goods, including electronic devices, clothing and footwear. In the case of Indonesia, large supplies of oil and gas helped to fund the growth of heavy industry, including shipbuilding, steel and petrochemicals. The economic expansion of the region gave rise to rapid urbanization and a depopulation of rural areas; vast numbers congregated in shanty towns surrounding the major cities.

The boom came to a sudden end in 1997. During preceding years, governments had acquired large budget deficits through over-borrowing; and unregulated banks had sustained huge losses through bad debts. In July 1997, heavy speculation against the region's major currencies forced them to devalue. Stock markets crashed and banks and businesses collapsed. Unemployment surged as the recession began to bite. The crisis sparked riots and toppled the 30-year government of President Suharto in Indonesia.

Below Burmese opposition party leader Aung San Suu Kyi addresses her supporters in Rangoon on 7 July 1989

BURMA

Some countries, such as Cambodia, Burma, Vietnam and Laos, did not share in the post-colonial economic transformation of the region. In the case of Burma, problems arose from the moment it achieved independence in 1948. The new government faced rebellions from communist and ethnic separatist groups. The conflict rumbled on until 1962, when a revolutionary faction under General Ne Win seized control, ending democracy in Burma. The Ne Win regime introduced socialist reforms, including a centralized economy. It banned free speech and foreign investment. Country-wide pro-democracy demonstrations in 1988 forced Ne Win to resign. The army overthrew the government and replaced it with the State Law and Order Restoration Council (SLORC), which put down the protests and arrested the pro-democracy leader Aung San Suu Kyi. SLORC renamed the country Myanmar in 1989. It promised elections once a constitution had been approved, but this never happened. The SLORC was renamed the SPDC in 1997. Aung San Suu Kyi was released from house arrest in 1995, rearrested in 2000, and again released in November 2010.

THE INDOCHINA WARS

1954–1979

French Indochina comprised the countries of Cambodia, Laos and Vietnam, which were united under French rule in 1893. The territory was occupied by Japan from 1939 to 1945. Following Japan's defeat in World War II, the Viet Minh, a Vietnamese nationalist-communist group led by Ho Chi Minh, occupied northern Vietnam. The Viet Minh founded the independent Democratic Republic of Vietnam (DRV), with its capital at Hanoi. France, determined to regain control of the territory, reoccupied the south. The First Indochina War, between France and the DRV, broke out in 1946.

Above *Under the leadership of Ho Chi Minh, communist North Vietnam succeeded in gaining power in South Vietnam*

Below *A soldier of the French Foreign Legion precedes a US tank in the Red River Delta in 1954*

First Indochina War

During the first three years of the war, the better-armed French forces made little progress against the guerilla tactics of the Viet Minh. To gain the support of the local population, the French established an independent Vietnamese government in the south under former president Bao Dai, in 1949. The US government, determined to halt the spread of communism in Asia, supported the French, while the new Communist government in China supported the Viet Minh.

In 1954, the Viet Minh captured a French military base at Dien Bien Phu. The French, tiring of the campaign, agreed to withdraw from Vietnam. At a peace conference in Geneva, it was agreed that the country would be reunified following elections in 1956. However, the new leader in South Vietnam, Ngo Dinh Diem, refused to hold elections because, he claimed, a free vote was impossible in the communist North.

The USA supported Diem's stance, preferring an independent non-communist South Vietnam to the most likely alternative: reunification under Communist rule.

Second Indochina War begins

Diem's government, based in Saigon, lacked popular support, and was opposed by many, especially in the countryside, who saw it as a puppet of the USA. An organized rural opposition emerged, called the Viet Cong, supported by the DRV. Open warfare between the Viet Cong and the South Vietnamese army (ARVN) broke out in 1959. The US government offered military advisers and financial support to sustain the Diem regime, but it grew increasingly vulnerable, especially after Diem himself was assassinated in a military coup in 1963.

America enters the war

In 1964, the US government under President Lyndon Johnson used an attack on US ships in the Gulf of Tonkin as an excuse to become directly involved in the conflict. US planes began bombing North Vietnam and in 1965, the first American combat troops were deployed to attack Viet Cong forces in the South. The DRV and Viet Cong avoided major battles where superior American firepower could be decisive, opting instead for guerilla tactics, including ambushes and bomb attacks. Prolonged and intensive US aerial bombing failed to demoralize the North, and despite suffering high casualty rates, the DRV and Viet Cong always managed to replace their losses. As the war dragged on with no sign of victory, it began to attract strong opposition from many in the USA, especially college students.

Tet Offensive

In early 1968, on the day before the Vietnamese celebration of Tet, the DRV and Viet Cong launched a major offensive, attacking military bases and the major cities in the South. The invaders were driven back, but the Johnson administration, stunned by the offensive, did agree to begin peace negotiations. The talks, in Paris, came to nothing. In 1969, faced with growing domestic opposition to the war, the new president, Richard Nixon, ordered a gradual troop withdrawal.

Final stages

Nixon also escalated the conflict, however, when he ordered, in 1970, an invasion of Cambodia, which was providing military supplies to North Vietnam. Anti-war protests intensified as news emerged in 1971 of a massacre of innocent Vietnamese by a US army unit at My Lai, and the American use of the highly toxic defoliant, Agent Orange, against the jungle bases of the Viet Cong.

North Vietnam launched another offensive in 1972, again successfully countered. Exhausted, both sides agreed to further talks, leading to a ceasefire in 1973 and US agreement to withdraw its forces. After US troops had gone, the conflict resumed, with the North now at a

KHMER ROUGE

In 1975, a Cambodian communist organization, the Khmer Rouge, under their leader Pol Pot, seized power and renamed the country Democratic Kampuchea. The Khmer Rouge had a vision of Cambodia as a peasant-run agrarian state. They marched all city dwellers into the countryside and forced them to take up farm labour. Intellectuals, merchants, bureaucrats, clergy and any ethnic Chinese or Vietnamese were slaughtered en masse. Millions more were forcibly relocated, deprived of food and tortured. During the four years that the Khmer Rouge were in power, some 1.7 million Cambodians were killed, which was more than a fifth of the population. The regime was overthrown by Vietnamese forces during an invasion in 1979.

decided advantage. The war ended in April 1975 when North Vietnamese forces captured Saigon, renamed Ho Chi Minh City. In 1976, Vietnam was reunited as the Socialist Republic of Vietnam. The war had left much of South Vietnam in ruins. The new government imprisoned thousands of South Vietnamese, and private businesses were forced to close, precipitating an exodus of around a million Vietnamese between 1975 and the early 1990s.

Above *Mass graves containing 8,895 bodies were discovered at Choeung Ek after the fall of the Khmer Rouge. The site is now a memorial*

CENTRAL AND SOUTH ASIA

1948 ONWARDS

The nations of Central and South Asia experienced major changes during the Cold War era and since. India, Pakistan and Sri Lanka embarked on a new road as independent nations in 1948. Bangladesh won independence in 1971, while the Central Asian republics had to wait until 1991 to gain their freedom. For Tibet, the wait continues.

Right *Benazir Bhutto, leader of the Pakistan People's Party, was twice prime minister of Pakistan but was assassinated during her campaign for re-election in 2007*

India

During the 1950s and early 1960s, under the premiership of Jawaharlal Nehru, India's agricultural and industrial production rose sharply, as did school attendance. Nehru improved the rights of women and outlawed discrimination against the 'harijan' (untouchables), a relic of the caste system. However, India's many languages and diverse cultures made it difficult to forge a widespread sense of national identity.

Under Indira Gandhi (1966–1984), India grew into a strong industrial and nuclear-armed power, but Gandhi's suppression of Sikh nationalism led to her assassination. The 1990s witnessed violence between Hindu nationalists and Muslims. A Hindu nationalist government, the BJP, came to power in 1998. During the 1990s and 2000s, India's economy expanded rapidly, helped by low taxes and a rising generation of well-educated, highly skilled professionals, transforming the country into a global economic power.

In the mid-1960s, India fought with Pakistan over the disputed territory of Kashmir. The conflict flared up again in the late 1980s, and the two sides nearly went to war over the territory in 2002.

Pakistan

Independent Pakistan comprised two territories, West and East, united by religion but separated by a distance of over 1,600 km (almost 1,000 miles) as well as a cultural and linguistic gulf. Resentful of West Pakistan's political and economic dominance, East Pakistanis rioted in 1971. Their protests gained momentum and in March 1971, East Pakistan declared its independence as Bangladesh. India supported the rebellion. After bloody fighting in which over a million people died, Pakistan surrendered.

Ruled by a military dictatorship throughout the 1950s and 1960s, Pakistan held its first elections in the early 1970s. Its first prime minister, Zulfikar Ali Bhutto, was overthrown by General Mohammad Zia ul-Haq, who imposed martial law. After

CENTRAL ASIAN REPUBLICS

Following the break-up of the Soviet Union in 1991, eight new nations, situated in the Caucasus and along the Iranian and Chinese frontiers, declared their independence: Armenia, Azerbaijan, Georgia, Kazakhstan, Kyrgyzstan, Tajikistan, Turkmenistan and Uzbekistan. While Armenia and Georgia adopted democratic constitutions and appear to be moving towards Western-style parliamentary democracy, most of these states quickly fell under the rule of autocratic regimes of varying degrees of corruption and repressiveness.

Zia's death in 1988, democracy was restored and two parties alternated in power, one being Bhutto's Pakistan People's Party, now led by his daughter Benazir. A 1999 military coup brought General Pervez Musharraf to power, and parliament was suspended. Under public pressure, Musharraf agreed to hold elections in 2008 and Pakistan returned to democracy again.

Bangladesh

One of the world's poorest countries, Bangladesh had to cope with enormous costs of reconstruction following its war of independence. Its fragile democracy was frequently interrupted by periods of military dictatorship during the 1970s and early 1980s. Democratically elected governments have ruled since 1986, although charges of electoral fraud have been common. In addition to political turmoil, the country often suffers floods caused by cyclones, which lead to widespread death and destruction.

Sri Lanka

Sri Lanka won its independence in 1948, along with India. From 1983, the government, representing the majority Sinhalese, fought a bitter civil war with the Tamil minority. The most powerful Tamil group, the Tamil Tigers, attempted to establish an independent state in the north of the island. From 2006, the government launched a series of military offensives, driving the Tamil Tigers out of the east and north. The Tamil Tigers finally surrendered in May 2009, ending the civil war.

Tibet

The staunchly Buddhist state of Tibet was occupied by the People's Republic of China in 1950. China's harsh rule and religious intolerance provoked an uprising in 1959. The rebellion failed and Tibet's ruler, the

Dalai Lama, fled to India, to be replaced by his deputy, the Panchen Lama. China imposed military rule, forcibly redistributing land and requisitioning grain to feed its troops. Chinese settlers took over senior administrative jobs. In the 1980s, the Chinese softened their approach, reopening some shrines and monasteries and giving farmers more freedom. At the end of the decade, however, reforms were halted; human rights issues continue to be a concern in the area.

Afghanistan

Afghanistan tried to maintain a neutral stance during the Cold War, but a communist coup in 1973 drove the country firmly into the Soviet sphere of influence. By 1978 the communists faced a major rebellion by Islamic 'mujahideen' (holy warriors). The Soviet Union sent in troops to shore up the regime, but suffered badly from mujahideen guerilla tactics and withdrew in 1988–1989. The Afghan government fell in 1992. A power struggle ensued between various mujahideen factions. In 1995, an Islamist group, the Taliban, won control of much of the country. They imposed a harsh Islamic regime and harboured the Islamist terrorist organization Al Qaeda. Following Al Qaeda's 9/11 attack, a US-led coalition invaded Afghanistan, toppling the Taliban. A provisional government, established in 2002 under Hamid Karzai, won a popular mandate in 2004–2005. Despite the continuing threat from Taliban insurgents, efforts to rebuild the war-torn country continue. But as the departure of NATO troops draws closer, many in Afghanistan are concerned about its future.

Above The Dalai Lama became leader of the Tibetan people at the age of 15, but has lived in exile since 1959

Below The Taliban seized control of much of Afghanistan in 1995

Australia and New Zealand

1914 ONWARDS

During the 20th century, Australia developed a national government, as well as a national identity, with its own distinctive culture. Both Australia and New Zealand played major roles and incurred grievous losses during the world wars; and both underwent major social and economic changes in the post-war years.

Above right
Australian forces land at Gaba Tepe on the Gallipoli Peninsula, Turkey, on 5 Oct 1915

World War 1

The constitutional development of Austalia into a single nation began with the federation of the six colonies as a commonwealth in 1901. However, it was World War I that really forged a sense of national identity for ordinary Australians. At Gallipoli, Australia and New Zealand lost more than 8,000 men. The battle was a military failure, but the heroism of the ANZACs (Australia and New Zealand Army Corps) passed into legend.

Interwar years

The Australian economy boomed in the 1920s, due to a high post-war demand for consumer goods, technological advances and the protectionist policies of the ruling nationalist coalition under prime minister Stanley Bruce. Some 300,000 immigrants arrived during this period, mainly from Britain. Then, in 1929, the worldwide depression hit. By 1932, a third of the male workforce was unemployed. Recovery did not take hold until 1936, helped by protectionist policies and government subsidies on wheat and wool. During this period, Aboriginals were removed from official reserves, especially in the north, and began to settle in cities. The first Aboriginal rights movements were established.

World War II

The 1931 Statute of Westminster granted Australia and the other dominions of the British Empire leglislative independence, yet Australia continued to be directed by Britain in matters of foreign affairs, and therefore entered World War II on the Allied side. But with Britain preoccupied with the fight against Germany, Australia became dependent on the USA for security. Japanese planes bombed Darwin a few times and a Japanese submarine entered Sydney Harbour, prompting fears of an invasion; however, the USA was able to provide effective naval protection. During the war, many thousands of Australian and New Zealand servicemen suffered harsh conditions in Japanese prisoner of war camps.

Post-war Australia

From 1949 to 1972, the conservative Liberal Party ruled Australia. The country retained close links with Britain, but also forged a strong defensive alliance with the USA. The economy grew, thanks to the government's pro-market economic policies and foreign investment in the manufacturing sector. Mass immigration from southern Europe and the Middle East began to change the face of Australian society. Ethnic communities created their own enclaves in the inner suburbs.

The early 1970s was a time of political activism in Australia, with demands for women's liberation, aboriginal rights and an end to the Vietnam War. A desire for change swept the country, propelling the Labour Party to power. Australian troops were withdrawn from Vietnam and social reforms were introduced. The government lasted just two years, but its Liberal successor continued the progressive domestic programme. Labour regained power in 1983 under Bob Hawke (1983–1993), then Paul Keating (1993–1996). During this period, the issue of aboriginal land rights was confronted and in 1993, aboriginals were given leave to file land claims.

In the 1990s, a growing movement to turn Australia into a republic, with an elected president replacing the British monarch as head of state, culminated in a 1999 referendum which the Republicans narrowly lost. The Liberals, under John Howard, won the election in 1996. A strong supporter of US President George W. Bush's War on Terror, Howard contributed Australian troops to the US-led campaigns in Afghanistan and Iraq. In 2010, Julia Gillard became Australia's first female prime minister; then, in 2013, the Liberals, under Tony Abbott, regained power once more.

NEW ZEALAND

New Zealand contributed 100,000 troops to the Allied war effort in World War I, and suffered appallingly high casualties of 60,000 out of a population of just over a million. The Labour Party was elected in 1935, in the middle of the Great Depression, and embarked on an ambitious programme of social reform, establishing a national system of social security, free health care and free education. During World War II, New Zealand was once again an enthusiastic supporter of the Allied cause, conscripting 200,000 troops, most of whom were placed at the service of Britain. After 1941, much of New Zealand's war effort was dedicated to providing food and equipment for US forces fighting the Japanese. After the war, the USA gradually replaced Britain as New Zealand's major economic and military ally, although economic links with Britain remained strong until 1973, when Britain joined the EEC. Between 1949 and 1984, New Zealand politics was dominated by the conservative National Party. The economy prospered from the 1950s to 1970s, despite heavy government regulation. During this period, the Maoris experienced a population boom, growing from 45,000 to over half a million. Many went to live in the cities and a movement for Maori rights developed. New Zealand abandoned its military alliance with the USA in 1987 because of its strong anti-nuclear stance.

Above *A troupe of Maori women arrive in Sydney from New Zealand on 9 June 1925, due to perform traditional songs and dances at a Sydney theatre*

THE MIDDLE EAST

1923 ONWARDS

When the Ottoman Empire collapsed following World War I, its former territories were partitioned between the victorious European Allies. Britain strengthened its hold on Egypt and won control of Iraq, Palestine (out of which a separate emirate, Transjordan, was carved in the east), Kuwait, Bahrain, the Trucial States (modern United Arab Emirates), Oman and Aden (now part of Yemen). France gained Lebanon and Syria. Greece, Italy and France divided up Asia Minor between them. But the Turks, led by Kemal Attatürk, fought a War of Independence (1919–1923) to establish the Republic of Turkey. By 1925, the only independent countries in the region were Iran, Yemen and the Arabian territories of the warrior statesman Ibn Saud, which he formed into the Kingdom of Saudi Arabia in 1932.

Struggles for independence

The colonial powers faced nationalist uprisings in Egypt (1919), Iraq (1920) and Syria (1925–1927). Britain granted partial independence to Egypt in 1922, while retaining control over military and foreign policy and the Suez Canal. Iraq was granted independence in 1932, Lebanon in 1943, and Syria and Transjordan in 1946. British forces withdrew from Egypt (except for the Suez Canal) and Iraq in 1947. The British mandate in Palestine ended in 1948, after which it became Israel (see pages 286–287).

Turkey

Under Kemal Attatürk, Turkey took a different path from the rest of the Middle East. Attatürk wished to turn Turkey into a modern, secular state on the Western European model. He abolished the caliphate and banned Islamic courts, and enforced Western dress and the Turkish language (in place of Arabic); he also introduced women's rights. Since then, Turkey has consistently regarded itself as part of Europe and is currently applying for membership of the EU. In 1952, Turkey joined NATO.

Oil

The discovery of crude oil in Iran in 1908, followed by a similar discovery in Saudi Arabia in 1938, and then in other Persian Gulf states, transformed the economic fortunes of the region. Oil was fundamental to global industry and it turned out that the world's largest and most accessible reserves of oil were located in the Middle East. Western companies flooded in to take control of the new industry, and the rulers of the oil states soon became immensely wealthy and powerful. In many cases, the ruling elites tended to use their wealth to fund lavish lifestyles rather than investing it in any economic and social development that might have benefited their people.

TIMELINE

1918	*Britain takes control of Iraq*
1932	*British control of Iraq ends*
1933	*Ibn Saud permits Standard Oil (US) to drill for oil in Saudi Arabia*
1946	*Transjordan wins independence*
1953	*US-sponsored coup in Iran reinstates Reza Khan Pahlavi (a US ally) as shah*
1968	*Saddam Hussein takes power in Iraq*
1970	*General Assad seizes power in Syria*
1980–1988	*Iran-Iraq War*
1991	*International coalition drives Iraq from Kuwait*
2003–2011	*The Iraq War*
2011–2012	*The Arab Spring.*

Arab nationalism and socialism

By the 1950s, the Middle East was free from direct colonial rule; yet because of the increasing importance of the oil industry, the West, particularly the USA, continued to exert influence on governments in the region. This angered many Arabs, who saw it as a new form of imperialism. Riding this wave of resentment, military officers seized power in Egypt (1954), Syria (1963), Iraq (1968) and Libya (1969). The new rulers were anti-Western Arab nationalists, seeking to end Western interference in Middle Eastern affairs, and to forge closer ties between the nations of the Arab world.

The new regimes favoured socialist reforms, including the nationalization of industries and the redistribution of land owned by foreign settlers. They regarded such measures as the most effective way of overcoming the legacy of colonialism and securing political independence. In the Cold War era, this naturally placed the new regimes in the Soviet camp; while the conservative monarchies of Saudi Arabia, Jordan, Iran and the Persian Gulf emirates remained staunch US allies.

The most influential of the new military leaders was Gamal Abdel Nasser of Egypt. In 1956 he nationalized the Suez Canal, taking it over from its joint owners, Britain and France. In response, Britain, France and Israel invaded Egypt, but pressure from the USA and Soviet Union forced them to withdraw. Nasser's victory in the Suez Crisis made him a hero in the Arab world.

Ultimately, Arab nationalism failed to bring prosperity to the Arab masses, and the regimes that promoted it retained power only by becoming increasingly autocratic. In 2011, a wave of popular uprisings known as the Arab Spring swept the Arab world, toppling regimes in Tunisia, Egypt, Libya and Yemen. Muammar Gaddafi's regime in Libya only fell after a six-month civil war, in which rebel forces were supported by an international military coalition. Following a brutal crackdown on protesters by the regime of Bashar al-Assad, the uprising in Syria evolved into an armed rebellion. By September 2013, the United Nations estimated that the civil war in Syria had claimed 120,000 lives.

Iraq and Iran

Saddam Hussein's regime in Iraq invaded neighbouring Iran in 1980, starting an eight-year war in which over a million people died. In 1990, Iraq occupied Kuwait, but was driven out the following year by a US-led international force. The West continued to view Saddam as a threat to the region's stability – intelligence reports indicated that he was developing weapons of mass destruction. In 2003, Saddam's regime was overthrown by a US-led invasion of Iraq. The invasion caused widespread anger in the Arab world, and US-led coalition forces struggled to contain a powerful insurgency in Iraq. Coalition troops finally withdrew in 2011.

Since its 1979 Islamist revolution, Iran has had tense relations with the West. It does not recognize Israel and it sponsors the anti-Israeli militant movement Hezbollah. Iran has a nuclear programme, which it claims is for peaceful purposes. However, the international community fears that Iran is planning to build nuclear weapons, and many countries have imposed sanctions against the country.

Above *Gamal Abdel Nasser was President of Egypt from 1954 until his death in 1970. He was a hero in the Arab world for his pan-Arabism*

Below *A US Marine drapes the American flag over the statue of Saddam Hussein in Baghdad*

THE ARAB-ISRAELI CONFLICT

1948 ONWARDS

The Arab-Israeli conflict is a dispute over the control of Palestine, or Israel, a narrow strip of land on the eastern coast of the Mediterranean. The Jewish claim is based partly on the ancient ties of the Jewish people to the Biblical kingdom of Israel, and partly on the fact that, in 1947, the UN granted them the right to establish a homeland there. The Palestinian claim relies on the fact that their people have lived on this land for many hundreds of years. The land is holy to three faiths – Christians, Jews and Muslims – and the conflict is also a religious clash between Jews and Muslims.

Above *The creation of the state of Israel was a disaster for the Palestinians; many became refugees*

Below *In 1993, Yitzach Rabin, Bill Clinton and Yasser Arafat signed an agreement for the autonomy of the Gaza Strip and the West Bank*

British Mandate

Anti-semitism in Europe and Russia during the late 19th century drove many Jews – known as Zionists – to seek sanctuary in Palestine, where they hoped to build an independent Jewish state. Under the British Mandate (1920–1948), clashes between Jewish settlers and Arabs became increasingly violent. Jewish emigration to Palestine accelerated during the 1930s, particularly following the Nazi takeover of Germany. After the Holocaust, the international community found it harder to ignore Jewish demands for an independent homeland. By 1947, the British wished to end their mandate and requested help from the UN. In November 1947, the UN devised a plan to divide Palestine into two states, one Jewish, one Arab. The Jews accepted the plan, but the Arabs rejected it.

Establishment of Israel

Fighting between the two sides broke out immediately. In the midst of this war, on 15 May 1948, the British departed Palestine and Jewish leaders declared the founding of the state of Israel. Six neighbouring Arab countries immediately invaded the new state. Although outnumbered, the well-organized Israeli forces held their own and even advanced into territory beyond that allocated to them by the UN plan. By the war's end, Israel controlled 77 per cent of Palestine, while its Arab foes took over the remaining portions. Transjordan occupied the West Bank (west of the River Jordan) and Egypt occupied Gaza in the south-west. The Palestinian Arab state proposed by the UN was never established. During the war, around 726,000 Palestinians fled Israel to become refugees in the West Bank, Gaza and neighbouring Arab states.

Israel versus the Arab states

None of the Arab states recognized Israel's right to exist, and the following years were marked by frequent border skirmishes. In June 1967, fearing imminent attack, Israel launched pre-emptive strikes against Egypt, Jordan (formerly Transjordan) and Syria. In just six days, the Israelis captured Gaza and the Sinai from Egypt, the Golan Heights from Syria, and the West Bank from Jordan; this action more than trebled its territory. Over 750,000 Palestinian Arabs found themselves under the control of the Jewish state. Many turned their support to the Palestine Liberation Organization (PLO), a coalition of Palestinian groups that began engaging in terrorist activity against Israel.

In 1973, Egypt and Syria launched a joint invasion of Israel. After making early gains, the Arab forces were pushed back. Israel won the war, but suffered heavy losses and was shaken by the surprise attack. In 1978, Israel and Egypt negotiated a peace agreement at Camp David in the USA, including the withdrawal of Israel from Sinai. In 1982, Israel invaded Lebanon, hoping to drive out PLO fighters who had been attacking in the north. After a long, costly operation, the Israelis succeeded in forcing the PLO from Lebanon.

Intifada

During the 1980s, Palestinians living in the West Bank and Gaza grew increasingly frustrated by the continuing Israeli occupation and in 1987, they began a mass uprising known as the 'intifada' (awakening). There were riots in many of the towns and cities of the occupied territories. By the time the intifada ended in 1993, over 1,000 Palestinians had been killed.

Peace process

In the early 1990s, Israel began peace negotiations with its Arab neighbours and the PLO, which led to the Oslo Accords, signed in 1993. Under its terms, Israel agreed to a staged withdrawal from the occupied territories. Israel would retain military control there while a newly established Palestinian Authority (PA) would take civil control. By the late 1990s, the peace process had stalled. Islamist groups within the Palestinian community – such as Hamas and Islamic Jihad – opposed any peace with Israel and carried out terrorist attacks against Israel. Israel continued to build Jewish settlements in the occupied territories. Renewed attempts to reach a peace deal in 1998 and 2000 both failed.

Recent developments

A second intifada erupted in September 2000. This time, as well as rioting across the

TIMELINE	
May 1948	*Declaration of the founding of the state of Israel*
1948–1949	*War between Israel and the Arab states*
1956	*Suez Crisis: Israel, France and Britain launch joint attack on Egypt, but are forced by the UN to withdraw*
1967	*Six Day War*
1973	*Yom Kippur War (launched on 6 October, the Jewish festival of Yom Kippur)*
1978	*Israel and Egypt make peace at Camp David*
1982	*Israel invades Lebanon*
1987–1992	*Palestinian intifada*
1993	*Oslo Accords: Israel agrees a staged withdrawal from the occupied territories*
1994	*Israel signs a peace treaty with Jordan*
2000–2005	*Second intifada*
2005	*Israel withdraws from Gaza*
2006	*The Lebanese Shi-ite Islamist group Hezbollah sparks a short war between Israel and Lebanon*
2008–2009	*Israel launches a three-week attack on militant Hamas in Gaza.*

occupied territories, there was a rise in terrorist attacks, including suicide bombings, inside Israel. Israel responded with ruthless acts of its own; reoccupying PA-controlled West Bank towns to destroy the terrorist bases there. In 2003, the UN drew up a 'road map to peace', detailing the route to a two-state solution to the conflict, but negotiations soon faltered in the face of renewed violence. Israel unilaterally withdrew from Gaza in 2005; the territory subsequently fell under the control of Hamas. In late 2008, Israel launched an offensive in Gaza in response to continued rocket attacks by Hamas militants, at a cost of over 1,000 Palestinian lives.

Above *Hamas, a Palestinian militant organization, was created in 1987 at the beginning of the first intifada*

THE RISE OF ISLAMISM

1979 ONWARDS

Islamism is a political movement within Islam that has attracted mass support among Muslims throughout the world since the early 1980s. Its adherents oppose the secular nature of much of the modern Muslim world and urge a return to an earlier, purer form of Islam when 'sharia' law governed all aspects of life. Islamism is anti-Western and anti-democratic. It does not recognize any authority beyond God and the Koran. It is opposed to women's rights and forbids homosexuality and the drinking of alcohol. Some Islamists wish for the return of the caliphate and a unified Islamic world. Others, like the Palestinian organization Hamas, wish to create an Islamic republic in just one country: in their case, Palestine.

Origins and causes

Modern Islamism has its roots in the teachings of the Iranian scholar Jamal al-Afghani (1838–1897), founder of the Islamic Movement. He saw the reintroduction of sharia law as a means of fighting Western colonialism. Another group, the Muslim Brotherhood, founded in Egypt in 1928 by Hasan al-Banna, spread a similar message. One of the Brotherhood's most influential thinkers was Egyptian-born Sayyid Qutb (1906–1966), who argued that it was the duty of every Muslim to engage in a jihad, or holy war, against the enemies of Islam.

The great upsurge of Islamism in 1980s was caused in part by the policies of Saudi Arabia, whose rulers follow a very strict and intolerant form of Islam, known as Wahhabism. From the mid-1970s, Saudi Arabia began pouring billions of dollars of its oil revenues

Below *Osama bin Laden with his deputy, Ayman al-Zawahiri (right). Bin Laden was killed in 2011 in a US operation led by President Obama's administration*

into the founding of 'maddrassas' (religious schools) and other institutions throughout the Muslim world to spread Wahhabi teachings, helping to create a generation of radical, anti-Western Muslims.

The establishment of Israel and displacement of the Palestinians in 1948 aroused great anger in the Arab world, and the eradication of the Jewish state became a rallying cry for Islamists during the 1980s. The 1987–1992 Palestinian intifada in the occupied territories was primarily led by the Islamist group Hamas, which since then has competed with the secular PLO for Palestinian hearts and minds.

Iranian Revolution

Although principally a Sunni movement, Islamism first came to world attention through the Shi'ite revolutionary movement, led by Ayatollah Khomeini, which took power in Iran in 1979. Khomeini's regime ruthlessly imposed sharia law on all aspects of life; it then tried to export the revolution to other countries, including Lebanon, where it sponsored the Hezbollah movement.

The Iranian Revolution inspired millions of Islamist militants around the world. The 1980s and 1990s was a time of radicalism and violence in many Muslim countries, from North Africa to South-east Asia. In most countries, the Islamists failed to achieve supremacy but in 1989, an Islamist regime was established in Sudan, while another – the Taliban – took control of most of Afghanistan in 1995.

Anti-Americanism

One of the major driving forces behind modern Islamism is a hatred of the USA, not least because of its consistent support of Israel (see pages 286–287). With its vast economic power, America can often persuade Muslim governments to act in its interests, and many perceive it as a latter-day colonial power. Anti-Americanism has been a radicalizing influence on numerous young Muslims because they feel their society is under threat from all-pervasive American culture, conveyed through movies, television, books, food and fashion. They are offended by 'decadent' Western attitudes to gender roles, sex and alcohol. The 2003 US-led invasion of Iraq, and allegations of torture and mistreatment of Muslim prisoners held at Cuba's Guantanamo Bay further fanned the flames of Muslim anti-Americanism.

Al-Qaeda

The best-known Islamist organization is Al-Qaeda, led until recently by Saudi-born terrorist Osama bin Laden, who rose to prominence as a mujahideen in the Afghan War against the Soviet Union. Here he developed a large network of Islamic militants, which later evolved into Al-Qaeda, an international terrorist organization dedicated to fomenting Islamist revolutions in Muslim countries.

Bin Laden was infuriated by the Saudi government's decision to provide a base for American forces there during the 1991 Gulf War. He moved his operation to Sudan and began to sponsor attacks, not just against regimes in Muslim countries but against US interests in the Middle East and North Africa. In 1995, bin Laden relocated to Afghanistan, where Al-Qaeda allied itself with the Taliban. From 1996, Al-Qaeda launched increasingly audacious assaults on American targets, culminating, in 2001, in the 9/11 attacks on the USA. Planes were hijacked and crashed into buildings, killing more than

3,000 and provoking President Bush to declare a 'War on Terror'. An American-led coalition toppled the Taliban and destroyed Al-Qaeda's bases, although bin Laden evaded US forces until 2011.

Al-Qaeda survived the assault by reforming as a highly dispersed network of Islamist terrorist organizations. Without a central command structure, it became much more difficult to attack. Al-Qaeda affiliate groups carried out major terrorist attacks in Bali (2002), Madrid (2004), London (2005), Egypt (2005), Jordan (2005), Algeria (2007) and Mumbai (2008). Since 2003, there have been numerous Al-Qaeda instigated bombings and suicide attacks on civilians in Iraq.

Above The twin towers of the World Trade Center burn on 11 September 2001 following the attack by Al-Qaeda

TIMELINE	
1928	*Formation of the Muslim Brotherhood in Egypt*
1938	*Muslim Brotherhood begins to engage in terrorism*
1960–1966	*Sayyid Qutb writes his influential works on the creation of a pure Islamic state*
1979	*Iranian Revolution brings the Islamist regime of Ayatollah Khomeini to power*
1982	*Islamists assassinate President Sadat of Egypt*
1983	*Hezbollah suicide bomber kills 299 American and French soldiers in Beirut, Lebanon*
1987	*Formation of the Palestinian Islamist organization, Hamas*
1989	*Islamist regime comes to power in Sudan under Hassan al-Turabi and Omar Hassan al-Bashir*
1989	*Khomeini issues a 'fatwa' (ruling) calling for the death of Salman Rushdie, author of the 'blasphemous' Satanic Verses*
1995–2001	*The Taliban rules Afghanistan*
1997	*Osama bin Laden issues his fatwa, calling for Americans to be killed*
2001	*In an attack organized by Al-Qaeda, passenger planes are flown into buildings in the USA, killing over 3,000 people.*

AFRICA

1914 ONWARDS

During World War I, British, French and Belgian forces invaded German colonies in Africa. After the war, the German colonies in South-West, East and West Africa were handed over to neighbouring colonial powers. The inter-war period saw rapid economic development in many parts of the continent. Colonial governments built hundreds of kilometres of roads and railways to link inland centres of agricultural and mineral production with the coastal ports. The development of a transport infrastructure and consequent growth of trade resulted in a dramatic expansion of towns and cities. Fascist Italy conquered Ethiopia in 1936. With British help, the Ethiopians drove out the Italians in 1941. World War II also saw major fighting in North Africa as Axis forces attempted to seize Allied territory and oil interests there. By May 1943, the Allies were victorious.

Above Nelson Mandela (1918–2013), imprisoned by the apartheid regime as a terrorist, is now one of the most highly regarded men in the world

Decolonization

Organized opposition to colonial rule had begun in some African colonies in the early 20th century. However, it was only after World War II that this grew into a mass movement, as an emerging class of educated, urbanized Africans led calls for independence.

In some cases, independence arose relatively peacefully; in others, it only occurred after a struggle. In 1951, the former Italian colony of Libya became the first African nation to achieve independence. Morocco, Sudan and Tunisia followed in 1956. The Gold Coast won its independence as Ghana in 1957, and by 1965 almost every other sub-Saharan colony had followed suit.

Struggles for independence

Conflict generally only arose in colonies with entrenched white communities. French colonists in Algeria were determined to hold onto the territory, and independence was conceded in 1962, after an eight-year conflict with nationalists that cost around a million lives. British rulers in Kenya were faced with the nationalist Mau Mau rebellion during the 1950s, which paved the way for independence in 1963. In Rhodesia, following the white minority's 1965 unilateral declaration of independence (UDI), it took 15 years of guerilla warfare

TIMELINE	
1949	Mau Mau movement founded in Kenya
1954	Gold Coast's National Liberation Movement begins
1958	French colonies hold referenda on independence
1961	Wars of liberation begin in Portuguese colonies
1962	Algeria wins independence from French rule
1963	Kenya wins independence from Britain
1965	Rhodesia's white minority declares UDI
1967–1970	Biafran war
1974	Marxists oust emperor Haile Selassie in Ethiopia
1975	Civil war breaks out in Angola
1984–1985	Major famine in Ethiopia
1992	Civil war in Algeria
1994	Genocide in Rwanda
2003–2009	Conflict in Darfur in Western Sudan
2010	Mali, Algeria, Mauritania and Niger unite to combat terrorism.
2013	Death of Nelson Mandela.

before the nation won its freedom as Zimbabwe. South African-controlled Namibia gained its independence in 1990.

In South Africa itself, the powerful white minority government imposed apartheid (racial segregation) in 1948 and ruthlessly put down the African National Congress (ANC) protest movement. In 1962 the anti-apartheid campaigner and leader of the ANC's armed wing, Nelson Mandela, was imprisoned. By the 1980s, the pressures of continued internal rebellion, combined with international condemnation, finally led the government to negotiate an end to apartheid and the implementation of multiracial democracy in 1994. Since then, the ANC has been South Africa's ruling party.

Belgium's hurried decolonization of Congo in 1960 left power in the hands of a weak government. Civil war led to the rise of Joseph Mobuto's brutal military regime in 1965. Portugal's colonies, Guinea-Bissau, Angola and Mozambique achieved their independence by 1975, after long and bloody guerrilla wars.

After independence

The euphoria that greeted independence was all too quickly dispelled. Few states were able to offer their citizens security or prosperity. The colonial borders they inherited bore little or no relation to the realities of ethnic settlement, and violence was the frequent outcome. Ethnic rivalry in Rwanda led to genocide in 1994, inflicted by the Hutu majority against the Tutsi minority.

With elected governments often ill-prepared for such challenges and democratic traditions still weak, many states fell prey to military coups. Among the more brutal and corrupt regimes were those of Jean-Bédel Bokassa in the Central African Republic, and Idi Amin in Uganda. During the Cold War, African nations often became the battlegrounds for rival interests, with brutal dictators kept in power by means of communist or Western aid. Rebel armies, assisted by South Africa and the USA, fought against regimes in Mozambique and Angola.

Africa suffered economically in the 1970s from a rise in oil costs and a drop in prices for home-grown commodities such as coffee and cocoa. National debt rose in most African countries, causing economic stagnation and extreme poverty. In Zimbabwe, the brutal land reforms of Robert Mugabe led to internal upheaval, population displacement and economic collapse. Disease remained another major challenge; by 2010, around 68 per cent of people infected with HIV/AIDS worldwide were in sub-Saharan Africa.

With the ending of the Cold War, the 1990s witnessed a resurgence of multi-party, democratic governments in several countries, including Mali, Malawi, Niger and Zambia (though most were shortlived). Political instability remained the norm in many places; civil wars occurred in Nigeria, the Congo, Algeria, Liberia, Sierra Leone and Sudan during the late 1990s and early 2000s. In the first decade of the 21st century, Islamist-led insurgents mounted attacks in several countries, including Somalia, Kenya, Algeria, Tunisia, Morocco, Mauritania and Mali.

Above *Soldiers guard suspected Mau Mau rebels in Kenya in November 1952*

Below *Idi Amin, President of Uganda (1971–1979), whose regime was marred by human rights abuses*

LATIN AMERICA

1910 ONWARDS

For Latin America, the 20th and early 21st centuries were a time of economic expansion and urbanization and a growing middle class. The vast majority, however, experienced few benefits from modernization, and for many rural dwellers, conditions grew worse. There was progress towards democracy, punctuated by frequent lapses into military dictatorship. It was a time of political upheaval, with revolutions in Mexico, Bolivia, Cuba and Nicaragua.

Above *Juan Perón, three times president of Argentina, with his wife Eva – a heroine to the poor of the country*

Mexican Revolution

In the early 20th century, economic growth and rapid urbanization created social tensions in many parts of Latin America. Workers demanded higher wages and better working conditions, while peasants resented the loss of their lands to hacienda owners and railroad companies. In Mexico, these tensions led to a revolution in 1910, in which liberal landowner Francisco Madero overthrew the pro-modernization, pro-US government of Porfirio Diaz. The new government curtailed foreign intervention in domestic industry; it also introduced land reforms, redistributing land to the peasants.

Populism

The worldwide economic slump of the 1930s brought mass unemployment and poverty to Latin America. In some countries during the 1940s, this led to the rise of political leaders known as populists, who promised higher wages and better working conditions for employees, and an end to exploitation by foreign businesses. In order not to alienate the business community,

populist governments kept firm control over labour unions, repressed communist groups, and promoted domestic industry. Leaders included Juan Perón of Argentina, Victor Haya de la Torre of Peru, Getulio Vargas of Brazil and Jorge Gaitan of Colombia. The populists, although elected, often became increasingly autocratic once in power. However, they were successful at mobilizing the working masses to their support; and in alarming the conservative, property-owning classes, sometimes sufficiently to back plots against them. Gaitan was assassinated in 1948, Vargas was forced to resign in 1954, and Peron was overthrown by a military coup in 1955.

US influence

During the Cold War, the USA sought to influence the politics of Latin America, backing anti-communist groups and regimes and undermining communist ones. A popular revolution was thwarted by US pressure in Bolivia (1952), and a CIA-backed invasion overthrew the government of Jacobo Guzman in Guatemala (1954) after he appropriated United Fruit Company lands. The USA armed and funded right-wing guerrillas in El Salvador (1980–1988) and backed an invasion of Cuba at the Bay of Pigs, but failed to oust the left-wing pro-Soviet government of Fidel Castro.

Military regimes

The success of the Cuban Revolution in 1959 inspired revolutionary and socialist movements in other parts of Latin America. Military leaders and conservative landowners feared revolution. A wave of military coups swept Latin America during the 1960s and 1970s. A coup in Brazil in

1964 ushered in 20 years of military rule and the elected socialist government of Chile was overthrown by US-backed General Augusto Pinochet in 1973. The leaders mercilessly suppressed communism and political opposition of all kinds. Their regimes presided over a growing debt crisis in the 1970s and their high defence spending diverted funds from social welfare programmes.

During the late 1970s and 1980s, armed uprisings overthrew several military regimes in Latin America. Others returned peacefully to civilian rule, including Argentina (1983), Brazil (1985) and Chile (1990). By 1990, Cuba was the only Latin American country not ruled by a democratic government.

Neoliberalism

In the 1990s most Latin American governments adopted neoliberal economic policies. These involved supporting free-market activity, privatizing industries; cutting back on social programmes; and encouraging foreign trade. In 1993, Mexico joined NAFTA, a trading bloc with the USA and Canada, which led many American companies to relocate to Mexico, where wages were lower. Many thousands of Mexicans have migrated to the USA in search of better employment opportunities. In 1995, Argentina, Brazil, Paraguay and Uruguay signed up to Mercosur, an economic and political free trade agreement; Venezuela joined as a full member in 2012.

Neoliberalism improved efficiency, but also produced unemployment and a growing discontent among the poor. Latin American economies remained largely driven by exports of raw materials. However, in the early 21st century, the economies experienced an average of 5.5 percent growth, despite the global financial crisis of 2008–2009.

TIMELINE	
1910	In the Mexican Revolution, liberal Francisco Madero overthrows the dictator Porfirio Diaz
1917	New Mexican constitution embodies the principle of land reform
1921	Guatemala, Honduras and El Salvador form the Republic of Central America
1932–1935	Chaco War between Paraguay and Bolivia
1940–1942	War between Ecuador and Peru over the Amazonia region
1946	Juan Perón elected president of Argentina
1954–1989	Pro-American Alfredo Sroessner rules Paraguay
1959	Cuban Revolution
1973	Chile's socialist president Allende is killed in a US-backed coup
1976–1982	The 'dirty war' is fought between the Argentinian military and guerrilla forces
1982	The Falklands War begins
1990	Chilean democracy restored under Patricio Aylwin
2002	Argentina defaults on its international debt repayments, resulting in inflation
2002	Attempted coup against Venezuelan president Hugo Chavez
2008	Fidel Castro hands over power to his brother, Raul
2009	Honduran president, Manuel Zelaya, is ousted.

Recent developments

In the 2000s, the gap between rich and poor became wider than ever, and the growing numbers of urban and rural poor put pressure on resources. A large illegal drug trade in countries such as Colombia and Bolivia led to a rise in organized crime. Left-wing or reformist governments came to power in the late 1990s and early 2000s, including Luiz Inácio Lula da Silva in Brazil (succeeded in 2011 by Dilma Rousseff), Hugo Chávez in Venezuela, and Michelle Bachelet in Chile. They all tried to improve social welfare for the poor and to reduce their countries' dependence on overseas investment.

Below *After an armed revolution, Fidel Castro ruled Cuba from 1959 until 2008*

ENVIRONMENTAL CHALLENGES

1970 ONWARDS

Human activity has always affected the natural environment, but the boom in industrialization, urbanization and population that began in the early 1800s has had an unprecedented impact. Visible effects include air and water pollution, desertification, deforestation and the extinction of plants and animals. Less evident until relatively recently, but potentially more serious than any other environmental change, is global warming.

Above right
A typhoon in the Philippines in 2013 brought torrential rain, winds and a storm surge that devastated coastal areas

Industrialization

Industrialization has provided human society with many benefits, including employment opportunities, better communications and a generally higher standard of living. But this has come at a cost. Producing the energy that powers industry, the consumption of industrial products such as motor vehicles, and the disposal of industrial and domestic waste, have all led to a massive increase in air and water pollution. For example, the increase in sulphur and nitrogen emissions falls back to Earth as acid rain, which damages trees, natural vegetation, crops and fish stocks. The intensivization of agriculture – necessary to feed a growing urban population – has transformed rural habitats, endangering wild plants and animals.

Population growth

The global population increases by around 77 million people each year. Overcrowding causes more pollution, greater habitat destruction and uses up ever more natural resources. Although population growth is now much slower in the developed sector than in the developing world, people in developed countries consume more resources per head and therefore have a greater environmental impact than those in developing nations.

Global warming

Arguably the greatest environmental challenge facing the human race in the early 21st century is global warming. Based

TIMELINE	
1970	*Millions gather in USA for first Earth Day*
1971	*Greenpeace is founded*
1972	*Formation of UNEP*
1975	*Convention on International Trade in Endangered Species of Wild Fauna and Flora*
1982	*International Whaling Commission agrees a moratorium on all commercial whaling*
1987	*Montreal Protocol on Substances that Deplete the Ozone Layer*
1989	*Basel Convention on the Control of Transboundary Movements of Hazardous Wastes and Their Disposal*
1992	*UN Conference on Environment and Development (Earth Summit) at Rio de Janeiro, Brazil*
1997	*Kyoto Protocol is negotiated*
1999	*World population reaches six billion*
2012	*Mean global temperature is 14.6°C, the warmest in hundreds of years.*

on current trends, many scientists estimate that the continued rise in average temperature of the Earth's surface could prove catastrophic for life on Earth. Already, scientists have observed a 40 per cent reduction in the average thickness of Arctic ice. If polar ice continues to melt, it could cause a rise in the sea level that would flood many low-lying islands and coastal cities. Global warming is caused by a layer of gases in the Earth's atmosphere, including carbon dioxide, that traps heat from the sun's rays in a process known as the 'greenhouse effect'. Most climatologists believe that human activity is the main driving force behind global warming. Since the Industrial Revolution, humans have burned vast amounts of fossil fuels – coal, oil and their derivatives – thereby greatly increasing the amount of carbon dioxide in the atmosphere.

International cooperation

Since the late 1960s, efforts have been made both at national and international level to protect and conserve the environment. The first major global conference on the environment, held in Sweden in 1972, led to the creation of the United Nations Environment Programme (UNEP). A major role of UNEP has been to encourage 'sustainable development', which means increasing standards of living without destroying the environment.

Many international agreements followed, including the 1975 Convention on International Trade in Endangered Species, and the 1982 moratorium on all commercial whaling. One of the most effective treaties was the 1987 Montreal Protocol on Substances that Deplete the Ozone Layer. The 1992 'Earth Summit' in Rio de Janeiro, Brazil, produced two major treaties; one being for nations to

THE GREEN MOVEMENT

During the 1970s, a powerful 'green' movement developed, pressuring political leaders to enact legislation to protect the environment.

Organizations such as Greenpeace and Friends of the Earth lobbied for change, sometimes adopting non-violent confrontation as a means of drawing attention to environmental destruction. Green political parties formed in many countries; the German Green Party even became part of the national government in 1998. By the 2000s, environmentalism had become a mainstream issue, and most major political parties in the Western world had strong green policies.

voluntarily reduce carbon dioxide emissions, and the other requiring nations to protect endangered species and habitats. By 1997 it was clear that the voluntary emissions targets set at the Earth Summit would not be met. At another conference in Kyoto, Japan, agreement was reached to reduce 1990 emission levels by 5 per cent by the years 2008–2012. By 2005 it had been ratified by the requisite 55 nations and became legally binding. However, many scientists believe that although many countries are on course to meet the Kyoto requirements, the reductions are too minimal to affect global warming, and that nothing short of a 60 per cent reduction in emissions is necessary to stabilize the world's climate. At the 2011 UN Climate Change Conference in Durban, South Africa, world leaders agreed to a legally binding deal on lowering carbon emissions, to take effect by 2020. Many scientists and environmental groups warned that this timetable was too slow to prevent global warming rising above 2°C by 2050.

Above Members *of Greenpeace stage a demonstration outside the Kowloon branch of China Light and Power in Hong Kong*

ADVANCES IN SCIENCE, TECHNOLOGY AND MEDICINE

1900 ONWARDS

The 20th and early 21st century was a period of spectacular achievement in science, technology and medicine. Thousands of scientists were engaged in ever-more specialized fields, while governments and corporations spent vast sums on research. The age of the lone inventor had passed, and most significant discoveries were made by research teams.

Genetics

In 1910, American biologist Thomas Hunt Morgan proved that genes are the units of heredity and are located in cell structures called chromosomes, which contain proteins and deoxyribonucleic acid (DNA). After James Watson and Francis Crick explained the structure of DNA in 1953, geneticists were able to see the chemical processes at work in heredity. Genetic engineering, that is making changes to the DNA of an organism – for example, to produce human insulin – became a valuable tool in medicine. In 2000, scientists identified the genome (the complete set of genetic instructions) of the human body.

Medicine

Early in the 20th century, biochemists learned how certain diseases were caused by deficiencies of essential amino acids, now known as vitamins. In 1910, German bacterioloist Paul Ehrlich developed the world's first anti-bacterial drug; and the 1921 discovery of insulin saved the lives of countless diabetes sufferers. Alexander Fleming's discovery of penicillin in 1928 paved the

Above *Albert Einstein, winner of the Nobel Prize for his services to theoretical physics, is best known for his theory of relativity*

way for the development of antibiotics in the 1940s and 1950s, now used to treat a wide range of once-deadly diseases. The same period saw the development of vaccines against viral diseases such as yellow fever, influenza and polio. Heart operations became possible with the 1954 invention of a heart-lung machine. The first organ transplants were also carried out in this decade. Since the 1970s, methods such as ultrasound, CAT and MRI scanning have given doctors and surgeons much clearer, three-dimensional views of the body's interior.

Medicine faced new challenges too, with the rise of antibiotic-resistant diseases, and the emergence of HIV/AIDS in the early 1980s. The expansion of international travel made the containment of infectious diseases increasingly difficult. More liberal attitudes to sex since the 1960s resulted in the greater occurrence of STDs. And in North America and northern Europe especially, a diet of processed foods has led to growing instances of heart disease, diabetes and obesity.

Physics

The world of classical physics was revolutionized in the early 20th century by a series of new insights. First, German physicist Max Planck showed in 1900 that energy was not released in a continuous stream, but in tiny, indivisible chunks, or 'quanta'. Five years later, another German, Albert Einstein, published his Special Theory of Relativity, which proposed that space and time are relative to the observer, thus contradicting Newton's laws. Einstein's discovery that matter is energy in a different form paved the way for nuclear power. In 1915, Einstein submitted his General Theory of Relativity, showing that gravity is not a force but a distortion in space-time created by the presence of mass. In the 1910s, Niels Bohr and Ernest Rutherford proposed theories of the atom; and in the 1920s, Werner Heisenberg and Erwin Schrodinger developed quantum theory, using mathematics to explain the physics of the subatomic world. Heisenberg's uncertainty principle showed that the attributes of a subatomic particle can never be completely known. In the latter part of the 20th century, physicists attempted to unite quantum theory with Einstein's General Theory of Relativity to create a unified theory to explain all physical laws. Many hoped to find the answer by experimenting with powerful accelerators, which smash particles together at very high speeds to reveal more about their nature.

Technology

The 20th century saw dramatic developments in communications, transportation and computing technology. Italian engineer Guglielmo Marconi sent the first radio signal across the Atlantic in 1901. Scotsman John Logie Baird invented the first television in 1920; and British physicist Robert Watson-Watt developed radar in 1935. The first computers were built in the 1940s, followed by the transistor (1947) and the microprocessor (1968). By 1981, the arrival of the PC transformed home and office life for millions. Communications continued to advance in the 1990s with the development of the Internet, email and mobile phones.

From the 1950s, as part of their Cold War rivalry, the USA and USSR began to compete in a 'space race'. The Soviets took an early lead, launching the first satellite,

TIMELINE	
1900	*Max Planck proposes his quantum theory of energy*
1903	*The Wright brothers achieve powered flight*
1905	*Einstein evolves his Special Theory of Relativity*
1909	*Rutherford and Geiger discover the atom's nucleus*
1910	*Ehrlich develops the first anti-bacterial drug, Salvarsan*
1911	*Biochemist Casimir Funk coins the name 'vitamin'*
1913	*Niels Bohr proposes his atomic model*
1915	*Einstein announces his General Theory of Relativity*
1919	*Rutherford discovers the proton*
1924	*Astronomer Edwin Hubble discovers the nature of galaxies and the expansion of the universe*
1927	*Heisenberg proposes his 'uncertainty principle'*
1928	*Alexander Fleming isolates penicillin*
1945	*The atom bomb is developed*
1953	*Watson and Crick discover the structure of DNA*
1957	*Launch of Sputnik*
1961	*Yuri Gagarin becomes the first man in space*
1969	*Neil Armstrong sets foot on the Moon*
1973	*Genetic engineering techniques are developed*
1983	*AIDS virus is identified*
1990	*Launch of Hubble Space Telescope*
1997	*Dolly the sheep is the first cloned mammal*
2000	*Publication of the human genome*
2012	*The Higgs Boson particle is discovered at CERN.*

Sputnik, in 1957, and sending the first man into space in 1961. But they were overtaken by the USA, which landed a man on the Moon in 1969, then sent out unmanned probes to explore the planets of the solar system in the 1970s and 1980s. In the 1990s, Russia and the USA joined forces to begin construction of the International Space Station. Human understanding of deep space has been immeasurably enhanced by the Hubble Space Telescope, launched in 1990. During the 2000s, the first extra-solar planets were discovered. More than 800 had been identified by 2013.

INTO THE FUTURE

The empires and dynastic states that dominated much of human history eventually gave way to the era of nation-states, with their defined borders and distinct social and cultural identities. In the early 21st century, the concept of the nation-state is itself under threat from the ever-growing forces of globalization.

Below *The ability to send cameras into space and thus see Earth in its entirety contributed to a new understanding of the environment*

A more integrated world

During the 1990s, the world started to become more integrated, both economically and culturally. Advances in tele-communications and transportation, the growth of the Internet, and the expansion of the free market and democracy following the fall of communism were all partly responsible for this trend towards 'globalization'. Furthermore, nations were increasingly faced with supranational challenges that they were ill-equipped to deal with on their own, including global warming, international terrorism, the drug trade, immigration, nuclear weapons proliferation and pandemics.

Many nations have felt it necessary to band together in international institutions, such as the UN, to address these concerns. Some are even prepared to surrender a portion of national sovereignty, handing over law-making powers to an international body, as in the case of the EU. Some see the gradual stripping away of national sovereignty by regional or global institutions as an inevitable trend, leading ultimately to a world government.

Others perceive a future in which multinational corporations – already mightier than many small states – will one day grow too powerful for any national government to control. With no democratic accountability, there will then be nothing to prevent these corporations from exploiting employees and destroying the environment. However, optimists claim that globalization actually increases economic prosperity and employment and promotes civil liberties in the developing world, just as the first wave of capitalist growth did in the developed world.

Scarce resources

As well as increasing globalization, the coming century is likely to be characterized by competition and conflict over scarce resources, particularly energy sources and water. Because of the threat of global warming, there could be a gradual shift away from the use of fossil fuels and towards nuclear power and renewable energy sources, as well as moves to reduce energy consumption (see pages 294–295). However, it seems likely that fossil fuels, especially oil, will remain the dominant energy source for decades to come. Yet oil is a diminishing resource – world oil production may have peaked in 2005 – and as the global population rises (projected to reach nine billion by 2050), it will become an increasingly scarce and expensive commodity. This may provide governments with a powerful economic incentive to switch to less environmentally damaging energy sources, but equally may lead to global famine, revolution and war.

Another vital resource in limited supply is water. Drinking water is very unevenly distributed around the planet, and countries in Africa and Europe, for example, face regular water shortages. Many experts claim this problem is going to get worse, due to population growth and our increasingly meat-based diets (meat farming requires much higher levels of water than arable). Technological or engineering solutions such as desalination, pipeline construction and fog harvesting may help to some extent, but water shortages are likely to become more frequent and may even lead to armed conflict.

Warfare and terrorism

There are ongoing conflicts in many parts of the globe today, and warfare is likely to feature prominently in the 21st century. However, the traditional pattern of armed conflict between sovereign states is giving way to a phenomenon known as 'fourth generation' warfare: conflicts between a state and a sub-national group, or insurgency. Fourth generation wars rarely take place on defined battlefields. The insurgency forces are decentralized, and often made up of small groups that unite to fight a common enemy. Recent and ongoing conflicts in Iraq, Sri Lanka, Israel/Palestine, Afghanistan, Syria and Sudan were and are all fourth generation wars.

Violent ideological groups that are too weak to attack government forces directly will continue to resort to terrorism. As with warfare, terrorism is constantly evolving. Future terrorist organizations may obtain weapons of mass destruction (chemical, biological, radiological or nuclear weapons). They may engage in

A GLOBAL CULTURE?

The Internet has become a powerful tool of cultural integration. People dress and eat more similarly than ever before; they watch the same films, play the same computer games and listen to the same music. This may be seen as a triumph of manipulative marketing by global corporations, or the beginnings of a truly global culture. Either way, many governments perceive the Internet as a threat to their political authority. China and Iran, for example, have attempted to restrict the access of their citizens to the Internet. Many French citizens have expressed concern about the erosion of their national identity by the global 'pop culture'.

cyberterrorism (sabotaging computer networks) and electronic warfare (targeting communications and power facilities).

Plus ça change

Whatever the future holds for the human race, it is clear that we are in a period of flux, with traditional ways of life increasingly under threat from globalization, environmental challenges and a growing population. Nevertheless, as any study of world history will show, political, social and economic structures may change, but the fundamentals of human society remain the same. We are not so different in evolutionary terms from the hominids who first appeared in Africa some two million years ago, and the same desires that motivated us then, to fulfill our basic needs, protect our loved ones and seek a better life, continue to drive us now.

Below Satellite dishes transmit signals to or from satellites, beaming information around the world

TIMELINE

4300BC—PRESENT DAY

ANCIENT WORLD

4300–2334BC	Sumer (Mesopotamia)
3100–1700BC	Indus Valley civilization (India)
c. 3000–1450BC	Minoan civilization and Cycladic culture (Greece)
2650–2150BC	Old Kingdom (Egypt)
2334–1000BC	Mesopotamian empires and kingdoms
2050–1640BC	Middle Kingdom (Egypt)
1766–1122BC	Shang dynasty (China)
1700–1500BC	Kerma (East Africa)
1700–500BC	Vedic Period India
c. 1600–1200BC	Mycenaean civilization (Greece)
1532–1070BC	New Kingdom (Egypt)
1250–1000BC	Olmecs (Mesoamerica)
1122–480BC	Zhou dynasty (China)
1000–612BC	Neo-Assyrian Empire (Mesopotamia)
c. 950–700BC	Cimmerians (Central Asia)
900BC–AD350	Kush/Meroë (East Africa)
890–800BC	Phoenicians (Mediterranean)
800–200BC	Chavin (South America)
712–332BC	Late Period Egypt
700–c. 350BC	Scythians (Central Asia)
627–539BC	Neo-Babylonian Empire (Mesopotamia)
600–400BC	Maya (Mesoamerica)
559–435BC	Achaemenid Empire (Persia)
500–202BC	Carthaginians (Mediterranean)

CLASSICAL WORLD

c. 800–350BC	Etruscans (Europe)
590BC–AD350	Kingdom of Meroë (East Africa)
509–27BC	Roman Republic (Europe)
500BC–AD400	Nok culture (West Africa)
500–435BC	Classical Greece
500BC–AD50	Mauryan Empire (India)
500BC–AD500	Celts (Europe)
336–321BC	Macedonia (Greece and Asia)
312–60BC	Seleucid dynasty (Asia)
306–168BC	Antigonid dynasty (Greece)
305–30BC	Ptolomeic dynasty (Egypt)

c. 300–53BC	Xiongu (Central Asia)
238BC–AD224	Parthian Empire (Persia)
221BC–AD220	Han Empire (China)
200BC–AD900	Classic Maya (Mesoamerica)
135BC–AD240	Kushan Empire (India)
c. 100BC–AD600s	Moche (South America)
27BC–AD476	Roman Empire (Europe, North Africa and Western Asia)
c. AD1–650	Kingdom of Axum (East Africa)
c. AD1–750	Teotihuacán (Mesoamerica)
c. AD200–800	Nazca people (South America)
AD224–637	Sasanian Empire (Persia)
AD320–550	Gupta Empire (India)
c. AD400–1000	Huari and Tiahuanaco (South America)
AD434–453	Huns (Central Asia and Europe)
AD400–553	Juan-Juan (Central Asia)
AD80–629	Byzantine Empire (Asia Minor)
AD553–600	Tujue (Central Asia)

MEDIEVAL WORLD

589–618	Sui dynasty (China)
600–814	Carolingian Empire (Europe)
618–907	Tang dynasty (China)
629–1453	Byzantine Empire (Asia Minor)
632–661	Islamic Empire (Middle East, North Africa)
661–750	Umayyad dynasty (Middle East, North Africa, Western Asia, Spain)
750–1037	Abbasid Empire (Middle East, North Africa, Western Asia)
793–1100	Vikings (Europe)
802–1440	Khmer Empire (Cambodia)
907–1279	Song dynasty (China)
939–1407	Dai Viet (Vietnam)
950–1168	Toltecs (Mesoamerica)
962–1806	Holy Roman Empire (Europe)
1000–1300	Feudal Europe
1030–1151	Ghaznavid Emirate (India)

1037–1194	Seljuk Sultanate (Middle East, Western Asia)
1095–1291	The Crusades
1144–1174	Zangid dynasty (Middle East)
1174–1250	Ayyubid dynaty (Middle East)
1200–1470	Chimú (South America)
1206–1526	Delhi Sultanate (India)
1204–1405	Mongol Empire (Central and Western Asia)
c. 1250–1464	Mali (West Africa)
1250–1517	Mamluks (Middle East)
1325–1521	Aztec Empire (Mesoamerica)
1336–1573	Ashikaga shogunate (Japan)
1337–1453	Hundred Years' War (Europe)
1400–1500	Renaissance (Europe)
1438–1533	Inca Empire (South America)

EARLY MODERN PERIOD

1350–1767	Ayutthaya Kingdom (Thailand)
1368–1644	Ming dynasty (China)
1415–1600	Age of European exploration
1464–1591	Songhai (West Africa)
1492–1905	Russian expansion (Asia)
1492–1918	Ottoman Empire (Western Asia, Middle East, Europe, North Africa)
1500–1700	Habsburg Empire (Europe)
1501–1722	Safavid dynasty (Persia)
1517–1618	The Reformation (Europe)
1521–1721	Swedish expansion (Europe)
1526–1765	Mughal Empire (India)
1531–1581	Taungoo Empire (Myanmar)
1550–1800	Spanish-American Empire
1600–1714	Dutch 'golden age' (Europe)
1603–1867	Tokugawa shogunate (Japan)
1607–1867	British colonization of North America
1608–1763	French colonization of North America
1618–1648	Thirty Years' War (Europe)
1643–1715	French expansion under Louis XIV (Europe)
1644–1911	Manchu Qing dynasty (China)
1650–1800	The Enlightenment (Europe)
1763–1783	American Revolution

MODERN WORLD

1765–1948	British Raj (India)
1770–1914	Industrial Revolution (Europe and North America)
1788–1914	British colonization of Australia and New Zealand
1789–1799	French Revolution
1790–1945	European colonization of South-east Asia
1796–1815	Napoleonic Empire (France)
1783–1830	Independence in Latin America
1783–1910	Westward expansion of the USA
1804–1903	Sokoto Caliphate (West Africa)
1815–1849	Growth of nationalism (Europe)
1815–1871	German and Italian unification
1861–1865	American Civil War
1880–1914	Rise of Germany
1880–1965	European colonization of Africa
1895–1945	Japanese expansion in East Asia and the Pacific
1911–1949	Republic of China
1914–1918	World War I
1917–1921	Russian Revolution and Civil War
1918–1938	Rise of fascism
1922–1991	Soviet Union
1929–1939	Great Depression
1938–1945	Nazi occupation of Europe
1939–1945	World War II
1942–1945	The Holocaust (Europe)
1945–1980	Decolonization in Africa, India, the Middle East and South-east Asia
1945–1989	The Cold War
1948–	The Arab-Israeli Conflict
1949–	People's Republic of China
1954–1975	Indochina wars
1957–	EEC and (from 1992) EU (Europe)
1979–	Rise of Islamism
1989–1990	Democratic revolutions in Eastern Europe
1990–	Globalization
2001	9/11
2008–2009	Global banking crisis leads to a world recession
2011–2012	The Arab Spring

INDEX

Abbas 120
Abbas I, Shah 176
Abbas II, Shah 177
Abbasid Empire 120–1, 124
Abraham 30
Achaemenid Empire 32–3
Adad-nirari II, King 28
Adolphus, Gustavus 159, 161
Aegean civilization 50–1
Afghanistan 265, 267, 281
Africa
  19th century 238–9
  and Axum 96–7
  and Bantu peoples 97, 130
  early farmers in 15, 58
  early modern 188–9
  European exploration of 154
  hominids in 8–10
  Homo erectus in 10
  Homo sapiens in 11
  independence 290–1
  and Kingdom of Kerma 59, 96
  and the Kush 59, 96
  and the Nok 97
  and the Nubians 59, 96
  Scramble for 240–1
Ahmose I, Pharaoh 38
Akbar 177, 178
Akkad/Akkadians 23, 24, 25
al-Afghani, Jamal 288
al-Din, Nur 125
al-Din, Salah 125
al-Hamid II, Abd 214, 215
al-Madjid, Abd 214
al-Malik, Abd 119
Al-Qaeda 289
al-Rahman, Abd 120
Alaric 75
Alexander II, Tsar 210–11
Alexander III, Tsar 211
Alexander the Great 39, 63, 64–5, 82
Alexius I Comnenus, Emperor 123
Alfred, King 106
Algeria 238, 290
Ali, Caliph 118
Ali, Mehmet 214, 238
Amenemhet I, Pharaoh 36–7
Amenhopet IV, Pharaoh 39
American Civil War 218–19
American War of Independence 197
Amorites 25
Anabaptists 157
Anasazi culture 144
Anastasius, Emperor 80–1
Angkor 142
Angola 291
Antigonid Dynasty 65
Antigonus 65
Antiochus III, Emperor 64–5
Antony, Mark 71
Arab-Israeli conflict 286–7
Arab Spring 285
Arabs
  Abbasid Empire 120–1
  and Arab-Israeli conflict 286–7
  and the Byzantine Empire 122
  and Islam 118–19
  Umayyad caliphate 118–19
Aramaeans 27, 28
Ardashir I, King 67
Argentina 225, 226
Arslan, Alp 124
Art
  in Ancient Greece 61
  in India 84, 85, 179
  in Upper Paleolithic period 13
Aryans 32, 42–3, 47
Ashoka Maurya 82–3
Ashurbanipal, King 29
Ashurnasirpal II, King 28
Ashurubalit I, King 27
Asia 11, 12
Assyria/Assyrians 25, 27, 28–9, 31, 39, 54
Athens/Athenians 52, 53, 60–1, 62–3
Attatürk, Kemal 284
Attila the Hun 79
Augustus, Romulus 75
Augustus, Emperor 71, 72
Aung San Suu Kyi 277
Aurangzeb 178
Austria 165, 167, 213
Austria-Hungary 212, 244–5
Australia 12, 91, 236–7, 282–3
Australopithecines 8, 9
Avars 79, 81
Axum/Axumites 96–7, 130
Ayyubid dynasty 125
Aztecs 146–7
Babur 177
Babylon/Babylonians 25, 27, 28–9, 31
Baghdad 120, 121
Bahamas 154
Bakr, Caliph Abu 118
Balboa, Vasco Núñez De 154
Balkans 212
Baltic region 160–1
Bangladesh 281
Bantu peoples 97, 130
Barbarossa, Emperor Frederick I 109, 126–7
Basil II, Emperor 122
Beg, Toghril 124
Beg III, Togril 124
Belgium 203, 206–7
Berlin 264
Berlin Conference 240
Bhutto, Benazir 281
Bimbisara 43
Bin Laden, Osama 288, 289
Bindusara 82
Bismarck, Otto von 209, 212, 213
Black Death 115
Boer War 239, 241
Bohemia 158
Bolívar, Simón 225
Bolivia 155, 225
Bonaparte, Napoleon 200–1
Boxer Uprising 231
Brazil 154, 191, 225, 226, 227, 292–3
Brezhnev, Leonid 268
Brihadrata 83
Britain
  alliance system 213
  Anglo-Saxon 104
  and Canada 222–3
  and the Celts 77
  and India 179, 228–9, 262–3
  industrial revolution in 202–3, 204–5
  and Napoleonic wars 200–1
  and North America 194–5, 196–7
  and Opium Wars 230
  and the Seven Years' War 167
  and South-East Asia 234–5
  and the Vikings 106
  World War I 244–5
  World War II 252, 253
Bronze Age 49, 50
Buddhism 83, 100–1, 150–1
Bulgars 122
Burma 142–3, 187, 230, 235, 277
Bush, George W. 267
Buwayhids 121, 124
Byzantine Empire 67, 122–3, 124, 172
  and the Arabs 122
  early 80–1
Cabot, John 155, 192
Cabot, Sebastian 155
Cabral, Pedro Alvares 154
Caesar, Gaius Julius 71, 77, 78
Calvin, John 157
Cambodia 142, 186, 235, 279
Cambyses, King 33
Canada 155, 222–3, 250, 267
Cape of Good Hope 154
capitalism 168–9
Carolingian Empire 104–5, 107
Carthage/Carthaginians 55, 70, 76–7
Cartier, Jacques 155
Casimir IV, King 129
Castro, Fidel 265, 292
Çatal Hüyük 21
Catherine II, Empress 163
Cathars 111
Cavour, Count Camillo di 208
Celts 17, 76–7
Central Africa 131, 189
Central America 15
  20th century 292–3
  and the Aztecs 146–7
  and the Maya 57, 92–3, 147
  and the Olmecs 56, 92
  and Teotihuacán 94–5, 146, 147
  and the Toltecs 146
  and the Zapotecs 57
Central Asia 46–7, 280
Chad 8
Chaldeans 27, 28, 29
Chandra Gupta I, Emperor 85
Chandra Gupta II, Emperor 85
Chandragupta Maurya 82
Charlemagne, Emperor 105, 107
Charles I, King 159
Charles II, King of Spain 165
Charles IV, Emperor 109
Charles V, Emperor 153, 156
Charles VI, King of France 128
Charles VIII, King of France 153
Charles X, King 161
Charles XII, King 161
Charles the Bold 128
Chavín 57, 95
Chechnya 269
Chen-la 142
Chiang Kai-shek 260
chiefdoms 18, 49
China 12
  Boxer Uprising 231
  Civil War 261
  Communist 272–3
  Han Empire 86–7
  and Japan 181, 233, 257, 261
  Jin dynasty 137
  Longshan culture 44
  Manchu dynasty 182–3
  Ming dynasty 180–1
  and the Mongols 137, 138
  Northern Zhou 89
  and Opium Wars 230
  Qianlong dynasty 183
  Qin dynasty 86
  Qing dynasty 182–3, 230–1
  religion in 100, 101, 151
  Shang dynasty 44–5
  Sixteen Kingdoms 88–9
  Song dynasty 136–7
Sui dynasty 134
Tang dynasty 134–5
technology 98, 99
Three Kingdoms Period 88
and Tibet 281
Toba 89
World War I 260
Yangshao culture 44
Xia dynasty 44
and Xiongnu 79
Chola dynasty 132
Christian II, King 160
Christian IV, King 159
Christianity
  in Africa 241
  and Ethiopia 97
  expansion of 110
  in Japan 185
  medieval 150
  Orthodox 110
  Reformation in Europe 156–7
  and Roman Empire 75, 103
Cimmerians 47, 79
cities 22, 23, 40–1, 44–5, 116–17
Cixi, Empress 231
Claudius, Emperor 72
Cleisthenes 53
Clovis, King 104
Cnut, King 106
Columbus, Christopher 154
Concert of Europe 206
Confucius/Confusianism 45, 101
Congo 189, 241, 291
Constantine I, Emperor 74, 103
Constantinople 123
Coronado, Vásquez 155
Cortés, Hernán 147
Counter-Reformation 157
Crete 18
Cromwell, Oliver 159
Crusader states 127
Crusades 123, 126–7
Cuba 154, 225, 226, 265, 292
Cultural Revolution 272–3
Cyclades 50
Cyrus the Great, King 29, 31, 32–3, 102
Czechoslovakia 270, 271
Dai Viet 143
Dalhousie, Lord 228
Darius I, King 33
Darwin, Charles 243
David, King of Israel 30
Davis, John 155
Delhi Sultanate 133
Delian League 61
Deng Xiaoping 273
Denmark 158–9, 160–1
Di-Xin 45
Diadochi, Wars of 64
Dias, Bartholomew 154
Diem, Ngo Dinh 278
Diocletian, Emperor 73, 103
Djoser, Pharaoh 35
Dorgon, Emperor 183
Dravidians 42
Eannatum, King 23
East Africa 130, 188, 238–9
Easter Island 145
Egypt
  and Alexander the Great 39
  and the Assyrians 39
  and the Crusades 127
  Early Dynastic Period 34–5
  and the Hebrews 30, 31
  and the Hittites 26
  and the Hyksos 37, 38
  and Israel 287
  and the Kush 39, 59
  Late Period 39
  Middle Kingdom 36–7
and the Mitanni 26
nationalism in 284, 285
New Kingdom 38–9
and the Nubians 96
Old Kingdom 35
and the Ottoman Empire 214, 238
and the Persians 39
and the Ptolemaic Dynasty 65
rise of chiefdoms 18
writing in 19
Einstein, Albert 296–7
Elam/Elamites 23, 24, 27
Elizabeth of Russia, Tsarina 167
Elizabeth I, Queen 157
England
  in 17th century 159, 164
  capitalism in 168–9
  Civil War 159, 164
  exploration of North America 155
  and the Hundred Years' War 115
  industrialization in 169
  Reformation in 156, 157
  Renaissance 129
  union with Scotland 164
  Wars of the Roses 129
environmental concerns 294–5
Epic of Gilgamesh 22
Eridu 21
Esarhaddon, King 29
Estonia 160
Etana, King 23
Ethiopia 8, 58, 96–7, 130, 188, 241, 291
Etruscans 55, 68–9
Eurasian steppe peoples 78–9
Europe
  1848 revolutions in 207
  absolute monarchy 165–6
  age of exploration 154–5
  alliance system 212–13, 244
  and the Black Death 115
  Bronze Age 49
  capitalism in 168–9
  Carolingian Empire 104–5, 107
  Christianity in 111
  cities in 116–17
  Cold War 265
  Counter-Reformation 157
  Enlightenment in 170–1
  and European Union 270, 271
  feudalism in 112–13
  French Revolutionary Wars 199
  Habsburg Empire 152–3
  Holy Roman Empire 107, 108–9, 115, 152, 158–9
  and industrial revolution 204–5
  inter-war 248–9
  medieval warfare 114–15
  and Napoleon Bonaparte 200–1
  nationalism in 206–7
  Neanderthals in 11
  Neolithic 48–9
  and the Ottoman Empire 172–3
  post-war 270–1
  Reformation in 157–8
  Renaissance 128–9
  rise of chiefdoms 18, 49
  Seven Years' War 167
  Thirty Years' War 158–9
  and the Vikings 106–7
  War of the Spanish Succession 165
  wars of succession 167–8
  World War I 215, 244–5
  World War II 252–3

European Union 270, 271
Ezana, king 96–7
farming
  in Africa 15, 58
  in ancient Egypt 34
  in Neolithic period 14–17, 48–9
  rise of settlements 16–17
  rise of chiefdoms 18
Fatimid caliphate 120
Ferdinand, Prince 158, 159
feudalism 112–13
Flinders, Matthew 237
France
  in 17th century 158
  capitalism in 169
  colonization of North America 194–5
  exploration of North America 155, 192–3
  Franco-Prussian War 209
  Franco-Spanish War 164
  and the Hundred Years' War 115
  and Huguenots 157, 158
  and India 179
  and Louis XIV 164–5
  and Napoleon Bonaparte 200–1
  nationalism in 206, 207
  Renaissance 128
  Revolution (1789) 198–9
  Revolution (1848) 207
  and the Seven Years' War 167
  and the Thirty Years' War 159
  War of the Spanish Succession 165
  Wars of Religion 157
  World War I 244–5
Franco, Francisco 249
Franco-Russian alliance 212–13
Frankish kingdom 104–5
Frederick I, King 167
Frederick II, King 167
French and Indian War 195, 197
Frobisher, Martin 155
Funan 91, 142
Funj 188
Gama, Vasco da 154
Gandhi, Indira 280
Gandhi, Mohandas 262, 263
Gaozu, Emperor 134
Garibaldi, Giuseppe 208–9
Germany
  alliance system 212–13
  Cold War 264, 265
  division into East and West 264, 265, 270
  Frankish kingdom 104–5
  Germanic peoples 78
  Nazi 249
  Reformation in 156
  reunification 271
  unification 209
  World War I 244–5
Ghana 131, 290
Ghaznavid emirate 121
global warming 294–5
globalization 298–9
Golden Bull 109
Gorbachev, Mikhail 265, 268–9
Great Depression 249, 251
Great Leap Forward 272
Great Northern War 163
Great Wall of China 181
Great Zimbabwe 131
Greece
  and the Antigonid Dynasty 65
  and Athens 52, 53, 62–3
  Classical 60–1
  colonies of 53
  and debt crisis 271

and the Delian League 61
and Macedon 63
and the Mycenaeans 51
and Ottoman Empire 207, 214
and the Persians 33, 60–1, 62
and Sparta 52, 53, 62–3
rise of 52–3
technology 98, 99
and Thebes 62–3
Gregory VII, Pope 109, 111
Guatemala 292
Guinea-Bisseau 291
Gupta Empire 85
Habsburg Empire 152–3, 165
Hadrian, Emperor 72
Haiti 224
Hakhamanish, King 32
Halafians 20
Hallstatt culture 76
Hammurabi, King 25
Han Empire 86–7
Han Gaozu 86–7
Hannibal 70
Hanseatic League 117, 160
Harappa 40
Harsha 132
Hassunas 20
Hawaii 145
Hebrews 30–1, 102
Henry IV, Emperor 108–9
Henry IV, King of France 158
Henry V, Emperor 109
Henry V, King of England 128
Henry VI, Emperor 109
Henry VII, King of England 155
Henry VIII, King of England 156
Henry the Navigator 129
Heraclius, Emperor 81
Hero of Alexandria 99
Hidalgo, Miguel 224
Hideyoshi, Emperor 184
Hinduism 43, 100, 151
Hispaniola 154
Hitler, Adolf 240
Hittites 25, 26
Hohokam culture 144
Holocaust, The 254–5
Holy Roman Empire 107, 108–9, 115, 152, 158–9
hominids 8–10
Homo erectus 10
Homo sapiens 10–11
Hongwu Emperor 180
Huang Di, Emperor 44
Huari 95
Huguenots 157, 158
Humayan 177
Hundred Years' War 115
Hungary 49, 129, 138, 264
Huns 79
Hurrians 25, 26, 27
Hussein, Saddam 285
Hyksos 37, 38
Incas 148–9
India 18
  and Britain 228–9, 262–3
  caste system 43
  Delhi Sultanate 133
  European influence 179
  Gupta Empire 85
  independence 262–3
  Indian Mutiny 228–9
  Indus Valley Civilization 40–1
  Kushan Empire 84–5
  Mauryan Empire 82–3
  medieval 132–3
  Mughal 177, 178–9
  post-independence 280–1
  Raj period 228–9
  religion in 100–1, 132–3, 150, 151
  technology 98, 99

Vedic Period 42–3
Indian Mutiny 228–9
Indochina wars 278
Indonesia 10
Indus Valley Civilization 40–1
industrialization/industrial revolution 202–3, 204–5, 221–2, 294
Iran 285, 288
Iraq 14, 267, 284, 285, 289
Ireland
  and Celts 77
  and Ulster plantation 159
Isabella of Spain, Queen 129, 154
Islam
  and Abbasid Empire 120–1
  and the Crusades 126–7
  and India 132–3
  Islamism 287, 288–9
  medieval 150
  rise of 118–19
Ismail I, Shah 177
Israel
  ancient 30–1, 102
  Arab-Israeli conflict 286–7
Italy
  Fascist 248
  Renaissance 128
  Triple Alliance 212
  unification 208–9
  wars in 153
  World War II 253
Ivan the Terrible 162
Jacobins 199
Jainism 101
James II, King 164
Japan
  and China 181, 233, 257
  early history 89
  inter-war 256–7
  medieval 140–1
  Meiji Restoration 232–3
  post-war 274–5
  religion in 101
  Russo-Japanese War 233
  Tokugawa shogunate 184–5, 232
  World War II 257, 258–9
Java 10, 143, 187, 234–5
Jayavarman I 142
Jayavarman II 143
Jehu, King 31
Jericho 20, 21
Jerusalem 31, 16, 127
Jin dynasty 137, 138
Jinnah, Mohammed Ali 263
Johanson, Donald 8
Johnson, Lyndon 279
Jordan 286
Joshua, King 31
Judah 30–1, 102
Judaism 102, 150–1
Justinian I, Emperor 81
Kadphises, Kujala 84
Kadphises, Vima 84
Kalinga 83
Kanishka 84
Kennedy, John 265
Kenya 8, 9, 290
Kerma 59, 96
Khaljis dynasty 133
Khan, Genghis 138, 139
Khomeini, Ayatollah 288
Khosru I, Emperor 67
Khrushchev, Nikita 264, 265, 268
Khufu, Pharaoh 35
Khwarizm, Shahdom of 125
Kim Il Sung 275
Kim Jong Il 275
Kim Jong Un 275
King George's War 194–5
King, Martin Luther 266

King William's War 194
Kish 23, 24
Knossos 50, 51
Köprülü, Mehmet 174
Korea 141, 181, 233, 264, 275
Kush 39, 59, 96
Kushan Empire 84–5
La Tène culture 76
Lagash 23
Lao Zi 100
Lapita culture 90–1
Late Stone Age 12–13
League of Nations 248, 249
Lee, Robert E. 219
Lenin, Vladimir 246, 247
Leo III, Emperor 123
Leo III, Pope 105
Leon, Juan Ponce de 155
Leopold II, King 241
Leszczynski, Stanilas 166
Li Hongzhang 231
Li Zucheng 181
Liao kingdom 136
Libya 285, 290
Lincoln, Abraham 218–19
Liu Xiu 87
Liu Yuan 88
Lomard League 109
Louis XIV, King 164–5
Louis XVI, King 198, 199
Louis the Pios 107
Lucy (Australopithecine) 8
Luther, Martin 156–7
Macedon/Macedonia 63, 65
Macedonian dynasty 122
Magellan, Ferdinand 155
Madmud II, Sultan 214
Mahmud of Ghazni 133
Majapahit 143
Malacca/Malacca Straits 187, 234
Malay Peninsula 234, 277
Mali 131, 188–9
Manchu dynasty 182–3
Manchuria 257
Mandela, Nelson 291
Mao Zedong 261, 272–3
Marathon, Battle of 33, 60
Marius, Gaius 70
Martel, Charles 103
Martín, José de San 225
Mary, Queen of Scots 157
Mary I, Queen 157
Maurice, Emperor 81
Mauryan Empire 82–3
Maximilian I, Emperor 153
May Fourth Movement 260
Maya 57, 92–3, 147
Mazarin, Cardinal 164, 165
Mazzini, Guiseppe 208
McCarthy, Joseph 266
Medvedev, Dimitry 269
Meiji Restoration 232–3
Mentuhotep II, Pharaoh 36
Merovingians 104–5
Mesopotamia
  early civilizations in 20–1
  empires of 24–9
  rise of chiefdoms 18
  and the Seleucid Empire 64–5
  and Sumer 22–3, 24, 25
Metternich, Prince
  Klemens von 206, 207
Mexico 94–5, 146–7, 226, 292
Micronesia/Micronesian culture 91
Middle East 284–5
Ming dynasty 180–1
Minoans 18, 50–1
Mississippian culture 144–5
Mitannis 16, 26, 27
Mithradates I, Emperor 66
Mithradates II, Emperor 66

Moche 95
Moctezuma II, King 147
Mogollon culture 144
Mohenjo Daro 40
Mongke 138
Mongols/Mongol Empire 79, 125, 137, 138–9
Morocco 130, 290
Moroë 96
Moses 30
Mozambique 291
Mughal India 177, 178–9
Muhammad 118
Muhammad ibn Tughluk 133
Muhammad of Ghur 133
Mursilis, King 25
Musa, Mansa 131
Muscovy 129, 162
Musharraf, Pervez 281
Mussolini, Benito 248
Mycenaeans 51
Myanmar 142–3, 187
Mysians 27
Nabonidus, King 29
Nabopolassar, King 29
Nan Chao 142
Nan Madol 145
Narmer, Pharaoh 34, 35
Nasser, Abdel 285
Natufians 20
Nazca 95
Ne Win 277
Neanderthals 11, 13
Nebuchadnezzar I, King 27
Nebuchadnezzar II, King 29, 31
Nehru, Jawaharlal 263, 280
Neolithic period 14–17, 20, 48–9
Nero, Emperor 103
Netherlands
  capitalism in 168–9
  independence from Spain 158
  Reformation in 157
  and South-East Asia 234, 235
New Deal 251
New Guinea 235
New Zealand 145, 237, 283
Nicholas I, Tsar 210
Nicholas II, Tsar 211
Nigeria 97
Ninevah 29
Nixon, Richard 267, 279
North Africa 130, 253
North America
  and American War of Independence 197
  early famers in 15, 144–5
  European colonization 193, 194–5
  European exploration of 155, 192–3
  modern humans arrive in 12
  Native Americans in 195
  and the Seven Years' War 191
North Atlantic Treaty Organization (NATO) 264, 271
North Borneo 235
North Korea 264, 275
Northern Zhou 89
Nubia/Nubians 59, 96
Nurhachi, Emperor 182
Obama, Barack 267
Occupy Movement 267
Octavian see Augustus
Ogedei 138
Olmecs 56, 92
Opium Wars 230
Orthodox Christianity 110
Ostrogoths 74–5, 81

Otto I, Emperor 107, 108
Otto II, Emperor 108
Ottoman Empire 125, 172–5, 214–15, 238
Oxus civilizations 47
Pachacutec, Emperor 148, 149
Pacific Ocean 90–1, 154, 155, 258–9
Pakistan 263, 280–1
Palestine/Palestinians 286–7
Panama 154
Paraguay 226
Park Chung Hee 275
Parthian Persia 66–7
Pasha, Enver 215
Pasha, Kara Mustafa 174
Patrick, St. 77
Pearl Harbor 251, 258
Pedro I, Emperor 225
Pedro II, Emperor 227
Peloponnesian War 62
Peninsula War 201
Pepin II of Herstal 105
Pepin the Short 105
Perry, Matthew 232
Persia/Persian Empire 29, 32–3, 39, 60–1, 62
and the Mongol Empire 138, 139
Parthian 66–7
Safavid Empire 173, 176–7
Sasanian 67
and Zoroastrianism 103
Peru 57, 95, 155, 224, 225
Peter (the Great) I, Tsar 161, 163, 174, 175
Philip II, Emperor 153
Philip II, King of France 127
Philip II, King of Macedon 63
Philip II, King of Spain 157
Philip of Anjou 165
Philippines 235
Phocas, Emperor 81
Phoenicians 54–5
Pinzon, Yanez 154
Pizarro, Francisco 149
Pol Pot 279
Poland 129, 160, 161, 162, 166–7
Polynesia/Polynesian culture 91, 145–6
Portugal 129, 154–5, 158, 188, 189, 201
Postumus, Emperor 73
Prussia 167, 200, 201, 209
Psamtik I, King 39
Ptolemaic Dynasty 65
Ptolemy 65
Puerto Rico 154, 225
Punic wars 70
Putin, Alexander 269
Pyrrhus, King 69
Qianlong dynasty 183
Qin dynasty 86
Qing dynasty 182–3, 230–1
Queen Anne's War 194
Qutb-ud-Din 133
Ramses II, Pharaoh 38–9
Ramses III, Pharaoh 39
Reagan, Ronald 265
Reformation in Europe 157–8
Rehoboam, King 30
Renaissance 128–9
Rhodesia 291
Richard I, King of England 127
Richelieu, Cardinal 158, 159
Robespierre, Maximilien de 199
Rome/Roman Empire
fall of Western Empire 74–5
and Germanic tribes 78
and Judah 102
later Republic 70–1
and Parthians 66–7
rise of 68–9

rise of Empire 70–1, 72–3
technology 99
Rudolf I, Emperor 109
Russia
alliance system 212–13
and Boris Yeltsin 269
and Catherine II 163
and the Cimmerians 47
expansion of 162–3, 210–11
Napoleonic invasion of 200–1
and Muscovy 129, 162
and the Ottoman Empire 174, 175
and Peter the Great 163
Revolution (1917) 246–7
Russo-Japanese War 233
'Time of Troubles' 162
World War I 244–5
Russo-Japanese War 233
Rwanda 291
Safavid Empire 173, 176–7
Sahara Desert 58
Saladin 126
Samarrans 20, 21
Samnite wars 69
Samudra Gupta, Emperor 85
Sargon I, King 24
Sargon II, King 29, 31
Sarmatians 79
Sasanians/Sasanian Persia 67, 81, 84
Satavahinahara 83
Saul, King 30
Scipio, Emperor 70
Scotland 164
Scythians 47, 79, 83
Seleucid Empire 64–5
Seleucus 64, 82
Seljuk Sultanate 124, 126
Sennacherib, King 29
Senusret III, Pharaoh 36
Seqenenre II, King 39
September 11th attacks 267
Serbia 207, 245, 271
Seven Years' War 167, 191, 195
Severus, Septimius 67, 72
Shah, Malik 124
Shah, Nadir 177, 178
Shalmaneser III, King 28, 29
Shamshi-Adad 25
Shapur I, Emperor 67
Shi Huangdi 86, 87
Shunga, Pushyamitra 83
Siberia 12
Sicily 55
Sierra Leone 154
Singapore 234
Singhasari 143
Sixteen Kingdoms 88–9
Skanda Gupta, Emperor 85
Sohshenq I, Pharaoh 31
Sokoto Caliphate 239
Solomon, King 30
Solon 53
Song dynasty 136–7
Songhai 188–9
Soto, Hernando de 155
South Africa 291
South America 12
20th century 292–3
and the Chavín 57, 95
and the Incas 148–9
independence movements in 225
and the Moche 95
Spanish colonization 190–1
South-East Asia 12
colonialism in 234–5
decolonization 276–7
early modern 186–7
and Hinduism 100
and Lapita culture 90

medieval 142–3
World War II 257
South Korea 264, 275
Southern Africa 131, 154, 189, 239
Soviet Union
Cold War 264–5
creation of 246–7
and Joseph Stalin 247
post-war 268–9
World War II 252–3
Spain 10
in 17th century 158
and Celts 76–7
Civil War 249
colonization of America 190–1
exploration of America 154–5, 193
Franco-Spanish War 164
Habsburg 153, 165
and independence in Latin America 224–5
and Islam 120, 121
Renaissance 129
War of the Spanish Succession 165
Sparta 52, 53, 60–1, 62–3
Sri Lanka 83, 151, 281
Srivijaya 143
Srubnayas 46
Stalin, Joseph 247, 264
Stonehenge 18
Stuart, John 237
Sudan 96, 238, 290
Sui dynasty 134
Suleiman the Magnificent 172–3
Sumatra 143, 234–5
Sumer/Sumerians 24, 25
invention of the wheel 15
writing in 19
rise of 22–3
Sun Yat-Sen 231, 260
Superbus, Lucius Tarquinius 68
Suppiluliumas, King 26
Sweden 156, 159, 160–1
Switzerland 157
Syngman Rhee 275
Syria 26, 119, 214, 284, 285, 286, 287
Tahiti 145
Taizong, Emperor 134
Tang dynasty 134–5
Tanzania 9
Taoism 100
technology
19th century 242–3
20th century 296–7
in Enlightenment Europe 171
metallurgy 98
in Neolithic period 15
power technologies 98–9
transportation 99
in the United States 221
in Upper Paleolithic period 12–13
Teotihuacán 94–5, 146
Thailand 142, 186, 276
Thebes 62–3
Theodoric the Great 80
Theodosius, Emperor 75
Theresa, Maria, of Austria 167
Thirty Years' War 158–9
Thule Inuits 145
Three Emperors' League 212
Three Kingdoms Period 88
Thutmose I, Pharaoh 38, 59
Tiahuanaco 95
Tibet 281
Tiglath-pilesa I, King 27
Tiglath-pileser III, King 29, 31
Tikal 92–3
Timur 139

Tito, Josep 270
Toba peoples 89
Tojo, Hideki 257
Tokugawa shogunate 184–5, 232
Toltecs 146
Topiltzin-Quetzalcóatl 146
Trajan, Emperor 67
Triple Alliance 212
Triple Entente 213
Tsuyoshi, Inukai 256
Tujue 79
Tukulti-Ninurta I, King 27
Tunisia 285, 290
Turkey 21, 121
modern 284
and the Mongols 125
Ottoman Empire 125
Seljuk Sultanate 124
Turkic peoples 79
Ubaids 20–1
Umar, Caliph 118
Umayyad dynasty 118–19
Umma 23
Unetice culture 49
United States of America
American Civil War 218–19
American War of Independence 197
anti-Americanism 289
Cold War 264–5
immigration to 221
industrialization in 220–1
inter-war 251
and Latin America 292
Native Americans in 217
New Deal 251
post-war 266–7
and September 11th attacks 267
and Vietnam 265, 266, 278–9
westward expansion 216–17
World War II 258–9
Upper Paleolithic period 12–13
Ur 23, 24–5
Ur-Nammu 24–5
Urban II, Pope 126
Urnfield culture 49, 76
Uruguay 226
Uruk 22, 23
Uthman, Caliph 118
Vandals 75, 81
Valens, Emperor 75
Valerian, Emperor 73
Vasa, Gustavus 156, 160
Vasily III, Tsar 162
Vedic Period India 42–3
Venezuela 154, 225, 293
Verrazano 155
Vespucci, Amerigo 154
Vietnam 91, 143, 187, 235, 265, 278–9
Vikings 106–7, 145
Visigoths 75, 81
Wang Mang 87
War of the Austrian Succession 166–7
War of the Polish Succession 166
War of the Spanish Succession 165
War of the Triple Alliance 226
Wars of the Roses 129
Watergate scandal 267
Wendi, Emperor 89, 134
West Africa 58, 130–1, 188–9, 239
Wilhelm II, Kaiser 212
Wilson, Woodrow 250
World War I 215, 244–5, 282
World War II 249, 250, 251, 252–3, 282
writing 19, 41, 45, 52, 56
Wu Zetian 134, 135
Wu of Zhou 45

Wudi, Emperor 88
Xerxes 33
Xian, Emperor 87
Xiongnu 79
Xixia kingdom 136–7, 138
Yang, Emperor 134
Yasovarman I 142
Yazid, Caliph 119
Yeltsin, Boris 269
Yongle Emperor 180
Yu the Great, Emperor 44
Yuan Shikai 231
Yugoslavia 270, 271
Zangi 124–5, 126
Zanzibar 238–9
Zapotecs 57
Zeno, Emperor 80
Zheng He 180
Zhu Yuanzhang 180
Zimbabwe 291
Zoroastrianism 103
Zulu kingdom 239
Zwingli, Ulrich 157